PEACEMAKING IN THE RENAISSANCE

PEACEMAKING IN THE RENAISSANCE

Joycelyne G. Russell

DUCKWORTH

First published in 1986 by
Gerald Duckworth & Co. Ltd.
The Old Piano Factory
43 Gloucester Crescent, London NW1

ISBN 0 7156 1937 3 (cased)

British Library Cataloguing in Publication Data

Russell, Joycelyne G.   Peacemaking in the Renaissance.
    1. Reconciliation   2. Europe—Foreign
relations   3. Europe—History—1492–1648
    I. Title
327.1'72'094   D234

    ISBN 0–7156–1937–3

Typeset by Input Typesetting Limited, London
and printed by Redwood Burn Limited, Trowbridge

Contents

Peace, with your depth of riches,
most beautiful of the blessed gods,
I long for you, and you are late coming.
I fear old age
may overtake me with its troubles
before I see your gracious beauty,
your songs and dances,
your revels and garlands.
Lady, come to my city;
and keep from our homes
hateful disorder
and that mad quarrelsomeness
that takes delight in a sharpened sword.

(Euripides, *Cresphontes*, fr.453Nauck[2])

Preface

This book has evolved from my researches in fifteenth- and sixteenth-century diplomacy, on which I first embarked as a post-graduate student in 1947. The theme was suggested by a brief period of employment by UNESCO, during which I was directly involved in international relations. The theme of peace developed from my study of the Congress of Arras in 1435, and of the Field of Cloth of Gold in 1520, and from lectures on more general topics.

My thanks are due to many colleagues and friends who have borne with my inquiries and discussions, particularly M. H. Keen, Mrs R. G. Lewis and M. B. Trapp; to the staff of the Bodleian Library, the Taylor Institution Library and the library of my own college; and to my husband, D. A. Russell, whose expertise in classical literature and countless other subjects, and unfailing encouragement, have made this book possible.

St Hugh's College,   J. G. R.
Oxford

Plates
(between pp. 118 and 119)

Abbreviations

Cal. For. I	: *Calendar of State Papers, Foreign Series, of the reign of Mary, 1553–1558*, ed. W. Turnbull (London 1861).
Cal. For. II	: *Calendar of State Papers, Foreign Series, of the reign of Elizabeth, 1558–1559*, ed. J. Stevenson (London 1863).
Cal. For. III	: *Calendar of State Papers, Foreign Series, of the reign of Elizabeth, 1559–1560*, ed. J. Stevenson (London 1865).
Cal. Span.	: *Calendar of Letters, Despatches and State Papers relating to the negotiations between England and Spain*, ed. G. A. Bergenroth, P. de Gayangos, A. S. Hume, and Royall Tyler (London 1862–1954).[1]
Cal. Span. F.S.	: *Further supplement to the Calendar of Letters, Despatches and State Papers*, ed. G. Mattingly (London 1940).
Cal. Ven.	: *Calendar of State Papers . . . in the archives and collections of Venice*, ed. Rawdon Brown and G. C. Bentinck (London 1864–).
Coll. des voyages	: *Collection des voyages des souverains des Pays Bas*, pub. par L. P. Gachard et C. Piot (Brussels 1876–1882), vol. IV.
Emm. Phil.	: Diarii d'Emmanuel-Philibert duc de Savoie, extracts, ed. by L. Romier: 'Les guerres d'Henri II et le traité de Cateau-Cambrésis (1554–1559)', in *Mélanges d'archéologie et d'histoire*, 1910, pp. 3–50.

[1] In order to have one sequence of citations for the whole period of this study, volume I: *Elizabeth 1558–1567*, has been referred to as *Cal. Span.* XIV. This series contains English translations of many of the Granvelle papers, and an English translation of the *Collection des voyages* entries for the reign of Queen Mary.

Forbes	:	P. Forbes, ed., *A Full View of the Public Transactions in the Reign of Queen Elizabeth*, 2 vols (London 1740).
Granvelle	:	*Papiers d'État du Cardinal de Granvelle*, pub. par G. Weiss, 9 vols., *Collection de documents inédits sur l'histoire de France* (Paris, 1841–1852).
Le Glay	:	A. Le Glay, ed., *Négotiations diplomatiques, entre la France et l'Autriche* (Paris 1845).
L.P.	:	*Letters and Papers, Foreign and Domestic, of the reign of Henry VIII, 1509–47*, ed. J. S. Brewer, J. Gairdner and R. H. Brodie (London 1862–1938).
Rawdon Brown	:	*Four years at the Court of Henry VIII*, ed. Rawdon Brown (London 1854). (Reports of the Venetian ambassador, Sebastiano Giustiniani).
Rel. Pol.	:	*Relations politiques des Pays Bas et de l'Angleterre sous le règne de Philippe II*, ed. Le Baron Kervyn de Lettenhove 11 vols (Brussels 1882–1900).
Ruble	:	A. de Ruble, *Le traité de Cateau-Cambrésis* (Paris 1889).
Traicté	:	*Traicté de paix fait à Chateau-Cambrésis l'an MDLIX le iii d'avril* (Paris, Camusat, 1637).[2]

---

[2] This contains the reports of the French ambassadors for the conferences of 1558 and 1559.

PART I

Ideals, attitudes and procedures

I

The way of peace: ideals, theories and propaganda

The Christian states of the late fifteenth century inherited a long tradition on the morality, legitimacy and practicalities of peace and war. On peace the religious and moral arguments were overwhelming: it was the ideal state to which all nations should aspire; the Christian community should not make war within itself. The ideal of universal peace was often a distant one; in classical legend there had been a Golden Age, the age of Saturn when there was eternal spring, all men were virtuous and there was universal peace. The silver age of Jove brought the seasons, extremes of heat and cold, and men began to till the soil. A third age of brass was followed by the iron age, when evil was let loose and wars came. The virgin Justice, Astraea, then left the earth, taking up her abode in the heavens as the constellation Virgo.[1] She might one day return to earth with a new age of peace. For the Christian, the prophecies of Isaiah concerned the latter days when there would be no war and nation would not lift up sword against nation; when the Messiah came, the lamb and the wolf would live together, the leopard and the kid, and a little child would lead them.[2] The peace which Jesus Christ left to his followers was a peace 'not of this world', a peace within themselves, and amongst them. The universal peace was to be in the New Jerusalem. Philo of Alexandria, in his *De somniis* took the word Jerusalem to mean 'Vision of Peace', a false etymology, but one which was to persist.[3] An eighth-century hymn gives us a vision of the city, bride of God:

---

[1] Ovid, *Metamorphoses* 1. 149–50; Hesiod, *Works and Days* 199; Aratos, *Phenomena* 96–136. The subject of Astraea is treated in F. A. Yates, *Astraea: the imperial theme in the sixteenth century* (London 1975).

[2] Isaiah 2:4; 11:6.

[3] *De somniis* 2. 250. Philo was a Jew, and wrote in the early part of the first century A.D.

Urbs beata Jerusalem dicta pacis visio,
Quae construitur in Caelis vivis ex lapidibus
Et angelis coornata ut sponsata comite,
Nova veniens a caelo, nuptiali thalamo
Praeparata, ut sponsata copuletur Domino;[4]

This distant vision of peace was echoed by the idealism of peace
on earth. For St Augustine, conscious of the classical and the Christian traditions, and writing his *City of God* in the period after Alaric's
sack of Rome in 410, the natural condition of mankind was attuned
to peace; the social good of peace was the highest of the goods of
this earth.[5] The search for peace within the *respublica Christiana*
was developed from Christian ideals of concord and charity, and
arguments from man's physical endowment and natural character-
istics, and the purpose of human societies. For Dante, universal
peace was the most excellent means of securing human happiness.
Man became perfect in quietude.[6] Such peace was seen as the
special concern of Christian rulers, particularly the Pope and the
Emperor. Christian religion could not flourish, nor could Christian
society, unless this happy state were achieved and maintained.

However, there were equally long traditions justifying and even
idealising war. Anthropologists and sociologists may argue for the
fundamental aggressiveness, competitiveness and violence of men,
individually and in groups. Whatever the reasoning, combative
warlike action became the object of ritual and of moral and legal
judgment. For Aristotle, war was a species of acquisitive activity,
like hunting. It was just (Aristotle introduced this concept) to use
it against animals or men who were natural subjects (i.e. less civi-
lised races) but unwilling.[7] In the Roman empire, the 'gates of war'
were usually open, and the concept of a just war developed: peace
was a form of contract, and the injured state had the right to avenge
injury inflicted by another state or its citizens. For Cicero, the just
war was occasioned by a just cause (a delict or injustice of the

[4] *The Oxford Book of Medieval Latin Verse*, ed. S. Gaselee (Oxford 1937), p. 36. [The
blessed city of Jerusalem, called Vision of Peace, which is built in heaven out of
living stones, and adorned by the angels as a bride for her husband, coming new
out of heaven, prepared for the marriage chamber, that the bride may be joined
with her Lord].
[5] *De civitate Dei* xiv.1; xv.4; xix. 12.
[6] Dante, *The Monarchy and Three Political Letters*, ed. D. Nicholl and C. Hardie
(London 1954), pp. 8–9.
[7] [Aristotle], *Rhet. Alex.* 1256b26.

enemy).[8] For Christians, the 'just war' no doubt began in the history
of the Jews, whose wars against the heathen were wars commanded
by God. St Augustine, a citizen of Rome, might postulate a state
of peace as the natural one among men, but he accepted the scourge
of war as a consequence of sin (avarice and greed) and also, on
certain conditions, a remedy for it. Wars were just when they were
waged on legitimate authority to redress injuries or to restore what
had been wrongfully seized. The holy war, commanded by God,
was also a just war.[9] St Augustine had accepted that Christians
might lawfully engage in war, and that the teachings of Christ did
not invalidate Old Testament injunctions on war. Thus war could
be regarded as an 'instrument' of peace, a lawful activity, upon
certain conditions.

In the medieval period canon and civil lawyers expanded and
refined theories of the just war. Gratian in his *Decretum* (*c.* 1140)
considered peace to be the desirable condition of mankind, but
allowed wars of pacification (*bella pacata*) to coerce the wicked or
sustain the right.[10] The Decretists of the twelfth century elaborated
the theory of the just war, waged on the just edict of the prince, in
defence of the *patria* or to protect the Church. For Aquinas, intro-
ducing the Aristotelian emphasis on the good of the community,
war's purpose was the conservation of peace; the common welfare
of the community was dependent upon peace.[11] By the later middle
ages, four categories of war were recognised: Roman war (war to
the death) waged on the authority of the Church against the Infidel;
public or open war, waged on the authority of the prince (in which
spoil and prisoners might be taken); covered or feudal war (between
holders of fiefs or lordships); and the truce, which was a condition
of war.[12] The Pope was the initiator of the Holy War, not only the
crusade against the Infidel but war against heretics and enemies of
the Church. The prince who could instigate open war was generally

[8] Cicero, *De officiis* 1. 11. 36; *De republica* 2. 23. 25.
[9] *De civitate Dei* xix. 12, 13, 15; *Contra Faustum Manichaeum* xxii. 74, 75, 76; *Epistulae* 189, 138.
[10] *Corpus Iuris Canonicis*, ed. A. Friedburg (Leipzig 1879–1881) i, 891–3 C 23 q.1, c.3, c.4, c.6.
[11] Aquinas, *Summa Theologica* 2–2, q.40 art. 1, q.123 art. 5. The theory of the just war, with copious citations, is dealt with by F. H. Russell, *The Just War in the Middle Ages* (Cambridge 1975).
[12] M. H. Keen, *The Laws of War in the Late Middle Ages* (London 1965) p. 104.

held to be not only the Emperor, but kings, great princes (such as the Valois Dukes of Burgundy) and, eventually, city states also.[13]

This concept of the just war must be seen within the context of the chivalric tradition which ennobled and commended military activity. It was no accident that all the nine worthies of medieval legend and romance were warriors: Joshua, David, Judas Maccabeus, Hector, Alexander, Julius Caesar, Arthur, Charlemagne and Godefroi de Bouillon. Hercules was sometimes added to the group. The military tradition, ennobled and romanticised in epic and romance, portrayed the knight as valorous, seeking activity in noble deeds dedicated to the service of the Church, his sovereign and the helpless in the community. The *chansons de geste* with their tales of Charlemagne, the metrical romances of Alexander and the Trojan war, the prose romances of the Arthurian cycle, were the embodiment of this tradition. The medieval orders of chivalry proclaimed a strict and onerous code of conduct for a select group: the twenty-four Knights of the Order of the Garter, the thirty Knights of the Golden Fleece.[14] The Burgundian order was created by Duke Philip the Good in 1430 to uphold the noble estate and order of chivalry, by which the true faith, the Holy Church, and public tranquillity and prosperity should be defended and maintained.[15] There were many motives for such foundations, not least those of practical politics and patronage. But the chivalric tradition was perpetuated and publicised in these orders, as it was also in the elaborate and romanticised tournaments of the time.[16]

This tradition, and these preoccupations, were reinforced and continued by the nature of war itself. For many it was an enjoyable, invigorating experience, and also a way to personal fame and advancement. In 1466 Jean le Bueil had written of the joyous quality of war, with its fine deeds and good lessons. It was a proper and useful career for young men; comradeship in arms was uniquely delectable.[17] Here we have the search for honour, blended with the

[13] Much argument centred on whether only princes who had no 'superior' could wage a just war.

[14] The Order of the Garter comprised the Sovereign, the Prince of Wales and twenty-four knights; the Order of the Golden Fleece was at first the Sovereign (the Duke of Burgundy) and thirty knights (later fifty knights).

[15] Statutes of the Order in *Chronique de Jean le Fèvre Seigneur de S. Remy*, ed. F. Morand, *Société de l'histoire de France* (Paris 1881) ii, 210–11.

[16] The subject of chivalry is examined in Malcolm Vale, *War and Chivalry* (London 1981) and in Maurice Keen, *Chivalry* (New Haven and London 1984).

[17] Quoted in Vale, op. cit., p. 30, from Bueil's *Le Jouvencel*.

search for profitable employment. It was perhaps no accident that
the wily merchant turned printer, William Caxton, who knew so
well the court of Burgundy, should have penned the eloquent but
down-to-earth appeal to the knights of his native country (1484) as
epilogue to his translation of Ramon Lull's *Order of Chivalry*. They
were now living in idleness, frequenting the stews, and playing dice,
when they should be reading of the Holy Grail, of Lancelot,
Galahad, Tristan and Gawain. They should recall the noble deeds
of Richard Coeur-de-lion, of Edward I and Edward III, should
read Froissart, and remember Henry V. How many of them now
had the use and exercise of a knight: to know his horse, and his
horse him, to ride a horse he has broken himself, and have his
armour and harness ready?[18] Caxton's output of romances, and
particularly the works of Malory, show what was popular, and thus
profitable to print, for the courtiers, knights and gentlemen, and
also aspiring merchants, of his own day. In Spain, the story of
Amadis de Gaula (the chivalrous adventures of Amadis, prince of
Gaul), was revised and augmented in the late fifteenth century
(printed in 1508). With its sequels, it was immensely popular in
Spain; it was praised by Cervantes.[19] In France, a French translation appeared in 1540; Blaise de Monluc testifies to a generation
still brought up on these tales.[20] Such romances of chivalric tradition
and ethic have been described as 'a fictional fulfilment substitute
through which people could live the ideals that human frailty denied
them'.[21] In moments of crisis, however, men might enact the ideal.

The cult of military honour survived and adapted to changes in
the technique of warfare: the massed pikemen, moving as units in
disciplined formation, the lighter mobile artillery for use in the field
(as at Ravenna in 1512), the portable firearms, particularly the
arquebus with its match-lock and later with the wheel-lock which

[18] *The Prologues and Epilogues of William Caxton*, ed. W. J. B. Crutch, (Early English
Text Society, London 1928) pp. 82–3.
[19] 'The best of all the books of this kind ever written', says the barber, when the
burning of Don Quixote's books is being discussed (*Don Quixote*, Part I, vi).
[20] Blaise de Monluc, *Commentaires et lettres*, ed. A. de Ruble (Paris 1864–7) III, 591.
Calvin had the book banned from Geneva; it might corrupt the young and was, in any
case, nothing but 'mensonge et rêverie' (cf. P. Burke, 'The two faces of Calvinism', in
J. Cruickshank, ed., *French Literature and its Background. 1. The Sixteenth Century* (London
1968) p. 53.
[21] *Spain: a companion to Spanish Studies*, ed. P. E. Russell (London 1973) p. 272.

made it a cavalry weapon (as at S. Quentin in 1557).[22] The massed troops seemed to inhibit individual deeds of glory. The new weapons aroused heated arguments on the morality of their use against Christians;[23] against the Turk, who had his own guns, there was no scruple.[24] The weapons were castigated by many as the invention of the Devil or of demons: thus Erasmus, Guicciardini, Monluc and Ronsard. As one would expect, the answer was not long in coming. Claude Colet, writing in 1544, allows Mars to argue that man has no need to be armed by nature, since he can himself forge arms. Battista delle Valle, in 1554, took this inventive power to be a gift of God.[25] Nevertheless there was a sneaking suspicion that such weapons were not those of chivalry, with its tradition of personal skill and personal combat with the enemy. The biographer of Louis de la Trémouille, who died in the Italian wars, asked what use was now the skill, prudence, strength and bravery of knights, and their desire for honour? On the death of La Trémouille's son at Marignano in 1515, he writes that it was a valiant death, in a just war, by the lance and not by cannon shot.[26] For Ariosto, the cannon was a cowardly weapon, striking at a distance; through its use martial glory had been lost, and the trade of arms had become a worthless art.[27] Blaise de Monluc (himself wounded seven times by the arquebus, which had killed three of his sons) castigated the weapon as an accursed engine, which killed many valiant men, and with which poltroons could kill at a distance those they dared not look in the face.[28]

But the weapons had come to stay; they were 'Christianised' and

[22] Already in 1513, the Venetian diarist Sanuto noted that a Frenchman thought he had lost his right arm if he found himself without a gun (M. Sanuto, *Diarii* (Venice 1879–1903) xvi, col. 462–3).

[23] J. R. Hale has discussed these problems in 'Gunpowder and the Renaissance' in *From the Renaissance to the Counter-Reformation*, ed. C. H. Carter (London 1966) pp. 113–37.

[24] The biographer of Louis de la Trémouille writes, à propos of the battle of Pavia (1525) in which his hero was killed, that most of the dead were killed by arquebusiers, light mounted cavalry with 'hacquebutes' (an early form of arquebus) 'dont les chrétiens ne devroient user fors contre les infidèles'. (Jean Bouchet, *Le panégyric du Seigneur Loys de la Trimoille*, in J. A. C. Buchon, *Choix de chroniques* (Paris 1838) p. 806).

[25] Colet quoted in J. Hutton, 'Erasmus and France, the propaganda for peace' in *Studies in the Renaissance* viii, 1961, p. 116; delle Valle quoted in J. R. Hale, loc. cit., p. 118.

[26] *Le panégyric du Seigneur Loys de la Trimoille*, loc. cit., p. 791.

[27] *Orlando Furioso* xi.23 and 26.

[28] Monluc ii.52. Yet Monluc wished his sons to go to the wars.

romanticised. Charles V and Henry VIII had artillery named after the Twelve Apostles. Alfonso d'Este, Duke of Ferrara, was painted by Titian with his hand resting on the muzzle of a cannon. St Barbara was made the patron saint of gunners (her father was struck by lightning at the moment of her execution). Charles V's artillery-men invoked the saint as they loaded their weapons.[29] For Roger Ascham, apologist of the long-bow, and schoolmaster to the Princess Elizabeth, the ideal pupil must learn 'to shote faire in bow, or surelie in gon'.[30] Thus the excitement of gunfire was added to the potent noises of battle: the battle cries, the neighing of horses, the clash of armour, the music of fife and drum. For many war was an intoxicant and a supreme experience.

It might be said, therefore, that the Devil had the best tunes, the best literature, the best propaganda. War is an activity; peace is a state or condition, ultimately upheld by the slow process of the law and the weight of moral suasion. It has few heroes, and in its entirety it may well be an impossibility, at least for the young and vigorous. This argument is, of course, here applied to the period under review, though it may have validity even in the atomic age. In the late fifteenth and the sixteenth century war, the just war of princes, or the Holy War against the advancing Turk, was continually fuelled by the ambition, restless energy and love of danger of large sections of the population. It was the habitual occupation of their rulers. Any prince worth the name could find a just cause for war, any pope could invoke crusading zeal (though usually with little success). That the prince should have just cause and enough artillery[31] was the renaissance version of 'Praise the Lord and pass the ammunition'.

One would expect, however, that such weaponry, and such battles, would invoke counter-propaganda. Ravenna in 1512 was held to be the bloodiest encounter since the time of the Goths. The greatest international figure in this debate was Erasmus. He had grown up in the period of the Italian wars and had witnessed the triumphal entry of the warring Pope Julius II into Bologna in 1506. The wars of the north would have impinged on him also. But he was seldom near actual battle scenes. During Henry VIII's campaign of

[29] J. R. Hale, loc. cit., pp. 126, 131–2.
[30] Roger Ascham, *English Works*, ed. W. A. Wright (Cambridge 1970) p. 217.
[31] Quoted by J. R. Hale (loc. cit., p. 125) from Robert de Balsac's *Nef des Princes et des Batailles* of 1502.

1513, for instance, Erasmus was fighting only the bad wine and the damp climate of Cambridge. Nevertheless detestation of war was a major theme in his works. In his *Education of a Christian Prince*, written in 1516 as a manual for the young Prince Charles (Charles V), he counselled first against misguided reading. The Prince should beware of being carried away by reading of Achilles, Xerxes, Cyrus, Darius and Julius Caesar; Seneca had called these men raging robbers.[32] The battles and butcheries of the Hebrews should be interpreted allegorically. His main argument rested on the nature of man: he was born for peace and goodwill, unlike predatory beasts.[33] The good prince should only go to war in self-defence, not on account of a mere title, a personal grievance, or stupid and youthful ambition. Erasmus did not propose to discuss the 'just war', for which prince did not think his cause was just? He preferred the teaching of Christ to the writings of St Augustine and St Bernard (who allowed war). Princes should not make their subjects suffer by pursuing personal claims; arbitration should be possible. If it were not, better to lose some claim than maintain it to the last. The costs of war should be weighed; often it cost more to destroy a town than to build a new one. Even against the Turk, there should be no rash war. A Christian prince who made peace (with other princes) would have done a more magnificent deed than if he had subdued the whole of Africa by arms.

In the *Adages*, of which many editions appeared between 1500 and 1520, the war theme recurs. In *Aut fatuum aut regem nasci oportere* ('Kings and fools are born not made'), Erasmus wrote that the glory of a prince did not consist in pushing back his frontiers by force of arms. He should shun war in every way; 'other things give rise to this or that calamity, but war lets loose at one go a whole army of wrongs.'[34] The adage *Dulce bellum inexpertis* ('War is sweet to those who have not tried it') was printed separately by Froben at Basel in 1517, as well as in Froben's complete edition of 1515. The theme was man's destiny for peace: his naked body and helplessness when born, his power of speech (for goodwill), his love of companionship, his learning, his inspiration by God. War was a

[32] *De Ira*, 3.16.3.; 3.21.1.
[33] *The Education of a Christian Prince*, trans. L. K. Born (New York 1936) pp. 201, 203, 249–51, 256.
[34] M. M. Phillips, *Erasmus on his Times: a shortened version of the Adages* (Cambridge 1967) pp. 41–2 (Adage I.i.1).

contagion, its instruments invented by the art of demons. It was murder shared by many; yet nowadays war was praised, even by preachers. Peace was the mother and nurse of all that is good, like springtime (a harking back to the Age of Saturn, when spring was eternal). Solomon, whose name meant 'peacemaker', was chosen to build the Temple, not David the man of blood; the angels sang of peace at Christ's nativity. The modern justifications of war were scathingly dismissed by Erasmus, taking as his touchstone the teaching of Christ. Nowadays, he wrote, 'one is suspected of heresy, if one earnestly tries to dissuade men from war'. Wars arose from some claim, some selfish treaty; to assert dominion over one town a whole realm was imperilled. Surely there could be arbitration by learned bishops and abbots, venerable peers? Even wars against the Turk were to be avoided; the Infidel should be converted by heavenly doctrine (an echo of Ramon Lull's teaching in the fourteenth century). Peace was to be made at all costs, and the pope was appealed to as the true giver of peace. In passing, the stupid tales and legends of war had been roundly condemned: 'our Iliad contains nothing indeed, but the heated folly of stupid kings and peoples.'[35]

Erasmus' *Querela Pacis* (Complaint of Peace), written in 1516 at the request of the Chancellor of Burgundy for a projected peace conference at Cambrai, was also published in 1517. It restated the arguments of the *Dulce bellum* in more formal style. Scarcely any peace was so evil that it was not better than the most just war.[36] The horrors of war, its causes and the remedies for it were set forth. There followed a great appeal to the Pope, the Emperor, Charles his son, and the Kings of France and England.[37] In 1522-3 when war broke out again, Erasmus included appeals for peace in prefaces to works presented to Charles V, to the Pope and to Prince George

[35] Ibid., pp. 108–10, 111–12, 116–18, 129, 131–7, 139–40 (Adage IV.i.1 of which the full text, in translation, of the 1515 edition is given; *Dulce bellum inexpertis*, ed. Y. Rémy and R. Dunil-Marquebreucq (Brussels 1953) pp. 20–30, 40–6, 72, 80–94, 98–102, the Latin text and a French translation of the 1703 Leiden edition). In the 1526 edition, passages were added against the preaching of war by the clergy, on the comparative 'humanity' of pagan warfare, and against the twisting of the scriptural texts to justify war (Rémy and Dunil-Marquebreucq ed., pp. 40, 64, 70); cf. J. Hutton, loc. cit., pp. 100–10.
[36] This came from Cicero (*Ad. Fam.* vi. 6.5), but his remarks refer to the evils of civil war, which he counselled Pompey to avoid.
[37] Erasmus, *The Complaint of Peace*, trans. by W. J. Hirten (New York 1946) (a modernised version of the English translation (1559) by Thomas Pagnell).

of Saxony.[38] In the colloquy *Charon* (1528) he wrote of three monarchs of the world bent on each other's destruction, and of himself who once wrote 'a sort of Hue and Cry after Peace, that was banish'd or driven away'. France, England and Spain were declaring a Holy War; there were bishops who were fitted only for war. Charon's boat was filled by the war dead, their spirits heavy, for they had been torn out of gross bodies. There was no reason for Charon to fear a peace for at least ten years. Erasmus makes a hit at the 'just war'; did not those killed in such wars fly bolt upright into Heaven?[39]

It seems that Erasmus' didactic, moralising eloquence was greatly to be feared. He had trounced the ancients, the scholastics, and the lawyers and theologians past and present, hitting hard at the whole apparatus of war apologetic, and at much else on the way. Not for him the admission of Old Testament 'war-mongering'. In Paris, Louis de Berguin's translations of Erasmus were seized in 1525, and the *Querela* itself in 1526. His old friend Josse Clichtove, who himself wrote on *Peace and War* (1523),[40] joined the Paris faculty of theology in the condemnation. Clichtove himself (a canon of Chartres) condemned war, but defended the 'just war', admitting some interpretations of Scripture which Erasmus rejected. Hence Erasmus' later additions to the *Querela*; he attacked Clichtove's writings as bigoted, 'begutarii libri'.[41] However, experience and disillusionment and perhaps also harsh criticism took their toll. By the 1530s Erasmus felt the need to stress that he had never argued that war was absolutely prohibited to Christians.[42] Princes were not forbidden to use the sword: 'they have the sword to defend the tranquillity of the republic, not to foster their own ambitions.' These words, in a letter to François I (1532) pleading for peace, were part of a painful acceptance of coercive force and hence of war, even among Christians. 'Perchance sometimes it is fitting for a prince to wage war, but only when reduced to extreme need, and if all other

---

[38] Quoted M. M. Phillips, *Erasmus and the Northern Renaissance* (London 1949) p. 149.

[39] Erasmus, *The Colloquies*, trans. N. Bailey (London 1878) II.139-45.

[40] J. Hutton, loc. cit., pp. 107-12.

[41] Ibid., p. 112.

[42] His letter 'Utilissima consultatio de bello Turcis inferendo' quoted in J. A. Fernández-Santamaria, 'Erasmus on the just war', in *Journal of the History of Ideas*, XXXIV, 1973, p. 219.

means have failed.'[43] The horror of war, and detestation of the soldiery, remain.[44]

Another great protagonist for peace was the Valencian Juan Luis Vives. He studied and worked in the Netherlands and in England from 1512, when he left the University of Paris, to his death in 1540. He was in turn tutor to the nephew of the Sieur de Chièvres (adviser to Charles V), professor at Louvain (where he met the future Adrian VI and Erasmus), lecturer at Oxford (1523) and tutor to the Princess Mary, leaving England to return to the Low Countries when royal proceedings against his patroness, Catherine of Aragon, made continued sojourn unbearable. His commentaries on St Augustine (dedicated to King Henry VIII in 1522) forced him to consider the contemporary problem of war. A letter from Louvain in that year, addressed to the Pope, urged him to declare that all war between Christians was unjust.[45] After the battle of Pavia, Vives appealed to King Henry VIII (from Oxford) to influence the Emperor to peace.[46] A dialogue of 1526 (written in Bruges) denounced the evils of wars among Christians, when war against the Turks was needed. His great work on concord, *De concordia et discordia in humano genere*, was dedicated to Charles V in 1529, the year of the Peace of Cambrai: 'only concord will reinstate the fallen, retain what is now fleeing from us, and restore what has already been lost.'[47] The Emperor was reminded of the immense sufferings of recent wars and of the need for a restoration 'quasi universali instauratione'. God had given him victory so that he could accomplish the divine will, which was that peace should be restored. For Vives man's ambition, his lust for power, influence, honours and fame, had brought discord and war to destroy the essential unity of human society. Concord brought human society together, founded cities, introduced the arts and the cultivation of human wisdom and virtue. Avarice and greed were at the root of wars, often caused by supposed insults to 'honour' and the desire

[43] Letter to François I (dated 1 Dec. 1532): Erasmus, *Opus epistolarum*, ed. P. S. Allen (Oxford 1906–1947) v, 354.

[44] Cf. *The Education of a Christian Prince*, p. 250; *Complaint of Peace*, pp. 33–7, 49.

[45] *Ioannis Ludovici Vivis, Valentini, opera omnia*, ed. G. Majansio (Valencia 1782–1790) v, 164–74. For Vives cf. J. A. Fernández-Santamaria, *The State, War and Peace: Spanish political thought in the Renaissance, 1516–1559* (Cambridge 1977) pp. 49–51; J. M. McConica, *English Humanists and Reformation Politics under Henry VIII and Edward VI* (Oxford 1965) pp. 53–5.

[46] *Opera omnia* v, 449–52. Another appeal was sent in 1526 (ibid., v, 175–86).

[47] Ibid., v, 187 (trans. from J. A. Fernández-Santamaria, op. cit., p. 51).

for revenge. Fools held that such 'honour' must be propitiated; relations between states were governed by such foolish vanity. Vengeance was bestial and diabolical. Charity should rule Christians and concord be re-established, for war did not even preserve the state, it destroyed justice and liberty, producing anarchy and rebellion at home. Vives hoped for the restoration of concord, the 'Golden Age of social unity' in Christendom. He castigated the inhumanity of war, particularly recent wars with their satanic, deadly weapons. Wars over territory were especially to be ridiculed; on such grounds there would be war for 6000 years.[48]

Erasmus and Vives were powerful apologists, able to write with vehemence and apostolic fervour. In England Thomas More, a friend of both, was to make his own practical comments in his *Utopia*, written partly in Antwerp, partly in London (1515/16), and first printed at Louvain, by Gourmont in Paris (?1517) and Froben in Basel (1518). Already in 1517 Cuthbert Tunstall had delighted in it, but there was no English edition for many years.[49] The Utopians, as is well known, detested war, counting nothing 'so muche against glorie as glory gotten in warre'. They would, however, defend themselves and help their friends, but in these struggles they would use first mercenaries, second the armies of their friends, and only as a last resort their own troops, who would be volunteers. They made no leagues; nature should induce men to love one another; if it did not, mere words would not suffice. Thomas More was pragmatic in temporal matters, his legal training and practical experience in public service showing very clearly.[50]

It was hard to argue for peace, entire and indivisible, at the court of Henry VIII, and particularly in court sermons. In 1513 the great reformer John Colet, Dean of St Paul's, had to face the King, who was lusting after victory over France and about to cross the Channel with his troops. Colet preached at Greenwich on Good Friday before the court, that Christians should war and conquer under Christ's

---

[48] Ibid., v, 187–403 especially pp. 218–19, 281–3, cf. Fernández-Santamaria, op. cit., pp. 144–50; R. Gibert, 'Juan Luis Vives (1492–1540) y la paz Europea', in *Recueils de la societé Jean Bodin, XV, La Paix*, II (Paris 1961) pp. 148–66.

[49] There was no English edition until 1551, when Ralph Robinson, goldsmith of London, brought out his translation.

[50] In 1516 he wrote to Erasmus of his beautiful dream of being made a prince by his Utopians; in the morning he had to return to the treadmill (the law courts) (*Opus Epistolarum Des. Erasmi Roterodami*, ed. P. S. Allen (London 1906–1958) II, 414).

banner; those who fought through hatred or ambition were fighting
under the Devil's. Few went to war unsullied by hatred or love of
gain; it was ordained that men should have brotherly love, not bury
the sword in a brother's heart. The sermon (which is reported by
Erasmus) allegedly made the King fear for the morale of his troops.
He met Colet in the gardens of the Franciscan convent nearby (of
which house the King and his Queen were patrons). In half an
hour's conversation, the Dean seems to have satisfied the King,
who returned with him to the palace, pledging him in wine: 'This
is the Dean for me.'[51] The King may have asked for another sermon,
on the just war, for he was, in his own eyes, fighting the schismatic
Louis XII, and was the Pope's ally in defence of the church. It was
left to the scholarly royal secretary, Richard Pace, to preach on
peace at St Paul's in October 1518, before King, Cardinal, Papal
Legate (Cardinal Campeggio), and the French ambassadors when
the 'Universal Peace' of London was proclaimed and ratified.[52] This
sermon, in Latin, was straightway printed in London and (in French
translation) in Paris. It is strongly Erasmian in tone: Christ was no
commander, riding gloriously on a white horse, but a Prince of
Peace. The calamities of war are set out, war achieved by ingenious
machines, to which are now added 'Bombards', truly a diabolical
invention which not only slays men, but whose noise produces
bewilderment, hallucination and total alienation of the senses. Some
fury must have produced war among men. The ancient proverb,
Dulce bellum inexpertis is quoted, a conscious tribute to Erasmus'
Adage, printed the year before. To Pace, war was the 'measureless
sea of all evils', peace the 'heap and accumulation of all good',
especially needful when the Turk threatened. The sermon did not

---

[51] Ibid., IV, 525–6; J. H. Lupton, *A Life of John Colet* (London 1887), pp. 188–93;
J. T. Scarisbrick, *Henry VIII* (London 1968) p. 33. Archbishop Parker recorded a
tradition that Colet did, in fact, preach a second sermon, justifying the King's war
(Mathew Parker, *De antiquitate Britannicae ecclesiae* ('Hanoviae' 1605) pp. 306–7).

[52] Pace, of a Hampshire family, had studied in Padua from about 1498. He there
met Cuthbert Tunstall, William Latimer, and the future cardinals Reginald Pole
and Gasparo Contarini. Erasmus stayed with him in Ferrara in 1508. He entered
the service of Christopher Bainbridge, Cardinal and Archbishop of York, in Rome
(1509). On his return to England he was in Wolsey's employ and then the King's,
serving as ambassador and as royal secretary. By 1518 he was considered by the
Venetian ambassador to be third in the royal council, after Wolsey and Thomas
Ruthall (Bishop of Durham and Lord Privy Seal) (J. Wegg, *Richard Pace, a Tudor
Diplomatist* (London 1971)). The relationships of these scholars and public servants
are of immense complexity; they were always in and out of each other's universities
and private houses, as of the households they served.

omit to humour the King. He must despise all glory and increase
of fortune that war could bring him; this will be all the more
remarkable since Nature has fashioned him as a great general. The
beauty of his body, its proportion, the compactness of his limbs,
'all breathes war'. Yet King Henry has inclined to peace, spurred
on by the Cardinal of York (the inference is that Wolsey is the
'rider'). The King of France is like-minded, and together they will
easily incline all Christian princes to peace. The two youthful kings
have, by reason and counsel, repressed their youthful spirits, wont
to be intent on extending frontiers. Wolsey's shrewdness, prudence
and dexterity are praised; posterity will marvel that England has
produced a man to whom not only her own king, but foreign kings,
entrust business.[53] Here the plea for peace is decked out in what
was apposite to the times; a young warlike king, a skilful and crafty
cardinal. It met with limited success, more accidental than heartfelt,
except perhaps in Wolsey's case.[54]

If it was difficult to confront Henry VIII on the subject of peace,
it was even more difficult to write or preach on the theme before
the kings of France: Louis XII, François I or Henri II. The great
Savoyard jurist and public servant, Claude de Seyssel, Bishop of
Marseilles, had treated of the subject in his political memorial *La
monarchie de France*: published in July 1519.[55] He thought that the
section of his work on living with foreign peoples was the most
useful part of the book, as it had been the most difficult to write.
All princes, he declared, should love and seek peace with their
neighbours and with strangers, except their enemies (by 'nature' or
by difference in laws, as the Infidel). There should be no war for
covetousness of dominion, or glory, or other disordered passion;
only to recover one's own (if one couldn't get it by other means),
or to redress an injury, or to aid and defend allies who had been

[53] *Oratio Richardi Pacei in pace* ... (London, Richard Pynson, 1518). An English
translation of this sermon is given in Appendix A below.

[54] See below, pp. 96, 126.

[55] De Seyssel, born *c.* 1450, was doctor of laws and then professor of Turin. He
moved from the counsels of the Duke of Savoy, his immediate sovereign, to those of
the King of France to whom he was counsellor in 1498. Service in Milan and on
diplomatic missions culminated in the period of French 'schism', the conflict with
Pope Julius II, to whom Seyssel took France's submission in 1513. While in Rome
(at the Lateran Council) he finished his translation of Thucydides, his greatest work.
He retired from royal service after the accession of François I, became Archbishop
of Turin, and again counselled the Duke of Savoy, Charles III (Claude de Seyssel,
La monarchie de France, ed. J. Poujol (Paris 1961) pp. 11–18).

unjustly attacked. Divine and human law allowed war in such cases. Seyssel admitted the naturally corrupt nature of man, ambitious and coveting 'dominion'. Princes should be on their guard against powerful neighbours with claims against them or bearing them ill-will. The best means to have peace was to show oneself to be strong and to have no fear of the enemy; feebleness or fearfulness merely incited him. A great prince should never humiliate himself before the enemy, nor ask for peace, except in extreme necessity. A reasonable peace was never obtained by begging. If a king were counselled by reason, and having a just cause, to conquer outside his realm, then he should carefully weigh the costs, and the likelihood that he could retain the lands. The Romans had refused provinces when they thought it unwise to accept. War, if it had to come, should be prompt, undertaken at the earliest and with all diligence. Here spoke the experienced counsellor, with the French involvement in Italy constantly before his eyes, and the need to pass on his hard-earned wisdom to the new ruler.[56]

In Spain the theologians and jurists were hard at work on the problems of Spanish dominion in the New World. The Dominican Francesco de Vitoria, Prima Professor of Theology at Salamanca from 1526,[57] wrestled with the political realities of Spain's dominion, achieved by conquest of Indian communities which he held to be perfect. For Vitoria, the right of self-defence was a fundamental privilege of all men; when the state or civil society came into being, this right was exercised on the community's behalf against all evil doers. Autonomous nation states were the reality of his day (he did not accept that the Emperor, or the Pope, had lordship over the whole world). War, therefore, an extension of the community's punishment of evil-doers, became a legitimate exercise of the right of self-defence. It was essentially a means (in the last resort) of settling disputes, an instrument of justice. Four basic reasons for waging war were self-defence, recovery of possessions, the avenging of wrong and the maintenance of peace and security. In such action 'offensive' war (as we should call it) was lawful. Vitoria faced the

[56] Ibid., pp. 189–208. Advice on how to govern conquered territory then followed (pp. 208–21).

[57] Vitoria, born in Burgos in 1492, became a Dominican in 1506, studied at the Collège de S. Jacques in Paris, first philosophy and then theology, taking his doctorate in 1522. He then taught at Valladolid before proceeding to Salamanca. In 1527 he and other theologians there condemned what they considered questionable passages in the works of Erasmus (J. A. Fernández-Santamaria, op. cit., pp. 63–4).

18   *Part I   Ideals, attitudes and procedures*

problem of the conflicting teaching of the Old and New Testaments.
The New Testament's message on peace was essentially directed to
the peace of the contemplative life. This did not supersede the Old
Testament's message, itself a guide to natural law, by which war
was permitted. In war, three ethical principles should be observed:
to avoid it as far as possible, not to destroy the enemy population,
and to be moderate in victory.[58]

Charles V's Spanish sojourns would have been enlivened and no
doubt permeated by these august pronouncements from Salamanca.
He eventually rallied to the defence of Indian rights; as to war, he
could never have doubted his authority to fight, though he was
probably well aware of the ethical problems of even imperial wars.

Writing in a different genre, and from differing standpoints, were
the contemporary poets. In the summer and autumn of 1521, French
disillusionment with war can be traced in the writings of Clément
Marot, who was at the camp at Attigny (in the Ardennes) during
the summer. The troops marched in the green countryside, feathers
waving, fifes and drums playing; 'la guerre est si doulce'. By
autumn, across the Scheldt, the countryside is no longer green,
winter comes, women and children flee, fire destroys all, even the
enemy are to be pitied. That pitiless Serpent, War, has darkened
the air, and Marot asks the prayers of the Princesses of France that
Peace, sacred daughter of Jesus Christ, may descend on French
lands. War itself may bring Peace again: Peace is followed by
Prosperity, Pride and Luxury; Contention and then War follow;
and from War springs Poverty, then Humility, and finally Peace
once more.[59] The poet is aware of a doleful cycle in human affairs;
he accepts war, and sees that peace itself may produce it.

After the peace of Crépy in 1544 the poet Claude Colet, in the
household of the Marquise de Nesle, wrote two poems: *L'Oraison de
Mars* and *Réponse des Dames à Mars*. Mars argues that war is a
universal principle; nation differs from nation, the arts contend with

[58] Ibid., pp. 69, 81, 115, 132–5, 139–41, in which Vitoria's views are expounded
from his *De potestate civile* (1527–8), *De Indes* (i) (1537–8), *De Indes* (ii) (1538–9), *De
jure gentium et Naturali, relectiones* or annual lectures given before the faculty or the
whole University between 1526 and 1540. The *relectiones* were not published until after
Vitoria's death (1557 edition from Lyons). They have been edited and translated in
many more recent works (cf. Fernández-Santamaria, op. cit., pp. xi–xii, 67.

[59] Clément Marot, *Oeuvres diverses*, ed. critique par C. A. Mayer (London 1968)
Rondeau xxxi, p. 100; *Les Épitres*, ed. critique par C. A. Mayer (London 1958)
Epitre iii, pp. 105–12, and Appendix i, pp. 280–2. For the 1521 campaign cf. below,
p. 91.

one another, men are divided, the planets have different orbits. The greatest honours are reserved for men in war. He himself claims to be born of Justice, but left behind when she fled the earth (it is the Age of Iron), to be nursed by Folly. Mars counters the argument that man's natural helplessness means that he is intended to be peaceful. Man did not need to be armed by Nature, since he can forge weapons at will.[60] The Ladies reply in an Erasmian defence of peace. The poem ends with a plea to the rulers of the earth to make perpetual peace.[61]

It is, however, with Ronsard that we meet the most eloquent 'occasional' pieces on these themes. In the summer of 1558, when Henri II's armies were encamped near Amiens but peace negotiations were beginning (see Chapter 5), Ronsard wrote two odes, one lauding the King's wars, the other urging peace. The first (commissioned by the King, he says) was to rouse the army: the enemy could be seen, their corpses lay unburied, let the soldiers fight and die as conquerors, or at least get honourable wounds. They should bathe and drink in the waters of the Rhine, treating it as familiarly as the Loire or the Garonne. The King would richly reward them. Ronsard hears the noise of war: the horses, the clash of armour, the cannon, the diabolical gun-fire. There is also the sound of the drum; let the pikemen brandish their weapons. The soldiers, children of Mars, were not fighting for a prize in a tournament, or any vile thing, but for themselves and their families. They must avenge S. Quentin. To die for one's prince and the defence of one's country was a holy war. If they fled the battle, they would die at home, of 'catarrh' or fever, or in secret anger over a lawsuit, or an ancient debt, or of plague or poison. Better far to die by 'bullet or the lance'. The God of camps and armies will help them.[62] The palinode is in contrary vein. Christians should love one another, not dip their arms in brothers' blood. They should lay down their arms, or use them against the Turk, whose lands were rich. Wars for twenty years have not yielded much. 100,000 men have died around one cold village or a poor town, or a small castle, trying to subdue it. Deaths in war are so many. Sometimes Earth has asked

[60] This is the earliest example I have found of an argument which became traditional.
[61] Extracts quoted in J. Hutton, 'Erasmus and France: the propaganda for peace', *Studies in the Renaissance* VIII, 1961, pp. 112–16.
[62] Pierre de Ronsard, *Oeuvres complètes*, ed. P. Laumonier (Paris 1924–1975) IX, 3–11 (*Exhortation au camp du Roy Henri II*).

to be free of a superfluity of men; Discord is then sent by Jupiter. The poet repeats the argument on man's helplessness and his peaceful destiny: he curses the discovery of iron, and of fire, and of gold (the means of providing for war). He sees the Moselle and the Somme blocked with dead horses, and the Meuse red with blood. Wars bring the destruction of all laws, of the Church, of justice. Would it not be better to live at home, with a beautiful and chaste wife in your arms, to play with the children and hear them call you 'Papa'? Better to die of old age at home, than have a dog's stomach as your tomb. Peace, daughter of God, must destroy the anger of kings.[63]

---

[63] Ibid., IX, 15–26 (*Exhortation pour la paix*).

Attitudes and obligations: the Popes and the Princes

The Popes

The prime obligation for the preservation of peace in Christendom fell upon the Pope, Vicar of Christ, protector of the faith, spiritual counsellor of princes. The peace of Christendom, both from heresy within, and the Infidel without, was the essential condition under which the Christian religion could flourish. Christians were in theory one community, which should not war within itself. The Pope, therefore, in addition to his combat against heresy and other 'ecclesiastical' disobedience (of the canon law on marriage for instance) came to be involved in secular affairs. Innocent III, attempting to impose a truce on the kings of England and France, in conflict over Normandy, had proclaimed that he could intervene in such disputes 'ratione peccati'. Peace was his concern, as it had been that of the apostles, and the breach of peace was a religious matter, a sin against peace, which was the bond of charity.[1] Hence the papacy came to intervene in the peacemaking process. There was the further point that treaties were promulgated at religious ceremonies, at which solemn oaths (often on a relic, or on the gospels) were taken. To break such an oath was perjury, itself an ecclesiastical offence. The Pope might act either personally or through legates, who were sent as 'angels of peace' to heal disputes. Admonition, and diplomatic and legal process was the normal first step. But in extreme cases the full papal armoury could be brought into play. Excommunication (of the individual) and interdict (against a community) might be used against the disobedient, even

[1] Innocent III, Letter to Philippe Auguste of France (31 Oct. 1203) in M. Bouquet, *Recueil des historiens des Gaules et de la France*, new ed. 1, M. Delisle (Paris 1880) xix, 441–2; the decree *Novit* of 1204 in *Corpus iuris canonici*, ii, 244. The King of France contended that the dispute was a feudal one, and therefore outside papal competence.

princes. A papal war might be declared, subjects released from their
oaths of obedience, and even the kingdom or principality transferred
to another.

Papal mediation between princes was, however, often feared as
smacking of 'judgment'. Pope Boniface VIII in 1298, and Pope
Clement VI in 1344, mediating between England and France, were
forced to admit that they were acting not as judges, but as private
persons.[2] Papal mediation, not arbitration, succeeded in 1435, when
the papal legate (assisted by a legate from the Council of Basel)
negotiated the reconciliation of France and Burgundy, absolving
the Duke of Burgundy from his sworn alliance with England. It did
not secure the three-party peace between England, France and
Burgundy which had been hoped for.[3] This legate (Nicolò Alber-
gati) was, however, a judicious and saintly Carthusian, and
conditions were favourable. Other legates were less fitted for peace-
making, and had a stormier passage, as for instance Francesco
Coppini, Bishop of Terni, sent to England as mediator in the
Yorkist-Lancastrian struggle of 1459–1461, but in fact a partisan
advocate and promoter of the Yorkist cause.[4] In 1479 the over-
powerful papal nephew, Cardinal Giuliano della Rovere (later Pope
Julius II) attempted in vain to pronounce judgment in the conflict
between Louis XI and Mary of Burgundy. Her husband, the Archduke Maximilian, in any case refused to receive the Cardinal, since
he was legate to France.[5]

The role of the papacy as peacemaker had been enfeebled and
compromised by this time. An aggressive Italian policy, intent on
restoring and strengthening the Papal State (stretching from Rome
and the surrounding Campania and Sabina, to Umbria, the March,
Romagna and Emilia, across the Appennines) alarmed the four
other 'great' powers: Venice, Milan, Florence, and the Kingdom of
Naples-Sicily (under Aragonese rule, but a papal fief which could
be transferred to the Angevin claimants, and their successors, the
kings of France). The papacy of the later fifteenth century was

[2] J. Dumont, *Corps universel du droit des gens* (Amsterdam 1728) I, 308; Adam
Murimuth, *Continuatio chronicorum*, ed. E. M. Thompson (London 1889) p. 136.

[3] Cf. my study (J. G. Dickinson, *The Congress of Arras* (Oxford 1955)).

[4] C. Head, 'Pope Pius II and the Wars of the Roses', in *Archivium Historiae Pontificae*
VIII, 1970, pp. 142ff.

[5] Philippe de Commynes, *Mémoires*, ed. N. Lenglet du Fresnoy (Paris 1747) III,
571, 598, 630. Della Rovere was Archbishop of Avignon and as Legate had a stormy
relationship with France at this time.

becoming more and more enmeshed in Italian politics. Even Nicholas V (the humanist Tommaso de Sarzana), who aspired to remedy
his failure to save Constantinople from the Turks, was not thereby
propelled into active work for an Italian peace. His half-hearted
attempts were overtaken by secret negotiations between Milan and
Venice, producing the Peace of Lodi (1454) by which the five Italian
powers were joined in mutual self-defence.[6] Pius II (Aeneas Sylvius
Piccolomini), his successor, also working for a crusade, was
observed at his Congress of Mantua (1459), to be obsessed by
Italian conflicts and interests.[7] Paul II (Pietro Barbo), told the
Milanese ambassador in 1465 that he did not mind what happened
in France, if there were peace in Italy.[8] The aggressive activity of
Pope Sixtus IV (Francesco della Rovere, 1471–1484) and his
nepotism were hotly resisted in Italy. His involvement in the Pazzi
conspiracy against Lorenzo de' Medici became enmeshed in his
bitter religious and political conflict with Louis XI, Lorenzo's ally,
and enabled the King to intervene energetically in Italian affairs
and to threaten the Pope with a General Council. Royal invective
rebuked the Pontiff, who should preserve the peace, as his predecessors had done, whereas his scandalous behaviour prevented war
against the Turk. The Pope, for his part, facing the ambassadors
of France, England and the Italian League (by now Milan, Venice
and Florence), persisted in his need to combat enemies of the
Church, and his desire for a Universal Confederation to preserve
peace.[9] This tension between papal commitments and alignments

[6] G. Manetti, in his life of the Pope, states that he acted tepidly, not to say coldly,
in these negotiations ('Vita Nicolai V', in L. Muratori, *Rerum italicarum scriptores*
(Milan 1723–1731) III (ii), 943.

[7] I intend shortly to publish a study of this Congress.

[8] P. M. Perret, *Histoire des rélations de la France avec Venise . . .* (Paris 1896) I, 442.

[9] Documents of the French embassy in Philippe de Commynes, *Mémoires*, ed. N.
Lenglet du Fresnoy (Paris 1747) IV, 163f.; A. Desjardins, ed., *Négotiations diplomatiques
de la France avec la Toscane*, (Paris 1859) I, 178. The Pazzi conspiracy is fully discussed
in J. Combet, *Louis XI et le S. Siège* (Paris 1903). The possession by the Pope's nephew,
Girolamo Riario, of Imola (in the Romagna), which was coveted by Florence; the
Pope's appointment of an unwelcome candidate to the Archbishopric of Pisa; the
Pope's favour to the Pazzi (banking rivals of the Medici) were all ingredients in a
conspiracy to remove the Medici. If the Pope did not intend to condone violence,
he did not prevail; Lorenzo de' Medici's brother Giuliano was assassinated in the
cathedral. The retaliation included the hanging of the Pisan Archbishop from the
windows of the Palazzo della Signoria, and the detention of the Pope's great-nephew,
one of the conspirators, and a cardinal, in prison. The Pope countered with the
excommunication of Lorenzo and his adherents, and made war on Florence, with
Neapolitan aid. Lorenzo's rejoinder was to appeal to a General Council.

in Italy, and the wider European obligations, became even more
marked under Alexander VI (Rodrigo Borgia), particularly since
his search for a secure territorial dominion widened into grandiose
schemes for his son Cesare Borgia. In this period, secular rulers at
variance with the papacy could always threaten a General
Council,[10] under cover of pleas for ecclesiastical reform. Their
political manoeuvrings could be wrapped up in ecclesiastical guise,
as could the Pope's own schemes. Conciliar traditions persisted
among those confident enough to use them.

When to these Italian distractions of the papacy was added direct
French invasion of Italy, first to claim Naples-Sicily, then to claim
Milan (1499), an imperial fief (but one which the house of Orléans,
and thus Louis XII, might claim against the Sforza), the flames of
war would engulf not merely Italy, but Europe. In these conflicts,
into which the Aragonese and their Hapsburg successors were inevitably drawn, the papacy could not sustain neutrality. It struggled
in the diplomatic war and in the military one, creating or joining
first one league and then another, as did Julius II against Venice
in 1508, and against France in 1511. Rome might be, as Ferdinand
of Aragon said, the 'plaza' of Europe, to which ambassadors came,
and from which special legates and resident nuncios were
despatched; but it was only occasionally the centre of international
arbitration. Secular rulers often enjoyed watching the popes struggle
in a net partly of their own making. They could resist papal
pressure, hector the Pope on his shortcomings and evil deeds,
perhaps threaten a General Council; or they could, if it suited them,
ally with him at a price. For the Pope, it was impossible to survive
such manifold pressure for long. If he was meak and mild, then he
was castigated for it. The Ferrarese ambassador referred to Innocent
VIII (Giovanni Battista Cibò), threatened with a General Council

---

[10] Pope Pius II in his Bull *Execrabilis* (1460) condemned appeals from the Pope's
authority to a General Council; all who so appealed would be condemned as 'fosterers
of heresy and guilty of high treason' (text easily accessible in F. A. Gragg and C.
Gabel, ed., 'Commentaries of Pius II', in *Smith College Studies in History* xxv, 1940,
pp. 276–7; *Defensorium obedientiae apostolicae et alia documenta*, ed. and trans. H.
Oberman, D. A. Zerfoss and W. J. Courtenay (Cambridge, Mass., 1968), pp. 225–7).
The Pope was attempting finally to scotch the conciliarist tradition which grew up
out of the papal schism of the early fifteenth century and the need for reform: that
a General Council could, in emergencies such as papal schism or papal heresy, act
as the residual authority in the Church, and should, in any case, meet at regular
intervals.

by the King of Naples, as a 'very rabbit'.[11] If, on the other hand, the Pope took a strong line, then he risked being opposed as a 'threat to peace'. Lorenzo de' Medici, up against the formidable Cardinal Giuliano della Rovere in 1486, declared that the ecclesiastical state would be the ruin of Italy, a view which Machiavelli later endorsed. On another occasion, Lorenzo opined that the Church would one day be more dangerous than Venice.[12] In 1492 he rejoiced that the Pope would, once more, be 'common father to us all';[13] what he in fact wanted, as often with such 'children', was that the Pope should be an indulgent father, granting favours and giving support in conflicts. If, in face of such pressures, the Pope was hesitant, or appeared to be so, as did Alexander VI in the unbearable tension preceding the first French invasion, then he was warned that he might simply end up as 'chaplain' of whichever power was victorious.[14]

In such times, papal neutrality was a rare sight. Perhaps partly because of this, papal censures were often resisted or disregarded. The interruption of religious services was one consequence of such censures, the other was the fact that interdict (on a community) and excommunication (of an individual) deprived the offender of legal protection and prevented him from performing any legal acts. For a merchant community, this was an open invitation to creditors or foreign competitors to seize the victims' possessions.

Florence had eventually disregarded papal interdict during the war of 1376, arguing that the censures were a 'political' act and that the papacy was usurping secular power.[15] The Florentines later disregarded the interdict imposed after the Pazzi conspiracy,

---

[11] *The Lives of the Early Medici as Told in their Correspondence*, trans. and ed. by J. Ross (London 1910) p. 283.

[12] Ibid., pp. 277, 287.

[13] Letter of Lorenzo de' Medici to the Florentine ambassador in Rome (18 January 1492), calendared in *Catalogue of the Medici Archives* (London 1918) p. 125. This catalogue is quoted since the edition of Lorenzo de' Medici's letters by R. Fubini and N. Rubinstein (Florence 1977–) has not yet reached the later years, to which this reference and others (below, pp. 76, 77, 81) relate.

[14] P. Negri, 'Studi sulla crisi italiana alla fine del secolo XV', in *Archivio Storico Lombardo* LI, 1924, p. 111. In 1499 the Spanish ambassador warned the Pope (then backing France's campaign against Milan in return for her help in the Romagna) that he was becoming the chaplain of the King of France (M. Mallet, *The Borgias* (London 1971) p. 152).

[15] W. J. Bouwsma, *Venice and the Defence of Republican Liberty* (Berkeley 1968) pp. 49–51.

appealing to a General Council.[16] Louis XI, on his own and their behalf, was to make the same threat. The Pope himself told the French ambassadors that it was not consonant with his dignity to lift censures at the request of the offenders; moreover, since the censure had been ridiculed and the interdict nowhere observed, it was thought absurd that a concession should be made which the offenders had taken for themselves. If the Florentines feared the censures, why did they despise them; if they did not, why ask for their removal?[17] In the end, after many months, the interdict was lifted, the Florentine ambassadors kneeling for absolution. The Turks' landing at Otranto was thought to have propelled the Pope into a settlement. Later, resistance to Pope Alexander VI over Savonarola was, in the minds of some Florentines, to put their goods at risk all over Europe.[18]

Venice likewise had a long history of papal censures. In the wars of the League of Cambrai, Julius II reinforced military action with spiritual penalties: interdict on the city and excommunication of the Senate (because of their seizure of papal territory and resistance over ecclesiastical appointments). The Venetian government acted as it had done in 1483; it described the censures as politically motivated and so unjust, forbade their publication, and prepared an appeal to a General Council. Eventually the city submitted and received absolution, but not before the Council of Ten had secretly declared that such absolution was void, because extorted by force.[19]

It is no surprise to find ambassador Giustiniani describing papal censures, proposed (by Wolsey) as an inducement to an anti-French league in 1517, as 'things really ridiculous, and rather calculated to furnish food for conversation, than to be carried into effect'.[20] Yet such penalties were a 'deterrent' which could not be entirely disregarded. Bologna in 1506 protested against the injustice of Julius II's interdict, yet was alarmed as the churches were closed and ecclesiastics left the city. If military action won the day, papal censures and the approach of the Pope himself did their work of

[16] Ross, op. cit., p. 209.

[17] Papal reply to the French ambassadors printed in Philippe de Commynes, *Mémoires*, ed. N. Lenglet du Fresnoy (Paris 1747) IV, 245. Cf. P. M. Perret, *Histoire des rélations de la France avec Venise . . .* (Paris 1896) II, 117–204; C. M. Ady, *Lorenzo dei Medici* (London 1955) pp. 64–79.

[18] F. Gilbert, *Machiavelli and Guicciardini* (Princeton 1965) p. 31.

[19] Bouwsma, op. cit., pp. 100–1.

[20] Rawdon-Brown II, 94–5.

intimidation.[21] Even Machiavelli, who frequently poured scorn on papal censures, 'displayed a nervous concern on the point, and a touch of indignation at the intrusion of such irrelevance into politics'.[22]

This blend of hostility, scepticism, and yet eventual submission to papal pronouncements, shows very clearly the difficulties besetting papal activity on the political and diplomatic scene. There was a continuous state of tension. The papacy had been drawn directly into, and had itself intervened directly in, the secular confrontations of first Italian and then European powers. This situation created, and was itself also partly the result of, the popes' concentration on their temporal power base, from which they could try to maintain their independence. The popes of the Renaissance were often engaged in a struggle for survival; this impinged at almost every point on wider schemes for peace in Italy or in Christendom, and hence also on any projects for a crusade, whose essential prerequisite was peace at home. To inject any altruism into the pressing commitments and endemic wars of European powers was a forlorn task. The advancing power of the Turk occasionally brought some feeling of urgency, but response to the crusading ideal among both popes and princes was half-hearted or endlessly postponed. Princes would go when their own wars were ended, the habitual cry, and 'crusading' popes like Calixtus III and Pius II could not stem this tide, even at the time of the fall of Constantinope.

Julius II (1503–1513)

Projects for peace were hardly in evidence in the time of the Ligurian Pope Julius II. As Cardinal, in exile from the Borgia power, he had abetted the schemes for the French invasion of Italy. As Pope, the bearded pontiff was terrifying in Consistory, still more so in war. His rapid changes of mood were alarming, and his cardinals

[21] C. M. Ady, *The Bentivoglio of Bologna* (Oxford 1937) pp. 131–2; cf. the 'salutary' example quoted by Henry VII to Sixtus IV when a London malefactor who mocked at papal censures (which he thought had not saved the King and his followers from defeat in the revolt of 1487) was struck down dead, his body turning black, and stinking horribly (*Letters and Papers of the Reigns of Richard III and Henry VII*, ed. J. Gairdner (London 1861) I, 94–5). The censures were no doubt the papal Bull threatening excommunication against any attempt to interrupt the King's succession to the throne (*Calendar of Entries in the Papal Registers relating to Great Britain and Ireland*, ed. J. Twemlow (London 1961) XIV, 14–28).

[22] Bouwsma, op. cit., p. 50.

complained at being treated like valets not brothers.[23] He could roar like a bull, and would constantly interrupt ambassadors, if necessary with a little bell. His main design was to reclaim lands lost in the Romagna and the Emilia. Shortly after his accession he had told Machiavelli that he intended to have the lands of the Church under his immediate control; to the Doge of Venice he wrote: 'From the beginning of our reign it has been our steadfast purpose to restore to the Church territories of which she has been despoiled.'[24]

In 1506, supported by the King of France, who sent troops, Pope Julius launched his 'thunderbolts' (the word is from the *Julius Exclusus*)—interdict and excommunication—to expel the Bentivoglio family from Bologna, where they had long been *de facto* rulers. The combination of censures and cannon fire had its effect.[25] Erasmus saw the triumphal entry of the Pope; it was November and the roses were still in bloom. Julius was borne in procession, his mitre and cope glistening with jewels, the procession led by infantry, light cavalry and regimental musicians. The author of the *Julius Exclusus* (perhaps, but not certainly, Erasmus) composed a dialogue of St. Peter's refusal of the Pope's entry into Paradise, as an enemy of the Church. The infuriated Pope protests at this condemnation:

'You would not say so had you seen even one of my triumphs, the one in which I was carried in state into Bologna, the one I held at Rome after the defeat of the Venetians, the one in which I returned to Rome in flight from Bologna, or finally the one I held here of late, when the French had been routed, beyond all expectation, at Ravenna. If you had witnessed the ponies, the horses, the host of armed men, the adornments of generals, the spectacle of hand-picked boys, the torches blazing on every side, the elaborate shows carried in procession, the pomp of the bishops, the pride of the cardinals, the trophies, the spoils, the acclamation of people and soldiery echoing to heaven, the universal roar of applause, the blare and thunder of the trumpets, the lightning of the bombards, the coins scattered among the people, and if you had seen me carried aloft like a god, the head and originator of the whole

[23] Cf. M. A. R. de Maulde-de-la-Clavière, *La diplomatie au temps de Machiavel* (Paris 1892–3) I, 42, 475; F. Gilbert, *Machiavelli and Guicciardini* (Princeton 1965) pp. 125–7; L. Pastor, *The History of the Popes*, English trans. by F. I. Antrobus (London 1950) VI, 211–15.

[24] Niccolo Machiavelli, 'Legazione alle corte di Roma' in *Le Opere*, ed. P. Fanfani, L. Passerini and G. Milanesi (Florence 1875–7) IV, 347; Pastor, op. cit., VI, 253.

[25] C. Ady, *The Bentivoglio of Bologna* (Oxford 1937) pp. 131–3, 198–9. The churches were closed and the ecclesiastics started to leave. The French connived at the escape of the Bentivoglio family and their supporters.

pomp, you would have said that Scipio, Aemilius and Augustus were poor, simple folk compared with me.'[26]

The Pope continued his onward march, joining the League of Cambrai (between the Emperor and King Louis XII), by which Venice was to be despoiled of all her conquests at the allies' expense. He regained cities in the Romagna (Ravenna, Cervia, Rimini and Faenza) and some settlement of ecclesiastical disputes, but the shock of her defeat had produced strong reactions in Venice; an appeal to a General Council, refusal to accept stringent peace terms,[27] and (from the young and inexperienced, we are told) the proposal that the Turk should be invited to attack Rome.[28]

In 1511, when the Pope had turned against the French and planned, with Venetian and Swiss help, to sweep them out of Italy, he campaigned again in person.[29] In the January snows he besieged Mirandola, the key to his coveted reconquest of an ancient papal fief, Ferrara. Political, military and ecclesiastical conflict with France produced, to European astonishment, the spectacle of dissident Cardinals supported by the King convoking a General Council (to Pisa) to establish peace among Christians, undertake a crusade and reform the Church.[30] Papal retaliation, a Council summoned to the Lateran (to promote the same causes), was overtaken by the French victory at Ravenna on Easter Day 1512, and the rival Council's denunciation of the Pope as 'disturber of the peace, contumacious . . . author of schism'. All Christians were urged to with-

[26] Translation of the Latin text in *Erasmi Opuscula*, ed. W. K. Ferguson (The Hague 1933), p. 118. An American translation has been made by R. Pascal, *The Julius Exclusus of Erasmus* (Bloomington 1968).

[27] See above, p. 26.

[28] Diary of Gerolamo Priuli, quoted in A. Bonardi, 'Venezia e la lega di Cambrai', in *Nuovo Archivio Veneto*, New Series VII, 1904, p. 244. The moral crisis in defeat has been examined by F. Gilbert, 'Venice in the crisis of the League of Cambrai', in J. R. Hale, ed., *Renaissance Venice* (London 1973) pp. 274–90.

[29] In his alliance with the Swiss, Julius II offered an annual subvention and diplomatic protection in return for a force of 6,000 men, on demand, and the promise to abstain from alliances not approved by him. He formed the Swiss Guard at the Vatican. (Pastor, op. cit., VI, 323–6, 340–1; John S. Bridge, *A History of France from the Death of Louis XI* (Oxford 1929) IV, 58–9.)

[30] Pierre Gringoire wrote satirical pieces against the Pope, at the request of the King. *La chasse du cerf des cerfs* is a play on the papal title *Servus Servorum Dei*, Pope Julius being the King Stag, the French the 'free' hunters (francs veneurs). (P. Gringoire, *Oeuvres complètes*, ed. d'Héricault and Montaiglon, I (Paris 1858), pp. 157–67).

hold obedience, and the Pope was suspended.[31] Julius had already reacted in March 1512 by preparing a brief deposing King Louis and transferring his kingdom and title of Most Christian King to Henry VIII (provided that the latter defeated his rival). The brief was, however, never put into force; there was no French defeat, and other events supervened.[32]

Yet this was the Pope who (after taking Perugia in 1506) had announced that he would deliver Constantinople,[33] and who protested, always, his work for the peace of Italy. His own appraisal of his work is clear-cut: 'the absolute independence of the Church, the maintenance of her prestige, the establishment of a balance of power in Italy, so that no one state may be stronger than any other, but all may co-operate with the Holy See in turning out the foreigner and making war on the Turk.'[34] Guicciardini put the edge on the argument: the Pope was worthy of great glory 'if either he had been a Prince secular, or if that care and intention which he had to rayse the Churche into temporall greatnesse by means of warre, had been employed to exalte it by mediation of peace, in matters spirituall'.[35] It was fitting that the Pope's statue on his tomb should portray him not in repose, but inclined on one elbow, restless and vigilant.

Leo X (1513–1521)

Pope Leo X, Giovanni de' Medici, was elected on the promise (his election 'capitulations') of Peace and a crusade. For his processional entry into the Lateran, a triumphal arch on S. Angelo bridge proclaimed him 'promoter of ecclesiastical unity and peace among Christian nations', while that year the Pasquin *festa* for poets had peace as its theme.[36] As the son of Lorenzo de' Medici, he would

---

[31] Pastor, op. cit., VI, 363–5, 390–3, 406–10ff.; Bridge, op. cit., IV, 95–119.

[32] D. S. Chambers, *Cardinal Bainbridge in the Court of Rome 1509–1514*, (Oxford 1965) pp. 38–9; J. J. Scarisbrick, *Henry VIII* (London 1968) pp. 33–4.

[33] Pastor, op. cit., VII, 271.

[34] A. Luzio, 'Isabella d'Este di fronte a Giulio II', in *Archivio Storico Lombardo*, Series IV, XVIII, 1912, p. 135.

[35] Francesco Guicciardini, *Storia d'Italia*, ed. C. Panigada and R. Palmarocchi (Bari 1929–1936) III, 257 (Lib.XI, cap. viii); the English translation is Fenton's (*The Historie of Guicciardin*, London 1579, p. 632).

[36] Pasquin, a statue erected near the Piazza Navona, opposite the house of one Pasquino, was the rendezvous for an annual poetic competition, on a given theme (it later became the 'placard' for any scurrilous or malicious lampoons). In 1512 the theme was War, appropriately. (D. S. Chambers, op. cit., pp. 121–4).

have known of his father's work for peace in Italy. His tutor, Politian (Angelo Poliziano) may have inclined his mind to the subject.[37] Politian's elegy on the death of Lorenzo (set to music by the great Burgundian musician Heinrich Isaac) lamented the passing of the physician of Italy, the giver of peace (a play on Medici, and Lorenzo, the laurel, symbol of peace). Pope Leo had grown to eminence during the stormy pontificate of Julius II; he had some experience of war, for instance he was Legate to the papal army at Ravenna in 1512, ministering to the dying. His wish for peace was genuine. After his accession, he declared that he wanted peace, and to mediate between princes; it was a function of the holy office to establish peace between all men and especially between neighbours.[38] His nuncio to England brought peace proposals to the victorious Henry VIII (newly returned from his first campaign against France).[39] The nuncio to the Emperor Maximilian was instructed to urge the Pope's strong wish for peace, as befitted the Vicar of Christ, and his own disposition, and as suited the need for action against the Turk. If the Emperor went to war, he should choose allies carefully; the Pope considered that war should be undertaken solely in order to restore peace.[40] The Pope had, meanwhile, accepted the submission of the French King, pardoned the schismatic cardinals, and, at the closing of the Lateran Council in December 1513, promulgated a Bull for the restoration of peace among princes and a crusade.[41]

Pope Leo succeeded in bringing pressure upon England and France, who responded in 1514 by a treaty of peace and a marriage

[37] The future Pope was confirmed, tonsured, and given a titular abbacy, at the age of 7; a cardinal at 13, he was not raised to the dignity until he was over 16. He was given a thorough classical education, though his tutor scorned his mother's (Clarice Orsini) prescription that he should read the Psalter. He studied at Pisa before leaving for Rome (1492). He was then counselled by his father to live unostentatiously, talk seriously with his new colleagues, acquire classical remains and rare books, eat plainly, exercise, and above all rise early and prepare the day's business the night before (H. M. Vaughan, *The Medici Popes* (London 1908) pp. 5–27; *The Lives of the Early Medici as Told in their Correspondence*, ed. J. Ross (London 1910) pp. 211, 216, 220, 273).

[38] R. Devonshire-Jones, *Francesco Vettori, Florentine Citizen, and the Medici Government* (London 1972) p. 93.

[39] Scarisbrick, op. cit., p. 51; Chambers, op. cit., pp. 50–4. There was an ambitious papal plan for a peace conference of King and Emperor, presided over by Cardinal Bainbridge. The latter had, in fact, been hoping for papal investiture of the King with the French Crown, as Julius II had secretly promised.

[40] Pastor, op. cit., VII, 63–4.

[41] Ibid., VII, 71–2.

alliance, but this did not prevent England's wish for military action
(this time against Ferdinand of Aragon). Nor could the Pope
prevent the new King, François I, from embarking on his Italian
campaign to regain Milan in 1515. As Guicciardini put it, the Pope
hoped that Milan would neither fall to France nor come into the
Emperor's hands: 'it was thus very difficult for him to know how
to proceed, or how to balance matters so that the means which
promoted one end did not prejudice the other.'[42] This basic problem
faced the Pope at every turn. In fact the princes of Europe went
their own way, making war and peace when it pleased them and
justifying their actions with consummate ease. The Pope himself
was not energetic—he was preoccupied first with his family's power
and security in Florence (where the Medici had been restored in
1512) and secondly with his personal pleasures and diversions: his
patronage of the arts (Raphael and Michelangelo were at work),
his musicians and buffoons, his players (Plautus and Machiavelli
were performed), and his passion for the hunt. Perhaps the over-
vigorous schooling, the parental precepts and the too early
promotion had blunted any appetite for political action, while his
natural indolence and indecisiveness increased. His exile with his
brothers at the age of nineteen, and the violent times of Julius II,
no doubt induced caution. He trusted to the mysterious working of
a balance of power, to his and other princes' diplomatic agents, as
resolvers of conflict. Inactivity was sometimes broken by a burst of
war; he risked war in 1516–17 to secure Urbino (a papal fief) for
his nephew, Lorenzo, whom he installed to replace the rebellious
Duke, Francesco Maria della Rovere.

In 1517 the Pope made another effort to fulfil his election promises. The logistics of a crusade had been exhaustively studied in
Rome (by eight cardinals, with foreign ambassadors), for the Turk
had returned to Constantinople having conquered Syria, Palestine
and Egypt. The crusade was proclaimed in March 1518, with a
five-year truce, which the Pope imposed upon the European
powers.[43] The peace project was, in the event, seized upon by
Wolsey and transformed into a universal peace treaty, a non-
aggression pact, in which the Pope was merely one of the contracting
parties (see below, p. 65). The Venetian ambassador in London
hoped that the inaudible mumbling of the treaty at the promul-

---

[42] Guicciardini, *Storia d'Italia* III, 326 (Lib.XII, cap. vii).
[43] Pastor, op. cit., VII, 213–35.

gation ceremony in St. Paul's was tantamount to the cancellation
of the preamble concerning an expedition against the Turk.[44] This
was no doubt wishful thinking, but the project of a crusade was, as
usual, endlessly postponed. For Henry VIII, the King of France
was the 'real Turk'; for the King of France, the clergy filled this
role; for Venice, a crusade was a threat to her understanding with
the Turk, renewed that very year. As for the Pope, his schemes of
peace had brought some success; but, more and more, the European
powers went their own way without his counsel or arbitration.

When Charles of Hapsburg inherited Aragon and Naples–Sicily
(1516) and the Empire (1519), the Pope's options became
immeasurably more difficult. His choice narrowed as the conflict in
Europe centred on a Franco-imperial struggle for predominance.
The papacy was, like Henry VIII or the Republic of Venice, forced
to ally first on one side and then on the other, though the Pope,
like his legate Wolsey, may occasionally have taken the lead. In
January 1519 he had concluded defensive alliances both with François I and with Charles, the future Emperor, defensive not only of
the papacy and the papal states, but of the Medici (in Florence and
Urbino).[45] On 8 May 1521 (rebuffing English pleas for continued
neutrality[46]), he came to an offensive alliance with Charles V for
the preservation of the faith, for peace, for war on the Infidel, but
first for the expulsion of the French from Italy. The Pope would,
as ambassador John Clerk reported, 'spend his mitre but he would
have them out of Italy'.[47] After a French attack in June on Reggio
(in the papal states and a centre for Milanese exiles) the Pope made
the alliance public (27 June); he could now claim that he was the
victim of aggression. By September, François I and his commanders

[44] Rawdon Brown II, 224–5.

[45] Pastor, op. cit., VII, 267ff.; F. Nitti, *Leone X e la sua politica secondo documenti e
carteggi inediti* (Florence 1892) pp. 143ff.

[46] The Pope told the imperial ambassador that neutrality was all very well for
Henry VIII; England was surrounded by the sea, but the Papal State was not an
island (*Cal. Span.* II, 343).

[47] Dumont, op. cit., IV, 3, 96; *L.P.* III (i), nos. 1402, 1430, 1466; Pastor, op. cit.,
VIII, 35ff.; Nitti, op. cit., pp. 425ff. The Sforza were to be restored to Milan, and the
Pope was to reclaim Parma, Piacenza, and Ferrara. The Emperor was promised the
investiture of Naples–Sicily (not traditionally granted to the holder of the imperial
dignity). The Emperor promised to protect the Pope against all enemies of the faith.
Some had counselled him to use the Lutheran problem to win his cause with the
Pope. In fact, the Edict of Worms was approved by the Emperor on 8 May. It was
celebrated in Rome, in early June, by the burning of Luther's writings in the Piazza
Navona.

were threatened with excommunication and interdict.[48] Papal,
imperial and Swiss forces conjoined to attack Milan, the capital's
fall (on 19 November) being celebrated by the Pope at his hunting
lodge at Magliano, near Rome, with gunfire, fireworks and music.[49]
Piacenza and other cities opened their gates to the papal army;
news of Parma's recapture came to the Pope on the day of his death
(1 December). He had been planning a thanksgiving service for
victory, and had told the imperial ambassador that he rejoiced more
over the taking of Milan than over his election.[50] It was an ironic
end to a pontificate committed to the cause of peace.

Adrian VI (1522–1523)

During the brief reign of Adrian VI (Adrian Dedel Floriszoon)[51]
peace was a central concern. He began by exhorting the Emperor,
France and England to peace, especially the first, who should accept
moderate terms for the greater good: action against the Turk. In
his first Consistory, he announced his wish for the union of princes
in a crusade, and for reform.[52] Vives, his friend, wrote from Louvain
in the cause of peace and reform, and Cardinal Campeggio, strong
for reform, also urged peace for the purpose of a crusade.[53] The
Turk had taken Belgrade (1521) and Rhodes (1522). Papal activity
continued; resistance to the Emperor's plea for an alliance against
France and urgent calls for help to relieve Rhodes. A commission
of cardinals met to plan for the restoration of peace and the collection of money for a crusade. The Pope then imposed a three-year
truce on the whole of Christendom in April 1523, supported by the
heaviest ecclesiastical penalties.[54] The Pope's letter to the King of
Portugal reveals his apprehensions: 'Woe to princes who do not

[48] The Pope alleged that the King had used crusading money for the war against
the Church (Dumont, op. cit., III (supplement) 70–3).

[49] Pastor, op. cit., VIII, 40ff.; the Marquis of Mantua commanded the papal army,
and Guicciardini (Governor of Reggio) was its Commissary-General.

[50] Pastor, op. cit., VIII, 60–1.

[51] The son of an artisan of Utrecht, schooled by the Brethren of the Common
Life, a professor and then Rector of Louvain (where Erasmus was his pupil). He
became the tutor of the young Charles V, counsellor to Margaret of Austria in the
Netherlands, Bishop of Tortosa in 1516, Cardinal in 1517, and Viceroy of Spain in
1520.

[52] Pastor, op. cit., IX, 92.

[53] Ibid., IX, 85, 89; quoting from *Ioannis Ludovici Vivis, Valentini, Opera Omnia*, ed.
G. Majansio (Valencia 1782–1790) V, 164–74.

[54] Pastor, op. cit., IX, 170–1, 189.

employ the sovereignty conferred on them by God in promoting
His glory and defending the people of His election, but abuse it in
internecine strife.'[55] Even this strong appeal met with hostility;
François I, who would not come to terms without securing Milan,
doubted whether the Pope could impose an unconditional truce
with ecclesiastical sanctions. The King berated the Pope, judging
his actions to be *not* against the Turk, but against France. He
reminded the Pope of Boniface VIII's fate; there were reports that
the King might set up an anti-pope.[56] Pope Adrian, on his part,
declared that he feared to side against France, for he would lose
great revenues, and the King might become the protector of the
Lutherans.[57] Only a final political rupture with France, and the
knowledge that French troops were assembling to cross the Alps,
drove the Pope to a defensive league against her; allied to the
Emperor, England, Milan and Florence, he promised money for the
expenses of war.[58] From the pronouncements and actions of Adrian
VI can be judged the deep conflicts, political, ecclesiastical and
military, in which the papacy had become involved. The Turk and
the new heresy were now the twin enemies against which peace in
Christendom was an essential first step. But even this first step was
often imperilled by the papacy's own commitments and the pressures of allies and enemies alike.

Clement VII (1523–1534)

Clement VII (Giulio de' Medici, the illegitimate son of Lorenzo de'
Medici's brother, Giuliano) faced the renewed problem of papal
territorial involvements in Italy, together with his family's rule in
Florence. He was hailed, on his accession, as 'restorer of peace to
the world and defender of the Christian name', but his hard work,
his knowledge of politics (he had ruled Florence before his
accession) and his commitment to impartiality, were hopelessly
vitiated by a fundamental indecision and lack of courage. The fatal
years 1524–6 are a case in point. Having refused to renew his
predecessor's league against France, sending legates to France,

---

[55] Ibid., IX, 176. The Pope hoped for peace negotiations in Rome.

[56] The papacy did, on occasion, impose a truce on secular powers or threaten
penalties if peace were not made. In 1473 this threat was made by the papal legate
to France and Burgundy (J. Combet, *Louis XI et le Saint Siège* (Paris 1903) pp. 125–6).

[57] Pastor, op. cit., IX, 197–201.

[58] Ibid., IX, 201–2.

Spain and England in the cause of peace, and again to François I
and the imperial commander in the weeks before the battle of Pavia,
the Pope was driven to a French alliance by the projected French
expedition to Naples, even promising free passage for French troops
through papal territory. Yet he had counselled François I to avoid
staking all on a battle at Pavia. The Emperor rightly declared that
with such a Franco-papal alliance, it was no time to discuss Luther
(it was the period of the Peasants' War).[59] After the French King's
defeat and capture at Pavia, the Pope was driven to a defensive
treaty with the imperial Viceroy. By 1526, however, after François
I had capitulated in the treaty of Madrid and regained his freedom,
the Pope came over to the side of France.[60] He defended his actions
to the Emperor in a bitter letter of June 1526, outlining his version
of events since his accession, and declaring that he had been forced
to take up arms to avoid servitude and to restore peace. The
Emperor should himself give peace to Christendom[61] (it was the
summer of the great Turkish victory at Mohacs on the Danube).

The Emperor's reply from Granada in September was even more
bitter. He had been taking counsel on the legality of withholding
papal revenues and making war on the Pope. He now wrote that
the Pope should sheath his sword; he should not permit one drop
of Christian blood to be shed in the acquisition of territory. He had
not protected Italy or Christendom or even the Papal State. His
conduct had given grave scandal; he should lay down his arms,
then it might be possible to combat heresy.[62] The letter was drafted
by the Emperor's secretary, Alfonso de Valdes.[63] The secretary had
a further chance in 1527, when Rome had been sacked by imperial

[59] Pastor, op. cit., IX, 257–8, 266–71.

[60] Ibid., IX, 278, 304–7. The accord (the League of Cognac) was largely the work
of Gian Mateo Giberti (Bishop of Verona), then at the height of his diplomatic
activity. Guicciardini, then holding office in the Curia, wrote a searching analysis
of current problems, in which he taxed the Pope with timidity and an easy-going
attitude which could only be described 'by its plain name ineptitude' (unpublished
memorandum cited by R. Ridolfi, *The Life of Francesco Guicciardini* (London 1967)
pp. 143–50.

[61] Ibid., IX, 316–16.

[62] Pastor, op. cit., VII, 352–5. By the time this letter was despatched the Pope had
been brought to heel; 5,000 imperial troops, in league with Cardinal Pompeo
Colonna, an ancient enemy of the Pope, and led by the imperial envoy Ugo de
Moncada, brought him to a treaty.

[63] Valdes, born at Cuenca about 1490, was taught by Peter Martyr, the Italian
humanist. He was at Aachen when Charles V was crowned, became a secretary at
the court, and in 1526 Latin secretary to the Emperor. He was a friend of Erasmus.

troops and the Pope made prisoner. The Emperor was held responsible by many; the grandees and prelates of Spain protested, in France and England elaborate plans were made to rescue the Pope, at a suitable price. Wolsey toyed with the idea of a meeting of cardinals at Avignon, and the exercise of papal authority, by delegation, from there. In the frenzied diplomatic and military activity, Valdes struck hard for the Emperor's case. His propaganda took the form of a dialogue (1527), *Dialogo de las cosas occuridas in Roma*, between Lactantius (himself) and an archdeacon, returned from Rome in soldier's dress and meeting his interlocutor in Valladolid. Lactantius argues that the Emperor was not responsible for the sack of Rome; God had allowed it, as a punishment of the Church for its sins. The Archdeacon states that even the Goths left St Peter's and the sacred relics unscathed. Both agree that Pope and Emperor should promote peace, but Lactantius argues that the Pope had destroyed the peace and started a new war, perhaps through evil counsel. He was warring for riches (material possessions) which even pagan philosophers despised, and at the very moment when the Turk threatened Hungary. Yet, objected the Archdeacon, the people of Italy would look down upon a Pope who did not wage war. The response was: 'Wouldn't it be better for the Pope to lose all his temporal power than to keep it at the expense of Christian suffering and dishonour to Jesus Christ?' The Church, which was all Christians, had been despoiled in these wars. Perhaps it would be better that the popes should have no temporal power? The Pope had done more to despoil the Church than anyone who might try to take away Church lands.[64] Valdes was here echoing Erasmus' Adage *Sileni Alcibiadis*, in which he had argued that the popes, having no heirs, were more given to plunder than their lay counterparts, who wished to leave their kingdoms prosperous. Why call a thing 'Peter's patrimony', which the apostle himself was proud not to have?[65]

---

[64] Alfonso de Valdes, *Dialogue of Lactantius and an Archdeacon*, trans. J. E. Longhurst (Albuquerque 1952), pp. 20ff. The papal legate, Baltasar Castiglione, answered Valdes' book: it was plain heresy.

[65] Erasmus, *Sileni Alcibiadis*, in Phillips, op. cit., pp. 92, 94 (Adage III.i.1). In the fifteenth century the distinguished humanist Lorenzo Valla had advocated the abolition of the Pope's temporal power. He did so in the course of his work on the Donation of Constantine (the mythical donation by Constantine of lands to the papacy) which he pronounced to be a forgery. (P. Partner, *The Lands of St Peter: the Papal State in the Middle Ages and the early Renaissance* (London 1972), pp. 443–4).

Advice on the temporal power of the papacy was again given in 1529. Gasparo Contarini, future cardinal and reformer, spoke to the Pope as a private person, not in his capacity of Venetian ambassador.[66] He suggested that the papal patrimony should be drastically reduced. The Church had been at her best before acquiring these dominions. The Papal State was like any other states of an Italian prince. The Pope should set in the forefront of his responsibilities the welfare of the true Church which consisted in the peace of Christendom, and allow the interests of the temporal state to fall for a time into the background. Contarini was speaking at a time when Venice had seized Ravenna and Cervia; he may not, however, have been disingenuous. He was one of the great reform commission of 1536, which roundly condemned unbridled papal power.[67]

For Clement VII, the counsels of 1529 were no doubt impossible to follow; he declared as much to Contarini. On peace, his efforts continued intermittently.[68] The papal legate at Cambrai in 1529 was able to prevent a breakdown of the negotiations between Margaret of Austria and Louise of Savoy (mother of François I), leading to the treaty of Cambrai.[69] The Pope himself met the Emperor at Bologna in 1530, where a reconciliation was proclaimed in the imperial coronation. By 1533, it was the turn of France: the Pope met François I at Marseilles and married his niece Catherine de' Medici to the King's son, the future Henri II. It was the time of England's 'apostasy'. In the midst of the conference, Dr Edmund Bonner, ambassador from Henry VIII, broke in upon the Pope. He was delivering the King's appeal to a General Council against papal excommunication (over his remarriage).[70]

[66] Pastor, op. cit., x, 35–7, quoting from *Regesten und Briefen des Cardinals Gasparo Contarini*, ed. F. Dittrich (Braunberg 1881) pp. 41–6.

[67] The reform commission pronounced that the doctrine that the Pope's will was law was the Trojan horse by which numerous abuses had crept into the Church (H. Jedin, *A History of the Council of Trent*, trans. E. Graf (London 1957) I, 422–4).

[68] The dilemma of the Pope, caught between the Emperor and the King of France, is well illustrated in the twin paintings by Giorgio Vasari in the Palazzo Vecchio, Florence (see Plates 1a and 1b).

[69] R. J. Knecht, *Francis I* (Cambridge 1982) p. 219; D. Moulton Mayer, *The Great Regent, Louise of Savoy 1476–1531* (London 1966) pp. 248–76.

[70] Scarisbrick, op. cit., pp. 319–20.

Paul III (1534–1549)

Like Clement VII, Paul III (Alessandro Farnese)[71] announced his intention, upon election, of working for the peace of Christendom. Such a peace was an essential preliminary to the Pope's two further aims: to assemble a General Council of the Church (to deal with heresy and reform), and to undertake a war against the Infidel.[72] Throughout his pontificate, the Pope was intent on preserving a strict neutrality between France and the Empire: 'Neutrality in Rome, like our daily bread, must be regarded as a necessity' he told Nicolas Perrenot de Granvelle, minister of Charles V.[73] It was an attitude which infuriated both Charles V and François I, who were at war in the years 1536–7 and 1542–4, constantly poised for war in the periods of 'peace', and forever seeking out new and old allies to tip the scales in the cold war of diplomacy.[74] Despite the Pope's great ambitions for his family (Titian's portrait of him with his grandsons[75] illuminates this concern and preoccupation), the Pope did not respond to the French offer of Milan as dowry for the marriage of a French princess and his grandson, Ottavio, nor to his son Pier Luigi's schemes in Tuscany.[76] He rebuffed the Emperor's plea for a strong alliance against the Turk and all Christian aggressors,

[71] The Farnese family were distinguished servants of the Church, particularly in the military sphere. Their lands stretched south from Lake Bolsena, but they had entered the ranks of the Roman nobility, marrying into the Gaetani family, as also the Orsini. Alessandro's sister Giulia (the wife of Orsino Orsini) was the mistress of Rodrigo Borgia; on the latter's elevation to the papacy, Alessandro (who had been educated in Rome, Florence and Pisa) had been given high office at the Curia. A Cardinal in 1493, he had been Legate of the March of Ancona, and later Legate of Rome. His palace in Rome was the centre of brilliant festivities. At his accession he was 66. His two natural sons were legitimised by Julius II; Pier Luigi, the elder, served as a condottiere, sometimes on the imperial side. Paul III was sagacious, shrewd and strong-minded.

[72] Pastor, op. cit., XI, 218–20; Knecht, op. cit., p. 236. The abortive Council of 1537 was to have dealt with heresy, reform, peace and a crusade. That it did not meet was largely due to French opposition, and their manipulation of Protestant hesitations (ibid., X, 70–2, 103).

[73] Pastor, op. cit., XII, 151.

[74] In 1536 François I concluded an alliance, probably a military one, with the Sultan, in preparation for his war with the Emperor. In the same year he invaded Savoy, claiming some territories once owned by his mother, Louise of Savoy. By March he had taken Chambéry and Turin, capital of Piedmont. The invasion was undoubtedly part of a scheme to regain Milan (Knecht, op. cit., pp. 274–8).

[75] In the Museo Nazionale, Naples.

[76] Pastor, op. cit., XI, 238, 315–18. Pier Luigi became Gonfalonier of the Church, and his lands in the papal patrimony were united into the Duchy of Castro.

and took no side in the war over Savoy in 1536–7.[77] This led to the famous imperial outburst in Consistory in April 1536. The Emperor, speaking in Spanish, put forward his whole case against François I, who had just invaded Savoy (an imperial fief) and laid claim to Milan (whose Sforza Duke had died leaving no legitimate heir). The Emperor proposed to fight a duel with the French King, which the Pope forbade. The Emperor requested a pronouncement from the Pope as to the rights and wrongs of the conflict; but the Pope wished to remain neutral. Only in this way could he preserve peace.[78]

In 1538 Pope Paul attempted a more positive solution. Acting on his own initiative,[79] he summoned the two enemies to a personal meeting at Nice, at which peace was to be negotiated. The Emperor came on his galley to Villefranche, François I lodged at Villeneuve. Neither would attend joint meetings with the Pope, who had been obliged to lodge in the Franciscan convent outside the city, since the Duke of Savoy would not hand over the citadel (one of his few remaining strongholds). The Pope accordingly met the two enemies separately. He met the Emperor four times, once in a pavilion in an orange grove near the sea. Pope and King met twice, and 'flying legates' sped between the parties. The Pope's proposal for a marriage alliance as a solution to French claims to Milan was accepted by the Emperor, if the King would break his alliance with the Turk and support the convening of a General Council. The King's refusal left a truce (based on the status quo) as the only feasible settlement; even over this, the King wished for a long truce (probably to retain Savoy), while the Emperor wanted only a shorter one. The truce, for ten years, was all that the Pope could obtain.[80] But when the Pope had left, the Emperor returned to meet the King at Aigues-Mortes. Cordial, direct discussions, an autumn meeting at Compiègne between the King and Mary of Hungary (Regent of the Netherlands), and a French embassy to the Emperor, marked three stages in the formulation of an accord.[81] It can only

[77] Pastor, op. cit., XI, 236.

[78] Ibid., XI, 246–9, 251–5. The Emperor spoke a second time, in Italian, to the French ambassadors.

[79] The Venetian ambassador at Nice reported that the Pope had summoned the meeting without consulting the cardinals (Alberi, 1st series, II, 84).

[80] Pastor, op. cit., XI, 286–92; Knecht, op. cit., pp. 291–2.

[81] The meeting of Aigues-Mortes seems to have concerned the treatment of heresy in Germany and war with the Turk. That at Compiègne concerned relations in the north; the French ambassadors to Spain offered marriage alliances and the King's co-operation in a crusade (Knecht, loc. cit.). The Emperor's journey through France

be concluded that papal involvement in the proceedings had been unhelpful or unwelcome. In any case, a full-scale 'summit', with direct three-party negotiations would have produced endless complications, not least over procedure and precedence. Nevertheless, the Pope's work for peace was lauded on his return to Rome.[82]

The Pope's search for neutrality was essentially a passive thing, yet it was the only hope of a peace initiative. It was also the product of fear; the Pope was haunted by the idea that a strong move against France would drive that kingdom into apostasy, following the English example. In 1542, when France again declared war, in alliance with the Turk, and in violation of the ten-year truce, the Emperor again attacked the papal attitude. The Pope was putting him, he wrote, on a level with the King of France, who had turned the sword of the Infidel against Christendom, supported the Protestants, hindered the meeting of a General Council, and broken the papal truce. The Emperor saw himself as the obedient son of the Church who had fought the Turk by sea and land. The 'prodigal' son was not set by his father above the elder, faithful one.[83]

The attempt to breach papal neutrality was made again when the Emperor met the Pope at Busseto (near Piacenza) in 1543. The Emperor declined to make peace with the King, unless the Pope abandoned his neutrality. He spoke scornfully of François I, who that winter had permitted the Turkish fleet to winter in Toulon. Against the Pope, he cited the six lilies of the Farnese coat of arms, but the 6,000 fleur-de-lys in the Pope's heart.[84] The subsequent mission of Cardinal Alessandro Farnese to both sovereigns met with equally tough imperial resistance. The Emperor would have no peace so long as an inch of Italian soil was in French hands. In Rome there were heated altercations between the Pope and a Spanish Cardinal who said that French alliance with the Turk was winked at, to which the Pope replied that the imperial alliance

---

in 1539, when elaborate festivities took peace as their theme, is discussed by V. L. Saulnier, 'Charles quint traversant la France', in J. Jacquot, *Fêtes et cérémonies du temps de Charles quint* (Paris 1960–1975), II, 207–33. Sir Thomas Wyatt was sceptical of these peace festivities: 'all these entries, joining of arms, knitting of crowns, and such like ceremonies' (*L.P.* XIV (ii), 174).

[82] The Senate and the people of Rome welcomed the Pope, 'to whom we owe peace among Christians and warfare against the Turk' (Pastor, op. cit., XI, 193).

[83] Pastor, op. cit., XII, 150–2; Jedin, op. cit., I, 457, 477–8.

[84] Pastor, op. cit., XII, 169–78. Cf. ambassador Nicholas Wotton's report, from the Diet of Speyer, in 1544: 'as long as there are apostolic nuncios, the King of France is not without his attorneys here' (*L.P.* XIX (i), 94).

with England was worse.[85] Peace with France was still the Pope's demand, but the peace when it came (the treaty of Crépy in 1544) was negotiated without papal help or representation.[86]

It was only in 1546, when the Emperor was preparing for war against the German Protestants (the League of Schmalkald), that the Pope came down on the imperial side. After lengthy bargaining, a treaty was made in June 1546 by which the Pope granted a subsidy and papal troops for a war 'against the Protestants, the Schmalkaldic League, and other German teachers of error'. There was also to be mutual assistance against any attack from a third party, and the granting of papal revenues from Spain and the Netherlands for the war chest. Ottavio Farnese commanded the papal troops. When, after a short campaign, the papal forces were withdrawn in January 1547, the Emperor's anger welled over. He told the Pope's nuncio, Girolamo Verallo, that the papal troops had been just a pack of Italian robbers. As for the Pope, he had the 'French' disease, no new affliction for him. French influence had been at work (it was true that Cardinal Jean du Bellay was, at this time, working hard for France's cause); the Pope had enticed the Emperor into war to destroy him.[87] The Emperor's victory at Mühlberg in April 1547 was thus independent of papal assistance; indeed the Pope may have been alarmed at this evident sign of imperial strength. He had hoped to induce the two rival sovereigns to unite and to reclaim England for the faith (Henry VIII had died in January), but Charles had stoutly rejected any war on the Pope's behalf. In an outburst ten days before Mühlberg, he had told Verallo that the Pope was working only to prolong his own days, to aggrandise his family and to heap up riches. He was neglecting his duty and working for the destruction of the Church.[88]

[85] Pastor, op. cit., xii, 184–9. At this time, the Pope came close to pronouncing on the Franco–imperial conflict. Because of the conflict, the Council of Trent had to be suspended; Charles V was not blameless in this since he forbade Spanish prelates to attend. France was, by long tradition, against the Council.

[86] Knecht, op. cit., p. 370.

[87] Pastor, op. cit., xii, 288–9, 319–31, 335–6; Jedin, op. cit., ii, 404–6. France's direct involvement in German politics was muted, in the final months of François I, due mainly to financial duress (the King had to raise money to regain Boulogne from Henry VIII), but also to differing attitudes in the French Council, and varying assessments of imperial power (Knecht, op. cit., pp. 375–6).

[88] Pastor, op. cit., xii, 358–60; Jedin, op. cit., ii, 413, 417–18. The Pope infuriated the Emperor by accepting the transference of the Council of Trent to Bologna (in papal territory, and thus probably unacceptable to the Protestants) in March 1547. Typhus was rampant at Trent, but the Emperor did not accept medical reasons for the move.

The impasse of 1547 clearly demonstrates the papal position: politically and diplomatically weak, with ecclesiastical problems reacting continually on his stance for peace. He could not, at the same time, propitiate France and the Empire; his work for reform and for the containment of heresy was perilously endangered by the political attitudes of the princes.[89] His own actions were embittered by family tragedy: his son Pier Luigi, whom he had installed as Duke in Parma and Piacenza, was assassinated on the instigation of the imperial viceroy, Ferrante Gonzaga in September 1547. The Pope, who feared an imperial expedition to Italy, was contemplating a definite alliance with France in 1549, the year of his death. His diplomatic policies had not, in the event, borne lasting fruit either on the European scale or in Italy, where Spanish domination could not be removed.[90] In fact the Pope had lost the initiative even in religious matters. The Emperor went his own way; the Diet of Augsburg, which produced the *Interim*, slighted the papal legate and excluded him from its deliberations.[91]

Julius III (1550–1555)

Paul III's pontificate, with the conference at Nice and the frequent legations in the cause of peace, had a faint echo in the time of his successor. Julius III (Gian Maria Cecchi del Monte)[92] was weak and vacillating, but still strove for 'neutrality' and for peace between Emperor and King. His search for peace, however, was vitiated by his war against Ottavio Farnese, Duke of Parma, a rebellious vassal of the Church. The Pope acted with imperial support against Farnese, the ally of France, to whom Henri II had promised money and arms. The French King threatened to withdraw obedience if the Pope persisted. Characteristically both Emperor and King claimed that they were not breaking the Peace of Crépy; the one said that he was acting in defence of the Church, the other that he

[89] Early in the reign of Henri II, the French made renewed approaches to the Pope. In October 1547 the young Charles de Guise, just promoted Cardinal, travelled to Rome to influence the Pope (and also to receive the Cardinal's hat) (Pastor, op. cit., XII, 383–4).

[90] Pastor, op. cit., XII, 385, 446.

[91] Ibid., op. cit., XII, 411–13.

[92] The del Monte, from Arezzo, had settled in Rome. The Pope had been trained as a lawyer at Perugia and Siena. He became Governor of Rome, Archbishop of Siponto, and one of the Presidents of the Council of Trent. His villa Giulia, on the Flaminian way, was famous for its gardens, its statuary, its grotto and its fountains. The Pope could reach it by barge.

was merely helping an ally. Papal defeat brought a truce with France in April 1552, but war again threatened Rome when the Sienese rebelled against Spanish rule and placed themselves under French protection.[93] King Henri sought papal support, although he pronounced that the pontiff was 'un homme inconstant, variable et léger'.[94] It was the period after the King's seizure of Metz, Toul and Verdun as ally and protector of the German Protestants. The Pope feared French apostasy, and made several efforts to secure a Franco–imperial peace. A commission of cardinals studied the problem in Rome, while legates travelled north to offer papal mediation in April 1553. The Pope constantly stressed his 'neutrality' and sent another legate in 1554.[95] King Henri had sent Cardinal Jean du Bellay to Rome to seek a papal agreement, and in the latter months of 1553 there were hopes of peace. The Cardinal's young relative, the poet Joachim, dreamt of the return of Astraea to the earth, in a new golden age of peace. His poem for the Pope hoped that Pallas (Minerva) would reign again, and that the Shepherd of the Roman flock would no longer see the country-side red with French, Spanish and German blood. The fields should run with milk, honey, manna and dew.[96] But there was no real success for the Pope's peace project. Matters had passed out of his hands.

Paul IV (1555–1559)

If Paul III made only a moderate impact on international politics, Paul IV (Gian Pietro Caraffa) was in its forefront. For him, however, peace had an essentially religious context: the peace of the Christian Church, victorious over heresy and safe in its temporal possessions. For this Neapolitan Pope, peace also meant the peace of Italy, which was to be secured by the expulsion of the Spaniards. The Pope, once a leader of a group of younger ecclesiastics who met

---

[93] Pastor, op. cit., XII 92–8, 130–3, 144–55. For the subsequent seizure of Siena by Duke Cosimo de' Medici, cf. below, p. 161.

[94] G. Ribier, *Lettres et mémoires d'Estat* . . . (Paris 1666) II, 474.

[95] Pastor, op. cit., XII, 145, 148–9, 152–3.

[96] Joachim du Bellay, *Poematum Libri quatuor* (Paris 1558), ff. 9, 22ᵛ; *Oeuvres fran-çaises*, ed. C. Marty-Laveaux (Paris 1866–7) I, 278, 283. The poet's view of Rome and Roman society is well known (cf. below, p. 69), as also is his castigation of the Pope, who had made his 'Ganymede' a Cardinal, 'un Ganymède avec le rouge sur la teste' (*Oeuvres françaises* II, 394–9; cf. Ribier, op. cit., II, 268, 357).

in the gardens of S. Giorgio Maggiore in Venice, 'vir sanctissimus et doctissimus' (as Reginald Pole, one of the group, called him), the co-founder of the Theatines and co-author of the 1536 *Consilium de emendanda ecclesia*, had become more and more alarmed by the growth of heresy. He suspected even his old friends, Contarini (after the negotiations with the Protestants at Regensburg)[97] and Pole. He saw the Emperor Charles V as the favourer of Protestants, making his own terms with them. Spaniards, in any case, he would dismiss as 'marrani' (converted Jews). He dedicated himself to fight for the preservation of the faith. He looked back with longing to the days of the medieval church, of militant orthodoxy in the work of the salvation of souls. Becoming Pope at seventy-nine, he was a 'man of iron' whose feet struck sparks from the stones (a Florentine view), overbearing, excitable, always poised for conflict.[98] Emperors and kings, he thought, should sit at his feet.[99]

As a Neapolitan, the Pope had grown up hating Spanish power, with which he had been in conflict; Charles V had opposed his appointment to the Archbishopric of Naples. Paul would recall the Italy of the fifteenth century, a well-tuned instrument of four strings (the Papal State, Naples, Milan and Venice), and wished that the new invaders, a mixture of Spanish and Flemings, could be driven out. They clung like couch-grass (*gramigna*) wherever they took hold. Only Italian should be spoken in Italy.[100] Yet, in the cause of sustaining the Church's Italian power, he was to precipitate a disastrous war.

A rebellion against papal authority grew out of a minor incident, the defection of two galleys commanded by two members of the hostile Sforza family of Santa Fiore in August 1555 and the support they received from the Colonna and Orsini. The flames of war

---

[97] Cf. P. Matheson, *Cardinal Contarini at Regensburg* (Oxford 1972).

[98] *Legazione di A. Serristori, ambasciatore di Cosimo I*, ed. G. Canestrini (Florence 1853) p. 375.

[99] Report of the Venetian ambassador in E. Alberi, ed., *Le relazione degli ambasciatori Veneti al Senato* (Florence, 1839–63), series 2, III, 380, 409. Using this, Ranke made much of the Pope's partiality for the very strong 'black' wine of Naples, 'mangia-guerra' (or more properly 'magnaguerra'), so thick that it could be cut with a knife, and his habit of finishing off with malmsey ('washing his teeth'). It seems, however, that the Pope ate and drank sparingly, though his banquets were famous (Pastor, op. cit., XIV, 65–6; L. Ranke, *The History of the Popes*, trans. E. Foster (London 1885) I, 217).

[100] Ibid., series, 2, III, 389, 405; P. Nores, 'Storia della guerra di Paolo IV' in *Archivio Storico Italiano*, series I, XII, 1847, pp. 307–8.

were fanned by the Pope's nephew, Cardinal Carlo Caraffa, himself seeking territorial gains (he would have liked Siena), and secretly in touch with Henri II.[101] An open alliance with France in December 1555 promised Naples and Milan for royal princes in return for money and troops should the Holy See be attacked.[102] This alliance did not prevent the King of France from signing the truce of Vaucelles with the Hapsburgs in February 1556. It is not certain, however, whether the Pope later absolved the King from this commitment, or whether Henri II simply disregarded it. A mission to France by Cardinal Caraffa produced a definite commitment to armed intervention. When the Duke of Alva (King Philip's Viceroy in Naples) was sufficiently provoked to invade the Papal State in September 1556, the first French contingent had already arrived in Italy; the second, commanded by the Duke of Guise, crossed the Alps in December.[103] The Pope had meanwhile threatened the Emperor and his son with deposition; the Emperor was a schismatic, a heretic, and coveted the whole of Italy. He was 'a cripple in body and soul'.[104] On the other side, opinions had been sought, and obtained, from the University of Louvain: it was no sin to embark on a 'defensive' war against the Pope. Valladolid said the same.[105] All papal legates were withdrawn from the dominions of the Emperor and his son in April 1557, and there was more talk of King Philip's deposition (he had taken his own anti-papal measures).[106] The failure of Guise's expedition, which never reached Naples, was followed by its swift recall just before the disastrous defeat at S. Quentin. The 'peace', mediated by Venice, compelled the Pope to abandon the French alliance and to remain 'neutral' in future, in return for King Philip's submission, performed on his behalf by Alva.[107]

The Pope's disastrous war was a last attempt to dislodge the Spanish power from Italy. In the struggle, Cardinal Caraffa had even sought Turkish help via the Turk's ally, the King of France. Instead of peace, the war had brought devastation and suffering

---

[101] Pastor, op. cit., xiv, 109–9, 116, 124–35, 138.

[102] Nores, loc. cit., pp. 36, 41.

[103] Pastor, op. cit., xiv, 119–25, 140, 152–3.

[104] *Cal. Ven.* vi (i) 518, 529, 534, 546. Philip had assumed the Crown of Spain and of Naples-Sicily in January 1556.

[105] Pastor, op. cit., xiv, 131, 138–9.

[106] Ibid., xiv, 156–8.

[107] Ibid., xiv, 166–7 (September 1557).

upon the papal dominions. On the wider front, there was the abortive peace mission of Cardinal Caraffa to Brussels late in 1557.[108] The Pope's concerns were, however, nearer to hand.[109] His last year was spent more and more in isolation (his nephews were dismissed on declaration of their many misdeeds). The English ambassador reported in June 1558 that the Pope would see no one; he spent his days with the hermits on the Belvedere or in solitary prayer.[110] Thursdays were, however, devoted to personal attendance at the sessions of the Holy Office, held in his room in his last weeks. The Index of prohibited books was launched by formal promulgation: all the works of Erasmus,[111] the works of Machiavelli, Dante's *De monarchia*, even the 1555 edition of the *Consilium de emendanda ecclesia*, which the Pope himself had written in 1536.[112] The papal concern was no longer action in Europe or Italy as arbiter of Christendom, it was the defence of the faith in the most belliose and reactionary manner. His agents took no part in the negotiations of 1558–9 for a general peace (see Chapters 5 and 6 below).

The Princes

It was declared by propagandists of the Holy Roman Empire that the Emperor was the source of peace in this world. The *Laudes* to Charlemagne (written *c*.796–800) have the prayer: 'To the most excellent Charles, crowned by God, great and pacific King of the Franks and the Lombards, patrician of the Romans; life and

---

[108] Ibid., XIV, 212–14, 223.

[109] As Cardinal Caraffa the Pope had been one of the initiators of the move to establish a commission of six cardinals (of which he was one) as General Inquisitors (1542), the beginnings of the Roman Inquisition, for which he is said to have fitted out a house (ibid., XII, 505–7). The Inquisition summoned the General of the Capuchins, Bernardino Occhino, who fled to Geneva, and Peter Martyr Vermigli, in Lucca, fled across the Alps to Zurich and then Oxford. Such 'apostasies' (and there were many) struck fear in the mind of the future Paul IV. Italy had many centres of Protestantism in the 1540s.

[110] *Cal. For.* I, 380, 384, 397.

[111] By 1564, only certain of Erasmus' works were included, the *Colloquies* and the *Praise of Folly* among them, but other works, treating of religion, were to be 'censored' by the Universities of Louvain and Paris (F. H. Reusch, ed., *Die Indices Librorum Prohibitorum des 16 Jahrhunderts* (Tübingen 1886) I, 183, 259.

[112] Ibid., I, 396; Jedin, op. cit., I, 432. There had been Protestant 'editions' of this work with heavily critical comments; Luther's German translation had sarcastic glosses.

victory.'[113] For Dante, the Emperor's mission was 'to provide freedom and peace for men as they pass through the testing-time of this world'. The Emperor, having no cause for cupidity, since his jurisdiction had no limit, was the purest incarnation of justice. He could assuage human cupidity; leave men free to enjoy the tranquillity of peace. In the words of the *Convivio*, there must be one prince 'who, possessing all, and not being able to desire more, holds kings content within the limits of their kingdoms, so that peace may be between them'. So men could live happily.[114] Medieval apologists looked to the age of Augustus, whose empire had been 'consecrated' by the birth of Christ. They repeated the prophecy of Anchises to Aeneas, in the underworld, that the mission of Rome was to rule over the nations, to establish peace, to spare the defeated, and to crush the proud.[115]

This concept of a supreme authority, source of justice and peace (often personalised as the daughters of Zeus) would only have been realisable in the medieval world had the Empire been coterminous with the known world (which it was not) and had the Emperor commanded sufficient power to enforce the rule of peace with justice (which he did not). England and France, for instance, were kingdoms whose monarchs claimed to hold their crowns of God alone. The Emperor was only the first among monarchs; in so far as he had armies, it was as ruler of his various dominions and dependent upon his financial resources in each. Nicolas of Cusa's hope that the Emperor would have some permanent force and some regular revenue[116] had not been realised either in his own time or later. His great plea 'law without force loses its binding power and its life'[117] was only too true.

Nevertheless, the ideal of universal empire continued to find expression. Frederick III took as his motto 'Austriae est imperare orbi universo' ('It is Austria's part to rule the whole world'). On his entry into Siena in 1452, he was welcomed as the 'prince of

---

[113] Quoted in R. Folz, *The Concept of Empire in Western Europe from the Fifth to the Fourteenth Century*, (London 1969) p. 179.

[114] Dante, *De monarchia*, loc. cit., pp. 14–15, 93–4; *Convivio* iv, iv.

[115] Virgil, *Aeneid* 6, 851–3.

[116] Nicolas of Cusa, *Opera Omnia*, vol. xiv, *De Concordantia Catholica*, ed. G. Kallen (Leipzig-Hamburg 1939–1959) iii, ch. 39, pp. 454–6.

[117] Ibid., iii, ch. 26, pp. 427–8. Cf. P. E. Sigmund, *Nicolas of Cusa and Medieval Political Thought* (Harvard 1963), for a general discussion of the great reformer's work.

peace' by a procession carrying olive branches.[118] In 1489 the University of Heidelberg welcomed the future Emperor Maximilian, lauding his 'power to bring together Christians in a bond of peace . . . so that you may destroy the enemies of Christ, curb the savageness of the Turks . . . and finally lead the wandering sheep into the sheepfold of Christ'.[119] The ideal seemed on the brink of fulfilment in the time of Charles V.

Charles of Ghent succeeded as a child to Castile, her dominions in the New World, and the Netherlands in 1506, to Aragon, Naples-Sicily and Sardinia in 1516, and to the Austrian lands and then the imperial dignity in 1519. Such a phenomenon seemed almost miraculous. It was proclaimed in the Emperor's proud device, the pillars of Hercules with the motto 'Plus oultre' ('More beyond' – taken by many contemporaries to refer to his empire, extending beyond the pillars, boundary of the Roman world).[120] The Piedmontese Mercurino di Gattinara, Charles V's Grand Chancellor, no doubt influenced by Dante's *Monarchia* (which he asked Erasmus to publish), wrote to the Emperor in 1519: 'Sire, God has been merciful to you: he has raised you above all the kings and princes of Christendom to a power such as no sovereign has enjoyed since your ancestor Charles the Great. He has set you on the way towards a world monarchy, towards the uniting of all Christendom under a single shepherd.'[121] Ariosto, in his *Orlando Furioso* (1516), inserted a prophecy of a universal monarchy, of the wisest and most just emperor since Roman times, fruit of the union of Austria and Aragon, a branch growing by the Rhine. Under this monarch, the virgin Astraea would return.[122] His choice of a Carolingian theme was in itself significant.

The pugnacious imperial secretary, Alfonso de Valdes, also

---

[118] Quoted in F. Heer, *The Holy Roman Empire* (English trans.; London 1968) pp. 125–6.

[119] Quoted in G. E. Waas, *The Legendary Character of Maximilian* (New York 1941) p. 41.

[120] Cf. M. Bataillon, 'Plus oultre: la cour découvre le nouveau monde' in Jacquot, op cit. II, 13–27. In the Royal Armoury of Madrid is the Emperor's round shield, on which is depicted an allegory of the Discovery of the New World, and his victory at Tunis. The Emperor, armed in classical style, stands on his ship which sails ahead, led by Fame and followed, overhead, by Victory. Hercules is moving his pillars forward.

[121] K. Brandi, *The Emperor Charles V* (English trans; London 1967) p. 112. Vives had the same view after the sack of Rome (J. Lynch, *Spain under the Hapsburgs* (Oxford 1964) p. 70).

[122] Canto XV, stanzas 21–25.

accepted the concept of a world monarchy, which would bring unity to the Church and lead a crusade.[123] In this context, he made his archdeacon in the *Dialogue of Lactantius and an archdeacon* say: 'My feeling is that the Emperor's duty is to defend his subjects; to keep them at peace, and to dispense justice by rewarding the good and punishing the wicked.'[124] For others, the concept of empire did not mean universal empire. Such was the conclusion of Vives, and also of Erasmus, who in 1517 wrote that the Roman empire had never been universal. The empire, he considered, was now too heavy a load for one man. Universal monarchy was not necessary if concord reigned among princes. The true monarch of the world was Christ.[125] This fragmentation of empire brought as its necessary corollary a fragmentation of peace. However, the emperor's responsibility was the greatest; as Vives declared, in the emperor's hands lay 'so great a share of human concord and tranquillity'.[126]

Were the emperors, in this period, conscious of a mission for peace? They were certainly conscious of their duties within their own lands. The various schemes for the establishment of a public peace, and the creation of zones or *Kreise* (eventually ten in number), which would share in the peace-keeping, as in other functions of government, made this clearly apparent. Likewise, for Charles V, the peace of his empire meant religious peace, some settlement, preferably after dialogue, but in the last resort after war, with the growing forces of heresy. But in external matters, the watchword was, surely, preparation to defend or to reconquer imperial territory, in other words, the 'just' war.

At his coronation in Aachen as King of the Romans, the emperor-elect gave his solemn undertaking, a six-part coronation oath, administered by the Elector Archbishop of Cologne. The fourth part of this oath ran as follows: 'Will you conserve and recover those rights of the kingdom and possessions of the Empire which have unlawfully been usurped?' The pontifical mass which followed was that for the Epiphany, with its epistle 'Surge illuminare Jeru-

---

[123] Official document on the battle of Pavia (written most probably by Valdes), quoted in M. Bataillon, *Érasme et l'Espagne* (Bordeaux/Paris 1937) p. 244.

[124] Alfonso de Valdes, *Dialogue of Lactantius and an archdeacon*, trans. J. E. Longhurst (Albuquerque 1952) p. 25.

[125] Letter to the Dukes of Saxony (Erasmus, *Opus epistolarum*, ed. P. S. Allen (Oxford 1906–1947) II, 586). This letter was brought to notice by Miss Yates (op. cit., pp. 19–20).

[126] *Opera omnia* v, 192 (quoted in Fernández-Santamaria, op. cit., p. 52).

salem' ('Rise and shine, O Jerusalem, for the Prince of Peace is come'). In this ceremony, in the Carolingian octagon of the cathedral beneath Frederick Barbarossa's great chandelier (with its twelve turrets, symbolic of the Heavenly City), the Emperor is at once hailed as prince of peace and committed to the defence and recovery of imperial rights and possessions.[127]

Maximilian I

This defence and recovery were surely the mission of both the Emperor Maximilian and his grandson Charles V. Maximilian, a 'very Proteus' as one ambassador called him, interpreted the mission in kaleidoscopic shifts and changes of policy and direction.[128] He had grown up, in Wiener-Neustadt, on tales of the Turkish threat. The crusade for him, as for many, was part of an attitude of mind. When he was not hunting or hawking, the Emperor was, therefore, preoccupied with war or preparation for war. He was, however, lacking in steadiness of purpose: in 1498, on the death of Charles VIII of France, the Milanese ambassador told him: 'Now is the time to let the chamois be and perform deeds worthy of your position'.[129] The long struggle with France, whose king had seized the Duchy of Burgundy, the Free County/Franche Comté (for a time) and Picardy after the death of Duke Charles the Bold, was the Emperor's preoccupation in the north. To the east it was the succession to Hungary, for which he provided by a double marriage alliance in 1515. To the south he had varied schemes for the reconquest of Lombardy and even of Venetia. Ulrich von Hutten saw him as the man who might finally assert the integrity of the empire against France, Italy and the Turks. In

[127] H. Heusch, 'Le sacre de Charles Quint à Aix-la-Chapelle', in Jacquot, op. cit., II, 165; Heer, op. cit., p. 151; M. David, 'Le serment du sacre du IXe au XVe siècle', in *Revue du moyen age latin* VI, 1950, pp. 251–2. This part of the oath had been introduced in 1309.

[128] Wolsey, speaking as a negotiator and a grammarian, remarked (on the Emperor's vacillations between England and France in 1516) that he 'doth play on both hands using the nature of a participle which taketh *partem a nomine et partem a verba*' (*L.P.* II, no. 2700, quoted by Scarisbrick, op. cit., p. 65).

[129] L. G. Pelissier, 'L'alliance Milano–Allemande à la fin du XVe siècle', in *Miscellanea di Storia d'Italia* XXXV, p. 339. The Emperor's hunting became an obsession, and took him often to the Tyrol. In 1501, for instance, he entered Trent preceded by two hundred dogs, with the bear and stag he had killed carried in a chariot (M. Sanuto, *I Diarii*, (Venice 1879–1903) IV, col. 151).

1507, a Milanese exile in Innsbruck declared that the Emperor was preparing not merely to recover Milan, but to conquer the world. In fact, Maximilian was soon to make 'medicinal' proposals to the French for the destruction of Venice.[130] But, as Guicciardini noticed, the Emperor deprived himself of what fortune brought him by inconstancy, extravagant ideas and his immense prodigality.[131] As Machiavelli declared, if all the leaves on all the trees in Italy had been ducats, they would not have sufficed.[132]

The Emperor no doubt saw himself as the knight errant, but on an imperial stage. The romances which he composed or partly composed show this very clearly. The *Freydal* had stories of the tournament; the metrical romance, the *Teuerdank*, was an adventure story whose hero, like Maximilian, hunted the chamois, had miraculous escapes and journeyed to claim his bride. The third, the *Weisskünig* (an allusion to Maximilian's white costume for the tournament), written between 1505 and 1516, told the strongly autobiographical story of a young king's defeat of his enemies.[133] It had 251 engravings. The great series of 137 wood cuts, the *Triumph of Maximilian*, proclaimed the Emperor's love of hunting, of music, of tournaments, but above all, of war. The hunt of the ibex, the chamois, the bear, and the stag, the falconer's sport, musicians, masqueraders and jesters, precede the personified representation of the Emperor's many lands. Those he had 'entered' in war are depicted in armour. The representations of his wars are preceded by *Landsknechte* carrying pictures of castles and towns (in the manner of Roman triumphs). The Emperor's much-prized artillery and his arquebusiers are depicted. Among the peoples conquered are those of 'Calicut', feather-clad inhabitants of the New World, with maize clearly drawn (and for the first time?)[134]

---

[130] A. Luzio, 'I preliminari della lega di Cambray', in *Archivio storico Lombardo*, series IV, XVI, 1911, pp. 250, 265–6. The Cardinal of Rouen was to be the 'doctor'.

[131] Guicciardini, *Storia d'Italia* IV, 117–18 (Lib.XIII, cap. vii).

[132] Niccolo Machiavelli, 'Rapporto delle cose dell'Almagna', in *Le opere* VI, 317.

[133] The King could design artillery and knew the secrets of making heavy armour.

[134] Sixty-six of the 137 woodcuts were by Hans Burgkmair of Augsburg (who did 117 of the 251 in the *Weisskünig*, and a few in the *Teuerdank*). Albrecht Altdorfer may have executed some of the others, and Albrecht Dürer 2 (S. Appelbaum, ed., *The Triumph of Maximilian* (New York 1964) cf. P. du Colombier, 'Les triomphes en images de l'Empereur Maximilien Ier' in Jacquot, op. cit., II, 99–112). The wars depicted show the long sequence: the first Guelderland, the Utrecht, the first Flemish, the Liège, the second Flemish, the Burgundian, the Austrian, the Hungarian, the Swiss, the Neapolitan, the Bavarian, the second Guelderland, the Milanese, the Venetian. Cf. G. Benecke, *Maximilian I* (London 1982), esp. pp. 7–30.

It was as a warrior, then, that the Emperor wished to be remembered. His speech to the Diet of Constance in 1507 shows his imperial and military ambition (he and Pope Julius II were hoping to drive the French from Milan). The Emperor declared that German divisions and sloth had emboldened the King of France. What could be more unhappy than to be reduced to such a state as to make it desirable not to be powerful? They had won the German Empire not by fortune but by valour, and must transmit the German name to their children in that grandeur and authority in which they had received it. The French remembered the Emperor's victory at Guinegate (while still a bare youth). The whole of Germany must be roused to arms. The more authority they gave him, the greater would be his power and force, the easier the defence of the Church. They would thereby exalt the imperial dignity, whose greatness and splendour are shown to all present, and to the whole body of this 'most powerful and warlike nation'.[135] The Emperor's tomb in the Hofkapelle of Innsbruck restates the chivalric, warlike tradition. The Emperor kneels at prayer. He is surrounded by more than life-size bronze statues of ancestors and kinsmen.[136] That of King Arthur, cast by Peter Visscher the Elder from a drawing by Dürer, shows the contemporary idealistic vision of a knight.[137] The Emperor had planned the mausoleum for Wiener-Neustadt, beginning his schemes in 1502; the eventual siting at Innsbruck came later and completion took many years. In 1515 ambassador Wingfield reported that, despite want of money, the Emperor went on building, making things for war 'and such other things as shall remain in perpetual memory after his death'. These things included

---

[135] Guicciardini, *Storia d'Italia* IV, 86–92 (Lib. VII, cap ix).

[136] The Emperor was deeply interested in genealogy. Jacob Mennel wrote the *Fürstliche Chronicle gennannt Kayser Maximilians Geburtsspiegel*, showing the Emperor's descent from Hector and from Aeneas. He was held to be Greek by birth, his empire Roman. The saints of the Hapsburg dynasty were numbered: 123 canonised, 47 beatified (Heer, op. cit., pp. 141–2).

[137] See Plate 2. The physiognomy and the guards' officer moustache have a peculiarly Edwardian connotation to English eyes, but may be based on Caesar's report that the Britons had hairy upper lips (*De bello Gallico* 5.14.3). The contemporary, chivalric, concept of King Arthur is demonstrated by the verses (in French) at the feet of the statue on the gateway of the 'theatre' built at Calais for the meeting of Charles V and Henry VIII in 1520: 'I Arthur, head of the Round Table chief of all valiant hearts, wish to receive, by deepfelt desire, all hearts ennobled by virtuous endeavour; powerful princes, brave and daring, loving honour, follow my deeds and my chivalry in your dominions' (*L'ordonnance et ordre du tournoy, ioustes et combat à pied et à cheval*, Paris 1520).

his father's tomb and his own sepulture, for which many statues were already made.[138] The report is a fitting epilogue for the Emperor Maximilian.

Charles V

The search for political peace in Christendom formed one theme in the policies of Charles V, but it was subordinate to the twin tasks of 'religious' peace, for which he worked through 'dialogue', but occasionally by war, and of war against the Infidel, to which Burgundian and Spanish tradition inclined him. The predominance of one goal or another shifted with the strength and activities of his enemies, Christian and Turk, and their temporary coalitions against him.[139] At the Diet of Worms in 1521 he spoke of his descent from Christian emperors of the German nation, Catholic kings of Spain, dukes of Austria and dukes of Burgundy, all faithful sons of the Church and defenders of the Catholic faith.[140] In war he inherited the chivalric and military traditions of Burgundy, Austria, Spain and Portugal; Brantôme wrote of him as the greatest emperor since Julius Caesar and Charlemagne, a master of the art of war. At his great victory on St George's Day 1547 over the German Protestants at Mühlberg, the battle cries were 'St James' (for Spain) and 'St George' (for the empire). Titian's equestrian portrait of the Emperor idealises the victor; he carries the long imperial lance, part of the state regalia, and not the shorter lance in actual use, he rides purposively, with no signs of the gout which crippled him in later life.[141] To commemorate his victories of 1535 at La Goleta and Tunis against the ruler of Algiers, Khair-ad-Din Barbarossa (ally and client of the Turk), the Emperor commissioned a set of tapestries. The artist Jan Vermeyen had been on the campaign, and made sketches (with precise topographical notes) which were used for the twelve great tapestries woven in Brussels by Guillaume de Pannemaker. The silk thread was brought from Granada, the

---

[138] *L.P.* II(i), no. 1006.

[139] Quoted by Heer, op. cit., p. 151. At the Diet of Augsburg in 1530, the Emperor spoke (in the context of religious peace) of the 'peculiar imperial grace and gentleness and desire for peace' (E. Armstrong, *The Emperor Charles V* (London 1910) I, 252).

[140] The interaction of the conflicts with the Turk and with the Protestants is studied by S. A. Fischer-Galati, *Ottoman Imperialism and German Protestantism* (New York 1972) p. 253.

[141] The portrait is in the Prado, Madrid.

gold from Milan; Castilian and Latin banderoles gave details of each event in 'Caesar's' campaign.[142] For the Emperor, whose armies' early victory over François I at Pavia in 1525 was likewise commemorated in tapestry, and in painting,[143] the three great enemies were the heretic, the Turk, and the French King. They were his total preoccupation, almost his obsession.

In the confidence of the years after Pavia, imperial propagandists, and no doubt the Emperor himself, could even defend the sack of Rome by imperial troops in 1527. Enemies thought this act the culmination of an 'open war' policy. The Emperor, however, wrote to his fellow sovereigns disclaiming all responsibility for this 'disastrous' event; the letter came from the pen of Valdes, whose *Dialogue* on the atrocity has already been mentioned. The letter declared that the Emperor's work for the peace of Christendom and for the honour and preservation of the Apostolic See was well-known. Yet the Pope, deceived by wicked persons around him, had allowed himself to start a new war. He and his French ally were intent on expelling the Emperor from Italy and dividing Naples between them. The imperial army, without consulting the Emperor, set out for Naples, part of which kingdom was held by the Pope. They distrusted the treaty which the Pope had made with the Viceroy and marched on Rome. They then performed the 'insult', which was not as bad as had been made out. God had allowed this to happen as revenge for the Emperor's sufferings. He allows great evils that greater good may come. So the Emperor will strive for the ending of 'civil' wars and turn against the enemies of the Christian religion.[144]

Yet the Emperor was constantly besieged by propaganda for peace. It came from all quarters, from the Netherlands, from Spain, even from distant England. In 1523, ambassador Richard Pace, who had negotiated the peace between the Emperor and Venice, reminded the Emperor that he had been elected by God to punish disturbers of the peace and to secure tranquillity to the Christian world, as Augustus did, during whose reign the temple of Janus

---

[142] Tapestries in the Alcazar, Seville (cf. J. Romero y Murube, *L'Alcazar de Séville* (Madrid 1971) pp. 76–93; the present set are eighteenth-century copies).

[143] Painting, by an unknown artist, in Hampton Court. Tapestry (after designs by Bernard van Orley?), in the Galleria Nazionale di Capodimonte, Naples. The arquebusiers, who took such a great part in the victory, are shown.

[144] Letter, August 1527, to King John III of Portugal, printed in Longhurst, op. cit., pp. 97–9. Copies of letters to Henry VIII, and to Sigismund I of Poland, survive (ibid., p. 7). The letters were sent on Gattinara's advice.

was closed.[145] But for the Emperor this peace must be 'peace with justice' (as the 1521 negotiations showed; see Chapter 4). In other words, peace must be on his own terms, with all his 'rights' sustained and acknowledged, or at the worst 'reserved' for the future. In the pursuit of such peace, he would resort to war, the 'just' war of the political theorists and lawyers.

A memorandum drawn up for the Emperor Maximilian by Jacob Mennel advised his grandson to remember the links between Hungary and Constantinople (Hungary was a bastion against the Turk and the springboard for a reconquest of Byzantium), and between Austria and Burgundy. Born in Ghent, the Emperor was unlikely to forget his Burgundian inheritance or its ancient claims against France. Gattinara, the Grand Chancellor, urged the Emperor never to give up Naples and Sicily, while Charles himself regarded Milan as the pivot of all activity against France. In this conflict, the Emperor saw the French King as the perpetual aggressor and responded accordingly. In 1523, for instance, his intention was to place France under the 'ban' of the empire, and to demand the cession of Arles, Dauphiné, Valence, Provence and Orange. In other words, he wished to regain the ancient medieval kingdom of Arles, a part of his 'ancestral' terrority. In 1526, after Pavia, he obtained the French King's promise that the Duchy of Burgundy should be restored, and although this was not achieved the claim was never abandoned. When, therefore, the Emperor declared in 1529 that princes seeking foreign conquests were tyrants, or that it was slander to represent him as seeking universal monarchy,[146] it was with the reservation that all ancient imperial, Burgundian and other claims might legitimately be pursued. Erasmus' plea that the Emperor might renounce some territory in the cause of peace went unheeded. Gattinara's vision of universal monarchy was often reflected in the Emperor's actions, particularly the elaborate marriage schemes,[147] Mary Tudor's marriage with Philip II being a last link in the chain.

[145] *Cal. Span.* II, 572–3 (Pace's report from Venice).
[146] Speech to the Royal Council in Madrid, and remarks to Gasparo Contarini, Venetian ambassador (Heer, op. cit., p. 161; J. Lynch, *Spain under the Hapsburgs* (Oxford 1964) p. 69). On the second occasion the Emperor had said that his intention was not to fight Christians, but the Infidel, and to see Italy and Christendom at peace, each man possessing his own.
[147] The Emperor's pride in his dynasty could be seen in the stained glass of the chapel of the Holy Sacrament and the transept of S. Gudule in Brussels, from designs by Bernard van Orley.

The Emperor's coronation at Bologna in 1530 symbolised an empire of east and west: the gospel was read in Latin and in Greek (by the Archbishop of Rhodes). The Duke of Savoy carried the imperial crown, the Elector Palatine the orb, the Marquis of Montferrat the sceptre, the Duke of Urbino the sword. In the 'triumph' which followed, Pope and Emperor rode under the same canopy; the College of Cardinals was led by Cardinal Boniface Paleologus, of the ancient imperial family. For some weeks, a united Christendom, at peace, seemed to be realised.[148]

It was, however, a reign of war and continuous conflict, yet, perhaps because of this, the Emperor's instructions to his son Philip in 1548 show that the message of peace had come home. The *Testamenta* shows the Emperor's concern: *conservar la paz*. God cannot be well served unless in peace; war must not be undertaken unless there is no alternative. 'Past wars have exhausted the realms of your inheritance, even though I have undertaken those wars in their defence. True, with God's favour I have succeeded in defending and adding to them: but at great cost, so that now they must be given a rest.' To avoid war, the help of good neighbours is needed. The old enemy, France, was not forgotten. Philip should be vigilant. He should offer peace to the new King (Henri II), for the sake of the tranquillity of Christendom. The Emperor had always wished to live in peace with France, but it was notorious that the King had never honoured truces or peace treaties. Philip should therefore live by past treaties and agreements but prepare for possible aggression. He should never abandon the claim to the Duchy of Burgundy, 'nuestra patria' (a final sting).[149]

Occasionally, a funeral oration gives a balanced and not unduly eulogistic view of the deceased. The oration for Charles V, at the requiem in Brussels in December 1558, ranged over the life's work of the Emperor, as seen by one of his loyal subjects. He had given peace to Italy, longer and firmer than any since the time of Augustus, he went to Aigues-Mortes in the cause of peace, he was magnanimous in victory to François I, he was slow to go to war, but when he went to war (the German war) he was like an eagle. His good fortune was like the eagle's, which is unharmed by light-

---

[148] Vicomte Terlinden 'La politique italienne de Charles Quint et le "triomphe" de Bologne', and A. Rodrigez-Morino, 'Vasco Diaz Tanco témoin et chroniqueur poétique du couronnement de Charles Quint', in Jacquot, op. cit., II, 29–43, 183–95.
[149] Quoted, with critical appraisal of the various versions, in J. A. Fernández-Santamaria, op. cit., pp. 244–5.

ning. He sought chiefly the repose of Christendom, the unity of the Church. He protected his kingdoms, he was the rampart of the Belgian provinces. Like David, he now hands over to Solomon. King Philip will rebuild the Temple.[150] It may be added that Philip in his own way did 'rebuild the Temple'. He also fought for his inheritance, though he was not the great soldier his father was. He did not forget, nor did his negotiators, 'nuestra patria'.[151]

France

The Kings of France shared the imperial obsession with defence of patrimony, by just war if need be. Their coronation oath had, for a time, included the promise to sustain inviolate the sovereignties, rights and lordships of the crown, and not to transfer or alienate them. By 1484 this had become a fundamental law, rather than a part of the coronation liturgy.[152] By that time, also, the Crown had reclaimed the Duchy of Burgundy on the death of Charles the Bold, and the Duchy of Anjou on the failure of the Angevin line. In addition, the Crown had seized the County of Provence, an imperial fief of the Angevins and outside the kingdom.[153] Charles VIII absorbed the Duchy of Brittany by marriage. He was, by this time, able to respond to invitations to intervene actively in Italy, a temptation which his predecessors had resisted, preferring skilful alliances and the domination of 'client' allies: Milan, Genoa and Florence. Charles VIII could take up his Angevin cousins' claims to Naples-Sicily, as Louis XII did the Orleanist claims to Milan. Italy, 'les fumées et gloires d'Italie',[154] became the obsession of French monarchs in these years, François I glorifying his momentous deeds at Marignano in 1515. The Italian ventures focussed

[150] Oration by François Richardot, suffragan Bishop of Arras, at the requiem for Charles V, 29 December 1558, in S. Gudule, Brussels (*Coll. des voyages*, pp. 47–62). One might query the 'magnanimity' to François I.

[151] For King Philip's attitudes to war and peace, cf. below, pp. 135, 180, 185.

[152] M. David, loc. cit., pp. 257–60. Seyssel quotes fundamental law against alienation of the demesne (ibid., p. 119), and Bodin cites the 'universal' law against alienation of the 'public domain', and also the French coronation oath (Jean Bodin, *Six Books of the Commonwealth*, ed. M. J. Tooley (Oxford 1967), p. 186 (Book VI, chapter 2)).

[153] Within living memory, boatmen on the Rhone have described the two banks as 'du côté de l'empire', and 'du côté du royaume'.

[154] 'The vain dreams and glories of Italy'. The words are Commynes' (*Mémoires*, ed. J. Calmette (Paris 1924–5) III, 20).

attention on Savoy, whose independence was jealously watched, and which was itself taken over in 1536 on flimsy pretexts. By this time the Franco-imperial conflict was in full swing: the French monarchy had been encircled by Hapsburg power since the Hapsburg succession to Castile (1506) and Aragon (1516) with its dependency the kingdom of Naples-Sicily. Since the French kings regarded themselves as the true successors of Charlemagne they might aspire to reclaim ancient Frankish territory. To the north, the claims to suzerainty over Artois and Flanders were still asserted until relinquished in 1526, in the north east, there might be expansion towards the Moselle and the Rhine by seizure of fortresses during the endemic wars or by skilful alliances (securing the imperial bishoprics of Metz, Toul and Verdun in 1552). It may be said, therefore, that the French monarchs in this period were aggressively expansionist, personally leading their wars, and in alliance with whomsoever they might secure to assist them: German Protestants, the Swiss, the Turk, not to mention their fellow sovereigns. In 1535 Thomas Cromwell said that the French King would not be deterred from bringing the Turk and the devil into Christendom, if it would help him regain Milan.[155]

Specious and legalistic arguments were used to justify such military action, for the King vied with his enemies in self-justification. On his invasion of Italy, Charles had declared that his purpose was to unite Italy, so that a campaign against the Turk could be launched, an argument earlier used to justify the diplomatic schemes of Louis XI in 1483. Louis XII, like the Emperor at a later date, was advised that he could resist a papal 'attack' by force.[156] In the imperial conflict, François I would argue in 1528 that he had always wanted peace, had been forced into war by his enemies, and that his recent advance into Italy was to protect France from further imperial attack.[157] He thus obtained support for a repudiation of the treaty of Madrid, forced upon him in captivity, and therefore, in his view, invalid. In later counter-measures against the Emperor, the King would, like his enemy, threaten confiscations: Flanders, Artois and Charolais in 1537, for instance.

---

[155] Quoted by Knecht, op. cit., p. 225 (from *Cal. Span.* v, 455). Cf. François I's boast, in 1540, that he could stir up trouble for the Emperor in Central Europe and the Mediterranean (Knecht, op. cit., p. 301).

[156] By the synod of prelates, theologians and jurists meeting at Orléans in 1510 (Bridge, op. cit., IV, 93–4).

[157] Speech to the 'assembly of notables' quoted by Knecht, op. cit., pp. 215–16.

Every trick of the game was used; the general argument was 'should war come, it will not be through any fault of mine'.[158]

As we have seen, Claude de Seyssel had defended the 'just war', and had considered the best way to rule over conquered territory. He had written for Louis XII, but his views, if not his person, would have been welcome to François I. Propaganda fed and responded to the expansionist theme. Ronsard could laud either peace or war. In the latter vein is his poem of 1558, an exhortation to the soldiers at the camp near Amiens of Henri II. He urged war; the enemy were occupying the inheritance of the soldiers' earliest ancestors, for France, Holland, Brabant and Artois then obeyed 'our kings'. They should bathe and drink in the Rhine, as if it were the Garonne or the Loire.[159] Later, in the *Franciade* for Charles IX, the poet struggled with the epic theme of the French kings, sprung from Francus son of Hector. Francus is promised that from Trojan blood, mingled with German, kings shall arise who will conquer the world, and whose virtues, triumphs and victories shall fill the universe with glory. The poet, however, concludes that princes and kings and their dynasties may vanish, nothing is eternal, virtue alone is secure.[160] No doubt the sixteenth-century kings of France were stirred by the mythology of their ancestors. In the heady days of Italian conquest, they might have used fifteenth-century terms for their wars, and called them 'magnificent'. 'War of magnificence is when princes proceed at the head of their feudal vassals to make conquest in distant and foreign countries, or to fight for the defence or extension of the Catholic faith.'[161] When the Italian ventures failed, it was again the defence of the patrimony which took precedence, and on these terms, the pursuit of peace was not entirely forgotten. In his own eyes, François I had always aimed for peace. The double standards were vigorously alive.

[158] Quoted by Knecht, op. cit., p. 279 (Guillaume du Bellay's reply to the imperial speech, in Consistory, denouncing the attack on Savoy).

[159] Ronsard, *Oeuvres complètes*, IX, 3–11.

[160] Ibid., XVI, 29ff. The *Franciade* did not get beyond the reign of Pépin. The death of Charles IX 'me veinquist le courage'.

[161] 'Debate between the heralds of France and England', trans. H. Pyne, in *England and France in the Fifteenth Century* (London 1870) p. 23. The treatise, written in the mid-fifteenth century, casts aspersions on the English, who did not fight wars of 'magnificence', but only against their neighbours, or at home ('common war', in the French view).

England

Henry VII of England claimed and won his kingdom by descent and by victory in battle, 'verum Dei judicium'.[162] His greetings to his kingdom were decked out in classical guise by his historiographer, the blind poet Bernard André from Toulouse, who came with him: 'Hail queen of war and mistress of peace, land adorned with sacred genius and endowed with all the gifts of fortune. You excel all countries that the mighty ocean encircles, and no one has praised you enough.'[163] Once established, Henry became a man of peace, perhaps because, like Charles II, he did not wish to go on his travels again,[164] and certainly because he was surrounded by enemies and pretenders. André presents these threatening adversaries, again in classical guise, in his strange poem *Les douze triumphes d'Henri VII*, modelled on the labours of Hercules. Juno, who imposed the labours on Hercules, is Margaret of York, dowager Duchess of Burgundy; the Boar of Arcadia (the third labour) is a natural disguise for Richard III, whose device was a white boar; the stag with golden antlers is John de la Pole, Earl of Lincoln, one of the pretenders. Margaret of York, who trained and supported Perkin Warbeck, appears as Hippolyta, Queen of the Amazons; the three-headed King Geryon is that three-headed monster the Emperor Maximilian, the Archduke Charles and the Duchess Margaret. The robber Cacus is Perkin Warbeck, who descended on the land with bands of robbers. The great dragon Maxillus in the garden of the Hesperides is, of course, the Emperor Maximilian, who is depicted as preventing Henry's friendship with France, or his entering France, the 'garden'. The King will, because of his virtues, overcome all his enemies.[165]

The King undertook only two continental expeditions, and they were very short-lived. In 1489 he sent a token force in defence of Anne of Brittany, whose father Duke François II had sheltered Henry in exile, and to whom he was bound by treaty. In 1492, after

[162] S. B. Chrimes, *Henry VII* (London 1972) p. 62.

[163] *Memorials of King Henry VII*, ed. J. Gairdner (London 1858) pp. 30–1. The poet witnessed the King's entry into London, which he celebrated in Horatian sapphics: the city is to rejoice, as a wife rejoices for her only husband. The realm's happiness is compared to that of the ploughman, when fine weather succeeds a long period of storm, and when Apollo drives his chariot (ibid., pp. 35–6).

[164] It is important to remember that Henry VII was living in exile in France and in Brittany from the age of fourteen (1471) until his accession in 1485.

[165] *Memorials of King Henry VII*, pp. 133–53.

Brittany's defeat and the marriage of the Duchess Anne with Charles VIII, Henry himself led an expedition to claim the French crown and to help recover Brittany's independence. It was a few weeks' campaign; the King accepted peace with Charles VIII in return for a renewal of the French pension granted to Edward IV in 1475, and settlement for the cost of Henry's aid to Brittany.[166] To establish his dynasty, and to make powerful marriage alliances for his children, was Henry's normal way of proceeding; the Spanish marriage for his son Arthur was the supreme achievement for a new and unproved dynasty, about which Ferdinand of Aragon made exhaustive inquiries. Dr De Puebla reported in 1500 that the kingdom was better 'situated' than for five hundred years. There had been 'brambles and thorns of such a kind that the English had occasion not to remain peacefully in obedience to their king', there being divers heirs to the throne and of such quality that the matter could be disputed. The realm was now thoroughly purged and cleansed; not a drop of doubtful royal blood remained.[167]

Henry VII's stance over war is revealed in his correspondence with Pope Julius II in 1507. He had proposed a crusade, and the Pope had replied on the difficulties of such an enterprise[168] (the Pope, though ostensibly working for a crusade, was planning a league against Venice). Henry, writing a second time, set out his own position and attitude. He had nothing more at heart than the peace of Christendom; he had treaties with almost all kings and princes, and was related to all of them. He had not accepted the policy of peace because he was lacking in valour, vigour, military talent or resources, soldiers or arms. He had always been contented with what he possessed, had never aspired to conquest nor even to regain, by force of arms, what he could claim by right. The shedding of Christian blood was repugnant to him; he was inclined to shed the blood of the enemies of the faith, and reconquer the Holy Sepulchre. He begged the Pope to use his authority to restore peace;

[166] In 1489 the King's ally, the Emperor Maximilian, had soon deserted him; in 1492, the treaty of Étaples ended the brief siege of Boulogne (Chrimes, op. cit., pp. 281–2).

[167] *Letters and Papers Illustrative of the Reigns of Richard III and Henry VII*, ed. J. Gairdner (London 1861) I, 113. King Ferdinand did not consent to address Henry as his 'brother' until after Perkin Warbeck's execution in 1499. Before that he had used the address 'my cousin' (normal in writing to an inferior in rank) (ibid., I, lxxv).

[168] The Pope stated that the King's letter had been read out in Consistory, and earned the praises of the cardinals. The King had offered to take part in a crusade.

then the united power of all Christian princes could be turned against the Infidel. Could the Pope invite all princes to send ambassadors to Rome where preparations could be concerted and commanders chosen? The Pope would earn eternal glory if he avenged the humiliations of centuries on the detestable Infidel.[169] Was the King genuinely committed to the peace of Christendom? He may certainly have recalled the Lancastrian crusading tradition[170] and was himself Protector of the Knights of Rhodes. His mother, the Lady Margaret Beaufort, may not have been without influence in this matter, as in so many others. She had often declared to Bishop John Fisher (sometime her chaplain) that 'yf the Cristen princes wolde have warred upon the enemyes of His fayth, she wolde be glad yet to go folowe the hoost and help to washe theyre clothes for the love of Jesus'.[171]

The attitude of Henry VIII to his membership of the Christian community was in general aggressive and disturbing. Sir Thomas More's gibe, made when there was war with France, was all too true: 'If my head could win him a castle in France, it should not fail to go.'[172] Against France, the ancient enemy, whose crown he still claimed, the King was always prepared: he would join in any web of alliances, and go to war in any scheme for the dismemberment of that kingdom. His 'chevauchée' in 1512 won him Tournai (a French enclave in Flanders), which he garrisoned and provided with a great citadel, as if to stay for twenty-five years or more.[173] In 1516, plans with Maximilian and the Swiss to invade France came to a swift end, and not before Wolsey had counselled caution.[174] In 1523, the grandiose campaign for the dismemberment

---

[169] *Letters and Papers Illustrative of the Reigns of Richard III and Henry VII* I, 174–9. The King mentioned the three kings at Christ's Nativity; a trinity of kings from the West should now go on crusade.

[170] Cf. R. Schwoebel, *The Shadow of the Crescent: the Renaissance image of the Turk* (1453–1517) (Nieuwkoop 1967) pp. 136–9.

[171] Quoted in C. H. Cooper, *Memoir of Margaret Countess of Richmond and Derby* (Cambridge 1874), p. 65. From Fisher's sermon at the Countess' month's mind, the requiem one month after her death (1509).

[172] William Roper, 'Life of Sir Thomas More', in *Two Early Tudor Lives*, ed. R. S. Sylvester and D. P. Harding (New Haven 1962) p. 209.

[173] C. G. Cruickshank, *The English Occupation of Tournai 1513–1521* (Oxford 1971). The citadel was built partly so that a smaller garrison would be needed; William Pawne did the designs, and a large work force was sent from England. Tournai had a governor (to replace the French *bailli*) and sent representatives to the English Parliament.

[174] Scarisbrick, op. cit., pp. 59–65.

of France (a force of 10,000 men crossed the channel) was short-lived and humiliatingly unsuccessful, its revival never accomplished, though never entirely put aside. In Henry's declining years, the war was again personally led; the King, racked by ulcers in both legs, was hoisted into the saddle. This time he took Boulogne, another bastion which he hoped to retain.[175] There had been more peaceful interludes; the great meeting, for mutual sport and entertainment, in 1520 at the Field of Cloth of Gold,[176] and the lesser gathering, to discuss the Divorce, in 1532 at Boulogne.[177] But the normal stance was warlike; the King would reclaim his crown of France, and revive ancient military glories. The mood is blazoned forth on a short sword or wood knife made for the King by the Spanish swordsmith and damascener, Diego de Çaias. On the right face of the blade is the siege of Boulogne, in gold damascening. On the left is the Latin verse inscription translated here:

> Rejoice Boulogne in the rule of Henry,
> Thy towers are now seen adorned with crimson roses,
> now are the ill-scented lilies uprooted and prostrate,
> the cock expelled, and the lion reigns in the invincible citadel.
> Thus neither valour nor grace of beauty will fail thee,
> since the lion is thy protection and the rose thy ornament.[178]

Against Scotland war was always expected: the 'guerre guerroyable' or feudal war in which France often intervened. Truces were intermittent and ill-kept. In 1511, it was said that the King expected his border troops to make one raid a week 'while the grass was on the ground'.[179] In 1521, Wolsey instructed the Warden (Lord Dacre of Gilsland) that if the Scots broke the truce, he should wage 'guerre guerroyable', especially at the time when the Scots sowed their barley.[180] Henry VIII, like his contemporary monarchs, regarded war as an essential right, a very part of his sovereignty. As Erasmus wrote (despairingly): 'once you have granted imperial rule, you

---

[175] Scarisbrick, op. cit., pp. 128–38.
[176] J. G. Russell, *The Field of Cloth of Gold: men and manners in 1520* (London 1969).
[177] P. A. Hamy, *Entrevue de François premier avec Henry VIII à Boulogne-sur-Mer en 1532* (Paris 1898).
[178] The sword, in the collection of H.M. the Queen at Windsor Castle, is described by Claude Blair 'A royal swordsmith and damascener: Diego de Çaias' in *Metropolitan Museum Journal* III, 1970, p. 168. I owe this information to Dr Sarah Bevan of the Tower Armouries, H.M. Tower of London.
[179] G. Brenan, *History of the House of Percy* (London 1902) I, 166.
[180] *L.P.* III (i) 1169.

have granted at the same time the business of collecting money, the
retinue of a tyrant, armed forces, spies, horses, mules, trumpets,
war, carnage, triumphs, insurrections, treaties, battles, in short,
everything without which it is not possible to manage the affairs of
empire.'[181]

Yet, even in the first flush of warlike activity, the Emperor and
the Kings of France and England could allow themselves to plan
for peace. It may have been largely Wolsey's vision, and also his
love of diplomatic solutions, that prompted the 'non-aggression
pact' (Mattingley's words) of 1518.[182] Papal commands for a five-
year truce as prelude to a crusade were translated in England not
only into an Anglo-French marriage alliance (the Princess Mary
and the Dauphin), but also into an ambitious 'perpetual peace', the
five confederates in which were to be the Pope, the Emperor,
Charles King of Spain, Henry of England, and François of France.
The purpose of the treaty was declared to be the need for united
action against the Turk. The five signatories therefore concluded a
perpetual peace, in which they would be friends of their several
friends, enemies of their enemies. If any of the five, or any of their
confederates, took any aggressive action, then the aggrieved power
should appeal to the others. The latter, and their confederates,
would then require the invader to desist and give satisfaction,
reminding him of the treaty. If the offender refused, or postponed
reply, then he would be declared an enemy within one month
following. Within two months, action would be taken to invade his
territory; all the signatories would provide forces for this. The treaty,
by a masterly stroke, was declared to supersede all previous treaties.
There was a very careful definition of aggression, and of the areas
in which action should be taken against it, by sea, by land, and on
fresh water. On the French side, the treaty might include the Kings
of Scotland, Portugal, Hungary, Navarre, the Dukes of Savoy and
Lorraine as also Venice, Florence, Urbino, Guelders, Ferrara,
Mantua, Montferrat, Saluzzo and the Swiss cantons. On the English
side, there were specified the Kings of Denmark, Hungary, Portugal,
Margaret Archduchess of Austria, Ferdinand brother of the King
of Spain, Venice, Urbino, Cleves, Julich, Florence, Ferrara, the

[181] Erasmus, *Sileni Alcibiadis*, in Phillips, op. cit., p. 93.
[182] Wolsey was by this date Archbishop of York (1514), Cardinal and Legate *a
latere* (1515), and Lord Chancellor of England (1518).

Hanse and the Swiss cantons. The Pope was to accede within four months and name his confederates.[183] Thus provision was made for a concerted unity of action against any aggression; though there was no defined obligation of the forces to be used in deterrence, and a fairly leisurely response was allowed for. In fact, the wider the application of the treaty, the more difficult it would be to operate; proliferation of allies can also mean proliferation of disputes. At the same time, agreement on what constituted aggression might divide the allies, as it did in 1521 when war started up again (see Chapter 4). Yet the treaty was an ambitious and imaginative project, even if, in the realities of Hapsburg-Valois conflict, it could not endure. It seems certain that Wolsey was the motivating force behind it.[184]

---

[183] T. Rymer, *Foedera, conventiones, litterae* (London 1704–35) xiii, 624–9; cf. G. Mattingley, 'An early non-aggression pact', in *Journal of Modern History* x, 1938.
[184] For Wolsey's work for peace cf. below, Chapter 4.

Peacemaking: the conventions and the machinery

Yet peace had to be made from time to time; as a result of victory (the imposed peace),[1] as a means of banding together against an enemy (the league or grand alliance),[2] as a way of purchasing a respite from war (the negotiated 'settlement' or the temporary truce which preserved the status quo),[3] and, very rarely indeed, the conscious effort for a peaceful community of nations (the non-aggression pact).[4]

Ambassadors

To achieve any of these settlements, experienced diplomats were the first need. By the end of the fifteenth century or the early sixteenth century, the powers of Europe had resident ambassadors at each other's courts. This development, from the use of 'special'

[1] The treaty of Madrid of 1526, which imposed heavy terms on François I, the Emperor's captive after Pavia. The French King subsequently denounced it. An earlier parallel is the treaty of Troyes of 1420, by which Henry V of England, victorious invader of France, secured the succession to the French crown. This treaty, also, was denounced as invalid by Charles VII, the lawful heir of Charles VI.

[2] The League of Cambrai of 1508 against Venice.

[3] The truce of 1521 (see below, Chapter 4), and the treaty of Cateau-Cambrésis (Chapter 6). An earlier peace, literally 'bought' by cash was that of Picquigny in 1475, by which Louis XI purchased the withdrawal of Edward IV and his great army, in return for a 'pension' (which the English excused as 'tribute' for their surrender of claims on France).

[4] The Peace of Lodi of 1454 between Milan, Venice, Florence, Naples and the Pope; it was for twenty-five years (with provision for renewal) and provided for military action (specifically quantitied) against any aggressor. Other Italian powers were invited to join, and did so. The non-aggression pact of 1518 (see above, pp. 65–6) was the most ambitious plan for a universal peace of European dimensions.

ambassadors with specific short-term missions, began in Italy and became normal after the Peace of Lodi in 1454. It was a way of obtaining and retailing regular information, adopted by the parties to this League in their struggle to maintain peace through a 'balance of power' within the peninsula. There were soon some Italian resident ambassadors north of the Alps; Milan, in search of alliance, sent to France after Louis XI's accession, as did Venice, after initial rebuffs in 1463 and 1470, from 1478. The system of permanent representation did not, however, become normal until the years after the French invasion of Italy and during the Hapsburg–Valois conflict. By the early 1490s Milan had resident representatives in Spain, in England, in France, and at the imperial court. Ferdinand of Aragon had blazed the trail with a resident in Rome by the 1480s, later one in Venice, and in England by 1495. His representation to the Hapsburgs was by 1495 the double one of an ambassador at the imperial court and another in the Netherlands. The Emperor Maximilian's network, built up before the end of 1496, collapsed through lack of money, as it did again in 1504.[5] The papacy eventually succumbed to this trend. Resident nuncios, who in a sense were the direct descendants of the tax collectors, were sent to Spain, France, England, Venice and the Emperor by the end of Alexander VI's pontificate (1503).

In Rome, the national procurators had been upgraded to ambassadors (*oratores* in Latin) by the last quarter of the fifteenth century. At the same time, members of the sacred college became cardinal protectors of individual nations, representing their interests and presenting ('relating') the evidence on candidates for papal provisions.[6] Both practices had been resisted by the papacy, Pius II wishing that ambassadors should only stay for six months and reluctant to allow the cardinals to assume extra responsibilities. But resistance proved vain.[7] There had been similar opposition by some secular rulers to the creation of resident ambassadors. Louis XI,

[5] Maulde de la Clavière, I, 26off.; G. Mattingly, *Renaissance Diplomacy* (London 1955) pp. 71–100, 121–44; D. Quellen, *The Office of Ambassador in the Middle Ages* (Princeton 1967) pp. 82–4. By 1502, the Signory of Venice had residents in Rome, at the imperial court, in France, England, Spain, Portugal, Hungary, Poland, Milan and with the Knights of Rhodes. The first English resident ambassador in France was Thomas Boleyn, father of Anne.

[6] W. E. Wilkie, *The Cardinal Protectors of England* (Cambridge 1974) pp. 5–10. The practice of using cardinal protectors was 'openly recognised' by the popes from the time of Julius II.

[7] Pastor, op. cit., III, 402.

who delighted in ambassadorial contacts, nevertheless argued in
1464 that in France a resident ambassador was not a sign of affection, but a matter of suspicion, the reverse of the custom in Italy.[8]
The King's confidant, Philippe de Commynes, advised caution in
the reception of ambassadors, except from friends.[9] As D. E. Quellen
has pointed out, resident ambassadors, once established, attracted
less notice than special missions; they were thus a useful tool to the
despatching power.

In this network, Rome became the central listening post, the
'plaza of Europe', as Ferdinand of Aragon called it. The delights
and miseries of curial life are most tellingly described by Joachim
du Bellay, in Rome as secretary to his relative, Cardinal Jean du
Bellay, from 1553–1557. One must follow one's Cardinal to the
Pope, to Consistory, to chapel, to meet an ambassador; at the palace
one found only pride, concealed vice, ceremonies, music, superb red
robes. One had to walk gravely, frown gravely, smile gravely, to
greet everyone, weigh every word, incline the head with a 'Messer
non', 'Messer si', 'E cosi', 'Son servitor', discourse on Naples or on
Florence. One had to conquer by kissing hands, and hide one's
poverty like a Roman courtesan. He watched the papal courtiers
wince when the Pope spat in a basin, as they looked, white-faced,
to see if there was blood in it (it was the time of the aged Paul
IV).[10]

It was, however, not only in Rome that news and rumours went
round, or that suspicions and temperatures rose. In 1481, for
instance, the Venetian Senate (renewing prohibitions of 1451) had
decreed that none of its members, nor members of the College or
the secret councils, should speak of affairs of state to ambassadors
or other foreigners in their own houses or elsewhere, on pain of a
fine or a period in exile.[11] Add to these sources the fact that resident
ambassadors often corresponded with their colleagues at other
courts, and one has an endlessly stirred whirlpool of information,
misinformation, and what we now call disinformation.

An ambassador was usually a distinguished public servant; he

[8] Report from ambassador Alberico Maletta in B. de Mandrot and C. Samaran,
ed., *Dépêches des ambassadeurs milanais en France sous Louis XI et François Sforza* (Paris
1916–23) II, 125, 241.
[9] Commynes, *Mémoires* I, 218–20.
[10] Joachim du Bellay, *Les regrets*, in *Oeuvres françaises* II, 209, 210, 232 (sonnets 84,
80, 110).
[11] Quellen, op. cit., p. 92.

was sent to 'say, advise and think whatever may best serve the preservation and aggrandisement of his own state'.[12] This not infrequently included the pursuit of peace. A basic requirement was the ability to communicate. Diversity of language was a powerful deterrent in this process. Biblical tradition asserted that diversity of tongues was a divine punishment for men's presumptuousness. Before the building of the tower of Babel all had spoken one language.[13] St Augustine wrote of the divisive flood of different languages, 'so that a man would rather be with his own dog than with another man of a strange language'. Rome, however, the Western Babylon, was endeavouring to communicate her language to all the lands she had subdued.[14] In the early fourteenth century Ramon Lull attributed the disputes between nations to their diverse languages; Latin should be learnt by all.[15] In the fifteenth century the humanist Lorenzo Valla dreamt of a purified Latin as the world language.[16] Certainly Latin was the *lingua franca* of renaissance ambassadors, just as Latin citations (from the Bible and the classics) were the essential ingredient of their formal speech-making. For this, a humanist education was required. The Florentine Vespasiano da Bisticci, praising one of his fellow citizens as of sufficient authority and reputation to be an ambassador, affirmed that he had 'a wide knowledge of Latin Letters'.[17] Richard Pace, himself a great ambassador, recalled (in his *De Fructu*, written in the public baths at Constance in 1517) a dinner in England at which, after much drink, one guest talked of his children's education. A noble, of the kind 'who always have a horn of some sort hanging from their back, as though they were going hunting in the middle of dinner' denounced literary learning. All learned men were beggars; Erasmus called 'damned poverty' his wife. The noble would rather

[12] From Ermolao Barbaro's treatise on ambassadors (quoted by Mattingly, op. cit., p. 109) written in the late fifteenth century. Mattingly contrasts this definition with the less pointed, less aggressive tone of Bernard du Rosier (1436) who wrote of ambassadors' ceremonial and negotiating duties (peacemaking one of the second) (ibid., pp. 34–5, 48).

[13] Genesis 11.

[14] St Augustine, *De civitate Dei* xv. vii.

[15] R. Gibert, 'Lulio y Vives sobre la Paz', in *Recueils de la societé Jean Bodin* xv, *La paix* (Brussels 1961) p. 142.

[16] Quoted from Valla's *De elegantia Latinae linguae* (1471) preface, by Yates, op. cit., p. 16.

[17] Vespasiano da Bisticci, *Vite di uomini illustri del Secolo XV*, ed. L. Frati (Bologna 1892–3) III, 36; trans. W. G. and E. Waters (London 1926), pp. 245–6.

that his son were hanged than learn literature; noblemen's children ought 'to blow a horn decently, know how to hunt, and carry and train a falcon nicely'. Literary studies were for 'the sons of country folk'. Pace interjected that the speaker was wrong: 'if a foreigner came to the King, of the kind that princes' envoys are, and a reply had to be made to him, your son, after the education you chose for him, would blow his horn I suppose and the learned sons of country folk would be called in to make the reply.' The noble relapsed into more drinking.[18] In fact, ambassadorial Latinity was quite often of a high order—Pace's, for instance, or Gasparo Contarini's,[19] and many another's—for the history of ambassadors is in some sense the history of humanism. There were exceptions. The first English resident in Spain, John Stile, spoke and wrote what Mattingly called 'hog Latin'. Even ecclesiastics were sometimes deficient. In 1519, the Archbishop of Cologne told ambassador Pace that 'he had not greatly exercised the Latin tongue'.[20] In the same period, some of the clerics of Verona needed the rubrics of the missal put into Italian.[21]

At the papal court, where 'so much violence, deceit and roguery' was disguised in beautiful Latin,[22] the language was essential, and elaborate attempts at elegance were called for.[23] Elsewhere, the

[18] Richard Pace, *De Fructu* (The fruits of learning), (Basel 1517) p. 15. The work is in the form of a dialogue, in which each of the Arts makes a speech on her own behalf.

[19] For Contarini, cf. below, Chapter 4 (his dinner party for Thomas More in Bruges in 1521 must have aired the Latin of both host and guest). Venetian skill is demonstrated in the Latin oration (by the captain of the galley moored at Southampton in 1518) to Henry VIII. Granted he was Andrea Priuli, of the patrician family, but ambassador Giustiniani noted that everyone was amazed that 'a professor of navigation and commerce could prove himself so able a rhetorician' (Rawdon Brown II, 192). The King himself gave an elegant Latin oration before Wolsey and Campeggio that year (*Cal. Ven.* II, 450).

[20] *L.P.* III (i) no. 283. Despite his august teachers, the Emperor Charles V was apparently ill at ease in Latin. In 1521, receiving a Latin letter from Henry VIII, he called on his Chancellor to look at it (*L.P.* III (i) no. 1328).

[21] W. Schenk, *Reginald Pole Cardinal of England* (London 1950) p. 55.

[22] Speech at the Diet of Frankfurt (1518) quoted by Pastor, op. cit., VII, 248.

[23] Cf. Richard Selling's oration in Rome, offering Henry VII's obedience to the Pope and his thanks for a marriage dispensation. The orator likened the King to Aeneas, in his struggle to win the throne, and to Theodosius and Constantine in his obedience to the Church (cited in Wilkie, op. cit., p. 12). In an oration, in 1471, in praise of the alliance between the Duke of Burgundy and King Ferrante of Sicily, the Burgundian chancellor cited Lactantius, Cicero, Seneca, the Book of Maccabees, Valerius Maximus, and Pythagoras (J. Bartier, *Légistes et gens de finances au XVᵉ siècle* (Brussels 1955) pp. 442–7.

language was the more essential the less the local and the visitor's vernaculars were mutually understood. Italians and French might use each other's tongues, as later did Spanish and Italians, but Latin was often resorted to. One French ambassador could still not speak Italian easily after seven years' residence.[24] In England and Germany Latin would be essential for communication with 'southern' ambassadors. One recalls Wolsey's Latin conversations with the Venetian and the Spanish ambassadors.[25] At the imperial and the Netherlands courts, the ideal situation in the time of the Emperor Maximilian was reported to be that English ambassadors should, between them, have both Latin and French.[26] In any case, oral communication made comprehension hard for the inexpert. In 1492, the Venetian ambassador in France did not know whether the Vice-Chancellor of Brittany was speaking Italian, French or Latin.[27] Long before Roger Bacon wrote of the necessity to know languages; one reason he posited was 'the securing of peace among princes . . . that wars may cease. . . . very often matters which have been set on foot with great labour and expense come to naught owing to ignorance of a foreign tongue.'[28]

The ambassador needed patience, agility, physical endurance, and the resourcefulness to deal with crises precipitated by all manner of hazards, from the vanity of princes and their counsellors to lack of money or personal affrays with the populace. Sebastiano Giustiniani, for instance, noted that three or four attempts were needed to obtain an audience with Wolsey; he had many audiences with the King, and before he left England (after a mission of four years) this very experienced diplomat, a Venetian patrician, was

---

[24] J. de Pins, 'Autour des guerres d'Italie. Un ambassadeur francais à Venise et à Rome (1515–1525). Jean de Pins, Eveque de Rieux', in *Revue d'histoire diplomatique* LXI, 1947, p. 226.

[25] Andrea Badoer (Giustiniani's predecessor in England) stated that he knew not only French and German, but English 'as little known in Venice as modern Greek or Slavonic is in London' (Rawdon Brown I, 64). Giustiniani needed an interpreter (his secretary) when he visited the French ambassadors (ibid., II, 233).

[26] *Letters and Papers Illustrative of the Reigns of Richard III and Henry VII* II, 108.

[27] Alberi, 1st series, IV, 13.

[28] Roger Bacon, *Opus majus*, trans. R. B. Burke (Pennsylvania 1928) I, 109. Henry VIII planned a House of Students (on the model of the Inns of Court) where pure Latin and French, and the Laws of England would be taught. Moots were to be held, alternately, in Latin and French. Significantly, students of this House were to accompany embassies abroad. (E. Waterhous, *Fortescue illustratus* (London, 1663), pp. 539–42.

addressed as 'father' both by the King and the Queen.[29] Pace was signally honoured during his missions to Venice; in 1522, he was allotted the Ca' Dandolo, was entertained aboard the Bucentaur (the Doge's state barge), and had dinner with the Doge's daughters.[30] Ferdinand of Aragon heard ambassadors personally, and sent abroad men of the calibre of Dr De Puebla.[31] Louis XI knighted ambassadors he favoured, but stiffly repelled those he did not: 'n'avons point agréeable le dit Jehan Pierre', he wrote of Panigarola, the Milanese ambassador whose recall he demanded.[32] The pitfalls were many; one needed to be 'well in' with the prince to whom one was accredited, but to keep a good reputation back home. Guicciardini had noticed that ambassadors often took the side of the prince at whose court they were.[33]

The physical stamina needed by such ambassadors might be considerable. First their outward journey, and their duty to follow the court (monarchs often evaded interviews by hunting or by travel), to assimilate to strange climates, customs, food and drink.[34] The hardships of travel bring to mind the journey of the ailing Cardinal Bessarion, in January 1460, sent from the Congress of Mantua to Germany as legate, and dragged over the Brenner on a sledge. Pace, on embassy to the Duke of Bourbon (commander of the imperial invasion force marching to Provence in 1524), described how, in the passes of the Col di Tenda (on the route from

[29] An analysis of Giustiniani's reports shows that during his sojourn in England (April 1515 to July 1519), he had thirty-three audiences of the King, some formal, some alone, and of considerable duration. He had sixty-six audiences of Wolsey, whose power he assessed; 'this man is King' was his parting shot.

[30] Wegg, op. cit., pp. 196, 201, 204–7, 212, 215, 255, 261.

[31] De Puebla, the first resident Spanish ambassador outside Rome, one of the *letrados* (jurists), a doctor of canon and civil law, a royal *corregidor* (municipal administrator) in Andalusia, is discussed by G. Mattingly, 'The reputation of Dr De Puebla', in *English Historical Review* 50, 1940. Thereafter, there was continuous Spanish representation in England until 1584.

[32] *Lettres de Louis XI*, ed. E. J. V. Charavay and B. de Mandrot (Paris 1883–1909) III, 283.

[33] Guicciardini, maxim 153, in *Maxims and Reflections of a Renaissance Statesman*, trans. M. Domandi (New York 1965) p. 80 (translations of his *Ricordi*).

[34] Perhaps one of the most eloquent pleas on this score came from ambassador Smith (1572), indifferent to the elaborate cooking at Catherine de' Medici's court: 'I would I were at home with you to eat a good piece of court beef and mustard, and cowsheel, and a piece of ling and sodden oysters, instead of all these pheasants and partridges . . . and young peacocks and all other such fine meats, covered and seethed with lard.' (M. Dewar, *Sir Thomas Smith, a Tudor Intellectual in Office* (London 1964) p. 133.)

Turin to Ventimiglia), he was obliged to crawl on all fours.[35] The Venetian Andrea Badoer, sent to England in 1509 at the age of sixty-two, injured his leg riding over the S. Gotthard in the dark. His horse fell on the ice, though fortunately not towards the precipice.[36] Stamina was also needed merely to fulfil the duties of resident. Daily reports home were often sent; a Venetian ambassador in Rome despatched 472 in a year.[37] The despatches had to be partially enciphered, usually by simple substitution of a numeral or an arbitrary symbol (Greek or Hebrew character for instance) for each letter. In Milan, in the mid-fifteenth century, the Chancellor Cicco Simonetta was a cipher expert; he ordered the use of separate ciphers by each ambassador, even those on the same mission. One such cipher used in 1461 had 229 symbols, perhaps the largest of its time. Occasionally meaningless signs or 'nulls' were inserted to deceive any investigator.[38] Some ciphers were very simple, that used by the Spaniard De Feria in 1558, for instance; De Puebla's was much more complex, one of his reports including 400 symbols.[39] The same cipher might be used for many years, even though in many cases it had been 'broken'.[40]

It was essential not only to send information home, but to receive it; otherwise the exchange of this vital commodity became inoperable. Badoer complained, in 1509, that he had received no letters for ten months; his successor Giustiniani was constantly protesting over lack of news. He stated baldly on one occasion that since he had no news there was 'consequently no inducement to negotiate'.[41] A Milanese ambassador to Burgundy in 1461 had even asked for a courier to be sent with blank papers, so that it would look as though some account was being taken of affairs in Burgundy.[42] Guicciardini, a young ambassador to Spain in 1512, complained both of lack of

[35] Wegg, op. cit., p. 236.
[36] Rawdon Brown i, 64.
[37] Despatches of Antonio Giustiniani, quoted by Mattingly, op. cit., p. 110. Milanese and Florentines were similarly copious.
[38] P. M. Kendall and V. Ilardi ed., *Dispatches with Related Documents of Milanese Ambassadors in France and Burgundy 1450–1483* (Athens, Ohio 1970) i, xvi–xviii, 342; ii, 4.
[39] Mattingly, op. cit., pp. 218–19, 314. The English ciphers caused difficulties in 1521 (see below, p. 120).
[40] Ibid., p. 249.
[41] Rawdon Brown i, 69. Even when letters did arrive, they were sometimes drenched and illegible (ii, 140).
[42] Kendall and Ilardi, op. cit., ii, 330.

information and of its falsification: Machiavelli, then secretary, had doctored the figures of the slain at Ravenna.[43] In addition to all this, letters might be intercepted and frequently were.[44]

This essential two-way information service could provide the conditions and sometimes the means of peaceful co-existence, alliance, or settlement of disputes between two powers. When, however, great matters were in hand, special impressive embassies would be despatched, sometimes to the opposite court, sometimes to a special peace conference. Career diplomats would often be included in such embassies, but high-ranking ambassadors were essential. A great noble, if possible a royal relative or minister, would head such embassies, plus one or two important ecclesiastics (for the formal speeches and the religious ceremonies by which treaties would be solemnised). In such matters, as Lodovico Sforza once remarked, the excellence of a power could be judged by the quality of its ambassadors, like the value of a bow from the arrows hurled from it.

For such special missions clear and sufficient but not too confining sets of instructions were needed. If the matter in hand was complex, then ambassadors needed very full guidelines on what they could offer, although often the sequence and timing of proposals would be left to them to decide. If they were not to change a single syllable, then this was, as Guicciardini commented, 'a method of negotiation most barbarous indeed'.[45] Normally, ambassadors would have some 'formal' instructions, which could be communicated to the other side, and 'secret' instructions, which were to be kept so. In 1497, for instance, the English ambassadors sent to negotiate with the Scots were given one 'book' of instructions to show to the Scottish ambassadors and another 'secret' book.[46] In 1503, Sir John

---

[43] R. Ridolfi, *The Life of Francesco Guicciardini* (trans. C. Grayson) (London 1967) pp. 30–7. Cf. the complaint of the imperial ambassador in Rome in 1524 that Pace (on the embassy in north Italy) wrote in 'a thousand colours', now saying that the imperial army prospered, now that it was ruined (*Cal. Span.* II, 660).

[44] Giustiniani complained that his letters, public and private, had been opened and read by royal officials at Canterbury (1516). He, however, had no scruples in reading letters of the papal nuncio (Francesco Chieregati) which he had 'come by' (Rawdon Brown I, 225, 314).

[45] Ridolfi, op. cit., p. 146. (Guicciardini's remarks on the rigid position of imperial ambassadors sent to negotiate with the Pope in 1526 after the treaty of Madrid); cf. the latitude allowed to the English ambassadors in 1558–9 (see below, pp. 189–90).

[46] *Letters and Papers Illustrative of the Reigns of Richard III and Henry VII* I, 109, 111–12.

Wiltshire, ambassador to the Netherlands, was told to 'revise' (i.e. re-read) his instructions frequently, so that he did not forget them.[47] In 1508 Margaret of Austria's ambassador to England begged the Archduchess to tear up his letters, or he would be taken (by the King of England) for a spy. She should write only 'good things' in her letters, other things in private notes.[48] In 1516 Florentine ambassadors to France had double instructions, one set to be shown to the King, the other for themselves.[49] The Turk evidently knew of the custom of multiple instructions; ambassador Ghiselin de Busbecq wrote that 'the Turks are prone to suspicion and have conceived the idea that the ambassadors of Christian princes bring different sets of instructions which they produce in turn to suit the circumstances and the needs of the moment, trying at first, if possible, to come to an agreement on the most favorable terms, and then, if they are unsuccessful, gradually agreeing to more onerous conditions'. For this reason, the Turks intimidated and threatened ambassadors, treating them almost as prisoners, so that their sufferings made them produce sooner the instructions which they wished to keep till last.[50] One could not find a better description of the normal use of instructions. Sometimes, as an additional ploy, an ambassador would be instructed to masquerade behind his private opinions; in 1454, a Venetian ambassador (to Milan) was to present the substance of his instructions as his private thoughts, pretending that he did not know if the Senate agreed.[51] The converse often happened; negotiators, in despair, would ask ambassadors their opinion as private individuals. Close observation of 'reactions' was always expected; in 1489 the Florentine resident in Milan was required to read out his letters, word for word, to Lodovico Sforza, and to report back not only the latter's words, but his gestures and expressions, so that it might be known whether he spoke from the heart.[52] Instructions were as divergent and intractable as circum-

---

[47] Ibid., I, 225.

[48] Ibid., I, 344, 349. The ambassador was the Provost of Cassel, who reports a three-hour conversation with Henry VII alone, the King on horseback, the ambassador riding a mule (ibid., I, 350).

[49] Devonshire-Jones, op. cit., p. 120.

[50] *The Turkish Letters of Ogier Ghiselin de Busbecq, Imperial Ambassador at Constantinople 1554–1562*, trans. E. S. Forster (Oxford 1968) pp. 141–2.

[51] F. Antonin, 'La pace di Lodi ed i segreti maneggi che la preparono,' in *Archivio Storico Lombardo* LVII, 1930, p. 254.

[52] *Catalogue of the Medici Archives*, p. 36. (Letter of the *Otto di Practica* to Pietro Alamanni, 5 June 1489).

stances and the instructing power dictated. Illness on mission was an expected hazard, but instructions to feign illness survive, as Lorenzo de' Medici's to the Florentine ambassador in Rome in 1491 (an illness or an attack of gout in the foot).[53]

The role of princes

It was sometimes suggested that princes should be their own ambassadors, though the desirability and the possibility of such 'summits' were hotly debated problems. On the former, there was some searching for the accord and understanding which princely encounters might produce. Georges Chastellain, the Burgundian chronicler, thought that Charles VII and Philip the Good of Burgundy did not understand one another because they never met.[54] Commynes, on the other hand, was convinced that princes who wished to preserve amity should never meet, except in extreme youth when bent on pleasure. Later, envy and spite would be added to danger. The princes or their followers might be consumed with jealousy or misunderstanding, and there was always the language difference. It was better, thought Commynes, to negotiate through loyal and wise servants.[55] In any case some princes considered this the correct way to proceed. The Emperor Maximilian, negotiating a double Austro-Hungarian marriage alliance with the Kings of Hungary and Poland in 1515, declared that 'it is not, however, fitting for our mutual dignity that we ourselves treat of such matters, but it is proper rather that all matters between ourselves and our two brothers be previously arranged and concluded, so that we come together merely to carry on friendly conversation'.[56]

[53] Ibid., p. 119. (Letter of Lorenzo de' Medici to Alamanni, n.d.).
[54] Georges Chastellain, *Oeuvres*, ed. Kervyn de Lettenhove (Brussels 1863–5) IV, 8. Duke Charles the Bold and Louis XI, who were two princes 'flying high', were also, he thought, estranged by not meeting (for fourteen years).
[55] Commynes, *Mémoires* I, 135–7. Commynes inserts this just after his account of the disastrous interview between Louis XI and Charles the Bold of Burgundy at Péronne in 1468. He also quotes the meeting of King Louis and the King of Castile in 1463, on the banks of the frontier river, the Bidassoa. Understanding was not promoted, and the French envied the luxury of Spanish accoutrements, saying that they had stolen rich cloth from churches. One may compare the rivalry over presents to ambassadors in 1467, when Edward IV's hunting horns and leather bottles were contrasted with the gold vessels given to the Earl of Warwick (Jean de Roye, *Journal, connu sous le nom de 'Chronique Scandaleuse'*, ed. B. de Mandrot (Paris 1894–6) I, 176).
[56] Letter of 20 May 1515, given in full by J. Strieder, *Jacob Fugger the Rich . . .* (English trans.; Archon 1966) p. 201.

Nevertheless, princely meetings were occasionally the order of the day. If so, elaborate security measures were much in evidence, particularly in time of war, as at the meeting at Picquigny between Edward IV and Louis XI to discuss the peaceful retreat of the English invasion force of 1475. The two monarchs met on a wooden bridge over the Somme, the bridge divided in the middle by a trellis (like a lion cage) through which they could talk and even embrace. King Louis had made Commynes wear identical clothes to his as a precaution (against assassination).[57] In 1495, after Charles VIII's retreat from Naples, Lodovico Sforza suggested a meeting on a bridge with a partition in the middle, as had been done at Picquigny. Charles VIII, however, rejected this proposal as unworthy of himself. Guicciardini records that Lodovico had proposed it either out of suspicion, or to raise difficulties (and thus please his allies), or to appear the equal of the French King.[58] The meeting did not take place.

There was inevitably much discussion over where to assemble for such meetings, whether in time of war or purely for pleasure. A 'neutral' place, in territory owned by neither power, or on the borders, was always preferred, both for security reasons and to avoid loss of face, i.e. the necessity for one monarch (or his diplomats) to travel into the other's dominions. During the Hundred Years' War between England and France, there was much partiality for places 'indifferent'. When, for instance, the Anglo–French–Burgundian peace congress was planned in 1435, the English wished it to be in Cambrai (a neutral city), or somewhere in Hainault or Brabant (Burgundian provinces).[59] Even for the pleasurable meeting of the Field of Cloth of Gold in 1520, the place selected was half way between Guines (in the English 'pale' of Calais) and Ardres (in France). In 1532 the two Kings had met first at Boulogne, then at Calais (five days in each) after a preliminary first encounter at Sandingfeld (S. Inglevert) just within the English 'pale'.[60] In the

[57] Commynes, *Mémoires* II, 60–9. One may compare King Louis' meeting with his own brother, with whom he was in dispute, on a bridge on the Sèvres river (in the Charente), with barriers dividing them (*Lettres de Louis XI* IV, 31).

[58] Guicciardini, *Storia d'Italia* I, 203 (Lib. II, cap.xii).

[59] Thomas Bekyngton, *Official Correspondence*, ed. G. Williams (London 1872) II, 266. The conference finally met at Arras, in Burgundian territory.

[60] Russell, op. cit., pp. 20–3, 94–6; Hamy, op. cit., p. 51. In 1550, there was wrangling over whether English and French diplomats should meet at Calais or Boulogne; the French won (S. R. Gammon, *Statesman and Schemer. William, First Lord Paget, Tudor Minister* (London 1973) pp. 169–71).

Hapsburg–Valois conflict, there was a partiality for meeting at Cambrai, or some place on the northern frontier, as in 1558–9.[61] The frontier with Spain was also a meeting point. Just as King Louis XI had met the King of Castile there in 1463, so, in 1526, François I was exchanged for his two sons (going to Spain as hostages) on the Isle of Pheasants in the river Bidassoa. A rowing boat set out from each bank towards the island.[62] Spanish and French royal brides were 'handed over' on this island: Élisabeth de France, Anne of Austria, Maria Teresa of Spain (brides of Philip IV of Spain, of Louis XIII and of Louis XIV).[63] A meeting of French and imperial ambassadors, in 1538, was at Salses, a fishing village on the lagoon of Leucate, on the borders of Roussillon (then Spanish) and France.[64] The 1538 meeting of the Emperor and the King (separately) with the Pope, was at Nice in the domains remaining to the Duke of Savoy.[65]

Sometimes ambitious projects for princely 'summits' were launched. There was often talk of princely meetings to bring peace or reform or both to the Church. During the great schism in 1381, Henry of Langenstein wrote: 'our kings and princes who are engaged in diverse wars and disputes, must, in accordance with the example and devotion of celebrated kings, faithfully and with obedient humility agree to the summoning of a General Council for the purpose of bringing about a general treaty of peace.'[66] Such councils, to be attended personally by the princes, to deal with recalcitrant popes, were a stock-in-trade political move, used by the Kings of France, for instance, in the late fifteenth and early sixteenth century. In 1517, the papal nuncio in England told ambassador Giustiniani that the popes were always against princely conferences, for the first thing that they discussed there was the reformation of the church which was to say of the pope and cardinals.[67] Yet there had been one grandiose scheme for princely summits to keep the peace of Christendom. In 1462 George Podiebrad, King of Bohemia,

[61] See below, p. 144.
[62] Knecht, op. cit., pp. 190–1.
[63] Velasquez decorated the pavilion for this last occasion. Margaret of Austria, on being returned to her compatriots in 1493, was handed over in a mill at Vendhuile, on the Scheldt, on the borders of France and the Cambrésis.
[64] Brandi, op. cit., p. 386.
[65] See above, p. 40.
[66] *Epistula concilii pacis*, in *Advocates of Reform from Wyclif to Erasmus*, ed. M. Spinka, *Library of Christian Classics* (London 1953) p. 111.
[67] Rawdon Brown II, 60.

advised by a Frenchman, Anthoine Marini, had urged a permanent alliance against the Turk (at first between Bohemia, France and Venice), which was to raise an army to retake Constantinople. There was to be a permanent court (*consistorium generale*) to regulate disputes and deal with aggressors, and a general assembly to discuss common affairs. A permanent 'secretariat' would manage matters between sessions of the assembly, which would itself meet in a different place every five years, under a president (one of the princes). Each nation would have one vote. The scheme was circumvented by Pope Pius II.[68]

The scheme of 'universal peace' of 1518 had no such institutional form, but was another attempt at some permanent provision for the keeping of peace, and on a European scale. In fact, as might be expected, peace came by individual treaties and alliances. There was always the possibility of leagues, or multiple alliances, but these usually proved of short duration, for they drew life from some confederation against a common enemy and lost vigour if the danger or threat were not abundantly clear to all. In fact, the general league for peace was itself vulnerable at every link in the chain: the wider the alliances, the wider the obligation and the commitment, a fact hardly lost on present-day commentators.

In such disputes and confrontations, princes would sometimes offer their personal services as arbiters or mediators. From the arbiter's point of view, such work could add immeasurably to his self esteem and honour; from the recipient's there was every reason for caution. The kings of France and England offered themselves as mediators in Italy in 1479 (between the Pope and Naples on one side, and Milan, Venice and Florence on the other).[69] King Louis XI was frequently on the verge of such intervention, being pleased to call himself arbiter of Italy. In 1463, he had arbitrated between the King of Aragon on one side and the rebellious Catalans and the King of Castile, whom the latter had called in, on the

<hr/>

[68] V. Vanecek, 'Deux projets tchèques des XVᶜ et XVIIᶜ siècles ... projets de Georges Podebrady et de J. A. Komensky', in *Recueils de la Société Jean Bodin, XV, La paix* (Brussels 1961) pp. 202–11; G. Mattingly, 'An early non-aggression pact' in *Journal of Modern History* x, 1938, p. 8. Podiebrad had hoped to reconcile the Bohemian church with Rome, on the basis of toleration for the Hussites as agreed by the *Compactata* of Prague of 1433. The King was himself condemned as a relapsed heretic, and deposed by Pope Paul II in 1466.

[69] Commynes, *Mémoires* iv, 241 (instructions to the French ambassadors).

other.[70] The Archduke Maximilian offered himself to Richard III, in conflict with Brittany (which harboured Henry Tudor and English 'exiles'), in 1484.[71] The Pope offered his services between France and Burgundy in 1491,[72] while in 1506 Henry VII proposed that he and Louis XII should arbitrate between the King of Castile (then ruler of the Netherlands) and the Duke of Guelders.[73] Henry VIII and Wolsey were wont to call themselves arbiters of Christendom; Wolsey's penchant for this role is well known. Yet Henry, in his turn, refused any notion that judges be appointed to arbitrate between England and France over Scotland in 1516. It was not customary among sovereign princes, and not 'for their dignity'.[74] Generally, arbitration was much favoured by propagandists, particularly Erasmus, but princes preferred the direct negotiation in which one could bargain and 'reserve' one's case, if one could not win it. The 1559 settlement was a good compromise; some matters decided, others reserved for future arbitration (see Chapter 6). In very hard cases, one reserved one's rights indefinitely. Papal mediation, as we have seen, was a particularly thorny subject. The Pope himself could take comfort from the maxim, *pontifex a nemine debet iudicari* (the Pope must not be judged by anyone), though conciliarists would not have agreed.

Treaties

Whether or not there were mediators, the negotiation of a solemn peace treaty brought the inbuilt peril of some 'judgment' over long-standing claims. An ancient 'querelle' or claim, for instance the English claim to the Crown of France, the French claim to Milan or Naples, the imperial/Spanish claim to Burgundy or Navarre, would be subject to the cut and thrust of diplomatic argument, and might have to be abandoned or modified in the realities of

[70] J. Calmette, *La question des Pyrénées et la Marche d'Espagne au moyen âge* (Paris 1947) pp. 112–13. The King met the King of Castile on the banks of the river Bidassoa, in that unsuccessful encounter which Commynes deplored (see above, p. 77).
[71] *Letters and Papers of the Reigns of Richard III and Henry VII*, II, 3–4.
[72] *Catalogue of the Medici Archives*, p. 87 (letter of Lorenzo de' Medici to Pietro Alamanni, 8 June 1491).
[73] *Letters and Papers of the Reigns of Richard III and Henry VII* I, 294–7; *Cal. Span.* I, 398.
[74] Rawdon Brown I, 159, 169. The King was referring to a French suggestion; the prospect of Venetian arbitration seemed, to Giustiniani, to be on Wolsey's mind.

peacemaking. Hence the disposition to 'reserve' ancient claims (as in 1559). Further, the solemn treaty was proclaimed (after a celebration of the mass) and ratified by solemn oaths, usually on the gospels or on some relic, of the contracting parties or their ambassadors.[75] In the latter case, the parties themselves subsequently took oaths of ratification. The treaty was therefore a solemn contract, and to break it was perjury, a stain on honour and an ecclesiastical sin, which might incur the ultimate ecclesiastical sanctions (excommunication and interdict). Hence the careful examination of treaties which had proved unworkable or unduly onerous to find legal loopholes.

A treaty which had been imposed under duress (*sub metu*) could, like other contracts, be repudiated as invalid.[76] Other legal difficulties might be cited. The French held that the treaty of Troyes of 1420 was invalid since King Charles VI had no power to alienate the throne to the victorious Henry V and disinherit the Dauphin. Canonists affirmed this and the invalidity of an act by a sick king in the hands of his enemy.[77] Further, the Pope had refused his ratification.[78] The 1526 treaty of Madrid was repudiated by King François I once he had regained his freedom. While still in captivity the King had made a secret declaration annulling the surrender of the Duchy of Burgundy, which he had then to accept in his public oath to the treaty.[79] Once returned home, the King and his Council repudiated the treaty: the French would not agree to surrender Burgundy, part of the royal patrimony, and the treaty had been concluded in captivity. A subsequent royal apologia invoked the fundamental law (on the patrimony) and the need for the consent of the inhabitants; the second principle was hotly denied in the

---

[75] Cf. Dickinson, op. cit., pp. 179ff.

[76] Cf. Cicero: 'who does not see that one does not have to stand by promises that one has made under compulsion of fear or deceived by guile? Many such promises are exempted by the praetor's ruling, some by law' (*De officiis* I, 32).

[77] P. Bonenfant, *Du meurtre de Montereau au traité de Troyes* (Brussels 1958); Dickinson, op. cit., pp. 61, 66–72, 175–6; T. M. Izbicki, 'The canonists and the treaty of Troyes' in *Proceedings of the Fifth International Congress of Medieval Canon Law, Salamanca 1976* (Citta del Vaticano 1980) pp. 425–34. The illegality of the disinheritance of the Dauphin Charles (i.e. the alienation of the Crown) was also asserted.

[78] E. Delaruelle, E-R. Labande and P. Ourliac, *L'église au temps du grand schisme et de la crise conciliaire* (Paris 1962) vol. XIV of A. Fliche and V. Martin ed., *Histoire de l'eglise*, p. 218; Izbicki, loc. cit.

[79] There had been a preliminary protestation some months earlier (Knecht, op. cit., pp. 185, 189–90, 206–8, 211).

imperial reply.[80] It was no wonder that Bodin, later in the century, pronounced that wise princes never impose unreasonable terms.[81] The converse was to take the Machiavellian view: princes need not keep their word. He added, however, that 'legitimate grounds' had never failed a prince who 'wished to show colourable excuse for the non-fulfilment of his promise'.[82] There lay the crux of the problem and the solution for a prince out-manoeuvred by some agreement. For one who wished to make a treaty hold there was much to be said for invoking the old-fashioned machinery in its entirety. In 1497 Henry VII, proposing a peace to the King of Scots, who harboured the imposter Perkin Warbeck and had twice invaded England on his behalf, instructed his ambassador that the King must be bound not only by his letter, great seal and solemn oath, but also upon pain of the censures of Holy Church, so that a breach might not, as of late, ensue upon 'light enformacion or suggestion'.[83]

Truces

The solemnities and the hazards of treaty-making predisposed combatants to the long-established device of the truce. A truce was a condition of war, a state of 'suspended animation', in which the status quo was to be rigorously preserved. During a truce, not one brick must be added to fortifications, no garrison reinforced, no act of war of any kind executed. The war, itself a 'kind of lawsuit', had been 'adjourned' and the territory covered by the truce was to be treated as neutral ground.[84] Matters in dispute were likewise suspended. Truces might be of very short duration (during the harvest, or during some peace conference, for instance, or in antici-

---

[80] Ibid. The Estates of Burgundy denounced the treaty as 'contrary to all reason and equity' (cf. H. Hauser, 'Le traité de Madrid et la cession de la Bourgogne à Charles Quint', in *Revue Bourguignonne* XXII, 1912, pp. 80–6. Gattinara had counselled against the French King's release on such harsh terms. Guicciardini wrote that this treaty was the first time that the Emperor had acted on his own (*Storia d'Italia* IV, 347; Lib. XVI, cap. xiv).

[81] Bodin, *Six Books on the Commonwealth*, pp. 178–80. Yet Bodin did not condone perjury in breaking such agreements. The work was printed in 1576.

[82] Machiavelli, *Il principe* XVIII.

[83] *Letters and Papers Illustrative of the Reigns of Richard III and Henry VII* I, 106.

[84] M. H. Keen, op. cit., pp. 206–9; K. Fowler, 'Truces', in *The Hundred Years' War*, ed. K. Fowler (London 1971) pp. 184–209.

pation of a peace conference[85]) or they might be long-term, literally a suspension both of hostilities and of the disputes which had caused them or might do so. Truces of a number of years were common.[86] Exceptionally even longer periods might be hoped for. In 1478–9 there were proposals for a very long truce between England and France, finally put at one hundred years after the death of Edward IV or Louis XI (whichever was first), with a renewal of the French 'pension' (paid to the King of England) for this period.[87] This was a postscript to the treaty of Picquigny of 1475, which was a truce for seven years. Such long-term projects were unusual. Whatever the length of time, the truce (unless it covered all the dominions of the contracting parties) defined the territory to be covered and whether the truce was on land only,[88] or was to hold on the seas or in fresh waters.[89] A truce 'with communication' meant that subjects of one power could travel into the territory of another, particularly important to merchants, and to students; normally there were restrictions over visits to fortresses or garrison towns. The truces between France and England, for instance, were normally 'trêve marchande' or 'trêve pêcheresse', to allow commerce or fishing.[90] In short-term truces, an instant renewal of war was contemplated; in 1474 Louis XI ordered all his men-at-arms to be at their posts when the truce with Burgundy should expire.[91] A

[85] The truce of Bomy (near Thérouanne) between the Emperor and the French, in 1537, for ten months, and then another three months, in expectation of a longer-term agreement (Brandi, op. cit., pp. 385–6.)

[86] The truce of Nice (1538) between the Emperor and the French was for ten years (ibid.; see above, pp. 40–1). That of Vaucelles in 1556 was for five (Pierson, op. cit., p. 31).

[87] J. Calmette and G. Périnelle, *Louis XI et l'Angleterre* (Paris 1930) pp. 223–38. King Louis denounced his ambassador's acceptance of the English terms, as beyond the powers given to him and contrary to the King's honour (cf. *Letters de Louis XI* VII, 253).

[88] E.g. the land truce between England and France in 1419; people and animals might move freely (Rymer, *Foedera* x, 818/2).

[89] E.g. the truce of 1416 between England and France, by sea from the pillars of Hercules to Norway, by land over certain areas in west Flanders and Picardy as far as the Somme (*Gesta Henrici Quinti*, trans. F. Taylor and J. S. Roskell (Oxford 1975) p. 169). The truce of 1463 was not to extend to the 'sea war', although harbours were included (*Lettres de Louis XI* II, 151, 184).

[90] The treaty of Picquigny of 1475 was a 'trêve marchande', as was Louis XI's nine-year truce with Burgundy concluded the same year (ibid., VI, 14; Commynes, *Mémoires* III, 397, 409). The 1478 truce between France and Burgundy was to be 'communicative et marchande' (*Lettres de Louis XI* VII, 114–15).

[91] Ibid., v, 270. Truces were often categorised as devices for reinforcing armies (cf. below, pp. 118, 121, 144).

truce was, of course, 'broken' by any act of war, in which case the hostilities could be restarted. In the truces between the Empire and the French, with their vast territorial extent, endless disputes would arise over such infringements of the agreements.

Marriage alliances

One often-used expedient in peace-making was the marriage alliance, though opinions varied as to the long-term benefits of such contracts. At the Congress of Arras in 1435, the English proposed a marriage alliance with France (with a long truce); it would unite the two realms, and the hope of issue would be a good augury for peace. But the French argued that such marriages had led to wars more bitter than those that preceded them.[92] There was truth in both contentions. The English claims to the throne of France sprang first from Edward III's French mother (the Princess Isabelle), and secondly from Henry V's right to the succession under the treaty of 1420 and his marriage to the Princess Catherine.[93] By these two claims or 'querelles', war and the dismemberment of France had been sustained for a very long period. There had been brighter hopes, on both sides, of the marriage of Richard II and the nine-year-old Isabelle de France in 1396. It had inaugurated a twenty-eight-year truce, and was to have been followed by a personal expedition of the two kings against the Infidel.[94] Again, it was hoped that the marriage of Henry VI and Margaret of Anjou would be followed by a meeting of the King with his uncle, King Charles VII, and a general peace settlement.[95] The Anglo–French marriages and marriage schemes continued: the marriage of Louis XII and Henry VIII's sister Mary, the projects for his infant daughter Mary in 1518 and 1520.[96] In 1550 secretary Paget, negotiating for the

[92] Dickinson, op. cit., pp. 146–7. The English at Arras quoted the advocacy of such a marriage by St Bridget (in her *Revelationes*). The contemporary historian Thomas Basin quoted a French proverb that French princesses had always found in England sad weddings and unhappy marriages. Through these marriages the English had asserted their claims to the French crown. (Thomas Basin, *Histoire de Charles VII*, ed. C. Samaran (Paris 1933–44) I, 293).

[93] Henry V had, in fact, predeceased Charles VI, and therefore there was legal doubt that he could transmit any claim to the succession to his son, Henry VI.

[94] J. J. N. Palmer, *England, France and Christendom 1377–99* (London 1972) pp. 169–75, 204–5, 242–4.

[95] R. A. Griffiths, *The Reign of King Henry VI* (London 1981) pp. 482–96.

[96] By 1521 she was affianced to the Emperor, whose son, Philip, she married many years later (see below, p. 134).

return of Boulogne to the French, was questioned on a French marriage for Edward VI. An Italian merchant, working for England, told him that a treaty with France without a marriage alliance was 'but a drye peax'.[97]

Similar projects, similar hopes and failures, could be cited in many other contexts. Awkward provinces, in dispute between two powers, could be treated to this 'medicine'. Imperial lands in the north or the 'imperial' duchy of Milan were offered to the Duke of Orléans in 1544, dependent on his marriage to either the Princess Mary, daughter of Charles V, or her younger sister. The death of Orléans removed this 'foundation for the peace'.[98] The negotiations of 1558–9 brought forth a 'marriage' solution for the problem of Calais.[99] The whole structure of the eventual treaty made a general peace hang on two marriage alliances.[100]

Whatever political result might follow, the marriage alliances of princes were fraught with problems: dowry, dower, cession of claims by descent (usually extracted from a princess in respect of her father's inheritance), and projected territorial endowment for children of the marriage. The preliminaries to all this were searching investigations of the most delicate kind. In 1505, when Henry VII was considering marriage to the widowed Queen Juana of Naples (niece of Ferdinand of Aragon), he sent a three-man embassy to the Spanish court. They were to inquire as to the 'estate' the Queen kept, whether she could speak any French or Latin (in addition to Spanish and Italian), her age, stature, the features of her body, visage, whether painted or not, her countenance (cheerful, frowning, blushing, etc.), clearness of skin, the colours of her hair, her eyes, brows, teeth, lips, her nose, the height and breadth of forehead, her complexion. Also they were to note her arms, her hands, fingers, neck, her breasts and paps, her lips (with hair or not?), the condition of her breath (they were to try to approach her when she had fasted), the height of her slippers,[101] her sickness or health, her

---

[97] B. L. Beer and S. M. Jack, ed., 'The Letters of William, Lord Paget of Beaudesert, 1547–1563', *Camden Miscellany* xxv (London 1974) p. 93.

[98] Knecht, op. cit., p. 371 (the treaty of Crépy).

[99] See below, pp. 155, 164, 186, 190.

[100] See below, pp. 151, 164, 204–5; the marriage alliance of François I and the Emperor's sister Eleanor (agreed in 1526, under the treaty of Madrid, but not realised until 1530), was no good omen for such hopes of peace.

[101] Heels could deceive as to height, hence the careful inquiries (the ambassadors, in this case, could only guess from the style of slipper then in fashion).

resemblance to the King her uncle, her diet, her finances. A portrait must be obtained.[102]

Margaret, Archduchess of Austria, the daughter of the Emperor Maximilian,[103] experienced the whole relentless machine at work, and three times over. As the child bride of Charles VIII of France, she had been repudiated and sent home when the match with Duchess Anne of Brittany (herself then affianced to Margaret's father Maximilian) seemed more profitable.[104] She was then married to Juan, Crown Prince of the Asturias, the only son of the Catholic King, and one-and-a-half years her senior.[105] The Prince died after only five months. Margaret's daughter was stillborn, and she returned to the Netherlands. There were suggestions of marriage with Lodovico Sforza, with the King of Scotland, and with Arthur Prince of Wales. She was, however, eventually married to Duke Philibert of Savoy, brother of Louise, the mother of the future François I. The Duke, a few months younger than Margaret, died after less than three years.[106] Margaret, not yet twenty-four, was a widow for the third time (if one counted her marriage to Charles VIII, which she certainly did). She returned to the north a second time, to be Regent of the Netherlands for her six-year-old nephew, Charles (now King of Castile, and later Emperor), taking up residence in Malines (Mechelen) the city from which Margaret of York (her grandmother by marriage) had 'ruled' the Netherlands. By this time Margaret was being courted by Henry VII, an ageing widower of forty-nine.[107] Her brother Philip had agreed to the

---

[102] *Memorials of King Henry VII*, pp. 223–39.

[103] See Plate 3.

[104] She was affianced at the age of two to the thirteen-year-old Dauphin (under the treaty of Arras of 1482 between France and Burgundy). Her dowry was to include Artois and Franche Comté. She travelled to France at the age of three, and lived at Amboise, first as Dauphine, then as Queen. Her nurse was the only Netherlander allowed to remain in her household, which was large, as became her rank. She was 'repudiated' in 1491, and the treaty of Senlis (1493) gave back her dowry to her father Maximilian. She had been kept hostage in France in the interim, but no longer at court.

[105] Under the double marriage alliance of Margaret's brother Philip the Handsome and Princess Juana of Castile-Aragon, and of herself with Prince Juan. The agreement was the price of Maximilian's adherence to the League of Venice, by which the French were to be driven out of Italy.

[106] The marriage contract provided for a dowry in money. In Savoy, Margaret took into her service Mercurino di Gattinara, future Grand Chancellor of the Empire.

[107] Some months earlier, Louis XII had been proposing that King Henry should marry Marguerite d'Angoulême, his niece, sister of the future François I (Chrimes op. cit., pp. 288–9).

marriage just before his death,[108] and her father the Emperor continued the campaign. The Archduchess, however, could withstand such politicking. Her refusal of the King is a masterpiece in blunt home-truths. She had had three husbands. The first had repudiated her, the other two she lost in youth. She would rather remain a widow. She feared that she might not bear children. The dowry which the King demanded was too large, and therefore too onerous for her 'subjects' to support. The terms were too favourable to England. The friendship with England could be maintained without marriage.[109] One might say, with her contemporary, Jean Lemaire de Belges, that Margaret had experienced the 'loyalty, service, gentleness and constancy of some; the deception, injury, meanness and fickleness of others; the perseverance and mutability of diverse human affections'.[110] It was no wonder that she took as her device 'Fortune, In fortune, Fortune', or that in pride at her highest and enduring rank, she styled herself 'Caesar's daughter'.[111]

The tragi-comedy of the marriage market entailed countless manoeuvres and diplomatic conspiracies. The results were often negative, if not positively harmful, in terms of international peace and concord. Erasmus was led to assert that princes would best marry within their own kingdoms. Marriages between different 'peoples' were not 'adamantine bonds of public harmony'. The greatest upheavals in human affairs sprang from them: broken betrothals, complaints of the terms, changes of mind. 'If the mutual alliances of princes would give peace to the world, I should wish each of them six hundred wives.' Marriages might secure peace, but they could not make it perpetual. When one party died, the accord was broken, and from the children arose further disputes.

[108] As a sequel to the treaty of Windsor between England and Philip, King of Castile, under which English armed assistance was promised to the King in Castile, on the seas, or in the Netherlands (*Foedera* XIII, 123ff., 127–32; *Cal. Span.* I, 351–2, 382–3, 393, 397, 400, 432).

[109] *Letters and Papers of the Reign of Richard III and Henry VII* I, 324–7. Cf. ibid., II, 156–8; A. F. Pollard, *The Reign of Henry VII from Contemporary Sources* (London 1914) III, 96–101, 124–8; Chrimes, op. cit., pp. 288–90.

[110] Jean Lemaire de Belges, *Oeuvres*, ed. J. Stecher (Louvain 1891) IV, 149. From the *Couronne Margaritique*, in which a crown is made of ten precious stones, corresponding to ten virtues or qualities, bearing the same first letters as the letters of the name 'Marguerite'. The tenth stone is the 'escarboucle' (ruby), and the tenth quality Experience. Margaret is compared to Dido. (For Margaret's patronage, cf. F. Thibaut, *Marguerite d'Autriche et Jehan de Belges* (Paris 1888).)

[111] Latin poem written by Margaret on the death of her brother Philip (cited in J. de Iongh, *Margaret of Austria* (London 1954) pp. 108–9).

Rights to rule were passed from one to another, and wars became more frequent. Through 'relationship', moreover, princes would stir up other kingdoms whenever they themselves were offended. He concluded that the prince might *sometimes* be strengthened by such alliances, but never his people.[112] Nevertheless, there was perpetual optimism on this subject; the temptations of immediate gain and endless future rewards were too great.[113] The negotiations of 1558–9 show the whole subject in strong colours.[114]

[112] Erasmus, *The Education of a Christian Prince*, pp. 241–3. Erasmus quoted the Anglo–Scottish marriage of James IV and Margaret Tudor, daughter of Henry VII. A Scottish invasion of England was not precluded by this.

[113] When Margaret Tudor's marriage to James IV of Scotland was being discussed in the English Council, there were those who objected that, should her two brothers (Arthur and Henry) die, then the King of Scots would inherit England. Henry VII is said to have replied that, if that happened, Scotland would accede to England, the greater kingdom drawing the lesser, which saying 'passed as an oracle' (quoted in W. C. Dickinson, *A New History of Scotland from the Earliest Times to 1603* (London 1961) p. 281). The succession of James VI to England would seem to have fulfilled the prophecy.

[114] Portraits are again in evidence (see below, pp. 138n14, 174n13). These, in themselves, were hazardous. For instance, Holbein the Younger (and not Cranach, who was ill) painted Anne of Cleves: 'a portrait by him [Cranach] . . . might have had a healthy deterrent effect [on Henry VIII]' (J. Pope-Hennessy, *The Portrait in the Renaissance* (London 1966) p. 198).

PART II

The actualities of peacemaking

An English peace initiative: the conferences at Calais and Bruges in 1521

The accession of Charles of Ghent to his grandfather's Austrian dominions, and his election to the imperial title as Charles V in 1519 intensified and widened the Hapsburg-Valois conflict. The 'perpetual peace' of 1518, the friendly encounters of the Emperor and Henry VIII at Canterbury and Calais-Gravelines, and of King Henry and King François I at the Field of Cloth of Gold in 1520, seemed to augur well for peace. Yet both powers were seeking to draw England into closer alliance against the other, and King Henry was tempted by imperial advances.[1] Gattinara, the imperial Grand Chancellor, declared that the King of England acted towards the Emperor and the King of France 'as a man that hath two horses, rydyng on the one, and ledyng the other in his hande'.[2] Between the Emperor and King François I hung the unfulfilled 'diabolical' treaty of Noyon of 1516;[3] each contemplated military action in Italy, the Emperor under cover of the journey to Rome for his coronation, the King as an expedition to Milan (which he had regained for France in 1515). The King of England counselled strongly against such enterprises, and warned that English aid would be given to

---

* This chapter is a revised and adapted version of my article 'The search for Universal Peace', in the *Bulletin of the Institute of Historical Research* XLIV, 1974.
[1] Russell, op. cit., pp. 1–21; Scarisbrick, op. cit., pp. 74ff. At the Field of Cloth of Gold, the Anglo–French marriage alliance of 1518 had been reaffirmed. The Emperor, however, also sought the hand of the Princess Mary (despite his commitment to a French marriage alliance by the treaty of Noyon); he wished for some new alliance with England, and a further personal meeting with the King (*L.P.* III (i) nos. 936, 1098, 1150, 1212, 1213, 1257; III (ii) no. 1340.
[2] *L.P.* II (i) no. 1162 (report of ambassador Tunstall).
[3] For the terms, see below, p. 115n78.

whichever of the two powers was first attacked.[4] This reaffirmation of the 1518 treaty and declaration of neutrality was also made clear to the Pope.[5]

Yet by 1521 François I was prepared for war. The moment may have seemed propitious since the Revolt of the *Communeros* in Castile had recently reached its height. By mid-May 1521 a double French offensive had been launched against the Emperor under cover of two localised disputes. In the north, royal troops and volunteers joined Robert de la Marck, Duke of Bouillon, in his attack on the Emperor in Luxembourg (in defence of his subjects who, he alleged, had been denied imperial justice).[6] In the south, the claim of Henri II of Navarre to recover the 'Spanish' province of his kingdom was supported by an expedition of 8,000 Gascons and 300 lances, led by Antoine de Foix, Seigneur de Lesparre. François I publicly denied involvement in the north, however, and considered help for Navarre lawful since the Emperor had reneged on his promises of 1516. However, the King is known to have personally planned both expeditions, with the Duke and with Lesparre.[7] His 'aggression' seems clear; it was certainly clear to the Emperor, who immediately planned retaliation and lodged a protest with Henry VIII.[8] The fighting continued.[9]

---

[4] *L.P.* III (i) nos. 936, 1098, 1212, 1213, 1270. To reinforce English neutrality, competing French and imperial requests that the English ambassador at Rome associate publicly with their own were refused. All three should act together.

[5] F. Nitti, *Leone X e la sua politica secondo documenti e carteggi inediti* (Florence 1892) pp. 251, 337–8. For the Pope's vacillating policy before his alliance with the Emperor (May 1521), see above, p. 33.

[6] *L.P.* III (i) nos. 1168, 1176, 1323.

[7] Ibid. III (i) nos. 1168, 1176, 1183.

[8] Ibid. III (i) nos. 1315, 1318, 1326, 1361.

[9] By May, de la Marck had withdrawn, but the French army in Navarre, at first victorious (at Pamplona), and entering Castile, made the Emperor warm to attack. His troops seized de la Marck territory: Musancourt, Jametz, Floranges and Bouillon itself. There was then a brief respite, allegedly for the conference, but in August, while Wolsey negotiated, the imperialists crossed the Meuse, taking Mouzon and laying siege to Mézières, both in France. This was to invite French accusations of 'aggression'. There was a further sector of activity in the region of the Upper Scheldt, along the Somme, by Valenciennes, Tournai (key and bulwark of Flanders, as the imperialists said) and Ghent, and a foray towards Calais, Ardres being taken on 9 September. Later that month the imperialists raised their siege of Mézières, allegedly at Wolsey's request. In October the French army, which the King had then joined (early in the month he was marching with his Swiss at the French camp, Attigny, near Vouziers in the Ardennes), crossed the Scheldt by building a bridge, to meet the Emperor and his army, then near Valenciennes. However, bad advice, or simply bad weather, prevented the French from joining battle, and the Emperor escaped.

King Henry and Cardinal Wolsey were thus faced with the implementation of the 1518 agreement. At first, a special embassy to France counselled the King against any invasion of the Empire, de la Marck having withdrawn his troops, and the imperial preliminary counter-attack being merely, in English eyes, an 'excorse' (expedition), such as often happened on frontiers.[10] King Henry himself may have contemplated immediate armed support for the Emperor, but his Council, considering the cost, and the lateness in the year, 'devised' that the King should offer to mediate between the parties, postponing the war until 'a more convenable season'.[11] This was, no doubt, a plan after Wolsey's heart, as it was in the spirit of the 1518 treaty; it also met the problem of England's naval and military unpreparedness.[12] The Emperor's 'final appeal', if made, could mean war within thirty days (under the 1518 treaty). King François accepted 'mediation', as far as was consonant with his honour: French Kings could not accept 'arbitration'; no other person but King Henry could have persuaded him.[13] He was willing to leave his crown at S. Denis and prove, as a gentleman (i.e. by force of arms) that the breach of the peace proceeded from the 'King of Castile' (his contemptuous term for the Emperor).[14]

The Emperor accepted the offer of mediation, but only under elaborate conditions and after first demurring on hearing of the Navarre campaign. He insisted that the conference should be interrupted while Wolsey journeyed to see him (at Bruges) there to conclude a defensive alliance, 'a stricter amity', and prepare for military action. King Henry accepted this plan; Wolsey must,

---

François failed to relieve Tournai, which surrendered on 30 November. An unsuccessful campaign in Ostrevant, between Scheldt and Scarpe, closed the season, the rains and the marshy terrain having done their worst. François disbanded his army, leaving a garrison and artillery at Amiens. The French campaign in the south had ended with Admiral Bonnivet's seizure of Fuenterrabia on 19 October, which embittered the negotiations perhaps more than any other single event.

[10] *L.P.* III (i) no. 1283.

[11] Ibid. III (ii) no. 1574, and following the deciphering of this ambassadorial report (John Clerk's from Rome) by J. J. Scarisbrick (op. cit., p. 83).

[12] Mattingly, loc. cit., p. 18 (using unpublished material from the *Haus-, Hof- und Staats- Archiv*, Vienna).

[13] *L.P.* III (i) nos. 1310, 1331, 1342; III (ii) no. 1385. Wolsey considered that the King's letters to King François, and his own to Louise of Savoy and Admiral Bonnivet, had turned the tables (ibid. III (i) no. 1329). King François protested that he had 'written' amity with the Pope, and all princes Christian, but the amity with King Henry was in his heart, and by spoken words (ibid., III (ii) no. 1385).

[14] *L.P.* III (i) no. 1331.

however, be empowered to mediate by both parties, and the imperial ambassadors should have powers to conclude a truce. The stricter amity could then be concluded, without exciting French suspicions, 'under colour of this meeting'. The Emperor would not specifically authorise Wolsey's mediation and jibbed at a truce before redress was made. He consented, however, to write officially asking that Wolsey be sent to Calais (where the mediation was to take place).[15] François I, meanwhile, gave Wolsey authority to mediate and accepted an 'abstinence' from fighting.[16]

The negotiators

Wolsey, therefore, had been bound to a double task: to mediating a peace settlement, and to a strict alliance with the Emperor. He had no choice but to accept these conflicting arguments. His undoubted concern for peace and his partiality for mediation (already the subject of rumour at the Field of Cloth of Gold and subsequently) made him hope that the King would 'pass between and stay them both'.[17] He was, equally, unable to escape the prospect of armed assistance to the aggrieved party, now being expanded into the strict alliance the Emperor expected. It is not necessary to accuse him of duplicity. He was the centre of a 'peace party', disparate and far-flung. With him to Calais went Sir Thomas More, now Sub-Treasurer.[18] Secretary Richard Pace was detained by his duties at home. Erasmus waited on events at Bruges.[19] Louise of Savoy, mother of François I, worked for peace as in 1520 when she had private talks with Wolsey at the Field of Cloth of Gold. Wolsey referred to her in 1521 as 'mother and nurische of peace', and she herself told the English ambassador (perhaps disingenuously) that her son was inclined to peace 'but would be prayed to it

[15] *L.P.* III (i) nos. 1340, 1357; III (ii) nos. 1382, 1383, 1394, 1415, 1422, 1423. The 'stricter amity' was to be concluded within six months of Wolsey's landing at Calais; the Emperor would not conclude any treaty with France during the conference.
[16] *L.P.* III (i), nos. 1126, 1311; III (ii) no. 1382. The truce was accepted largely on the insistence of the King's mother, Louise of Savoy.
[17] Ibid. III (i) nos. 1213, 1254, 1255; *Cal. Span.* II, 310, 313.
[18] *L.P.* III (ii) no. 1437; cf. below, p. 107.
[19] A new edition of the *Querela Pacis* was printed at this time. Erasmus wrote to his friends on the need for peace (Allen, op. cit., IV, 565–6, 569, 576), and hoped to meet Pace (*L.P.* III (ii) no. 1499).

often'.[20] At the imperial court, Margaret of Austria, Dowager
Duchess of Savoy and lately Regent of the Netherlands, was urgent
for peace, as also for the 'neutrality' of the former Burgundian lands
(as in 1511 and 1513). It was said that she was 'like a mother' to
the Emperor; she was also Wolsey's 'good mother', and did not
resist the title 'bonne Englese'. She had most probably encouraged
the English marriage alliance in 1520, and had promised to inform
Wolsey of any misunderstanding between the Emperor and the
English.[21]

A major problem for historians is Wolsey's own ambitions as a
cleric, which were certainly fostered in imperial circles. The prospect
of the papacy was mentioned to him both by the Emperor and by
the Duchess. Whether or not he actually coveted the honour—and
modern research suggests that he did not—it was a flattering offer,
and he was moved to state that he would only desire it 'to exalt
their Majesties' (Charles V and Henry VIII). He declared that if
he were Pope, he would crown the Emperor, exalt his own King
and make war in person, first against the French, and then against
the Infidel.[22] As mediator for both sides, he no doubt dreamt of a
general settlement and a crusade. Perhaps this sense of supreme
opportunity, and his undoubted supreme authority, accounts for his
long and wearisome labours at the conference and his stately
mission to Bruges. There was also the hope of personal triumph.

In 1521 Pope Leo was hardly fulfilling 'the good and virtuous
purpose of achieving the pacification of Christendom' (to use
Wolsey's definition of papal obligations).[23] In May of that year he
had concluded an offensive alliance with the Emperor; the French

[20] Russell, op. cit., p. 92; *L.P.* III (ii) nos. 1442, 1651, 1696; she styled Wolsey
'mon fils et bon amy' (cf. below, p. 127).

[21] Ibid. III (i) nos. 1213, 1255; III (ii) nos. 1388, 1417, 1603, 1637, 1694, 1707,
1749, 1763, 1776, 1810. The Duchess had two representatives at Calais; one was her
counsellor Nicolas Perrenot de Granvelle, future minister of Charles V, and father
of Granvelle, the negotiator in 1558–9 (ibid., III (ii) nos. 1437, 1603).

[22] *L.P.* III (ii) nos. 1876–7, 1892, 1906, 1934, 1952, 1960. Cf. D. S. Chambers,
'Cardinal Wolsey and the Papal tiara', in *Bulletin of the Institute of Historical Research*,
XXXVII 1965; Scarisbrick, pp. 107–10. At Calais, Wolsey told the French that he
already had more possessions than a man of the Church should have (Le Glay II,
515). In 1522, John Clerk, ambassador in Rome, did not stir because 'your grace
at my departing showed me precisely that ye would never meddle therewith'. In
1523, Wolsey declared that he would rather be in the King's service than be ten
popes (*L.P.* III (ii) nos. 1960, 3372). His youth was supposedly against him (ibid.,
no. 1952, report of Campeggio).

[23] *L.P.* III (ii) no. 3389.

attack on Reggio (in June) brought heavy counter-attack. The papal, imperial and Swiss troops marched on Milan, whose capital fell in November.[24] Although, in 1520, the Pope had hoped for English mediation between the Emperor and the King of France, and although both parties wished for his participation in the 1521 conference,[25] the Pope was in no mood for negotiation. He considered that arbitration would be futile.[26] He declined to send a special nuncio to the meeting; the resident in France or England would suffice. In the event, his nuncio to England, Geronimo Ghinucci, Bishop of Ascoli (in the March of Ancona) came to Calais. Initially, he appears to have had no special powers; he was, in modern parlance, mainly an observer, and was told to procrastinate.[27] The Pope was no friend to Wolsey, nor Wolsey to him.[28]

At Calais, Wolsey faced his two peers, both lawyers, and much his senior: Mercurino di Gattinara, Grand Chancellor of the Empire, and Antoine Duprat, Chancellor of France.[29] Gattinara's vision of the Emperor as supreme peacemaker clearly had its practical counterpart: the defence of imperial claims and rights. In 1521 he was for war; the French objected to his leadership of the imperial embassy on grounds of his hostility.[30] A Piedmontese, he was devoted to the welfare and quiet of Italy, as ambassador Contarini reported; Wolsey thought that he sought his own advancement there; the Duchess Margaret saw his plan for the Emperor's journey to Rome as very 'prejudicial' (to northern interests).[31] Certainly the fate of the northern Italian states (particularly Milan) and the new alliance with the Pope were central to Gattinara's concerns. He wanted affairs in the north to be quickly settled by force of arms, and

[24] See above, pp. 33–4.
[25] *L.P.* III (i) nos. 1123, 1339; III (ii) no. 1534. The Emperor had written to the Pope in August, promising that he would make no agreement with the French without papal sanction (Pastor, op. cit., VIII, 47).
[26] Ibid., III (i) no. 1366; III (ii) no. 1430.
[27] Cardinal Campeggio had hoped to be sent (ibid., III (ii) no. 1404) as he had been in 1518.
[28] Russell, op. cit., pp. 83–5; *Cal. Span.* II, 309–10, 313–14, 360.
[29] Wolsey was then about forty-six, Gattinara fifty-six, and Duprat fifty-eight. For Gattinara cf. G. Clarette, 'Notice pour servir à la vie de M. de Gattinara', *Mémoires et documents publiés par la société savoisine d'histoire et d'archéologie* XXXVII (Chambéry 1898).
[30] *L.P.* III (ii) no. 1413.
[31] *Cal. Ven.* III, 189, 204; *L.P.* III (ii) nos. 1479, 2001; cf. no. 1695 for Wolsey's views on the Emperor's Italian plans.

the Emperor on his way over the Alps. Just before the imperialists proceeded to Calais, Gattinara wrote a long memorandum from Dunkirk on 30 July for the Emperor on the way of peace and the way of war. The memorandum put the reasons for peace under the heading of the seven deadly sins and the reasons for war under that of the ten commandments. On the side of peace, he argued on the uncertainty of war, the immense cost, the suppression of de la Marck's rebellion and the readiness of the English to negotiate a peace. For the cause of war, Gattinara showed how the Emperor was committed to the Pope, who had invested him with Naples and would help in the expulsion of the French from Milan, admittedly at the price of cessions of north Italian territory to the Papal State. The imperial army was almost mobilised, and it would be wiser to go forward with the war; clearly God was on the Emperor's side, and it was Charles's duty to win honour and glory. Italy called for help, Spain was quiet again, Germany feared and loved him. Perhaps Charles responded; there is a French report that in August he 'preached' to the people of Ghent, asking their help and declaring that he would leave the King of France in his shirt, or else suffer a like fate.[32]

Both Emperor and Grand Chancellor were intent on the intransigent defence of every imperial claim: to Navarre, to Naples-Sicily, to Milan, citing the treaty of Noyon as unfulfilled.[33] They were watching the progress of fighting, waiting for news from Italy, Navarre and the northern front, in the hope that the French would be compelled to submission. Peace negotiations were to be dragged out in the hope of a better solution through the war, which had begun to favour the Emperor. Everything meanwhile hung on proving that the French were the aggressors, and on securing maximum commitment from the English. The Emperor worked tirelessly, from six or seven in the morning until mass, from an hour after 'dinner' until supper.[34]

The French Chancellor, Antoine Duprat, a lawyer from the

---

[32] Le Glay II, 473–82; *L.P.* III (ii) no. 1456.

[33] In disputes over French 'suzerainty' over Flanders and Artois, and on the Somme towns, they were prepared to disinter the history of Boniface VIII and Philippe le Bel, not to mention fifteenth-century treaties. They even cited evidence from the time of Pépin.

[34] *L.P.* III (ii) no. 1357. He was said to have done this ever since his Great Chamberlain and adviser, Guillaume de Croy, Sieur de Chièvres, had died on 29 May.

Auvergne, was by 1521 seasoned in diplomacy and statecraft, but found the English Cardinal somewhat too subtle for him. He tried hard to follow Wolsey's mood and wrote to his master that they were 'lowering their sails' until the Cardinal commanded.[35] He stoutly opposed any arbitration by Wolsey—this was not used among princes, he said—and drove a hard bargain where he could. Louise of Savoy described him as too much the man of law, always driving things at length; the imperialists found him defending his points—to them, his untruths—'au bec et aux ongles' ('tooth and nail'), while Ruthall, Bishop of Durham, declared that Duprat's arguments on the invalidity of the treaty of Noyon would invalidate any treaty.[36] Evidently the Chancellor was driven to desperation and hence to blunt expletives by the imperialist claims at Calais. He offered his head if it could be proved that François I had helped de la Marck (to which Gattinara replied that he would rather have a pig's head), and again offered his head if some letter of the King's contained the implications alleged by the other side (he had composed the letter, he said), to which Gattinara replied that the Chancellor was very free with his head, and would already have lost it if it were possible to give it. In fact Duprat had protested before the conference at the choice of imperial representatives, Gattinara, Berghes and Hanneton, as too anti-French, and may well have approached the meeting with distrust. He had not, as far as I can discover, met Gattinara before.[37]

The French King, also intent upon war, had, like the imperialists, a long list of grievances and claims. His ambassadors brought with them a 'petit cayer' (a small booklet) citing all their grievances, which they presented to Wolsey early in the negotiations.[38] They were to stick to their claims to Milan and Naples-Sicily, under recent treaties, and to reject imperial pretensions based on the treaties of Arras (1435) and Péronne (1468), agreements negotiated by force and therefore invalid. Imperialist efforts to reopen ancient '*querelles*' going back to the time of Pépin, or of Pope Boniface VIII, were stoutly resisted.

Wolsey had set out for Calais with multiple authority from his

[35] A. Buisson, *Le chancelier Antoine Duprat* (Paris 1935) pp. 166, 370; Russell, op. cit., pp. 68–9.

[36] *L.P.* iii (ii) nos. 1551, 1946.

[37] Granvelle i, 184, 189; *L.P.* iii (ii) no. 1413. cf. below, p. 102n48.

[38] Before the conference, the King's long list of grievances had been rehearsed by his ambassador to England (*L.P.* iii (i) no. 1310).

own King. Documents dated 29 July empowered him to conclude
a settlement of the differences between François and Charles, a
closer amity with François, a confederation between Pope, Emperor
and King, a marriage between Charles and the Princess Mary, a
treaty with the Emperor for the defence of the two realms and for
carrying on war against France to recover English possessions
there.[39] François I gave the Cardinal the same authority as last
time, at the Field of Cloth of Gold: Wolsey had powers to act for
François with the English and for Henry with the French.[40] The
Pope had conveyed his desire for the Cardinal to mediate; he had
also renewed Wolsey's legateship (for England) for another two
years.[41] The Emperor had bound himself not to make separate
peace with France without the express consent of the Pope and
King Henry, until the closer amity with England was concluded or
the conference dissolved. Holding the imperial letters patent,
Wolsey boasted to his master: 'he [the Emperor] is now bound,
your Grace is at large'.[42]

The proceedings at Calais and Bruges are very well documented,
for there was constant reporting by the ambassadors.[43] While the
conference proceeded, King Henry busied himself with military and
naval plans for the war he no doubt expected and perhaps desired.[44]

[39] The first, second and fourth in duplicate, the third in triplicate (*L.P.* III (ii) no.
1443.
[40] Ibid., III (i) nos. 1126, 1254.
[41] Ibid., III (i) no. 1123; III (ii) no. 1403.
[42] Ibid., III (ii) nos. 1418, 1439.
[43] The imperial procès-verbal (French translation of the Latin, made for Margaret
of Austria) is printed in Granvelle I, 125–241. The French equivalent, and texts of
letters are included in the journal of Jean Barrillon, secretary to Chancellor Duprat
(*Journal de Jean Barrillon, 1515–21*, ed. P. de Vaissière (Paris 1897–9); letters and
memoranda are printed in Le Glay. English reports and letters are in *L.P.* There is
an English narrative of Wolsey's journey to Calais and Bruges, by no means a
procès-verbal, but written from outside the conference room, probably by an officer
of arms (Corpus Christi College, Cambridge, MS. 111, pp. 383–95). The suggestion
that the author was York Herald (Thomas Writh or Wryth), whose part is highlighted, is tempting. The Venetian ambassador to England, Antonio Surian,
accompanied Wolsey to Calais; Gasparo Contarini was ambassador with the imperial
court and at Bruges, while Giovanni Badoer, ambassador to France, was with the
French court, itself in the north-east, near to the army's campaigning. (cf. *Cal. Ven.*)
[44] The King at first planned to send a force of archers to aid the Emperor, and
his own entry into France by way of Reims. Then he began to favour a naval war
to destroy France. He was in dispute with Wolsey over the logistics; the Cardinal
saw many difficulties, and was able to sustain an independent course (*L.P.* III (ii)
nos. 1393, 1429, 1440, 1462, 1474, 1488, 1519, 1523, 1536; Scarisbrick, op. cit., pp.
86–8).

The Emperor was playing on his ambitions.[45] Meanwhile the King eluded work and Secretary Pace by 'hunting the harts'. Occasionally there were personal letters to write; to King François (in French) and to the Duchess Margaret (presumably also in French). The latter task was advised by Wolsey 'though to your pain': 'Ye know well enough that women must be pleased.'[46]

The first conference at Calais

Wolsey arrived in Calais on 2 August,[47] the imperial ambassadors[48] meeting him at the waterside, and the guns of Risebank, those of ships in the harbour and of the town, firing salutes. Wolsey lodged in the Staple Hall, where the conference was held. The French ambassadors[49] arrived on Sunday 4 August, bringing with them gentlemen, spears and men of the guard, to the number of 300 horse. They had been met at the turnpike, half a mile outside Calais, by the Lord Chamberlain, the Lord of St. John's, Sir Thomas Boleyn, Sir William Sandys and York Herald. Right from the start, there was suspicion. A servant of one of the French ambassadors was found on the walls of Calais with a rope and a leaden weight; he was thought to be measuring the walls, but turned out only to be fishing. In the mouth of the Thames, an English and

[45] The Emperor promised to make good the loss of the French pension, which Henry's entry into the war would entail (*L.P.* III (ii) nos. 1340, 1371).

[46] *L.P.* III (ii) nos. 1424, 1425, 1459.

[47] Wolsey travelled accompanied by the Lord Chamberlain, the Earl of Worcester (Charles Somerset), the Bishop of Ely (Nicholas West), the Bishop of Durham (Thomas Ruthall), the Lord of St John's (John Docwra, Prior of the Hospitallers at Clerkenwell), Lord Ferrers (Walter Devereux), Lord Herbert (Henry Somerset), Sir Thomas Boleyn (former ambassador to France, and father of Anne Boleyn), Sir William Sandys, the Master of the Rolls (Cuthbert Tunstall), Thomas More, York Herald (Thomas Writh or Wryth), and others. The King instructed that 'as old men decay greatly', Sandys and More were to be privy to the negotiations (*L.P.* III (ii) no. 1437). These were all present at the Field of Cloth of Gold (Russell, op. cit., p. 194 wrongly cited Lord Ferrers of Groby).

[48] The imperial ambassadors: the Grand Chancellor, Mercurino di Gattinara, Jean Seigneur de Berghes (Margaret's special envoy), Jean de Luxembourg, Seigneur de Fiennes, Philippe Hanneton, Audiencier. Berghes and Hanneton were replaced on the return from Bruges by Bernard de Mesa, Bishop of Badajoz and Elne and J. B. Spinelli, Count of Cariati (in the Kingdom of Naples). The imperialists demanded war from the first moment of arrival (*L.P.* III (ii) no. 1462).

[49] The Chancellor, Antoine Duprat, Jacques de Chabannes, Seigneur de la Palice and Marshal of France, Jehan de Selva, Seigneur de Cormières, President of the Parlement of Paris, and Robert Gedoyn, Seigneur de la Tour, Secretary of Finances. For Duprat and Chabannes, cf. Russell, op. cit., pp. 68, 72.

a Spanish ship, the latter charged with wines, some for the Lord of St. John's, were seized by Frenchmen, perhaps from Le Tréport. John Hopton, captain of the king's bark, which was at Calais to 'protect' the meeting, evidently sailed out to deal with this. Bonnivet, Admiral of France, declared that things must be going badly with the English if they stuck at such trifles. It was not a good beginning.[50]

How did matters proceed? The parties met before the Cardinal from Monday 5 August until Thursday the 8th, beginning with the customary but poignant pleas for peace. The Cardinal protested that he would travel to the King of France and to the Emperor, and on foot as far as Rome if need be. The imperial ambassadors stated from the outset that they had no powers to negotiate peace, but had simply come to declare their master's injuries. The papal nuncio said he had no powers; the French said that they were there at the request of the English, but they could not negotiate if the others had no powers. Both sides invoked English aid under the treaty of 1518, and Wolsey countered by declaring that it must first be determined which side was the aggressor. Meanwhile there must be an abstinence of war. There were discussions on the seating (l'assiette), evidently left to Wolsey's discretion. At one meeting the imperial ambassadors and the papal nuncio sat on Wolsey's right—the place of honour, thought the French—and the French ambassadors and the ambassador of Venice on the left. Wolsey had suggested that, to avoid disputes, he should seat the ambassadors so that it would not be known who was first and who last.[51] We are not told what happened, but for once negotiations did not founder on this favoured debating point. There was far worse disagreement; an unwillingness to give way on any point under discussion.

The French had a full record of the treaties which they said had been broken: they presented the 'petit cayer' of their case to Wolsey. The imperialists said that they had the letters of the French King and his servants to prove his aid to de la Marck. Wolsey communicated the evidence of one side to the other. The imperialists did not

---

[50] Barrillon, op. cit., II, 214; *L.P.* III (ii) no. 1489; Corpus Christi Coll. MS. 111, pp. 384–5. There may have been only one ship (a Spaniard) (cf. *L.P.* III (ii) no. 1473). On the fishing incident, the French protested that the young man was an Irish boy, given to La Bastie, a member of the embassy, by an English gentleman shortly before, and that he used the lead to weight the bait.

[51] *L.P.* III (ii) nos. 1549, 1574; Barrillon, op. cit., II, 205, 217ff.; Granvelle I, 125ff.

reply to the French document, rather they presented what the French termed 'une invective', giving their case: princes should keep order on earth; the Emperor had worked for peace, and against the Turk, but the French were always the aggressors, even fomenting Luther. They were like a raging lion, or a wolf in sheep's clothing. The French reply stressed equally that kings should keep peace for their subjects. Homer called kings gods, as protectors of justice and piety. Yet the Emperor had failed: he had refused homage for Flanders and Artois, had denied royal rights there, had conspired in Milan, had sought marriage in England, despite his commitment to a French princess, had attacked in Navarre, and had seduced the Pope (a good man, if only he would follow his own counsel) from the French alliance. The King of Spain (the Emperor) would wage war like a fox, having stitched a fox's skin on to a lion's.[52] Amidst all this, Wolsey laboured for the beginnings of an agreement. As the anonymous English narrative states: 'my lordes grace toke mervilous great busines in hering thes complanyes every daye amoungst thes imbasators and every daye feasting them one after an other.' Discussion, liberally spiced with eating and drinking, was Wolsey's way with the intractable.[53]

Despite his impressive labours, Wolsey was working to a plan. On 6 July the imperial ambassadors to England had reported that the King agreed with 'Wolseys plan': that he should be sent to Calais under cover of hearing the grievances of both parties, and when he could not 'arrange' them, should withdraw to the Emperor to treat of alliance. The imperial officers would conduct him to Bruges. The Cardinal had proposed an alliance of the Pope, the Emperor, England, Portugal, Denmark, Hungary, Savoy, the Swiss and others. Already on 22 July the Emperor had declared his wish that Wolsey should come to him speedily to arrange secret affairs. There was no time for delay, since the Emperor would already have 8,000 men under arms by 8 August, and a long stay at Calais would prejudice his affairs. Besides, Henry should now strike to claim his own (in France). Writing from Rome, ambassador Clerk records that Wolsey had arranged that the imperial ambassadors at Calais should say they had no powers to conclude peace, so that he could then proceed to the Emperor. The truce there being discussed is

---

[52] Barrillon, op. cit., II, 217–50; Granvelle I, 125ff.
[53] Corpus Christi Coll. MS. III, p. 385. The King sent 2 harts, baked, which he had killed himself (*L.P.* III (ii) no. 1473).

termed a 'colour' to deceive the French King.[54] The plan was neatly followed and on 12 August Wolsey set out for Bruges, escorted by the imperial embassy and leaving the French to await his return.

The conference at Bruges

Travelling by way of Gravelines, Dunkirk, where he slept the night, the great abbey of the Dunes and then Nieuport, and being welcomed by local processions in each stopping place, by the prince of Orange at Nieuport and by the Pope's nuncio at 'Oysbrough' (Oudenburg?), Wolsey entered Bruges in great state. His company included many nobles, his gentlemen, in crimson velvet with gold chains about their necks, and a contingent of Yeomen of the Guard in their red and black livery. In all there are said to have been 1,000 horse: two eye-witnesses run to this figure. The Emperor himself had waited outside the city for about two hours, and when they met Wolsey did not dismount, but greeted Charles 'from the saddle, raising his bonnet'. They rode in procession into the city, where the streets were lined with people and hung with tapestries.[55] Wolsey was taken to the Emperor's palace, the Princenhof, former residence of the Dukes of Burgundy. He was lodged 'on the backsyde of the sayde palace that my lordes grace myght at everytime goe to the emperores at his pleasure thorowe a garden'. From this it seems clear that Wolsey occupied the Hôtel Vert (from its green tiles), across the garden at the back of the palace. In the time of Philip the Good it had been the residence of the heir, the Count of Charolais. We are told, from another source, that Wolsey occupied the lodgings normally used by the Duchess Margaret; this would not invalidate the previous statement, since Margaret may well have taken over the Hôtel Vert, there being no heir at this time.[56]

In the general arrangements for Wolsey's embassy, the Emperor bore all the costs, in return for his own entertainment at Canterbury the year before. No house was allowed to charge for expenses; the Emperor's officials came every evening with the 'livery': a baking

[54] *L.P.* III (ii) nos. 1395, 1393, 1421–2, 1439, 1574.
[55] Corpus Christi Coll. MS. III, p. 386; *Cal. Ven.* III, 160–1. Compare Wolsey's stately processions in 1520 at the Field of Cloth of Gold (Russell, op. cit., pp. 86–7).
[56] See Plate 4. The residence of the Count of Charolais can be clearly seen. Unfortunately hardly anything remains of the Princenhof, enlarged by Philip the Good and again by Charles the Bold. It lay between the modern Rue Nord du Sablon and the Rue du Marécage.

of bread, two great silver pots with wine, a pound of fine sugar, white lights and yellow, a bowl or goblet of silver and a tall candle or torch. In the morning the same officials came to settle with the host for the previous day's expenses. Men and women of Bruges visited the Cardinal's lodgings to see his plate and to drink wine. His household, lodged at the Bishop of Tournai's palace, brought their hosts to drink wine and beer. In the market the English found victuals ready for oven or grill, especially ducks, pigeons and hens. The English narrative wonders at the cleanliness of the streets and at the marvellously fair women, with the best hair in the world.[57]

Here began a whole round of visits and discussions, the latter 'interminable', according to Contarini. It was a combination of state functions and personal diplomacy such as Wolsey loved and in which he excelled. The day after his arrival, he rode with the Emperor in solemn procession across the city to mass at Notre Dame. The Lord Chamberlain and other English lords wore rich gowns 'for the honour of England'. The Cardinal and the Emperor shared the same traverse, and Wolsey gave the benediction from the high altar. There followed a dinner at the Princenhof and about two hours in discussion. Later the Duchess visited Wolsey in his lodgings, a signal mark of honour, but not, as far as I can judge, something which Wolsey had demanded, as Brandi suggested. On another occasion, Wolsey visited the Duchess 'in her secrete chamber the space of ii howers'. He wrote home that the Emperor and the Duchess had come to his lodgings 'familiarly', and that he had been entertained in 'delicate, plenteous and sumptuos manner'. One afternoon the Emperor and the Duchess came to Wolsey's lodgings; he met them in the garden, took them to his privy chamber and 'there sate at council ii longe howers and more and that was familerly done of so great a prince and after made lustie cheere with in and with ought with great bowels of wyne and freute'. Another time, Wolsey was with Charles and Margaret the whole day, and returned home about 9.30 p.m. in high spirits. At another time he went riding with the Emperor. On the first Sunday, 18 August, there was another solemn procession to mass, this time in the nearby church of S. Jacques, Wolsey wearing crimson satin and the Emperor gold brocade, a thing never seen before, said the Venetian

[57] G. Cavendish, 'The life and death of Cardinal Wolsey', in *Two Early Tudor Lives*, ed. R. S. Sylvester and D. P. Harding (New Haven 1962) pp. 22–3; Corpus Christi Coll. MS. III, pp. 385–7.

report. It was a mass of the Holy Spirit, which the papal nuncio interpreted as indicating that an alliance had been agreed, for it was customary to have this mass when treaties or alliances were promulgated. After the mass, there was dinner at the palace, and then a council. The next day, at 5 o'clock, the Emperor and the Duchess Margaret again visited Wolsey in his lodgings. Seeing them coming, he met them at the garden steps ('the gresing in the garden'). They sat familiarly in council, and stayed until 10 o'clock, being served with hippocras and all manner of dainties.[58]

There was also mutual entertainment and discussion between the English and imperial counsellors: Wolsey entertained Gattinara and Berghes and others on one day, the imperial minstrels and the Cardinal's 'chapel' singing for the guests. The Duke of Alva gave dinner for the English, and Wolsey reciprocated. At another time the papal ambassadors—the nuncio to the conference, Ghinucci, and the resident, Carraciolo—were brought by York Herald to Wolsey's privy chamber, and sat in council for two hours, proceeding thence across the garden to the Emperor. However, counsellors and nuncios were for the more routine occasions. As Contarini reported, the main business was dealt with by four persons; Charles, Margaret, Wolsey and Gattinara. Contarini himself could not secure an interview with Wolsey; he had to be content with riding alongside the Cardinal as he left Bruges. He did, however, have dinner with Gattinara, and himself secured as dinner guest one Thomas More, whom he found 'learned and discreet', but who dropped no hint of any treaty, only speaking of the peace between France and the Empire.[59]

Meanwhile the Anglo-imperial accord was worked out. Clearly Margaret took a leading part: on 16 August the Emperor empowered her, with her adviser Berghes, to arrange a treaty of

[58] Corpus Christi Coll. MS. III, pp. 386–91; *Cal. Ven.* III, 160–2, 162–4.
[59] Ibid.; Corpus Christi Coll. MS. III pp. 386–91; *L.P.* III (ii) no. 1493; Edward Hall, *The Triumphant Reigne of Kyng Henry VIII*, ed. C. Whibley (London 1904) I, 227–31. Wolsey gave audience to the King of Denmark, brother-in-law of the Emperor, who visited the conference, perhaps with the hope of mediating, but also to win Charles to his schemes in the north. Wolsey 'made difficulty' over the first meeting, to avoid conceding precedence to the King, and in fact they had converse in the garden, the King looking 'solemply and another time grimly', Wolsey making 'a mery countenance of a salutacion', and a doctor of Scotland acting as interpreter. For the second meeting, York Herald fetched the King to Wolsey's lodging (Corpus Christi Coll. MS. III, pp. 387–8; *L.P.* III (ii) nos. 1419, 1432, 1495). Dürer painted the King during his stay in the Netherlands.

marriage and ratify any stipulation for war against France which it might contain. The minutes of deliberations in the imperial Council show hesitation over publicising the marriage alliance until Henry declared himself. They also reveal counsellor La Chaulx's opinion that Wolsey must be firmly dealt with: if he gained one point, he would expect always to do so. The Council agreed that details of the proposed accord should be discussed, after dinner, in the presence of Duchess Margaret, who was to debate with the Cardinal afterwards. Wolsey certainly discussed with 'my lady' the marriage alliance and the indemnity for the loss of the King's French pension which would follow it. The terms of the dowry were, as usual on such occasions, keenly debated. No doubt the Emperor kept matters under close scrutiny. He had promised Wolsey that the two of them would do more in one day than his ambassadors in a month. On 25 August, the date of the treaty, he visited Wolsey secretly with but six counsellors, Wolsey returning the visit, and attending a 'council' in the Emperor's lodgings. The details were no doubt worked out by the counsellors, and during the last few days of the deliberations the two papal nuncios had been present. Gattinara's role was as important as Wolsey's. On 24 August he had been closeted with the English counsellors until nine in the evening. Giving dinner to Contarini, he spoke of Wolsey, who had expected to find the Emperor a lad in leading strings as in the time of Chièvres, but had discovered a different disposition in him. It may be that the Cardinal had found the imperialists tougher than he had expected: he wrote simply of the Emperor as coldly and circumspectly using himself, as a discreet prince, in pondering and regarding his affairs.[60]

Whoever prevailed, a marriage alliance and a clear offensive alliance was the result. In a treaty of 25 August, which it was hoped the Pope would approve, a tripartite alliance was made. The Emperor and King Henry were to meet on the former's journey to Spain, their two fleets were to conjoin at Falmouth for this journey. By March 1523 there was to be war on sea and land against France; the Pope would lay the whole realm under interdict. Henry would cross the sea in person, he and the Emperor each providing 10,000 horse and 30,000 foot (the English might hire some of their contingents from the Emperor). The two naval forces would each have

---

[60] *Cal. Ven.* III, 160–4, 167–71; Corpus Christi Coll. MS. 111, pp. 388–91; *L.P.* III (ii) nos. 1475, 1491, 1493–4, 1507.

3,000 men. The two princes would put down heresy and reform abuses in spiritual things in any lands they might conquer (clearly a high-sounding motive for their personal war of reconquest under ancient claims). They would then turn their attention to the Turk. A marriage would be concluded between Charles and the Princess Mary, then aged five, the Pope giving dispensation from previous contracts. The treaty, which was to be kept secret from all but the most intimate counsellors of the two rulers, was to be ratified by the Pope, then publicly by the two princes.[61] A second, bilateral treaty was also agreed. It set out the detailed terms of the marriage alliance (12 articles), the war measures, and an undertaking for the Emperor to pay Henry's French pension (until he had reconquered territory to that value).[62]

A whole world order was thus to be arranged, with England and the Empire dividing France and reforming her into the bargain. It was all cut and dried; Contarini saw Gattinara hand to Audiencier Hanneton some numbered sheets, the text of an agreement.[63] Wolsey's plea for peace must thus have been set aside. Edward Hall gives a long version of an opening speech in which the Cardinal had set forth the calamities, misery and wretchedness of war, and the commodities, benefit and wealth that came by peace. The cardinal's Italian secretary, Peter Vannes, told Contarini of his master's desire only for peace. But Hall's version of the Emperor's reply to Wolsey's speech shows the way the discussions went. Charles is reported as invoking the law of God, which bound every man to claim his right, and bound no man to hold or keep or withstand another's right. His cousin of France had withheld his (the Emperor's) rights and patrimonies. Margaret also took a firm line. Wolsey reported that she demanded that England should declare war against France immediately. Willingly or unwillingly, the Cardinal was evidently committed before he left Bruges.[64]

Wolsey left the city after a hurried meal with the Emperor, at which the other guests had taken the last course into another room, because of his departure. Charles escorted him out of the city, and

---

[61] *L.P.* III (ii) no. 1508; signed by Wolsey, the Duchess Margaret and the Seigneur de Berghes. It was ratified by the sovereigns (*L.P.* III (ii) no. 1509 is the Emperor's ratification).

[62] *Cal. Span.* II, 365–71; signed by the same negotiators. It was later ratified by the sovereigns (ibid., 380; *L.P.* III (ii) no. 1571).

[63] *Cal. Ven.* III, 169–70.

[64] Hall, op. cit., I, 228; *L.P.* III (ii) no. 1493.

the English cavalcade arrived back in Calais on 28 August having slept at Nieuport and then at Dunkirk, and being escorted by Gattinara, with the Bishop of Badajoz and Elne, Bernard de Mesa, and the Count of Cariati, who replaced Berghes and Hanneton.

The second conference at Calais

Wolsey found the French in an ill humour, for he had been away sixteen days and not eight, and his interim message, telling of his six hours a day with the imperialists to 'induce' them to peace, failed to convince. In fact England began to supply gunpowder to the Emperor: Wolsey promised 200 barrels, and the King swore by St George that it should be sent. Only French knowledge of these transactions eventually compelled a surcease.[65]

It is most difficult to determine whether Wolsey still hoped for a peace. The Anglo-imperial accord was already concluded. Yet Wolsey told Contarini that the imperialists were returning to Calais with powers to conclude a peace, which they had not had before. The Cardinal would almost certainly have talked with Erasmus at Bruges, and he may still have hoped against hope that the ideal of universal peace could be achieved. He may still have wished to prove to all the world that he could succeed where others failed. However, Hall—no doubt after the event—comments: 'immediatly after his arivying he treated with them [the French ambassadors] of peace, yet not so ernestly as he did before and that perceived well the sayd Ambassadors and wrote therof to the Frenche kynge.'[66]

Let us look at the final discussions, from 29 August to 27 November, when Wolsey crossed the sea for home. They are closely documented, almost daily reports being sent by one or other of the participants. Wolsey's first effort was to assemble the conference (30 and 31 August) and to secure agreement on four points relating to fishing rights and communications.[67] Even these had to be referred to Charles and François, Wolsey trying to obtain answers

---

[65] Corpus Christi Coll. MS. 111, pp. 391–2; *Cal. Ven.* III, 160–1; On the gunpowder, *L.P.* III (ii) nos. 1523, 1536, 1547, 1539, 1606, 1634.

[66] Hall, op. cit., I, 231.

[67] The four points were: freedom of fishing rights (it was the herring season), freedom of communication for the ambassadors and their messengers, freedom of access to Calais for the victuallers, and an undertaking by both parties that the havens, ports, rivers and lands of the king of England would be free of attack, and safe for all (Le Glay II, 487–95; Granvelle I, 139; *L.P.* III (ii) no. 1534).

in eight days. Meanwhile the old wrangles recommenced. The papal nuncio said he had no powers, the French said they had no powers to negotiate with him and would send for others. The imperialists burst out in accusations against the French, who had injured the Pope. Spiritual and temporal swords should help one another, and therefore the Pope had turned to the Emperor. It was unpropitious. From the outset Wolsey attempted private persuasion. He had a long talk with Gattinara, then summoned Duprat to his 'garde robe' where they sat down together and talked familiarly. Wolsey promised that Henry would never fail the French. He pleaded for the neutrality of Burgundy, as Margaret had asked, referring to her as a good woman who hated war. Duprat's letter to his king was cautious and advised all safety measures. On Sunday 1 September, all three diplomats rode to Notre Dame for mass, and Wolsey took his colleagues back to dine with him.[68]

The public sessions proceeded dismally. On Monday 2 September, Wolsey summoned the parties to put their 'querelles'. There was preliminary fencing over who should speak first, for traditionally it was held that whoever made the first 'offer' in a peace conference was the weaker side, who had asked for the meeting. Wolsey secured that the French should speak first. Their terms were based on the upholding of the marriage alliance with the Emperor and the treaty of Noyon regarding Naples, and on the recovery of Navarre. Gattinara answered charge by charge. The French denied that any help had been given to de la Marck; their King had not given permission for even a hen to be taken on imperial land: Gattinara asserted their guilt, they had rolled the stone, while feigning to take away their hand. All ancient 'querelles' were reopened by the breaking of treaties. Wolsey declared that the affair was 'doubtful' since neither side would admit being the aggressor, and the English therefore did not know whom to help. After four hours, he adjourned the meeting until the morrow, when Duprat did not attend, for he had taken the discussions very ill (the English narrative's view). Gattinara wrote home that his powers,

---

[68] Granvelle I, 135–40; Le Glay II, 487–95; Corpus Christi Coll. MS. 111, p. 393. Wolsey made arrangements for the conference: the imperialists should sit on the right and the French on the left, and take the same side on passing through the town. The Cardinal himself would be accompanied by one ambassador from each side, as he went through the town (*L.P.* III (ii) no. 1534).

presumably for a peace, had still not arrived, but he was not displeased, since the object was to gain time.[69]

Problems did not diminish in these daily meetings; Duprat interpreted the royal letter to Alberto Pio, Count of Carpi (in the March), which seemed a clear admission by his King that he had helped de la Marck. Was the vital verb in the indicative or the subjunctive?[70] The imperialists asserted the former, and Duprat, who had dictated the letter, upheld the subjunctive, offering his head to prove his point. Other records were analysed. Gattinara spoke on the treaty of Cambrai, which he had 'dictated': Duprat disclaimed knowledge of the treaty of London, as he was not there. Imperial reports record the French as saying it was a time to sharpen knives.[71]

Wolsey struggled on; they had met for peace, and he did not wish to give judgment or to say who was aggressor. Since neither side would admit aggression, they must find another way to peace or they would labour in vain. Finally, on 4 September, Wolsey broke up the meeting; he felt unwell and must purge himself; his deputies

[69] *Cal. Ven.* III, 172–3; Hall, op. cit., I, 231; Granvelle I, 135–90; Le Glay II, 487–95; *L.P.* III (ii) nos. 1534, 1541, 1544; Corpus Christi Coll. MS. 111, pp. 392–4; Barrillon, op. cit., II, 251ff. The 'sessions' referred to in the imperial procès-verbal are not dated, but as far as can be determined the sessions here discussed are those numbered 1–5 in the record.

[70] This famous letter, printed in Granvelle I, 116–24, was dated 19 June and referred to the King's war on three fronts and his expenses, among others, his help for de la Marck. He stated: 'ce ne seroit honnesteté à moy laisser fouler, en ma présence, un mien serviteur qui n'eust voulu espargner sa vye et ses biens pour obeyr à mes commandemens.' This seems clearly to mean that François could not omit to help someone who 'would not have' (rather than—'had not') spared his life or his goods to obey the King's commands. 'N'eust' could sometimes be used as a variant of the past indicative, but not here, with a conditional sense clearly indicated. François' supposed help for de la Marck and incitement of his rebellion could not be fastened upon this passage.

[71] The conference well illustrates the problem of information and news. Charles V's posts were available to Wolsey, while the English ambassador at the French court used the French service. There was constant interception of letters, and breach of confidence as between one side and the other: imperial letters to the Swiss intercepted by the French, Venetian letters intercepted by the imperialists, English ambassadorial reports sent by Gattinara to the Emperor, French complaints that Wolsey had shown the King's letters to the papal nuncio before the conference (*L.P.* III (ii) nos. 1610, 1580, 1625, 1662, 1126; *Cal. Ven.* III, 177, 180, 184). The complexities are shown in the case of letters from the French King and Bonnivet to l'Esparre their commander in Navarre. The letters were taken from him when he was made prisoner, translated from French into Spanish, sent to Henry VIII, and translated into English by the chaplain of Catherine of Aragon. In this version they were forwarded to Wolsey (*L.P.* III (ii) no. 1582).

would discuss the treaties with the ambassadors, they might meet every two or three days.[72] There followed a week during which the Bishop of Ely and the Master of the Rolls grimly went through the evidence with the parties. The letter to the Count of Carpi took up a whole session, then the treaties of Noyon and London. Gattinara had a copy of the former, on paper, Duprat boasted the originals. Discussing the treaty of London, both sides claimed that God was with them, quoting the news from the battle-fronts, the imperialists taking the blinding in battle of the French commander l'Esparre as divine judgment. The imperialists were privately pleased at the prolongation of the discussions, and the English fell in with this scheme. The Bishop of Ely admitted to Gattinara that he was satisfied with the imperial case under the treaty of Noyon, but was working to gain time, as the Emperor wished to see what his army could do. They should therefore discuss the treaty of London (the 1518 peace treaty).[73]

Wolsey did not reappear in the conference room until 1 October, but was not inactive behind the scenes, despite an illness which appears genuine but convenient. He admitted to Gattinara that his illness had gained them time, but he seems genuinely to have suffered. He was feverish on 30 August, on 9 September Duprat saw from his face that he was ill, a flux is mentioned on the 10th, and tertian fever on the 19th, while on 4 October he went for an airing outside the town for the first time since his illness, Gattinara accompanying him. The next day, however, he is reported as 'malade jusqu'a mort', and later confided that he would never enjoy perfect health in Calais.[74] His words 'until I am on my feet again' are perhaps literally true of these days.

Yet intermittent activity continued. On Sunday 8 September, Wolsey went to mass in Notre Dame with Gattinara and the papal nuncio, and afterwards asked them to dine. He had wished to ask the French also, but the imperial demand for precedence for every member of their party seems to have decided him against it.[75] He

<hr>

[72] See above, p. 112n69.
[73] See above, p. 112n69; *L.P.* III (ii) nos. 1560, 1580, 1568, 1584, 1634, 1735. Many Englishmen were with the imperial army, according to the English narrative, and more would have gone 'yf they might be suffered' (Corpus Christi Coll. MS. 111, p. 394).
[74] *L.P.* III (ii) nos. 1525, 1560, 1580, 1590, 1593, 1595; Le Glay II, 521; Granvelle I, 191; Barrillon, op. cit., II, 273.
[75] Corpus Christi Coll. MS. 111, p. 394; *L.P.* III (ii) no. 1557.

cultivated Duprat, however. There were several meetings in private; one, a long dialogue when the two men dined in Wolsey's chamber, is reported almost verbatim by Duprat (and there seems no reason to doubt him). Wolsey began by stressing the Emperor's strength in Italy, showing letters just received from there. Henry would never waver in friendship for France, and Wolsey's own aim was to serve his master loyally, make his people live in love and fear, enrich his King, and maintain his allies. The King had desired this meeting because of the evils of war, and because he would eventually have to declare for one side or the other. He and Wolsey were inclined to France, but the English nobility and people, difficult to lead, favoured the other side. The imperialists were proud and hard, but might soften. The French had not shown him their letters from their King, as the other side did. He would have his head cut off if he did not lead the Emperor to peace within six months. Now was a time to 'lower sail'; the honour of the King of France would be safeguarded, and Wolsey would appeal to Louise of Savoy, who loved peace. Telling Duprat: 'See what I have to do to content these people', Wolsey drew his own colleagues into the conversation, showing how the French had supplied England with corn when others, who were thought to be her friends, did not, and how the French would accept a truce. He would rather lose his head (perhaps he caught this mode of speech from Duprat) than lose what he had achieved. He referred to the fate of the Duke of Buckingham who had opposed his work for amity with France. If Wolsey's advice had been followed, and François had not moved against the Emperor until the latter was in Spain, then things would have gone better.

Wolsey ended with an appeal for Duprat's personal friendship. They must meet often and be entertained by their singers. They were both Chancellors and must have perpetual fraternity. Duprat declared himself but the servant of one who was Legate, Cardinal and Lieutenant of his king. From the behaviour and countenance of the Cardinal's entourage, and from reports from England, however, he advised his master that it was a time for a sharp eye, a ready foot, and for not trusting people too much.[76]

---

[76] Le Glay II, 514–20. This was the occasion when Wolsey declared that he did not want the papacy. At another meeting later in the month, Duprat found Wolsey ill in bed; the occasion was made known at the French court, where Treasurer Robertet praised Wolsey's zeal (*L.P.* III (ii) nos. 1595, 1602).

The French were in fact despairing; all the time was spent in comings, goings and words ('en allées, venues et parolles'). But it is clear that these delays suited the Emperor and Wolsey. On 24 September, the Cardinal apologised to Gattinara for not meeting the ambassadors for so long; it was on account of illness, otherwise he could not have gained time without arousing suspicion. He would shortly proceed to make offers for new treaties of peace, and this could give Gattinara the opportunity to raise old claims. Gattinara himself intended delay, and reported, somewhat cryptically, that Wolsey could make a better bargain at the fair in England—perhaps a reference to proposed adjournment of negotiations. Gattinara would propose on 30 September that all treaties should be considered void, that the King of England should mediate on all quarrels, and that a truce should be made meanwhile with the Pope's consent. He hoped to refer these proposals to the Emperor to gain time for the enterprise of Tournai. It was on this that Charles had fixed his attention; even on 8 November he was still asking for delay of negotiations for another fifteen days. Wolsey was said to have offered half his blood to have the city taken; he had already prolonged discussions and stayed longer than was good for either his master's or the Emperor's affairs.[77]

Nevertheless, there was still talk of peace. On 1 October Wolsey assembled all the ambassadors and made a majestic plea (the eighth session recorded in the imperial procès-verbal), addressing the ambassadors as 'magnificences'. He referred to the treaty of Noyon as diabolically conceived, for which one must blame the authors; it had led to war.[78] Treaties had been broken, and meanwhile the Turk, like a ravenous lion, had invaded Hungary, the strong and firm bulwark of Christendom (the Hungarian ambassador had just visited Wolsey). All Christians must be moved by this, if they were

---

[77] *L.P.* III (ii) nos. 1560, 1568, 1584, 1605, 1612, 1632, 1640–1, 1748.
[78] It must be admitted that Wolsey was right. The treaty (cf. J. Dumont, *Corps universel diplomatique du droit des gens* (Amsterdam 1726–31) IV, 224–8) provided that, within six months, Charles should either restore Navarre to the d'Albret king, or 'content' him, and that France might go on assisting the latter if he was not contented. The marriage alliance of Charles and Louise of France (or, if she died, a younger sister) was based on the cession of French rights to Naples, in return for an annual pension paid by Charles to the French king. The endless disputes over French support of Navarre, and over the intention of a marriage alliance with a younger sister (since Louise died), bringing into play ancient claims to Navarre and Naples, show that the negotiators, the Grand Master, de Boisy, and Chièvres, had bequeathed an unworkable settlement to their successors.

not as hard as marble or iron; they must be moved, if only by the danger.[79] It was best, therefore, to consider the treaties as broken—neither side would admit breaking them—and to make new ones to restore peace. There should be a campaign against the enemies of the faith. Wolsey promised to go to see François, as he had visited the Emperor. But again the disputes started. Gattinara spoke of the Emperor's will to peace; he would agree, if the terms were reasonable. But Justice and Peace were sisters (they were daughters of Zeus), and could not exist for long without one another. So he spoke of the ancient 'querelles'. The claim for the Duchy of Burgundy was one: Louis XI, posing as the protector of Mary of Burgundy, had by his usurpations left only the County to the heiress. The Emperor should hold all these lands, exempt from suzerainty, as Charles the Bold had held them since the treaty of Péronne. There were also the old claims of the Crown of Aragon to Toulouse, Narbonne and Montpellier and the claims of the Crown of Navarre to Béarn, Foix, Bigorre, Champagne and Brie. The ancient imperial claims to Dauphiné, Arles and Provence were also put forward. Charles V had instructed them to raise all the old claims, and they certainly left no stone unturned, even that of the reparations for the murder of Duke John the Fearless.

Duprat replied that the imperialists were claiming what they knew they would not get. Their claims were derisive, particularly the alleged cession of French lands to the Emperor by Boniface VIII. The French, in their turn, could equally claim Aragon, Catalonia, Roussillon, Naples, Sicily, the County of Burgundy, Flanders and Artois. Louis XII had been invested with Milan by Maximilian. But such things only reopened old wounds. The French had powers only to discuss the non-observance of treaties. It was best that they all went home and saw to their affairs. Gattinara replied that his propositions did not remove the hope of peace, but aimed at the true foundation of it: justice. If things were not decided, there would only be an imaginary peace ('ymaginacion ou conglutinacion de paix'). Previous treaties had often led to war, and the French only made them to gain time and deceive the enemy. The Emperor might claim the whole realm of France, since Boniface had promised it to Albert. This claim had, however, been omitted because of Henry's claims on France. Wolsey again pleaded for

[79] Belgrade had fallen on 29 August.

peace: before all these quarrels had been discussed there would be much shedding of Christian blood and much suffering. Gattinara's claims were like those of the man who asked his king for a forest when he only needed seven or eight trees. It would be a great grief to him if they had all laboured in vain. Another way must be found; he besought them to find a way to peace. They should meet with his deputies on the next day, since his health was still troubling him. Gattinara said that the papal nuncio was ill, but he would meet the French.[80]

At the next session, the ninth in Gattinara's record, each side wanted to avoid speaking first: let he who first broke the peace speak first. The imperialists still insisted that they were not empowered to make peace or a truce, but only to find out who broke the treaties, and then invoke aid. Wolsey's deputies insisted that the first require-ment was peace between the three powers, but each side still contended that the other had insufficient authority to negotiate. The mediator in any case must make the peace offer. Gattinara, speaking only as a private person, said that peace could only be made if firm and stable. Within six months both sides should produce their 'querelles' before the King of England.

This time it was the imperialists who admitted that they might as well all go home. The French, still fighting, reminded Gattinara that the treaty of Noyon, to which they doggedly adhered, had been negotiated by Chièvres, and should be observed. This was their 'commission'; they had no powers to discuss old quarrels, which in any case were not normally submitted to 'compromise' (mediation). The imperialists protested that they did not intend to revive the dead or rekindle what was extinguished. The breaker of treaties lost all rights under them. One must either observe them or revert to older 'querelles'. Rights of kingdoms might be judged either by law, by friendship (mediation), or by war. Since the French rejected mediation, they must return to war. The Cardinal's deputies were aghast at these proceedings. He would be very displeased and angered. He would find a way of peace, concluding a truce or

---

[80] Granvelle I, 209–28 (8th session); Le Glay II, 551; Barrillon, op. cit., II, 265–7; *L.P.* III (ii) nos. 1578, 1579, 1609. There was much talk of the treaty of Arras of 1435, the imperialists saying that it was negotiated by a papal legate, and confirmed by the Pope, and therefore a valid basis of their claims. The French ruled it out of order, since the King of France at that time was deprived and destitute of his kingdom (Granvelle I, p. 221). The bishop of Ely wrote home that all the practices of the French 'be but fraskes [tricks] and loose ends' (*L.P.* III (ii) no. 1551).

abstinence of war meanwhile. After this, according to the imperial procès-verbal, the nuncio and the imperial ambassadors did not meet the French; the Cardinal met first one side and then the other. There being no hope of peace, they turned to a truce or abstinence.[81]

At some time, perhaps ever since his return from Bruges, Wolsey saw that a truce would be all he could obtain. On 24 September he told Gattinara that he thought Louise of Savoy would prefer a peace to a truce, but would give powers for the latter if peace could not be obtained.[82] A truce, in fact, often suited contestants the best.[83] How could it be achieved? Even over this temporary measure the parties were not agreed. The papal nuncio was sent powers in November, but would only use them if the terms were favourable to papal security; in August he was said to be against either peace or a truce. The French, and particularly Louise of Savoy, were reported in favour of peace, but would accept a truce for Wolsey's sake, if they might do so with honour. This became a point of resistance, for François found Wolsey's truce 'vitupérable, honteuse et dommageable'. Charles would agree, for the repose of Christendom and the repulse of the Turk, because of his promises at Bruges and for the sake of Hungary. Gattinara warned that Charles must write to Wolsey, showing all deference; on 1 October Wolsey had, said Gattinara, accused the imperialists of being as cold with him as if he were a Frenchman.[84]

Even the period of truce was not easily agreed. At first the French wanted a long truce of ten years, and then suggested four years: they did not want a short truce while the Emperor prepared for war. Wolsey suggested two years, but the Emperor favoured one year or eighteen months. Wolsey thought a truce essential to the Emperor, because of his military position and his projected journey to Spain. There were reports of the imperial army diminished by death, sickness and 'departures'. Gattinara reported that, otherwise, Wolsey would desire nothing more than war, which would benefit England and ruin France; perhaps here he was projecting his own views on to the Cardinal. The Emperor certainly admitted the need for truce, but still tried to hide the necessity from Wolsey: he sent

[81] Granvelle I, 228–39.
[82] *L.P.* III (ii) no. 1605.
[83] See above, pp. 83–5.
[84] *L.P.* III (ii) nos. 1569, 1574, 1602, 1620, 1624, 1634–5, 1640, 1765; *Cal. Ven.* III, 167–8, 170–1, 183; Barrillon, op. cit., II, 277.

1. *Above:* Clement VII and François I, by Giorgio Vasari. *Below:* Clement VII and Charles V, by Giorgio Vasari. (Sala di Clemente VII, Palazzo Vecchio, Florence)

2. Statue of King Arthur, 1513, by Peter Visschner the Elder. (Emperor Maximilian's funeral monument, Hofkapelle, Innsbruck)

3. Margaret, Archduchess of Austria, by Bernard van Orley. Copy of lost original, probably dating from 1515-18. (Musées Royaux, Brussels)

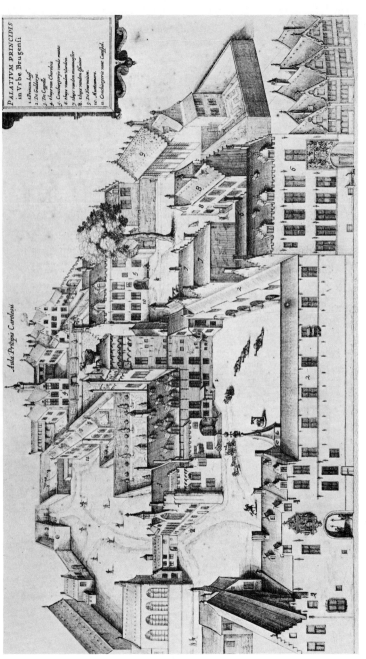

4. Engraving of the Princenhof, Bruges, from Antonius Sanderus, *Flandria Illustrata*, Cologne 1641. Bodleian Library, Oxford.

5. Drawing of Charles de Guise, Cardinal of Lorraine. Artist and date unknown (probably soon after Lorraine's promotion in 1547). (Musée Condé, Chantilly)

6. Antoine Perrenot de Granvelle, Bishop of Arras, 1548-9, by Titian. (The Nelson Gallery – Atkins Museum, Kansas City, USA)

7. Allegorical drawing of the Peace of Cateau-Cambrésis, 1565, by Jan van der Straet (Stradanus). (Ashmolean Museum, Oxford)

8. Marguerite de France as Minerva, Goddess of Peace and Wisdom, seated on the orb of the world, Limoges enamel, 1555, by Jean de Court. (Reproduced by permission of the Trustees, the Wallace Collection, London)

special letters for Gattinara to transmit to the Cardinal, which concealed this need. The Duchess Margaret advised a truce of eighteen months, and Gattinara admitted, though not to Wolsey, a chronic shortage of money. Eighteen months became the suggested term, with Henry as conservator, who would adjudicate on appeals against infringement. Even then there were problems: which allies should be included—for truces normally included the allies of each side—and should the truce be only on the northern side of the Alps? On the first point there were endless arguments: on the second, general agreement was reached on the restriction, though Wolsey feared that it would open the way to a French attack on the Pope. Throughout there was resort to the favourite device of 'inadequate powers', since both sides wished to prolong matters, eagerly awaiting news of the war, particularly the siege of Tournai, which François even on 19 November gave a further fifteen days' hope of relief. In intervals between hawking and other pastimes, Henry was pleased to advise the Emperor not to besiege the city: he himself wanted a truce concluded before the last vintage in France.[85]

In this situation, Wolsey tried more diplomatic exchange. He despatched embassies to both courts. Docwra, Lord of St. John's, Sir Thomas Boleyn and Richmond Herald went to the Emperor, the Lord Chamberlain (the Earl of Worcester), the Bishop of Ely and Clarencieux King of Arms to the French. Under letters of 20 October Wolsey instructed the ambassadors. Those to the Emperor were to dissuade him from leaning to the advice of young folk around him to continue the war. They must contrast the sickness and long service of Charles's army with the magnitude and freshness of the French. The Emperor must not pay such attention to matters of Italy and the Pope as to damage the rest of his dominions for their advancement, clearly a dig at Gattinara. The ambassadors were to point out 'humbly' that if Wolsey's advice had been followed the Emperor's affairs would be in a better state. Earlier he had told Gattinara that a truce in time would have obviated raising the siege of Mézières. To François, the companion embassy was to declare that Wolsey would have come in person, if he could have done so

---

[85] *L.P.* III (ii) nos. 1594, 1606, 1640–1, 1643, 1651, 1663, 1665–6, 1676–7, 1680, 1707, 1715, 1780, 1724, 1729, 1779; *Cal. Span.* II, 377–9. The French admitted that Wolsey knew they had a double set of powers, and therefore could negotiate to include their allies, Florence and Mantua, if they chose (Barrillon, op. cit., II, 280–3, 301–6).

without great danger. The King of England had accepted a truce with Scotland, notwithstanding his advantage, which favoured war. The ambassadors must approach Louise of Savoy, 'the mother and nurische of peace'.[86]

The ambassadors to François, who found him encamped near Cambrai, reported him as very 'difficile'. He wanted first one period of truce and then another, while Tournai should be revictualled, and was not disposed to tell them what he intended. He eventually consented to halt his army for three days, although he said the Emperor did not do the same. The war raged near; one night the ambassadors were woken by the King himself, as there was a fire alarm. 'We lie in terrible war . . . our folk lie every night in their clothes on the ground . . . writ in haste in the field upon a bank without the town, which was set on [fire] before we could depart out of the town.'[87]

The ambassadors to the Emperor, who addressed them in French, found a willingness to make a truce. There had been debates in the imperial council, the Duchess Margaret and Berghes had advised truce, and Alva had declared that if he were at Calais a truce would already have been accepted, the trouble was Gattinara. Fitzwilliam, resident ambassador, was called in to discussions, weary as he was of the whole diplomatic game. His servants were ill, his clerk likely to die, he had trouble with his despatches: 'an ye wold gyf me all thow goud (gold) in thow world I cannot lerne to make thes syfers'. Eventually the Emperor's terms were established: eighteen months' truce, with the Pope's consent, without French sovereignty in Flanders and Artois, with mutual reservations about allies or former rebels, all possessions to remain as at present, except that the French were to restore Fuenterrabia and all towns taken in Navarre and Spain, in return for which Charles would surrender all towns taken in France. No promises were made about the Emperor's journey to Italy, which the French were inclined to oppose. From France, where the ambassadors communicated both with Wolsey and with their companion embassy to Charles, through the officers of arms, it was learnt that the King would accept a truce, but would not surrender Fuenterrabia (in which Duprat strongly supported him). Richmond Herald reported that by 2 November François had in

[86] *L.P.* III (ii) nos. 1693–4, 1696 (cf. no. 1624).

[87] Ibid., nos. 1698–9, 1702, 1708–9, 1707. The Captain of Rheims escorted the ambassadors to the King.

fact abandoned Tournai, and would destroy and ravage in Artois and then retire. 'Here is the most piteous destruction of towns, and spoiling of so fair a country as never have been seen among Christian men.' François declared that he would make 'guerre garriable'[88] and be first in the field next year. The fires still raged, despite a proclamation against burning which the King made at the ambassadors' request; fires were seen even while they talked to the King.[89]

At Calais, Wolsey was still having difficulty. He reported that the more the French gave way, the more obstinate he found Gattinara, who was not only declining the truce, but even the articles on fishing rights which the Emperor had agreed to. Wolsey was endeavouring to bring matters to a 'narrow point', but he was

> as sore tempestyd in mynd by the on [towardness] of the chauncelers and oratours on every side, putting so many diffi[culties and] obstacles to condescend to any reasonable conditions of treux and abstinence of war . . . nyght nor day I cowd have no quietnesse ne rest.

He complained of 'obstinat dealing and frustatory delays', and of opposition on the imperial side, where he had felt most secure. In his opinion his own policy was a 'schote [sheet] anchor' of peace. He found Gattinara rather inclined to continue the war; perhaps, like François, he occasionally felt that Gattinara was only abusing and mocking both kings. On the other hand, the French insistence on retaining Fuenterrabia 'discomforted' Wolsey more than all the diseases and incommodities he had sustained.[90]

Discussions were protracted between Calais and the two courts. Wolsey's articles of truce, produced on 6 November, were to be ratified by the Pope within ten days and by the Kings within six. These terms had been difficult. Duprat had written to Louise of Savoy that the imperialists had couched their articles in captious and dubious wording, and would not accept the French minutes of points agreed. In addition the mediator could not be moved either by remonstrance or by gentleness. Truce would only be the nursemaid of greater war, and war itself more difficult to embark on in time of truce. François refused to cede on the inclusion of his allies

---

[88] See below, p. 190n77.
[89] *L.P.* III (ii) nos. 1710, 1714, 1727–9, 1732, 1736, 1742, 1752, 1758, 1762–3. French disillusionment with the war can be traced in the writings of Clément Marot: see above, p. 18.
[90] *L.P.* III (ii) nos. 1728, 1735–6, 1742.

in a truce, and would not give way to include the Milanese who favoured the Emperor, the 'rebels' of Milan. Wolsey pointed out that these rebels had declared for the Pope, and must be covered. Finally he proposed that his terms should be discussed with the French by the Master of the Rolls, that an agreed version should be produced and sent to the French King, and then if he agreed it, to the Emperor. If not agreed, the Cardinal would return to England. The French thought this procedure very long: 'il nous semble que ce circuit qu'il prend sera bien long'. Wolsey complained that the French terms had given him a bad night: 'disait que nostre plume luy avoit donné une mauvaise nuit'. The French were patently nonplussed by his remarks.

The final proposal was eighteen months' truce with 'communication' (the normal phrase to cover the comings and goings of merchants, students, and what we should now term bona fide travellers), to include the Venetians. Fortresses held might be provisioned (an obvious stipulation for Tournai), French suzerainty in Flanders and Artois would be waived during the truce, and each side would nominate those they wished to be included. The truce was to stand even if the Pope did not ratify, and Henry was to be conservator. Each side was still continuing the diplomatic contest: François would like Duprat home in view of the news from Italy, but might agree to the truce so that Wolsey would not go home with nothing.[91] The Emperor advised toughness with the French; if they could not be persuaded, a truce might be negotiated in England. Margaret thought that Wolsey was driving the Emperor too hard, trying to make him accept what he could not accept with honour. He was treating Charles as the Emperor had told him to treat the French. She wished for two hours' conversation with Wolsey to clear up the difficulties.[92] Even the marriage alliance was being pressed too far, for Charles had said that there was no want of wives, he need not buy them so dear. On the truce Charles felt that the *status quo* on possessions was not honourable to him. Fuenterrabia must be restored, and the English would find it most helpful in a campaign in Guyenne. There were long discussions in the imperial Council,

[91] In November, John Stuart, Duke of Albany, heir presumptive to the Scottish throne, returned to Scotland. He had been detained in France, at the request of the English, and their suspicion that he would and did escape with French connivance undoubtedly embittered Anglo-French relations at Calais (*L.P.* iii (ii) nos. 1613, 1631, 1761, 1811, 1833).

[92] Barrillon, op. cit., ii, 316ff. *L.P.* iii (ii) nos. 1749, 1752, 1758, 1762.

and Charles admitted that their advice was a truce, even without
Fuenterrabia, since he owed money, could not afford to guard his
frontiers, and would not take Tournai that year.

Finally, however, the Emperor instructed the diplomats at Calais
that a truce could not be accepted. He had found French modifica-
tions of Wolsey's terms too stiff; these presumably were the 'apostils'
which Duprat added to the margins of Wolsey's proposals, and
which the Cardinal admitted wiped away the substantial part of
the agreement. The French insisted that Tournai should be victu-
alled during the truce, that Charles should not go to Italy to be
crowned, that there should be French sovereignty in Flanders and
Artois, that their allies, Lorraine, Guelders, Ferrara and Venice,
should be included, but not the 'rebels' of Milan. François protested
that while Charles was an enemy he would do with him the worst
he could, but that when they should be friends he would treat him
as a friend.[93] There was some talk of exchanging Fuenterrabia for
Tournai, but otherwise, clearly, agreement was no nearer, and the
nuncio still had reservations. The truce, that 'narrow' point to
which Wolsey had brought negotiations, eluded him. He consoled
the King and himself by arguing that delay, even in this, might be
helpful; the French would be weakened in Tournai and Navarre,
and it was better to 'suffer these princes [the imperialists] to ruffle
with the said French King, and infest him in all parts for the
consumption of his treasure which is almost clearly extenuate, than
suddenly to take this truce now, when he can do no more harm'.[94]

Wolsey and the Emperor then fell back on the final way out:
postponement. There should be embassies sent to England, where
the matter would be settled. François clearly wished his ambassadors to depart. In this atmosphere Wolsey made his last efforts on
20 and 21 November. The French ambassadors dined with the
Cardinal, where they found the imperial ambassadors and Audiencier Hanneton, newly arrived from the Emperor with the rebuff
that Charles must consult Spain before accepting a truce. Wolsey

[93] *L.P.* III (ii) nos. 1749, 1758, 1762, 1776, 1765; Barrillon, op. cit., II, 283ff.
Duprat's obstinacy in small matters was mentioned to François by the English
ambassadors, with the request that he be instructed not to be so difficult.

[94] As conservator of the truce, Henry had objected to taking an oath to it, thinking
this would endanger Wolsey's oath to the stricter alliance at Bruges. Wolsey agreed,
praising the King's judgment; the whole council could not have 'more deeply
perceived or spoken herin'. As conservator, the King could declare against whoever
broke the truce.

then proposed a simple truce, presumably with no detailed provisions on territory, sovereignty, etc. The French proposed a simple truce excluding Italy, and if necessary the handing over of Tournai to Henry, if they themselves were too hard pressed there. Wolsey then put three proposals: an abstinence of six weeks, a simple truce for eighteen months this side of the mountains, and the handing over of Tournai to Henry. He would wait until Monday 25 November for answers. Secretly he told Gattinara that he hoped Tournai would fall by then, in any case Charles could buy the city from Henry. The French record states that there were many discussions on peace, the repose of Christendom and its defence. Wolsey declared that Fuenterrabia had been the greatest hindrance to peace. He offered to forego an instalment of the French pension, and to secure the payment of the imperial pension for Naples, if the French would disgorge Fuenterrabia. Finally, he was content that the French should leave, if one of them remained behind. Wolsey had taken Duprat aside, and spoken things which the latter promised to report verbally to his master. If the effect followed Wolsey's words, said Duprat, then François would be well content with the Cardinal. He should write often to him, as did the King of Spain.[95]

This was the end of the effort at negotiations, with Wolsey clearly approaching first one side and then the other, and making confidential remarks to each in turn. As Gattinara's procès-verbal states, what pleased one side did not please the other, though the Cardinal had worked without ceasing. Wolsey finally invited ambassadors to go to England with him, hoping to accomplish in winter, with its cold, what had been prevented by the heat of anger and indignation, inflaming the hearts and wills of princes. By 26 November Ambassador Surian reported that the truce had vanished into smoke.[96]

---

[95] *L.P.* iii (ii) nos. 1793–4; Le Glay ii, 524ff. Tournai fell on 30 November, perhaps with some treachery, for the Emperor had been informed that the former master of the works, who had built the castle, would tell him how to take the city (*L.P.* iii (ii) nos. 1786, 1789). The city could be battered in two places (a plan was sent to the Emperor); the wall was rotten at one side and water could be drained out of the ditch.

[96] Barrillon, op. cit., ii, 326; Granvelle i, 239–41; *Cal. Ven.* iii, 191.

The treaty of Bruges

The French departed from Calais on 22 November, leaving behind Duprat's brother, Thomas, Bishop of Clermont and one Denis Poillot. The stage was now set for the final acts. Already on 19 November the Duchess Margaret had written to Henry at Wolsey's suggestion praising the Anglo-imperial alliance as contributing to the universal good of Christendom. Charles also was primed to do this, while Henry wrote to the Emperor recapitulating the terms of agreement. At Calais Wolsey further elaborated on his peace efforts, the need for truce, and his own need to be in England. From Oudenarde the Emperor wrote hoping that Wolsey might accomplish in England what he had failed to achieve at Calais; the resident imperial ambassador might continue the work. For the last time, the Emperor pleaded for the neutrality of Burgundy, which Wolsey had promised at Bruges to secure. The County/Franche Comté, from its confidence in Wolsey, was unprovided with troops. At Calais on 24 November, Gattinara, de Mesa and others on one side, and Wolsey and the papal nuncio on the other, put their hands to the agreement, the 'treaty of Bruges'.[97] They had gone to mass together:

> On Sunday our lady daye my lord went then solemly to our lady churche and with him the popys ambassator and the emperoure and that daye dined with my lorde, but the frenchmen [the ambassadors left behind by Duprat] would not appere for disdayne that daye.

Wolsey wrote the next day to Charles emphasising that he would have as much regard to imperial honour as to that of his own master. Charles was elated by news from Italy, and awaiting that from Tournai. He kept the feast of St Andrew, patron saint of old Burgundy, at Oudenarde. Wolsey in his turn left Calais on 27 November, proceeding to the King at Bletchingly. Ironically, François had on 24 November accepted the abstinence, and the handing over of Tournai to Henry; the Anglo-French marriage alliance must stand, however. At Dover, Wolsey, forced no doubt by events, dismissed the news as a French ruse to sow dissension among the

---

[97] This was a reformulation of the tripartite treaty of 25 August (*L.P.* III (ii) no. 1802). The undertaking to put down heresy was now to extend to all the dominions of Emperor and King.

new allies, and to renew the Anglo-French alliance, and as a
confession of their inability to succour Tournai.[98]

Conclusion

Here ended the supreme effort of Wolsey's diplomatic career. Was
he genuinely working for peace? How much conscious deceit was
there in his conduct? It is most difficult to say. That he was moved
and motivated by a wish for peace is certain, but it was to be a
peace on advantageous terms, an alliance of profit if not a universal
peace, and certainly something for his own and his master's honour;
it was difficult to tell which came first. It seems clear that he often
exaggerated the degree of unity which might be achieved, and
sometimes the degree of unity even between himself and Henry.[99]
For Wolsey peace was, at best, a grand design of universal peace,
to be followed by a crusade. The 1518 treaty had been a blueprint
for this. But the machinery to control aggression was, in 1521, being
turned to wider uses. To establish aggression had been to open the
door to a recital of all ancient grievances against the aggressor,
while each side accused the other of the initial aggressive act. Thereafter, the war to 'punish' aggression was likely to prove extensive
and long-lasting. To enlist allies, particularly England, became part
of the bargaining process and took time. In all this, the hope of
universal peace had disappeared. Political realities and ambitions
proved too strong.

Perhaps the final word on Wolsey himself should be that he

---

[98] *L.P.* III (ii) nos. 1796–8, 1801, 1803, 1806, 1808, 1811, 1815, 1839; Hall, op.
cit., I, 232; Corpus Christi Coll. MS. 111, pp. 394–5. François had earlier declared
that he would rather have Princess Mary for his son than the daughter of the King
of Portugal 'with all the spices that her father hath' (*L.P.* III (ii) no. 1303). After
the breakdown of the conference, François issued a declaration of his own work for
peace, and a justification of his own conduct, the Emperor having defied him without
reason (ibid., no. 1815). He was still hoping to deflect England from the imperial
cause. In May 1522, just before the English declaration of war, he told the English
ambassador that he wondered at the English alliance with the Emperor, who had
no money, and would need two purses to continue what he had begun (ibid., no.
2226).

[99] During the conference, Henry fought back at Wolsey's proposals on the armed
help for the Emperor, and also at his sanguine hopes of peaceful continuance of the
wine trade with France (*L.P.* III (ii) nos. 1594, 1611). At home, Pace was driven out
of his mind with loss of sleep and appetite: 'It was lately the King's pleasure to
dispute with your grace, and now it is his pleasure to hold his peace, whereof I for
my part am right glad' (ibid., no. 1629).

enjoyed diplomacy, and that universal peace was the supreme aim of a diplomatic career. It was a delight to him to negotiate with the great, to feel that Emperor and King, Louise of Savoy and the Duchess Margaret, waited on his words, would even write at his dictation. In November 1521, both the Emperor and his aunt wrote, at Wolsey's request, to Henry, praising the Anglo-imperial alliance. Charles, on being informed that his letters were 'plus maigres' than Wolsey's draft, protested that he had kept as close to the substance as possible, only changing points of language; however, he sent another version, word for word as in the draft, and said that the Cardinal might use either. Margaret also wrote her letters to order, changing only 'l'adresse du langaige'.[100]

The years 1520 and 1521 were the period of close personal relationships: Margaret refers to herself as Wolsey's good mother, and wishes for two hours conversation to clear up difficulties. Louise calls him 'mon fils et bon amy' and he no doubt remembered his discussions with her in 1520. She herself knew the value of personal contact: François would perhaps agree to peace if he and Henry could meet, but not 'upon mere letters'. François declared that Wolsey was the person on whom he relied wholly in the matter of the 'amity'. He declared his faith in Henry and in Wolsey, hoping only for good from them, and protesting that if England declared war on the Emperor's side, he would take treaty with no other princes, but trust only in God and revenge himself. The Emperor, in his turn, drew Wolsey to Bruges, and took care to visit him frequently. Elated by imperial confidences,[101] the Cardinal wrote to Henry that he (the King) was now not only ruler of his own realm, 'but by your wisdom and counsel Spain, Italy, Almayne and these Low Countries, which is the greatest part of Christendom'.[102]

No doubt there was positive delight in his own power to mediate, to suit his manner to the occasion, to win confidence and extract agreement. The secret interview, the aside in the closet, the meeting on the garden steps, the quiet meal in private; all these were meat and drink to him, as were the more public occasions with which he is mainly associated: his processions with cross and pillars and golden trappings, his entries at the Field of Cloth of Gold, or into

[100] *L.P.* III (ii) nos. 1782, 1787, 1808.

[101] By 1522 the Emperor was addressing Wolsey as 'mon bon et loyal amy' (Rymer XIII, 776–7).

[102] *L.P.* III (ii) nos. 1202, 1517, 1904, 1954, 1993; Barrillon, op. cit., II, 277.

the city of Bruges, his part in the great church ceremonies at which treaties were proclaimed and oaths taken. The Calais-Bruges conference was particularly his affair. Perhaps in 1520 he had been overshadowed by the young monarchs, with their tournaments, dancing and royal triumphs. In 1521 he was mediator and still papal legate; his was the key position and he exacted it to the full. He represented his King 'en pompe et triumphe magnifique et sumptueux', 'furnished in all degrees and purposes most likest a great prince, which was much to the high honour of the King's majesty and of his realm'. The King was thankful to God that he had such a chaplain, 'by whose counsel, devotion and industry, he had been able to achieve greater things than all his predecessors in so many wars and battles'.[103]

What of Wolsey's diplomatic methods? Brandi has him listening with indifference to the extravagant demands and insolent speeches of either party. This is too cold; the accent was on restraint. Wolsey was there to mediate, and his restraint rather than his indifference is what the French and imperial records reveal. His career in this field was already distinguished. Cavendish wrote of him: 'he had a special gift of natural eloquence with a filed [polished] tongue to pronounce the same, that he was able with the same to persuade and allure all men to his purpose.' At Calais and Bruges his variant manner came into full play.[104] He himself wrote that he had countered the arguments of the imperial council 'sometimes with sharp words, and some time in pleasant manner'. His capacity for flattering promises was apparently well known. Charles warned him, after his return to Calais from Bruges, that he would not win the French by fair words alone; he must use threats. Wolsey evidently used both, for Gattinara mentioned his threats and fair words. He had his blunter style. Charles asked, so the English ambassadors wrote, for 'some of your sober countenances and sayings' (to be used on the French), and on an earlier occasion

[103] Granvelle I, 125; Cavendish, op. cit., pp. 14, 23, cf. Wolsey's state on his 1527 embassy to France (ibid., p. 50); *L.P.* III (ii) no. 1519. The expenses of Wolsey's embassy, including purchase of black velvet, scarlet, and red cloth for his gentlemen, yeomen, clerks and children of the chapel, amounted to £2346 13s. 6d. (British Museum, Harley MS. 620; abstracted in *The Chronicle of Calais*, ed. J. G. Nichols (London 1846), pp. 94–9). He was recompensed by the King with the Abbacy of St Albans (*L.P.* III (ii) no. 1759).

[104] Brandi, op. cit., p. 161; Cavendish, op. cit., p. 14 (cf. ibid., p. 12).

Wolsey was asked to use his 'round and plain fashion' to the Pope.[105] In such manner he could no doubt tell home truths, as when, at Calais, he told the French that it was not worth putting all Christendom at war for the sake of a young prince (Navarre). He expatiated on the diabolical character of the treaty of Noyon. He boasted, cryptically, that he could make a better bargain at a fair in England, presumably than the terms being discussed. He could, indeed, rail and rant; in 1522 he told the Venetian ambassador that the French must be exterminated, and later inveighed against the Venetians themselves, promise-breakers, lowest of all potentates. He did not always choose his occasion, as in 1522 when, during high mass at Canterbury, and with the King and Emperor present, he sent for the Venetian ambassadors to both princes and argued about the galleys to be commandeered for the imperial voyage to Spain.[106]

On other occasions, it was the telling, and often homely, anecdotes which pointed his argument. At Calais, discounting a report of papal duplicity, he reminded the ambassadors of the boy Papirius, who shamed his mother's curiosity by reporting to her that the Senate was to introduce a law permitting men to have two wives. At one stage he compared imperial demands to those of a man asking for a forest when he only needed seven or eight trees.[107] The general impression at Calais and Bruges is of reticence, restraint and unremitting labour in face of the uncompromising and overwhelming demands of both parties. The Doge wrote of Wolsey's incredible fatigue and vigils in order to make peace, and the Venetian ambassador, Contarini, thought he would have secured peace had he not been thwarted. Marguerite Duchess of Alençon spoke of his labours for peace, even to the day of battle; the French were impressed by his handling of Duprat, his interview even when illness kept him in his bed. An imperial ambassador was received at 8 a.m. in the final days of negotiation. The Cardinal himself wrote of how he laboured and reasoned with both sides, and how his appetite and sleep were taken away.[108] There seems no reason to deny him the title which he won in 1527, when on embassy to France 'there

---

[105] *L.P.* III (ii) nos. 1502, 1652, 1717, 1765, 2103.

[106] Barrillon, op. cit., II, 280; Le Glay II, 209; *L.P.* III (ii) no. 1584; *Cal. Ven.* III, 237–9, 230–7, 276.

[107] See above, p. 117.

[108] Granvelle I, 159; Barrillon, op. cit., II, 297; *Cal. Span.* II, 360, 389; *L.P.* III (ii) nos. 1602, 1728, 1793, 1581; *Cal. Ven.* III, 182, 212–13.

were made divers pageants for joy of his coming, who was called there and in all other places within the realm of France as he travelled, Le Cardinal Pacifique; and in Latin, Cardinalis Pacificus'. We may allow this even if, as Professor Scarisbrick has suggested, the scheme for peace was 'over-laid with vanity and power lust'. In 1521, as in 1527, Wolsey was sometimes carried away, perhaps by his own eloquence, into grandiose schemes which had a strong element of advantage for England and his own glory. But he had held the conference together, kept alive some reminders of the need for peace, and of the duties of princes to secure it. Perhaps his mood was throughout over-confident, but he made a laborious attempt, and, as in 1527, found disillusionment. Duprat reported him as very discontented with what he had achieved. The final sour reflection came in 1524, by which time he wished that 'he had broken his arms and legs when he stepped on shore to go to Bruges'. Skelton's harsh words may have rung in his ears:

> Treatinge of trewse restlesse,
> Pratynge for peace peaslesse.
> The countrynge at Cales
> Wrange us on the males (purses).[109]

Even after the commitment to the treaty of Bruges (kept secret from the French), Wolsey laboured for peace. Both parties had agreed to continue discussions through ambassadors to England; the Cardinal even hoped that the three princes might meet. He never relaxed his campaign for peace.[110] At all costs, the Emperor's final appeal (under the 1518 treaty) must be postponed, for this meant entry into the war within thirty days. When the appeal came in February 1522, the King, no doubt under pressure from the Cardinal to receive it; Wolsey accepted it privately.[111] But when the Emperor visited England (28 May to 6 July 1522) two further treaties provided for a joint attack on France and the

---

[109] Cavendish, op. cit., p. 53; Scarisbrick, op. cit., p. 143; *Cal. Span. F.S.*, p. 392; John Skelton, 'Why come ye not to court', in *The Poetical Works: with some account of the author and his writings*, by A. Dyce (London 1843) II, 29.

[110] *L.P.* III (ii) nos. 1946, 1992, 2036, 2092, 2129, 7139. The imperial ambassadors in England were highly suspicious of Wolsey's peace moves (Mattingly, loc. cit., pp. 26–7, quoting unpublished material from the Viennese archives).

[111] *L.P.* III (ii) no. 1838; *Cal. Span. F.S.*, pp. 2, 33, 38, 41, 46, 53, 56.

conquest of territories claimed by the allies.[112] An English herald, Clarencieux, took England's declaration of war to King François in Lyons.[113] Henry began to speak of the French Crown; King François would make way for him, as Richard III did for Henry VII.[114] Wolsey feared French designs to separate the allies; as much must be gained (from the French) as they might offer the Emperor: 'for loth would I be that, your grace [the King] being so expert in archery, the Emperor should have more strings to his bow than ye.'[115] England's entry into the war (apart from two minor engagements) came in August 1523. Again, war strategy was to provoke argument between King and Cardinal; Wolsey hoped that a speedy war would bring peace.[116] The claims of peace and war continued in 1524: the new Pope, Clement VII, appealed for peace, but the imperialist invasion of France (led by the traitor, Charles Duke of Bourbon) provoked the French King's retaliatory expedition, and hence the disaster of Pavia.

The peace movement seemed to have collapsed. Rather, it went underground. Wolsey would revive it when he could. In 1524 he had talked of abandonment of claims: the Emperor's to Milan, the King of England's to France. [117] Two great ladies, Louise of Savoy and Margaret of Austria, were still peacemakers. In late 1521 the Emperor had heard that they planned a joint pilgrimage, out of which might come some arrangement for peace.[118] Their chance came in 1529, with the 'Ladies' Peace' of Cambrai, negotiated personally by them.[119] But in 1521 they could not prevail. As Queen Catherine of Aragon told Ferdinand of Hapsburg's envoy (in 1522,

[112] *L.P.* III (ii) nos. 2333, 2360; *Cal. Span.* II, 434. The new Pope, Adrian VI, would have no part in the war, nor in the ecclesiastical censures on France which were hoped for (above, p. 34). As for the marriage alliance, it was reaffirmed, and the English still invoked it in 1525. In 1526 the Emperor married Isabella of Portugal.

[113] The King of France had already stopped the English pension. English students in Paris were returning home, as also was Anne Boleyn (*L.P.* III (ii) no. 1994).

[114] *L.P.* III (ii) nos. 2243, 2292, 2555. Scarisbrick drew attention to this hope of another Bosworth Field (op. cit., p. 128).

[115] *L.P.* III (ii) no. 2450.

[116] Scarisbrick, op. cit., pp. 128ff.; *L.P.* III (ii) nos. 3135, 3225; cf. *L.P.* IV, no. 61.

[117] *Cal. Span. F.S.*, p. 417.

[118] *L.P.* III (ii) no. 1915. Margaret wrote to Wolsey, early in 1522, two letters in her own hand (on peace between the Emperor and King Henry); she had not received a reply (*L.P.* III (ii) no. 2091).

[119] They had met as children (aged seven and three) at the French court in 1483; they shared the same governess, although, at that stage, Margaret's 'household' as 'Queen of France' was on a much more lavish scale (cf. above, p. 87).

when the Turks were besieging Rhodes), the Emperor and the King of England considered the King of France to be the true Turk, the chief menace to the liberties of Christendom.[120]

---

[120] *Cal. Span.* II, 433, 448 (cited by Mattingly, loc. cit., p. 28).

The Peace of Cateau-Cambrésis: negotiations at Cercamp, October–December 1558

The background to the negotiations

The negotiations of 1558–9 at Cercamp and Le Cateau achieved a settlement of the long series of Hapsburg–Valois wars, in which French and imperial/Spanish claims (the French to Milan, Naples-Sicily, overlordship of Flanders and Artois, the imperial/ Spanish to the Duchy of Burgundy, Auxonne, Maconnais, and the Somme towns) had been fought over and encapsulated in treaties. The 1559 settlement was achieved, as one Spaniard remarked, by leaving most of these ancient quarrels and concentrating on questions which had arisen during the previous twenty-five years. During this period, France had, in 1536, seized and retained the domains of the Duke of Savoy (Savoy and Piedmont); in 1552 Henri II had seized the 'imperial' bishoprics of Metz, Toul and Verdun, the reward for his alliance with the Protestant German princes against the Emperor Charles V.[1] The French had shown great ardour to fight, and to 'see the river Rhine'; but, having 'watered their horses' in the river, they turned back from Alsace. In 1558, the Duke of Guise had retaken Calais from the negligent English; later he captured the great fortress of Thionville on the Moselle, key to Luxembourg. Philip II had succeeded his father in 1555/6 as ruler of the Spanish kingdoms, the Spanish New World, the Netherlands (including Luxembourg), the kingdom of the two

---

[1] For Ronsard, the King is 'liberator' of Germany, lord of the German waters of the Rhine; the King and his horses drink from the river (Pierre de Ronsard, *Oeuvres complètes*, ed. P. Laumonnier (Paris 1924–75) V, 215; VIII, 20; IX, 104).

Sicilies (Naples-Sicily), Sardinia and the Duchy of Milan. By his marriage to Mary Tudor he was King of England, but they had no heir. In 1556 his armies had repulsed a French expedition to reconquer Naples, and in 1557 they had seized the great fortress of S. Quentin on the Somme. This was a disastrous defeat for France: her army, outnumbered by at least two to one, lost two-thirds of its infantry and over one-third of its cavalry. Ham and Le Catelet were also taken, but the great victory of S. Quentin was not followed up; lack of will, of money and victuals held back a projected march on Paris.

By 1558 the two powers were beset by difficulties. The government of Henri II was in financial, social and religious crisis. Philip II was in financial straits; virtual bankruptcy had been declared in 1557, when revenues were committed three years ahead and loans cost up to 54 per cent. Yet the two monarchs kept their armies in the north on a collision course. A French attack at Gravelines was repulsed in July. On 8 August, Henri II reviewed his great army of 40,000 (including 10,000–11,000 cavalry) at Pierrepont in Picardy between Montdidier and Amiens. The army then moved north nearer Amiens and was reinforced. By late August the French had crossed the Somme.[2] They faced King Philip's army, also reinforced and about the same size. It had marched into Picardy and was encamped near Doullens, a frontier town still held by the French. The two armies were only five leagues (about fifteen miles) apart. Both, but particularly the Spanish, had problems of supply, and foraging was difficult. The Spanish accordingly moved to the other side of Doullens and then, by 5 October, to within sight of Auxy-le-Chateau between Doullens and Hesdin, on the river Authie, known as the 'second ditch' of France (the Canche being the first). Skirmishes were inevitable as troops moved to reconnoitre and in search of food, though the Duke of Guise had forbidden such encounters under heavy penalties.[3]

---

[2] F. Lot, *Recherches sur les effectifs des armées francaises des guerres d'Italie aux guerres de réligion, 1494–1562* (Paris 1962) pp. 176–86. Blaise de Monluc (Blaise de Lasseran-Massencombe, Seigneur de Monluc, from north Gascony), the veteran soldier, was present at Pierrepont and vividly describes the scene (*Commentaires et lettres de Blaise de Monluc*, ed. A. de Ruble, *Société de l'Histoire de France* (Paris 1864–72) II, 302–6). Selections from his commentaries have been edited by Ian Roy, *Military memoirs, Blaise de Monluc.* (London 1971) from the English translation of Charles Cotton (1674).

[3] *Cal. Span.* XIII, 451–2; Granvelle V, 172, 215; *Cal. Ven.* VI, 1524–7, 1530.

Preliminaries

In spite of this warlike stance, the two monarchs were, during this summer, turning to peace negotiations. Henri II may only have bowed to necessity, including the urge to obtain the release of his favourite, the veteran Constable of France, Anne de Montmorency, whose incompetent generalship had lost the battle of S. Quentin, at which he was taken prisoner.[4] The King, 'with little conscience, ambitious, sombre, warlike', was dominated by the Guises: François, Duke of Guise, and his brother Charles, Cardinal of Lorraine. Their gradual acceptance of the necessity for peace may only have been a temporary expedient to gain a respite. In King Philip's case, a desire for peace may have been more sincere. He was not of warlike ambition; probably, as the Venetian ambassador wrote in 1559, his aim was 'not to wage war so that he can add to his Kingdoms but to wage peace so that he can keep the lands he had'. King Philip himself stated that he was 'doing everything compatible with my honour and reputation in order to achieve this end [peace]'.[5]

If there was to be peace, then subsidiary issues would be drawn into the principal Hapsburg–Valois disputes. France was committed to the restoration of the d'Albret-Bourbon house of Navarre to the 'Spanish' part of the kingdom south of the Pyrenees. As consort and ally, Spain was committed to England, which had entered the war on the Spanish side in 1557. King Philip was also committed to the restoration of the Duke of Savoy, serving in exile as his Captain General in the north. The Duke's motto, 'Spoliatis arma supersunt' ('those who have been despoiled still have arms'), perhaps indicates his attitude to the recovery of his lands, so long postponed. Hence Navarre, Savoy and above all the English claims on Calais would immensely complicate the task of the negotiators.[6]

The diplomats were to meet under the mediation of Christina of

---

[4] *Cal. Ven.* VII, 40, 44; letter to Montmorency in F. Decrue, *Anne de Montmorency connétable et pair de France sous les rois Henri II, François II et Charles IX* (Paris 1889) p. 211.

[5] *Relazioni degli ambasciatori Veneti al Senato durante il secolo decimosesto* ed. E. Alberi (Florence 1839–63) 1st series, III, 379; *Cal. Ven.* VII, 6; Granvelle V, 453–4; *Cal. Span.* XIII, 440. Cf. The Duke of Alva's views of King Philip's desire for peace (*Cal. Ven.* VII, 63).

[6] The Duke of Savoy (see below, p. 158) would have liked to attend the conference, but the French countered that if he did, then the Duke of Guise must also be present. The King of Navarre sent representatives (see below, p. 163).

Denmark, Dowager Duchess of Lorraine. A niece of the Emperor Charles V, and therefore cousin of King Philip, she had been brought up at the court of her great-aunt, Margaret of Austria, in the Netherlands. She had been married to the Duke of Milan at fifteen, widowed at sixteen, and again came to the Netherlands. Her marriage to François, Duke of Lorraine, in 1544 ended in widowhood.[7] Renewed exile came in 1552, when her young son and his duchy were taken under French protection. He was brought up at the French court and married Claude de France in January 1559. His ducal house was the senior line of that 'brood of Lorraine', whose junior line was the ducal house of Guise. Christina might, therefore, have been seen as the potential ally, if not tool, of France. But she was born a Hapsburg, and her long periods of residence at the imperial court could hardly have failed to influence her opinions and style. She had wit; in 1538, when Holbein drew her, she rebuffed Henry VIII's courtship by remarking that, if she had two heads, she would gladly place one at his disposal. She knew the political scene well, though no commanding impression is gained of her part in the 1558–9 negotiations. Perhaps, as the Venetian ambassador reported, she lacked the vigour ('vivacita') and experience (of government) of her aunt Mary of Hungary.[8] Yet it seems to have been on her initiative that the whole process began.

In mid-April 1558 the Duchess interceded with King Philip, asking that the Marshal S. André (Jacques d'Albon), a prisoner since the battle of S. Quentin, might be released on parole to go to France. He returned with a royal commission for himself and Montmorency to meet Spanish representatives to talk of peace. In May the Cardinal of Lorraine accompanied the young Duke of Lorraine to Péronne to see his mother, then at Cambrai. The Cardinal was attended by two powerful secretaries of state (Fresne and de Laubespine); secret interviews were arranged at Marcoing in Cambrésis with the Duchess and the Bishop of Arras, Granvelle, who had left court for a supposed visit to his diocese. At this meeting, the French made definite proposals on their terms for peace, mentioning the restitution of territory and the problems of Savoy and Calais; the Spanish spoke of restitutions, of Savoy, and

[7] C. M. Ady, *A History of Milan under the Sforza* (London 1907) pp. 244–5, 312; K. Brandi, *The Emperor Charles V* (London 1967) pp. 190, 324, 343, 445, 617.
[8] *Cal. Ven.* VI, 1533.

of marriage alliances.[9] It is possible that the problem of the suppression of heresy was discussed, but no contemporary evidence has been found.[10]

During the summer there was other secret activity. Marshal Vieilleville, governor of Metz, sent a monk to King Philip to suggest a peace based on a marriage alliance.[11] The Duke of Savoy recorded in his journal that a Burgundian Hieronomite from Spain came to visit him in August and was sent on to the King to tell him of Henri II's wish for peace.[12]

By August, at the Duchess of Lorraine's request, the two French prisoners S. André and Montmorency proceeded to Lille, and from 9 to 18 September they had discussions with King Philip's representatives: the Prince of Orange, Ruy Gómez de Silva, Count of Melito, and Bishop Granvelle. They met in the palace of the Dukes of Burgundy, and, again, there was talk of peace terms. The French were already protesting that the Spanish wished them to restore all that they had won since the Peace of Crépy (1544) in exchange for places in Vermandois (S. Quentin, Ham and Le Catelet) and marriage alliances. Simon Renard, councillor of King Philip, acknowledged that the French would find the terms difficult; they would have to surrender what they had won, by loss of men and heavy expense, during the last twenty-four years. On their side the French declined to discuss Metz, Toul and Verdun, Corsica and (if possible) Calais also, as not King Philip's concern. Montmorency, however, showed a clear commitment to peace. He remarked to the Spanish that he would do all he could for peace; he wished he were

---

[9] *Traicté*, pp. 2, 12; Granvelle v, 181, 240; *Cal. Ven.* vi, 1489, 1491–2, 1494 (the editor's note that this meeting was at Cercamp is an error).

[10] The tradition of the heresy discussion seems to come from the early seventeenth-century historian and royal librarian, Jacques-Auguste de Thou, who is usually impartial and reliable. He states that Granvelle declared heresy to be a greater problem than the Turk; Lorraine was attracted by these views (J.-A. De Thou, *Historiarum sui temporis volumen primum* (London 1733) xx, 9 (p. 687); cf. N. Sutherland, *The French Secretaries of State in the Age of Catherine de Medici* (London 1962) p. 90, and see below, p. 217). The Cardinal of Lorraine and his brothers had no doubt been reared on stories of the victory of their father, Duke Claude, over the two marauding armies of German Lutheran peasants who crossed the Rhine in 1525, victories seen as the defence of order and religion, which earned congratulations from the Pope and the Parlement of Paris, and the creation of the Guise dukedom and peerage.

[11] François de Scepeaux, Sire de Vieilleville, Marshal of France (cf. Vincent Carloix, 'Mémoires sur Vieilleville', in *Nouvelle collection de mémoires*, ed. J.-F. Michaud and J. J. F. Poujolat, 1st series, ix (Paris 1854) p. 272).

[12] Emm. Phil., p. 31 (the memoirs of the Duke, written day by day in Spanish).

at court and the Guise in his place. He did not care who had the honour, even if it were only a kitchen scullion, so long as peace was made. He thanked God that he had been present at many other 'good undertakings', a reference to his diplomatic work in the past. An English ambassador, Nicholas Wotton, was present at Lille, but only on the sidelines; he learnt of the French views on Calais.[13] But matters were only at a preliminary stage. The two French prisoners were closely controlled by the Spanish; King Philip would permit only limited meetings between the two, and there is clear evidence that their letters were being opened, although Montmorency gave thanks for receiving a royal letter 'vierge et entière'. Secretary de Laubespine came and went, and the Bishop of Limoges visited the Spanish camp to make arrangements for the full-scale meeting which was to follow.[14]

The negotiators

The full-scale meeting, scheduled for October, was of three powerful embassies. Henri II sent the Constable and Grandmaster Anne de Montmorency, Peer of France, Duke of Montmorency (just north of Paris), and the Marshal S. André, Jacques d'Albon, Marquis of Fronsac (on the Dordogne), both released on parole; with them were Charles de Guise, Cardinal of Lorraine, Archbishop and Duke of Reims and Peer of France, Jean de Morvilliers, Bishop of Orléans, and the royal Councillor and Secretary of State, Claude de Laubespine.[15] The Constable, a contemporary of François I, was by now

[13] Granvelle v, 169, 172–4, 187, 196, 205–27; *Traicté*, pp. 2, 5–7; *Cal. Span.* XIII, 451–2; *Cal. Ven.* VI, 1528; *Cal. For.*, I, 393–6.
[14] Granvelle v, loc. cit. The Spanish clearly took copies of Montmorency's letters and of Lorraine's letters back, and held up S. André's letters (ibid., v, 181, 195–7, 204). They feared what information might be included in such letters, and what information envoys from France might collect as to military strength etc. Hence their seeming obstinacy over the visits by a secretary of state. Ruy Gómez hoped that his men taking Montmorency's letters might see the French camp. Bishop Granvelle was on the alert, and was exasperated by references, in S. André's letters to Lorraine, to 'portraits' and 'fine cloths'. Were these code words? he asked the Duke of Savoy (Granvelle v, 193–7).
[15] De Laubespine, of a family of lawyers from Orléans and the Beauce, was Seigneur d'Hauterive (on the Tarn); he owned the famous house of Jacques Coeur, *argentier* of Charles VII, in Bourges. He was one of four secretaries of state nominated in 1547 by Montmorency, with whom he worked closely thereafter. His importance grew in the later years of Henri II, as did that of his office, by 1558 given the title of 'Secretary of State' (Sutherland, op. cit., pp. 20–2, 29).

sixty-five; he was a veteran soldier, politician and diplomat; he was also a patron of the arts. He had worked for peace in 1538–40, and again in 1556 (the truce of Vaucelles). He took a leading part in 1558–9. He was closely befriended by the King and the Queen. The shrewd diplomat, Simon Renard, recorded that Montmorency was devoted to the King, knowing his humour and instincts.[16] The Marshal S. André (from the Roannais) had served the King from his youth, earning his friendship, following him in war, and becoming governor of the Lyonnais, Beaujolais and Bourbonnais. His greater military daring and decision might have saved the day at S. Quentin.[17] The young Cardinal of Lorraine, then 33, was already marked by his learning and his ability in diplomacy and finance (see Plate 5). He not only knew Greek and Latin, but spoke Italian amazingly well, and had become an eloquent and formidable orator. A fellow student of Ronsard's at the Collège de Navarre, he was perhaps not over-praised by the poet, whose patron he had become, as 'Sage Mercure' or 'Mercure de France' (Mercury being the God of Eloquence), his persuasiveness balancing his eloquence, which bubbled over and was like the pirouetting of a Spanish horse. Lorraine's eloquence was also likened to a weapon of war.[18] The Bishop of Orléans, sometime ambassador to Venice, was less

---

[16] For Montmorency, cf. Decrue, op. cit.; Simon Renard's comments are in Granvelle v, 226. The Constable (whose first name came from his godmother Queen Anne of France) was a great builder. At Écouen, just north of Paris, Jean Goujon worked for him, Rosso Fiorentino's team from Fontainebleu did frescos, and there was grisaille stained glass. In the 1550s, Jean Bullant designed the north wing; under its monumental porch once stood the two slaves by Michelangelo, originally intended for the tomb of Pope Julius II, and now in the Louvre. There was a fantastic grotto by Bernard de Palissy, whose first patron was Montmorency. At Chantilly, further to the north, was the Constable's great library. A new Petit Chateau was built by Bullant in the period after the 1559 peace. In Paris, Montmorency had four residences, one, in the present Rue du Temple, had a painted gallery by Niccolo da Bologna. Montmorency was a Knight of the Garter, and of the Order of S. Michel.

[17] L. Romier, La carrière d'un favori Jacques d'Albon de S. André, Maréchal de France (Paris 1909). He was a Knight of the Order of S. Michel.

[18] Négotiations diplomatiques de la France avec la Toscane, ed. A. Desjardins (Paris 1859–1886) iii, 215; Alberi, 1st series, ii, 433–4, iii, 440–1; Ronsard, viii, 27, ix, 44–46, 59; Brantôme, iii, 256; H. O. Evenett, The Cardinal of Lorraine and the Council of Trent (Cambridge 1930). The Cardinal, an Archbishop at fourteen (though consecration was delayed) was promoted to the Sacred College in 1547 (his titular church, S. Apollinare). At his sumptuous residence at Meudon, near Paris, he employed Domenico del Barbieri and Francesco Primaticcio. In Paris, he occupied the Hôtel de Cluny, being Abbot of that foundation.

impressive; he was learned but somewhat timorous.[19] However, it is difficult to agree with Romier's judgment that the embassy as a whole, possibly excepting Lorraine, was 'd'une incapacité navrante'.[20] It was the problems, not the negotiators, which proved intractable.

King Philip was represented by the Duke of Alva (Alba de Tormes near Salamanca), Don Fernandez Alvarez de Toledo, grandee of Spain, High Steward of the royal household, Viceroy of Naples and Knight of the Golden Fleece. He had accompanied Philip II to England and was an experienced soldier, diplomat and administrator of fifty-one. Twenty years older than his royal master, he had been inclined (as the Emperor Charles V predicted) to treat the King as a child.[21] His slight deafness does not seem to have inhibited his commanding role at the conference.[22] With him came the Prince of Orange, William of Nassau-Dillenburg, Knight of the Golden Fleece, a rising young man of twenty-five, richly endowed with estates stretching from the North Sea to the Rhine and the Rhone. Educated and advanced at the imperial court, Orange's high favour with the Emperor was not matched by King Philip's regard. In 1558 his head was filled with 'the feates of Chivalrie, hunting and other exercises' rather than with the thoughts of salvation.[23] He was an eligible widower, hoping for a daughter of the Duchess of Lorraine in marriage.[24] King Philip's favour went to another ambassador, the Portuguese Ruy Gómez de Silva, Count of Melito (Calabria), Councillor of State and future husband of the

[19] The Bishop, from Blois, had risen in royal service, under the protection of the Guise. As Bishop, he had insisted on retaining his beard, obtaining some royal dispensation when the Chapter complained (*Biographie Universelle*, ed. M. Michaud, Paris 1843). He was uncle by marriage of de Laubespine.

[20] Emm. Phil., p. 17.

[21] Cf. W. S. Maltby, *Alba; a biography* . . . (California 1983). For Alva in England, cf. D. M. Loades, *The Reign of Mary Tudor* (London 1979) pp. 213, 222.

[22] The French remarked on his deafness (*Traicté*, p. 37).

[23] *The Apologie of Prince William of Orange* . . . ed. after the English edition of 1581 by W. Wansink (Leiden 1969) p. 60.

[24] William, the future William 'the Silent' (see below, p. 216) was born at Dillenburg Nassau (between Hesse and the Rhine). His principality of Orange lay between Provence and Dauphiné, an enclave in the Comtat Venaissin. He inherited the Nassau palace in Brussels, a favoured residence, the Kasteel, at Breda in north Brabant, and the great fortress of Vianden in Luxembourg. He was sent to the imperial court at the age of eleven. Motley is still worth reading on the family history and social life (J. L. Motley, *The Rise of the Dutch Republic* (London 1897) pp. 119–21; cf. G. Parker, *The Dutch Revolt* (London 1977) pp. 51–2; P. Pierson, *Philip II of Spain* (London 1975) pp. 161–2; C. V. Wedgwood, *William the Silent* (New Haven 1944)).

Princess of Eboli. He had negotiated the King's English marriage, and went with him to England. Antoine Perrenot de Granvelle, Bishop of Arras, was the chief spokesman of the embassy (see Plate 6). A Franche-Comtois, he was the son of Charles V's minister Nicolas Perrenot;[25] he had studied at Dôle, Padua, Paris and Louvain (philosophy and theology). As a rising ecclesiastic, he had accompanied his father to the colloquies at Worms and Ratisbon in 1540, and was a delegate to the Council of Trent in 1543. By 1559 he was an experienced and trusted royal servant, soon to be the first Archbishop of Malines (Mechelen) and a Cardinal. His meticulous and perceptive method of work is mirrored in his voluminous correspondence. His motto, 'Durate', taken from Aeneas' counsel to his shipwrecked men ('endure and keep your-selves for prosperous times'), displayed on his buildings, his arms, and his books, fitted well with his way of life, and particularly his staying power.[26] He knew Spanish, Italian and of course Latin. There was to have been a fifth ambassador, Ulric Viglius van Aytta van Swichum, the Frisian President of the Privy Council of the Netherlands, but illness detained him. He was a trained lawyer, skilled in negotiating contracts, and his advice was asked during the negotiations.[27] Of these diplomats Granvelle was held to be the

---

[25] The Perrenot family came from Ornans. Granvelle's father Nicolas, lawyer and statesman, was Seigneur de Grandvelle (Grandvelle near Gray); the family home was at Besançon, where Antoine was born and where Nicolas built a sumptuous palace with a great picture gallery (later rifled by Louis XIV). Antoine was patron of artists, men of letters and printers. His papers, having been carelessly treated after his death, were saved for posterity in the seventeenth century by a learned Franche-Comtois, the abbé Boisot (Cf. Granvelle I, xvi–xix; L. Febvre, *Philippe II et la Franche Comté* (Paris 1970) pp. 83–5); M. Van Durme, *El cardenal Granvela* (Barcelona 1957).)

[26] *Aeneid* I. 207. Granvelle had a residence in Brussels and another, east of the city, at S. Josse-ten-Noode, once a favoured retreat of the Dukes of Burgundy, and more recently of the Nassau, Croy and Marnix families. In this countryside, with its large ponds, these nobles had villas. Granvelle's 'La Fontaine', bore his motto 'Durate'. The retreat was called 'the Smithy' by Granvelle's enemies, a reflection on his origins, for his great-great-grand-father had been a blacksmith (*Mémoires de Pontus Payen*, ed. A. Henne (Brussels 1861) I, 64. Payen, a lawyer, échevin of Arras, and Seigneur des Essars (near Neufchatel-en-Bray, in Picardy) wrote his *De la guerre civile des Pays Bas* sometime after 1581. It is a valuable and colourful near-contemporary source. Cf. also P. C. Hooft, *Nederlandsche Historiën* (Amsterdam 1650) I, 56; Van der Vynckt, *Nederlandscher Beroerten* (Amsterdam 1823) I, 164; A. Wauters, *Histoire des environs de Bruxelles* (Brussels 1855) III, 25).

[27] The Venetian ambassador referred to him (March 1559) as the 'wearer of the long robe', a doctor of laws, versed and experienced in treaties of peace (*Cal. Ven.* VII, 54). For Viglius, cf. *Biographisch Woordenboek der Nederlanden* (Haarlem 1852), and *Biographie nationale pub. par l'Academie royale . . . de Belgique* (Brussels 1866).

most experienced in negotiations with France and was allowed to speak first on that subject in the royal Council.[28] As for the King, he kept a close watch on the proceedings at the conference, but probably needed continual prompting to action judging from the remarks of an experienced royal servant that the King 'expects to be tired out [by importunities] before he does anything great or small'.[29]

Mary Tudor despatched as ambassadors three members of her Privy Council. The Lord President, and Lord Steward of her household, Henry Fitzalan, 12th Earl of Arundel and Knight of the Garter, led the mission. A soldier, courtier, sometime Lord Deputy of Calais, negotiator with France and the Empire in 1555, he was also an antiquarian and bibliophile. His residences at Arundel House in the Strand and Arundel Castle were now supplemented by Royal Nonsuch.[30] Despite his attainments, he proved purely a figurehead at the negotiations. With him came Thomas Thirlby, Bishop of Ely, a Cambridge man (in both senses), Doctor of Civil and Canon Law, and experienced in diplomacy. Cardinal Pole thought him a good jurist and an able negotiator.[31] The third ambassador was Dr Nicholas Wotton, of a powerful Kent family, graduate of Oxford and probably of some Italian university (perhaps Perugia), Doctor of Theology and Canon and Civil Law. He was Dean of both Canterbury and York, but had refused higher promotion. He had travelled widely, first to Italy on his studies, then as diplomat; he was at the imperial court in 1543–4, and ambassador resident in France from 1546–9, and again from 1553–7. He knew French, Italian and German, in addition to Latin.[32] His small stature made the French call him 'the little ambassador'. He was immensely learned, but by 1559 (when he was sixty-three) he

---

[28] *Emm. Phil.*, p. 36.

[29] *Cal. Span.* xiv, 88 (letter of the Count of Feria, July 1559; cf. below, p. 157).

[30] *Dictionary of National Biography.*

[31] Thirlby was a conservative in religion and politics (cf. T. F. Shirley, *Thomas Thirlby, Tudor bishop* (London 1964)). He had been on many embassies: to France (1533, 1538, 1545), to the Emperor (1542, 1545–8, 1553), to Scotland (1543) and to the Curia (1555).

[32] *Dictionary of National Biography*; epitaph at Canterbury (printed in *Illustrium virorum elogia sepulchralia*, ed. E. Popham (London 1778), p. 320). Wotton's seniority provoked amused comment from the young. In 1560 the Duke of Norfolk, aged twenty-four, wrote to Cecil of 'mine uncle Wotton'. The same expression (el tio) was used of Alva by the much younger Requesens. One may compare this usage with the fool's in King Lear (iii. vi).

was tired and timorous. In 1560 Cecil wrote, 'Mr Wotton is very wise, and loveth quietness, but this matter [negotiations with Scotland] requireth travail [exertion]'.[33] It might have been so, also, in 1558–9. Both Thirlby and Wotton were fearful of their mission and of the likely turn of events at home, where Mary Tudor was in her last illness.

The Duchess of Lorraine came to the meeting as the officially designated mediator. Henri II's safe-conduct stated that she had decided 'with the good pleasure of King Philip, to attend the meeting to mediate and facilitate accord and union of the two Princes, according to her long demonstrated affection'.[34] The diplomats referred to her as 'nostre moyeneresse', and she may, indeed, have intended to act as a true neutral. In articles submitted at the conference on Lorraine's position, the Duchess claimed that the Duke had not merely 'regalian' but 'sovereign' rights (see Appendix D). The position, as seen by the English, was this: the Duchess had procured the meeting by her labour and travail, she being a Princess not subject to either Spain or France; they used her therefore as 'indifferent' between all parties.[35] Meetings at Cercamp and Le Cateau were in her lodgings, and she presided. Granvelle wrote to her of her sacred task and stressed that she must take what part she wished in the negotiations.[36] Yet she herself wrote of her 'service and obedience' to King Philip, her submission to his will and her fears that the French bore her no goodwill.[37] Whatever the truth on this latter point, the Spanish clearly saw her as under their instructions. She signed herself King Philip's most obedient cousin and servant; his ambassadors expected her to fit in with Spanish negotiating manoeuvres, and not to act on her own initiative.[38] In fact there is little evidence of her part in the peace-making process, though she several times prevented a rupture, perhaps an indication that she achieved more than the professional diplomats liked to reveal.[39]

[33] Conyers Read, *Mr Secretary Cecil and Queen Elizabeth* (London 1955) p. 184.

[34] *Traicté*, p. 15.

[35] *Cal. For.* II, 124; Forbes, I, 40.

[36] Granvelle v, 231–4.

[37] Ibid., v, 228–9.

[38] See below, pp. 192–4.

[39] An intercepted letter from King Philip to one of his military commanders stated that the Duchess had sought the deliberations in order to postpone the fighting for which the King was not ready (*Cal. Ven.* VI, 1504).

The negotiations, in the hands of an officially 'neutral' mediator, were also, as might be expected, in a 'neutral' place, both for safety and for the honour of the two kings.[40] The French had demanded a place equally distant from the lands of the two kings, and the Spanish favoured one not too near the camps, for security reasons. Cambrai was the Duchess' choice; she had asked Lorraine to visit her there in May, and the city was suggested at the Lille meeting. Eventually the Cistercian abbey of Cercamp was chosen. It stood on the left bank of the river Canche, the 'first ditch' of France, dividing French Picardy from Artois (in King Philip's domains). Experience at Cercamp prompted a change in the New Year, and negotiations were resumed at Le Cateau in Cambrésis, in the territory of the bishops of Cambrai, and one of their favoured residences. For French and Spanish this was truly neutral territory, since Cambrai and the Cambrésis were technically imperial land and had a long tradition of neutrality as between France and the rulers of the Netherlands.[41]

First, there was the practical problem: to separate the armies and provide for security. A truce covering the areas on both sides of the frontier was declared and subsequently renewed for limited periods, always including six days after the end of negotiations. Short truces were favoured by the Spaniards, who feared that the French preference for long truces masked some warlike designs. The truce was, as the Spanish requested, 'non-communicative', i.e. it did not permit normal freedom of travel. King Henri's safe-conducts for the Duchess, the Spanish and the English gave protection from Arras, on the highroad to the Spanish camp and thence to Cercamp, or direct from Arras to Cercamp. The great problem was to move the camps, so perilously near each other. In October the area was inundated with rain, so that the roads were broken up, the artillery needed to be moved, and there was much sickness. The Spanish wanted to get their camp under cover and to dismiss troops or send them to garrisons. There was also great shortage of food for men

[40] The negotiations are very fully documented. The reports of the Spanish ambassadors are in Granvelle, those of the French in *Traicté*, those of the English in *Cal. For.* Most of the English documents are printed verbatim, with the original orthography, in *Rel. Pol.*, and some are in Forbes (see Abbreviations).

[41] *Traicté*, p. 8; *Cal. Ven.* VI, 1491–4; Granvelle V, 222–3. Cambrai was chosen for the meeting of the arbiters under the treaty of Cateau-Cambrésis (Appendix B, articles 14 and 17: disputes over Bouillon, and general disputes between France and Spain over 'border' territories).

and horses, and Spanish foraging in French territory (i.e. around their camp) was much resented. It was decided that the camps be moved; the French were to withdraw across the Somme and King Philip back into his own lands.[42] Henri II's camp was 'broken' in late October and moved, tardily, across the Somme. Some of the troops were disbanded; the remainder dispersed to frontier posts and into Champagne and Burgundy. The King himself was first at Beauvais, then, by 7 November was moving to S. Germain, and in Paris by the end of the year.[43] King Philip was with, or near, his army until mid-October. By November he had returned to Arras, in his own lands, having 'broken' camp. By mid-November he was at the Augustinian abbey of Groenendael[44] in the forest of Soignes, about eight miles south-east of Brussels, to which city he moved for Christmas. The disbandment of the Spanish troops was complicated by shortage of money; in October the Duke of Savoy reported that the King had only one month's ready money in his coffers, and in mid-November, the army not yet disbanded, money was being obtained from Genoese at Antwerp.[45]

These itineraries of the two kings demonstrate that communication with Cercamp could be relatively easy and quick. The Spanish needed only one or two days to get a reply from their King. For the French, a two-day interval was normal until the King moved south; six days were needed by November. There were 'express' delivery services; a swift messenger ('homme exprès') would be used, and sometimes an ambassador might travel 'post-wise' (i.e. on swift horses). The Spanish had 'posts', but payment was often limited to short journeys, as from Brussels to Cercamp. The Duke of Alva paid privately for some messengers to England.[46] Only the English languished for want of information or instructions. Letters could reach them at Cercamp or Le Cateau in six or seven days, but this meant at least two weeks' delay for a reply, and their problems increased in the final days of Mary Tudor's life. The route, also, was less certain than in the past; Calais had once been the normal way, but now Dunkirk (in King Philip's domains) was

---

[42] *Traicté*, pp. 12, 14–24, 49–50; Granvelle v, 263–5, 267, 321, 362, 414, 418, 422–8, 436; *Cal. Ven.* vi, 1533 (referring to withdrawal four leagues (about twelve miles) from the frontier).

[43] Granvelle v, 288, 297; *Cal. For.* i, 272, 396; *Cal. Ven.* vi, 1536–7, 1543.

[44] The foundation of Jan van Ruysbroeck, the Flemish mystic (1350).

[45] Emm. Phil., p. 42; *Cal. Ven.* vi, 1545.

[46] Granvelle v, 281, 338, 342, 344, 358, 484–5; *Cal. For.* ii, 8; *Traicté*, p. 40.

used, Calais being refused as unsafe when the French offered that
facility.[47] There was much use of information-gatherers or spies,
though even the experienced Granvelle feared that one of his agents
was a 'double' ('que nostre homme ne soit double').[48] Rumours
were encouraged by frantic searching for information, particularly
by the foreign ambassadors at the courts.

Foreign ambassadors were, indeed, cut off from the scene of
negotiations. The Venetian ambassadors to Henri II and Philip II
give us detailed and very frequent reports of all they could glean in
Paris or Brussels. Occasionally the ambassador to France followed
the King to his 'camp', as in the summer of 1558. The ambassador's
secretary was at Beauvais with the King in October, and the
ambassador himself was at La Ferté Milon with the King in
February.[49] The ambassador in Brussels remained there but
received news from the conference, for instance from Alva's
secretary and from Granvelle's brother, and on one occasion saw the
letters from one of the Spanish negotiators. There was no Venetian
ambassador to England at this time, Mary Tudor deciding in 1556
to use her husband's envoys abroad. Some letters of Alvise Priuli,
lifelong friend of Cardinal Pole and in his household, concern final
days. For the first months of the new reign, a Mantuan, Il Schi-
fanoya, servant of the English Grand Prior of the Hospitallers, is
informative.[50] The Venetian reports tell us that ambassadors from
Florence and Mantua to King Philip were at Cercamp but not at
Le Cateau, though this has not been substantiated. The Florentine
certainly had letters from Le Cateau and was consulted by King
Philip on the treaty.[51] The Genoese ambassador was also consulted
by the King. The Ferrarese ambassador's son visited Le Cateau in
March.[52] In France, Alfonso d'Este, brother of the Duke of Ferrara,
brother-in-law of the Duke of Guise, and son-in-law of the Duke of
Tuscany, was at court. He was stated to be there for medical
treatment, but the Venetian view was that he had been sent to offer

---

[47] *Cal. For.* I, 404; II, 122, 153, 199; Granvelle v, 470. Francisco [sic] Thomas 'the
post' was one messenger (*Cal. For.* II, 2).

[48] Granvelle v, 198.

[49] La Ferté Milon, on the Ourcq, north-east of Paris.

[50] *Cal. Ven.* VI, 1533, 1535, 1545, 1555; VII, 26, 30, 39, 41, 61. Venice offered to
arbitrate on Calais (ibid. VII, 1539).

[51] *Cal. Ven.* VII, 1, 34–6, 55, 60–1; Granvelle v, 565. Florentine 'exiles' appealed
to Henri II (*Cal. Ven.* VI, 1546).

[52] Granvelle v, 565.

his brother's mediation between France and Spain in return for a marriage alliance.[53] Sienese representatives were at the French court in November, canvassing their city's wish for independence from Florence.[54] Chiaponi Vitelli, Marquis of Cremona, kept a secret agent at Le Cateau.[55] From this surviving detail, one may gauge the secret comings and goings, the desperate search for news by Italian powers whose fate, in many cases, hung in the balance. In all this the lesser personalities at the conference should not be discounted, particularly the secretaries. We know of Montmorency's secretary and of Alva's; the latter corresponded with the Venetian ambassador in Brussels.[56] John Somer, Wotton's secretary, who had served with him in Paris (where he taught other secretaries the language) must certainly have been in touch with his opposite numbers.[57]

A basic problem is the languages used in negotiation. It is an intractable one, since contemporaries did not record much, probably because usage was taken for granted. One is concerned with language as a tool for discussion and decision, where both flexibility and precision are needed. This is not the language of formal compliments or occasional airy phrases, the 'small firkin of salutation [in Italian]' which an English ambassador craved for use on Catherine de' Medici. The language of hard bargaining, and the common understanding which this requires, as between Spanish, French and English in 1558–9, was clearly Latin. We know that this was the case; on 24 October, for instance, the French reported that the 'other Spanish' (i.e. not Granvelle) only half understood the French use of Latin. Significantly, this meeting was one attended by all three parties.[58] But Latin placed a heavy burden on lay ambassadors unless they were university educated and had continued to use the language, for instance in professional work. Few others could have used it as a vehicle of *discussion*. The ecclesiastics, or humanists, would therefore be in command, and the normal spokesmen for their colleagues: Granvelle, Lorraine and Ely (or Wotton) spoke regularly in the debates. But it is inconceivable that French was not the 'runner up' as the common daily instrument of communication.

---

[53] *Cal. Ven.* vi, 1526, 1543, 1546; vii, 45; Granvelle v, 565.
[54] *Cal. Ven.* vi, 1543; vii, 49 (cf. below, p. 202).
[55] *Cal. Ven.* vii, 41.
[56] Ibid., vi, 1539–41.
[57] *Cal. For.* i, 138; ii, 187.
[58] *Traicté*, p. 43.

Granvelle was a native of Franche Comté, who had learnt Spanish to serve his career. French was the normal language of government in the Netherlands; the Spanish ambassadors wrote their reports in French and official replies came in French, sometimes with a post-script, in Spanish, in the King's own hand. Philip II's working language was Spanish (Castilian); he could sustain a conversation in Latin and knew a little Portuguese; Granvelle and the King corresponded in Spanish, as did Granvelle and Alva, Granvelle and the Duke of Savoy.[59] Alva spoke at the negotiations in Spanish, once rebuking Montmorency, who had not rightly understood his Spanish.[60] Orange spoke French, Dutch and German, and knew some Spanish. On the French side, Lorraine would have spoken formally in Latin, but no doubt informally in his own tongue; Montmorency, who often took the lead, must surely have spoken in French. Lorraine's amazing proficiency in Italian would have given him an easy understanding of Spanish. It is doubtful that his colleagues shared this linguistic gift.

As for the English, they were out on a limb; no one would have understood their language save possibly Ruy Gómez.[61] The Spanish refer to the English speaking together, at the table, in 'their English'. Lord William Howard, who replaced Arundel, addressed the assembly in French, apologising for his use of the language.[62] Thirlby's experience of French may not have been recent; he does, however, appear to have spoken in French to secretary Courte-wille.[63] Wotton, twice resident in France, and once as recently as 1557, was at home in French. For the English and Spanish, Latin would normally be the common ground; the English Privy Council had used it when King Philip was present, they used it with his ambassador in 1562, as did Cecil with a successor in 1569. We must presume, therefore, much use of Latin and of French in the

---

[59] An analysis of the Granvelle papers shows this. The Duke of Savoy, whose journal is in Spanish, had been at the imperial court since he was seventeen. For King Philip cf. Pierson, op. cit., pp. 16, 18, 29–30, 118, 145. The Emperor had strongly urged a good command of Latin (in 1543) since his son would have to govern many lands, separated by language barriers (Fernández-Santamaria, op. cit., p. 240; cf. above, p. 71n20).

[60] Granvelle v, 341.

[61] For his service in England, cf. D. M. Loades, *The Reign of Mary Tudor* (London 1979), pp. 123–6, 211–12, 227.

[62] Granvelle v, 455; *Traicté*, pp. 83, 88.

[63] This seems to be the implication of a reported conversation, in which the Bishop added some words in Latin (Granvelle v, 416–17).

deliberations. But what of the Duchess? We do not know how she ranked as a Latinist; her crucial interventions may well have been in French. A general conclusion would therefore be that Latin was used when all three parties met together. French may, however, have been the common language between the Spanish, the French and the Duchess. 'Lay' ambassadors would generally speak their own language, but this option was scarcely open to the English. They were, therefore, at a disadvantage and in isolation; those most favoured were Granvelle and Lorraine; Ronsard has the Cardinal as the 'divine interpreter' between Flemings, English and Spanish at the negotiations.[64]

At Cercamp the Duchess and the diplomats were all lodged in the abbey itself; Granvelle noted that her arrival would restrict the lodgings of the others. The participants frequently refer to their 'quarters' ('nostre quartier') or to the quarters of the Duchess, where they met for discussions in a room set aside for this ('la salle à ce destinée'). They sat around a table, the Duchess presiding; the Spanish appropriated the right-hand side of the table, the more 'honorable', even before the Duchess arrived. Breaks in the discussion allowed the diplomats to confer more privately and then return to the table ('et après retournons à la table'). The monastic chapel was used for daily masses, and, like the cloisters, for occasional private meetings. Awkward points could often be ironed out, or hints dropped of likely solutions, by intercepting representatives of the other side on their way to mass or on their way back. The formal meetings were held at about one o'clock, after 'dinner'.[65] The presence of several heads of royal households (Arundel, then Howard; Alva; Montmorency) must have been intimidating for lesser officials concerned with accommodation and food.

The Spanish arrived at Cercamp first; the French travelled by way of Doullens (9 October), where they met the two 'prisoners', Montmorency having already discussed his own release with the Duke of Savoy en route. The French were greeted by the Spanish as they dismounted (probably on 12 October). Arundel and Ely, having travelled to Dunkirk, met Wotton at Béthune; Ely was there detained by illness, so that all three were not at Cercamp until 20

[64] Ronsard XIII, 22.
[65] Granvelle v, 234–6, 247, 250, 277, 280, 340, 342–3, 402; *Traicté*, pp. 19, 74; Emm. Phil., p. 43.

October. The Duchess had arrived on 19 October.[66] The Spanish
had powers to negotiate a peace and marriage alliances for King
Philip's son, Don Carlos, and for the Duke of Savoy. The French,
whose powers clearly refer to offers already made (at Marcoing and
Lille), had authority to confer about the means of obtaining a
peace, to come to an agreement, and to negotiate marriages 'for our
children and relations [Savoy]'.[67] The English powers, for peace
with France and with Scotland, have survived, as granted by Queen
Elizabeth, but not the initial powers from Queen Mary.[68] The
Spanish had with them the royal secretary Josse de Courteville, a
Fleming who had long served Charles V and his son. He sat behind
the ambassadors at the deliberations, since he was not one of them.
In the same position was the Bishop of Limoges, Sebastion de
Laubespine (brother of secretary Claude), known as Bassefontaine,
since he was Abbot of that Premonstratensian house near Bar-sur-
Aube. He travelled, on occasion, to see King Henri and returned
with information needed.[69] The embassies were in great need of
'documents'; this was particularly true of the English. Ely wrote
from Dunkirk anxiously asking for copies of treaties with France of
the later years of Henry VIII and Edward VI, which his own
collection lacked. Wotton found that the papers sent to him included
only one whole treaty; the remainder were simply extracts. The
French had an analysis of recent treaties made; the Spanish may
have done likewise, but no doubt found it convenient that their
records on Navarre were in the archives in Spain and thus out of
reach.[70]

Early negotiations

How did the negotiations proceed? The French and Spanish were
already forward in discussions and proposals after the earlier meetings at Marcoing and Lille. The English presented the main
problem, they insisted on the restoration of Calais, lost in the war
begun in support of Spain, and also on payment of 'arrears' owed

---

[66] Granvelle v, 234, 262, 281; Emm. Phil., pp. 41–2; *Cal. For.* i, 398–9. Arundel
and Ely left on 2 October to see King Philip (*Cal. For.* i, 396, 400–1).

[67] *Traicté*, pp. 160–5.

[68] T. Rymer, *Foedera, conventiones, litterae* ... (London 1713) xv, 510–11, 515–16
(powers dated 20 January 1559).

[69] *Cal. For.* i, 97.

[70] *Cal. For.* i, 398–9; Decrue, op. cit., pp. 214–15; *Traité*, p. 65.

by France (two million écus, they reckoned, made up of arrears of
the French 'pension' and debts contracted by François I). The
Spanish were committed to the support of England, their King's
ally and consort, and to securing England's inclusion in any treaty.
The French would have preferred direct and separate negotiations
with England, or, as second best, the exclusion of the English from
continual presence at the negotiating table.[71] Henri II saw his
opportunity for direct talks when Queen Mary's death removed the
personal bond between England and Spain, but he was not able to
'sink' the Cercamp/Le Cateau negotiations. Savoy and Navarre
added still further strains to the negotiating process, which already
covered the whole area of Hapsburg–Valois conflict. The agreement
at Lille, to limit discussions to events of the last twenty-five years,
allowed reference to the French conquest of Savoy (1536). It did
not prevent reference further back in time, for instance French
invocation of the treaties of Madrid (1526) and Cambrai (1529).
There was, therefore, endless opportunity for bargaining, for
switching the essential demand from one item to another . . . Calais,
Corsica, Piedmont. Or one could refuse settlement on one item
unless another were linked with it (Piedmont and Milan, for
instance). Marriage alliances could paper over the cracks; Lorraine
said that all could be settled this way, but the Spanish feared that
the French 'enveloped' their claims (to Milan, for instance) in such
proposals; dowries, and settlement of lands on the future children
of a marriage, were the very stuff of such agreements.[72]

At Lille in September the French declared that the time was good
for negotiation, since things were 'in balance' between France and
Spain. There was much in this argument. At Cercamp the French
were adamant that there should be equivalent restitution of 'places
patrimoniales'.[73] They would have preferred that nothing be
reduced to writing until all was agreed, not seeing this as incompat-
ible with their demand that nothing be done until Calais was
settled.[74] On the other side, the Spanish refused to go ahead without
the English; they also insisted on full restitutions of conquests in
the recent wars.[75]

---

[71] Granvelle v, 221, 131; Emm. Phil., p. 43.
[72] Granvelle v, 243, 324, 360; *Traicté*, p. 5.
[73] Granvelle v, 271; *Traicté*, p. 4.
[74] Granvelle v, 271; *Traicté*, p. 30.
[75] At Lille, already (Granvelle v, 282).

It is clear that the English were in isolation. Their case and their proposals were normally put by the Spanish. The main pattern of negotiation therefore consisted of Franco–Spanish discussions, formally before the Duchess, informally in private interchange. Between 15 and 31 October when negotiations were suspended, the French and Spanish met before the Duchess in fourteen formal sessions; only one of these included the English. There were at least eight informal meetings of French and Spanish. Before the English arrived the Cardinal of Lorraine gave supper to the Duchess and the Spanish.[76] At least five separate meetings of Spanish and English are recorded. The French had no recorded meeting with the English save the one just mentioned, and a morning's session in Granvelle's room, as witnesses of the English recital of their treaties with France. English and French appear to have made no effort at informal encounters, as they did at Le Cateau, when Howard replaced Arundel and the pace of negotiation quickened. Before the recess of 1 to 6 November, French proposals had been sent to England; some of the ambassadors then left Cercamp. In the following sessions, from 7 November to 2 December, there were seven recorded Franco–Spanish meetings plus, inevitably, some informal encounters. The English, who had visited King Philip, were now without Arundel. At Cercamp they kept to their quarters, even celebrating mass there.[77] They anxiously awaited news of the Queen and avoided questioning. She died on 17 November. Another, longer, recess was agreed from 2 December. The English Queen's death left her ambassadors 'powerless', although new authority was on its way.[78]

Calais

Calais was the main stumbling block throughout these negotiations, 'le principal nœud et difficulté de tout ce négoce'. Both sides were entrenched in their position that it was theirs by right, and while the French revealed that the Spanish laughed at these disputes,[79] they could refer to their cause as 'cette noble querelle'.[80] The

---

[76] Granvelle v, 280.
[77] *Traicté*, p. 75.
[78] Granvelle v, 443.
[79] *Traicté*, p. 38, 43.
[80] 'Querelle' is used in the lawyer's sense of a claim or cause.

English, who were literally weighed down with evidence, invoked the treaty of Brétigny of 1360, in which King Jean II of France renounced all right to Calais, in return for English renunciations of claims in France; to Normandy, Touraine, Anjou and Maine. They then invoked their right by prescription, for 198 years; in fact, as they also mentioned, they had been in possession for 210 years, since 1347. They also contended that Calais had been confirmed to them, by implication, in treaties made by Henry VIII with France in 1527 and 1546, and by Edward VI. They referred to the town as 'this jewel', although one councillor (Sir John Mason) and perhaps others, thought that it might have to be surrendered.[81] Bishop Thirlby spoke at length at the solemn meeting of 24 October, before the Duchess.[82] The French case was that Calais was the King's 'yours and of your crown', part of the ancient patrimony of the crown. The treaty of Brétigny, they said, was invalid, since it was made by King Jean when a prisoner in England, and some provisions (on the renunciations) had never been fulfilled, were linked to the terms of his release, and thus annulled by his death. He had died after returning to England, as a prisoner in French eyes, as a free man in English. Any recent Anglo–French treaties were irrelevant, since England had broken them by entering the war on the side of Spain. The English referred to their 'reserved' rights in such circumstances. In French argument, there was no right of prescription between princes who had no 'superiors', since there was no competent judge between them. Calais was theirs and should remain so.[83]

Many home truths come out in the discussion. The French spoke of the wisdom of Providence which had put the sea between England and France; they would never let the enemy into the realm again, for peace was easier to make when they were not such near neighbours as they would be if the English had something on this side of the sea. The English reported 'vain words and stiff affirmations' from the French. Gloomily, at Lille, Wotton had foreseen great trouble; he thought that the Spanish only wished the English to be

[81] *Cal. For.* II, 6–7.

[82] Ibid. I, 402–3; Granvelle V, 299, 307–9. The English were not, at this stage, basing their claim on right of war (*Cal. Span.* XIII, 453).

[83] Granvelle V, 312, 354; *Cal. For.* I, 402–3; *Traicté*, pp. 40–5. The Spanish accepted the 'reservations' under the treaty of 1544, and the two later treaties (Granvelle V, 354). Charles V had sent a herald to the French King, forbidding the taking of Calais, during the Boulogne campaign of 1544.

present at negotiations when they realised that Calais would be
lost, and to avoid the blame falling on themselves. He could not
sleep for worry, as Themistocles was kept awake by thoughts of
Miltiades' trophies from Marathon. It was now or never if Calais
was to be regained.[84] At Cercamp, the English insisted on rehearsing
all the evidence for their case; a full morning's session, assembling
at 8 a.m. in Granvelle's room, in the presence of the two French
bishops and de Laubespine, was given to reading out all the relevant
articles of treaties with the French. The English had brought 'leur
traictez et un monde de papiers et tiltres'.[85]

Spain's view was that there was no possibility of proceeding
without satisfying the English, however difficult they might prove.
The Spanish thought, privately, that Calais had been so 'carelessly'
lost ('tan mal perdida').[86] King Philip stated that the loss was
England's fault, for he had warned of imminent attack and had
offered reinforcements; Spanish plans to retake the town had been
prevented through lack of money. The Spanish, at Cercamp, tried
every means to solve the dispute, for the French would not proceed
until it was settled. The English case was good, 'more solid', in
Spanish eyes; the French complained that Granvelle was helping
the English very much. The Spanish several times asked for private
talks with the French; after mass one day, for instance, or walking
after one of the meetings, the Constable with Alva, Lorraine with
the other three, or Alva with Montmorency on another occasion.
The Spanish hoped for some unofficial break-through 'en devises
familières'. War seemed the only outcome if discussions failed; the
Spanish also feared separate Anglo–French talks. They saw themselves as mediators in the process, committed to the English, and
putting their case to the Duchess and the French, except for the
three-party meeting on 24 October. Hard work went on behind the
scenes; Granvelle got secretary Courtewille to spell out, for the
King, the reasons, from Spain's point of view, for England's

[84] *Cal. For.* I, 394–6; *Rel. Pol.*I, 245–9. The reference is to Valerius Maximus (VIII. 14 ext. 1). Wotton feared that Spanish fortification at Gravelines (on their frontier with the Calais pale) indicated their assumption that Calais would remain French.
[85] *Traicté*, p. 40; *Cal. For.* I, 404; Granvelle v, 307. The English wanted this session to be a full assembly, which Granvelle prevented (*Traicté*, pp. 43, 45–6).
[86] Cf. D. M. Loades, op. cit., pp. 375–6. The information of spies had assisted Guise's campaign (above, p. 133). In December 1557 Secretary de Laubespine reported that every page at court knew that an attack was imminent (letter of 28 December, cited in Sutherland, op. cit., p. 88). The English had, of course, no ambassador resident during the war.

regaining Calais, based on information from local inhabitants and captains.[87]

Ingenious solutions became the order of the day. King Philip suggested that Calais be the dowry for the proposed marriage of Don Carlos and the daughter of Henri II;[88] Granvelle jibbed at this, it would simply imply acceptance of the French claim. In any case, the French did not respond, even when any other dowry was waived. The Duke of Alva, whom King Philip designated as the specialist on Calais among the ambassadors, suggested, as a private person, that the matter be referred to arbitration, perhaps to the Pope, or to the Emperor, or to the imperial Electors, or to Venice? King Philip should hold Calais meanwhile. The French refused: no judge would be agreeable to both sides, and they had definite reservations about the Emperor's neutrality. They would not refuse arbitration if really neutral judges could be found; perhaps they could keep Calais meanwhile (Lorraine's suggestion)?[89] The Spanish feared that Guise ambition, and the activity of young men at the French court in search of 'trouble', was behind French intransigence. Granvelle had little confidence in the Duchess of Lorraine's power to influence her Guise relations. The Duke of Guise, who was the victor of Calais, was the leader of the war party in France; he also had a personal interest in Calais. Lorraine admitted at Cercamp that Calais concerned Guise honour as well as the King's. The Duke and the Cardinal had been given a house there, which was gilded with the Guise coat of arms and had been registered as theirs by the Parlement of Paris. The Spanish felt that honour, rather than reason, prevailed with the French; they hoped that the Constable, known to favour peace, might intervene with the King, but at this stage he feared to be sent on such a mission. The French ambassadors were adamant: the King would never give away on Calais; any other expedient for peace would be acceptable. They

---

[87] Granvelle v, 271, 277, 303–5, 319–20, 323, 331, 339–40, 474; *Traicté*, pp. 43, 45–6, 48; *Cal. Span.* XIII, 440. For King Philip's part, cf. S. R. Gammon, *Statesman and Schemer, William, First Lord Paget, Tudor Minister* (London 1973) pp. 241–2.

[88] Montmorency was suggesting this to the Duke of Savoy at the end of October, i.e. after King Philip's suggestion (Emm. Phil., p. 45).

[89] Granvelle v, 289, 311–17, 321, 347; *Cal. Span.* XIII, 440; *Traicté*, p. 48. In September the Duke of Savoy had drawn up his own plan for Calais, but we have no details. In November, he records that Alva suggested the division of the Calais territory between England and France (a later English proposal, cf. below, p. 189), but that this was refused by the Duke of Guise. There is no corroborating evidence of this incident (Emm. Phil., pp. 37, 46).

referred to the King during the discussions.[90] When Mary Tudor's death was known, there was a strong temptation for the French King to barter recognition of Queen Elizabeth for her 'surrender' of Calais.

The English coupled their demand for Calais with that for two million écus, the sum they reckoned to be owing from France under previous treaties and as a result of loans to François I. They had been promised this sum in 1525 by the treaty of The More, compounding old debts, and in return for helping to secure the release of François I from prison in Madrid. In 1546, in the treaty of Ardres, they were promised the same sum for the cession of Boulogne, although in fact Edward VI's government finally accepted 400,000 écus. The French argued that all these debts were cancelled by acts of war, by Edward VI and Queen Mary: the English rejoined that the Scots had started the war in King Edward's time, and that Queen Mary had lawfully been enabled to support Spain, despite treaties with France. The English also hoped for renewal of the pension paid by France to the King of England intermittently since the treaty of Picquigny in 1475, in 'compensation' for English renunciation of ancient claims to the Crown of France. This, again, was repudiated by the French.[91]

There was, therefore, stone-walling on both sides. When the English were told of French intransigence, they feared for their lives. Arundel stated that he would not be the negotiator of the loss of Calais, for he feared the hatred of the English people and judged that neither the Queen nor her Council could consent unless they had express mandate from Parliament.[92] The Bishop of Ely said that the ambassadors would be stoned on their return to England; he would rather go home in his shroud than agree.[93] The only solution was urgent reference home; the ambassadors would have

[90] Granvelle v, 320, 323–5, 331, 348. The Spanish argued that the Constable desired peace, as an old man, a prisoner, and to firmly establish his family (ibid., v, 375–6.)

[91] Granvelle v, 312–15; *Cal. For.* i, 403, ii, 10. The best treatment of the 'pension' is in F. C. Dietz, *English Government Finance 1485–1558* (Urbana, Ill. 1921). Cf. also J. G. Russell, *The Field of Cloth of Gold* . . . (London 1969) pp. 89–90.

[92] On 4 and 8 November the English Council decided that their ambassadors should remain at Cercamp, while the matter of Calais was referred to Parliament (cf. below, p. 189n74).

[93] Granvelle v, 319, 329, 331. The fears were well grounded. On the eve of her accession Queen Elizabeth told Feria that she would have the ambassadors beheaded if they made peace without Calais ('The Count of Feria's dispatch to Philip II of 14 November 1558', ed. and trans. by M. J. Rodriguez-Salgado and Simon Adams, *Camden Miscellany* xxviii (London 1984) p. 333).

liked to return personally, but the King of Spain did not wish it. Instead, his trusted ambassador the Count of Feria (Don Gómez Suárez de Figuerosa), who had been in England earlier in the year, returned to explain matters. The 'hardness' of the French was to be stressed by him, and, most important, by the ambassadors themselves in their reports. Feria might take with him a copy of the Spanish ambassadors' reports to the King, which had been shown to Ely. King Philip was aware that the English had lost Calais during a war which they had entered in his support. However, both he and Granvelle stressed that English entry into the war was a treaty obligation (under the treaties of 1543 and 1546); it must never be admitted that the English had taken up arms 'to please the King'. He and his ambassadors knew, however, that he could not, without shame, treat with the French unless the latter restored Calais. They knew also that Calais, in French hands, was a threat to the Netherlands, compounded by French power over Scotland. The King could not break the English alliance ('cette société'), but his Council thought Calais a useful tool with the English. Some (Feria, Francheville, and Antonio de Toledo, Alva's relative) did not think Calais was worth the losing of the peace. Granvelle wrote gloomily that perhaps French obstinacy was a punishment for Spanish sins. As a diplomat, he felt they had been too slow, too accommodating and too irresolute, despite their resolutions to speak bluntly ('que l'on parlast sec avec les Francois'), and this had made the French more insolent and difficult. Perhaps the English would become weary of war and counsel peace, while winter might worsen the French position and bring them round.[94]

In the meantime, negotiations were suspended. The French wanted to return home, leaving some representative behind; the Spanish wondered whether negotiations should not be broken off entirely. In fact the French secured six days' recess. The English visited King Philip during the recess,[95] while Montmorency, S.

[94] *Cal. For.* I, 403–5; Granvelle v, 315–16, 321–5, 344, 346, 350–1; *Cal. Span.* XIII, 437, 440; ibid., XIV, 4, 13–16; Emm. Phil., pp. 44–6, 49. For discussion of England's obligations under these treaties, cf. R. B. Wernham, *Before the Armada* (London 1966) pp. 152–3, 161; D. M. Loades, *Mary Tudor*, pp. 122, 241, 368.
[95] Granvelle v, 325, 344, 348, 356, 358. The English left for Arras on 31 October. They visited the King, who instructed Ely to return to Cercamp, Wotton to remain at Arras. Arundel returned to England, on hearing of Mary Tudor's death, but first he met the special ambassador from England, Lord Cobham (Henry Brooke). The English also met Feria, before he left for England. Arundel did not cross until 6 December; during the stormy voyage he wept like a child, so that his tears 'floated the ship to port' (*Cal. Span.* XIV, 7).

André and Lorraine had long consultations with their King at Beauvais. Montmorency, the confidant and favourite, had his bed in the King's 'wardrobe'.[96] Alva reported to King Philip; according to a Venetian report, he had prevented a complete rupture which would shame the diplomats before the world. He had counselled a reference to the two kings (in fact he acted on King Philip's personal instructions on this).[97] Granvelle and Ruy Gómez meanwhile kept their feet on the ball ('tiendrons pied à boule'), while the Duchess of Lorraine left to see her daughters.[98] An extension of the truce protected the peace.

Savoy

Calais had not been the sole object of debate, though it was the dominant one. Franco–Spanish discussions began before the English arrived, and, after the recess, continued from 7 November to 2 December (seven meetings). The first problem, almost solved at Cercamp, was that of Savoy,[99] already discussed at Marcoing and Lille. The exiled Duke, Emmanuel Philibert, Captain General of King Philip's army and victor of S. Quentin, had inherited only Aosta, Nice, Cuneo and Vercelli (which served as his capital) from his father, Charles III, in 1553. Promises of restitution had been made by François I on his death bed, but negotiations between Henri II and Charles V, including the offer of a French marriage for the Duke, proved abortive.[100] At Lille the French had made clear that they wished to hold on to Piedmont at all costs, unless they regained Milan (a most unlikely event). They would give compensation for the province, would give back Savoy itself and Bresse, and offered a marriage alliance with a daughter of Henri II. The Spanish, speaking for their King and for the Duke, rejected any compensation for Piedmont; they feared that, in any case, it would be deferred until the marriage, or even until children were

---

[96] *Traicté*, p. 52; *Cal. Ven.* VI, 1540–1.

[97] *Cal. Ven.* VI, 1541; Emm. Phil., p. 45.

[98] Granvelle V, 353.

[99] By 'Savoy' is meant the Duke's dominions as a whole: the Duchy of Savoy, the County of Bresse, and the Principality of Piedmont being the main territories.

[100] Emm. Phil., p. 7. Charles III was brother-in-law of the Emperor Charles V (they both married Portuguese princesses), and uncle, by marriage, of François I. His son, born in 1528, joined the imperial court in 1545, was given a pension, and became a Knight of the Golden Fleece (1546). He was always in financial straits.

born. The French switched from a marriage alliance with the King's daughter to one with his sister, Marguerite, S. André hinting privately to Ruy Gómez that if this were accepted, they would be more generous over Piedmont. Before going to Cercamp, Montmorency had attempted to persuade the Duke to the less prestigious match; it was also less favourable, since Marguerite was thirty-five, five years older than the Duke, and might not bear children.[101] On the Duke's demurring, Montmorency promised to work for the alliance with the King's daughter; it would be difficult, he said, but he promised 'marvels'.[102]

In the early days at Cercamp, the French offered to restore only a part of Piedmont, perhaps only Savigliano and Carignon. They brought out their map and measured out what their King wanted, looking at the map again and again,[103] while Alva and Granvelle pretended not to follow. Alva was, in fact, an expert on Piedmont. An agreement was drawn up by 17 October and a draft marriage contract. The French, however, insisted on the King's sister, Marguerite, being the bride; a royal daughter was not on offer;[104] Alva reported that terms on Piedmont would be more generous if the sister was accepted. The French would not then insist on retaining twelve or ten places. On 22 October Alva visited King Philip and the Duke of Savoy with the terms; the Duke agreed to the retention of four or three places, according as to whether the French King's daughter or sister were offered. The towns were, however, not to include all the territory surrounding them. The matter remained unresolved at Cercamp, the French sticking to a demand for six towns plus Villanova d'Asti. On 24 November King Philip's Council decided that they would not demur over Villanova d'Asti, since there was no money to continue fighting; it would be better to break off over Calais than over Piedmont, for in this way

---

[101] For Marguerite, cf. below, pp. 205, 222–3.

[102] Emm. Phil., pp. 37, 40; *Traicté*, pp. 2–5, 4–8; *Cal. Span.* XIII, 450–2; Granvelle V, 196.

[103] The French were 'map-minded' by the time of the Italian wars (cf. C. T. Allmand, ed., *War, literature and politics in the late middle ages* (Liverpool 1976), p. 112). In 1552, when Metz was taken, they had a map of the course of the Rhine (du trait du Rhin) (H. Noel Williams, *The Brood of False Lorraine* (London n.d.) I, 129.

[104] Marguerite de France (born in June 1523) had been suggested as a bride for Henry VIII and for the Emperor himself. In 1553 she had refused the Duke (W. Stephens, *Margaret of France, Duchess of Savoy* (London 1912) p. 166). Ronsard gives Montmorency the credit for negotiating the marriage (Ronsard IX, 123).

they could alienate England from France and have a lever to urge England to renew the war.[105]

The whole issue was of deep concern to the Spanish. They feared French designs on Italy, for to let them keep Piedmont gave them a springboard for Milan, which they had renounced under the treaties of Madrid (1526) and Cambrai (1529). Indeed Milanese designs had probably been behind the French seizure of Savoy in 1536. The French at Cercamp quizzically denied that the Duke of Savoy needed fortresses; had they been reading Machiavelli, whom Montmorency revered?[106] They contended that they were making restitution, as of grace, and not by absolute will, for their King (through his grandmother, Louise of Savoy) had claims to Savoy. The Spanish countered that the French could, by keeping Piedmont, drive the Duke out of Savoy and Bresse in three days; he would only be able to get to Vercelli or Asti by their permission.[107] At all costs, the Spanish wished to keep the French out of Italy. They made much of the argument that mountains were natural frontiers, and that holding provinces beyond them was perilous and uncertain. This the French disputed, as well they might, given their ambitions in Italy and Navarre. The general conclusion of the Spanish was that either the French wished for Piedmont for their own defence, which the 'frontier' argument invalidated, or they wished for it because they had some new design on Italy. They probably wished to stir up Italy again ('remuer l'Italie'). The French mocked at this old Spanish song ('leur chanson accoustumée'). There was much historical argument, the French referring to the ancient Angevin claim to Piedmont; in fact it had been ceded by the Angevins to Savoy in 1382. The practicalities of war were not forgotten; the Spanish noted that Ivrea (which the French wished to keep) guarded the pass to Aosta. The French thought that the Spanish needed Piedmont and Montferrat to nourish their men-at-arms, and as an outlet for Milan.[108] In fact Savoy was essential to Spain's lines of communication with the north.[109]

---

[105] Emm. Phil., pp. 43–7; *Traicté*, pp. 27–38, 53; Granvelle v, 246–7, 272–3 (articles of agreement offered to the French, and the Duke of Savoy's terms), 277–8. In mid-November, the Duke sent the Count of Stroppiano to Cercamp to negotiate the marriage.

[106] Machiavelli, *The Prince*, Book i, xx.

[107] *Traicté*, pp. 55–6; Granvelle v, 244–6, 268–70, 292–3.

[108] Granvelle v, 244–6, 268–70, 292–3; *Traicté*, pp. 27–8, 33, 61.

[109] See below, p. 215.

Corsica

Calais and Savoy were stumbling blocks; Corsica became another, since the French did not succeed in excluding it as they had intended at Lille. The French invasion of the island in 1553, with the help of a Turkish fleet, had been welcomed by the Corsican patriot Sampiero Corso, a veteran of the French army in Italy. The Genoese, who had held the island since 1453, and had been involved in its history since the eleventh century, were not completely driven out. Corsica in French hands was a threat to King Philip's position in Italy and in the Mediterranean.[110] It might serve as a springboard for Italy, and, under stress, the Spanish brought forward ancient Aragonese claims to the island dating from a grant of Pope Boniface VIII. The French persisted; King Philip should support them and not the Genoese. At first they would grant nothing until Calais was 'settled', then they made Corsica their sticking point and would not proceed to other problems. By the end of November, the Spanish reported that the French wished everything to hang on Corsica. They themselves were adamant; Milan could not survive without Genoa, and Genoa depended on Corsica.[111]

Other Italian problems

The dispute over the Marquisate of Saluzzo was left to 'justice'; sovereignty was claimed by the Emperor, and by the Duke of Savoy as his vicar, but the French (the occupying power) had incorporated it in Dauphiné.[112] Montferrat was to be restored by the French to the Duke of Mantua, whose father had acquired it by marriage in 1536.[113] The French were to withdraw from any places they still held in Tuscany, and in particular from the *contado* of Siena. Siena had been taken by Florentine and imperialist troops in 1555 and formally ceded to Duke Cosimo by King Philip in 1557, as the price

[110] Cf. Pierson, op. cit., p. 31.

[111] *Traicté*, pp. 4–5, 29–34, 39–41, 62, 63, 69–72; Granvelle v, 293–4, 361–3. The Duchess of Lorraine was upset by the French attitude (*Traicté*, p. 63). Henri II's Council discussed Corsica in November and their instructions to the ambassadors. A Corsican representative met the King (*Cal. Ven.* vi, 1543).

[112] Granvelle v, 270; Sutherland, op. cit., pp. 128–30; Ruble, p. 56 (a treaty of 1562 incorporated it in Piedmont).

[113] Article 19 of the 1559 treaty (below, Appendix A); Ruble, pp. 62–3; Granvelle, v, 221. Casale was also restored to the Duke.

of his alliance.[114] The whole discussion on Italy and Savoy led the French to protest that Spain was doing nothing for France's allies (Navarre), but everything for her own (Genoa and Savoy). Discussions sometimes went on until late, once until 8 p.m., so that the French remarked that they were learning to sup 'Spanish style'. There were also private meetings, in the chapel, in the cloisters, and in the ambassadors' quarters.[115]

Problems in the north

Discussions on the restitutions in the north ambled along. In September the French had already protested that the Spanish required restitution of all their conquests in the recent wars, in return for three places in Vermandois (S. Quentin, Ham and Le Catelet were in that ancient county, the first two fortresses on the Somme, the third on the Scheldt). Agreement on these restitutions had probably been reached by the end of October, when King Philip informed the English that the two sides were 'well near agreed upon the whole . . .' The Spanish offered these three fortresses plus Thérouanne, a French enclave in Artois, known as the King's pillow, which the imperialists had seized and razed to the ground in 1553.[116] On the French side, restitution was to be made of Mariembourg, a fortress near the French frontier, built by Charles V and named after Mary of Hungary. There was also to be restitution of Yvoir, on the Bocq, near Dinant, and of the great and ancient fortress of Bouillon on the Semois. In Luxembourg, Thionville, guardian fortress of the province, was to be restored; it had been taken by the French in that very year. There was also to be restitution of Montmédy and Damvillers (on the Meuse), both near the frontier. There was eventual agreement that, since Thérouanne had been razed by the imperialists, Yvoir should be dismantled before

---

[114] Siena, garrisoned by French troops under Blaise de Monluc, had been attacked in 1554, the province devastated, and the town taken (April 1555); the French left, and most of the inhabitants sought refuge in Montalcino. The King, however, retained the Tuscan fortresses or *praesidi* of the Maremme (see Appendix C, p. 253). These arrangements were implicitly, but not explicitly, confirmed by the treaty of 1559 (cf. Ruble, pp. 59–61). The Sienese from Montalcino appealed again for independence from Florentine rule, at the French court in June 1559 (*Cal. For.* II, 303; cf. above, p. 147).

[115] *Traicté*, pp. 56–7, 61–3, 64–7, 68, 74–7.

[116] The Duke of Savoy had taken a lead in this conquest (cf. Ronsard IX, 163).

being handed over.[117] The Spanish had insisted on full restitutions; they pointed out that with S. Quentin and Ham in their possession, the French could well, and with advantage, re-open the war. They themselves were to keep Hesdin, in Artois, part of the ancient patrimony of the Dukes of Burgundy, its castle their 'pleasure palace'. Charles V had destroyed the town in 1553 and built a new Hesdin, at great expense, it was said. The County of Charolais, ancient patrimony of Burgundy, was to be restored, but under French suzerainty.[118]

In November the case of Navarre was heard.[119] Antoine de Bourbon, Duke of Vendôme, had married the d'Albret heiress to the kingdom, Queen Jeanne. He sent to the conference the Bishop of Mende, Nicolas Dangu, and Jean Mesmes, Seigneur de Roissy. His Queen wrote to the King of France and to Montmorency, asking for help. At Cercamp, the case was merely 'noted'. Alva had been told by Lorraine that the French could not avoid speaking of Navarre, but would not persist. The plan was to leave it to 'justice', a euphemism for indefinite postponement. Spain insisted that the case be heard. The Seigneur de Roissy made a long speech on 12 November, rehearsing the whole history of Navarre from the time of King Thiebaut, whose grand-daughter Jeanne had married King Philippe IV of France. An unbroken succession was traced down to the present Queen. Invasion by Spain in 1512 was the capital crime in the story; since then, the 'Spanish' part of Navarre had never been regained. The Spanish indicated that they could not discuss Navarre; they had not been instructed on this, and had no papers with them; the documents were in the archives in Spain. The French preserved the full text of de Roissy's speech, their

---

[117] Granvelle v, 180, 220–1, 272, 277; *Traicté*, p. 2; *Cal. For.* i, 405; *Cal. Span.* XIII, 452 (a report that all was already settled, by 15 October). Thérouanne, seat of an ancient diocese, provoked dispute since the Spanish did not accept French suzerainty over the ruined Benedictine abbey of S. Jean-au-Mont, north-west of the town. The treaty (articles 12 and 13) provided for the division of the diocese (below, pp. 201–2). No services had been held in the ruins of Thérouanne.

[118] Granvelle v, 271–2; articles 15 and 19 of the treaty.

[119] The ancient kingdom bestraddled the Pyrenees; in 1484 the heiress of Navvare, Foix and Béarn married into the d'Albret family. Her son, Henri II, was, however, only titular King of Navarre (1517) since in 1512 Ferdinand of Spain had invaded Spanish Navarre and in 1515 annexed it to the Kingdom of Castile. The d'Albret and then the Bourbons ruled their remaining lands from Pau, in the ancient Viscounty of Béarn.

only tribute. Meanwhile the hapless King approached the German Electors and led an abortive expedition across the Pyrenees.[120]

The marriage alliances

At this stage in the negotiations the Spanish wished to break off; the French sent the Bishop of Limoges to King Henri, who returned on 16 November with firm instructions, so that the ambassadors were very 'enlightened' and 'well instructed'. By 18 November some general articles of agreement (including provision for Thérouanne) were considered by King Philip's Council. The basis was the marriage of Don Carlos and Élisabeth de France, once promised to Edward VI and now thirteen. As far back as 1555, when England tried to mediate, ambassador Paget had proposed two marriage alliances to solve the two problems of French claims to Milan and the restitution of Savoy.[121] Such marriages had been discussed at Marcoing and Lille, and the ambassadors at Cercamp, both French and Spanish, had powers to conclude. The royal marriage was immediately 'on the table'. On arrival, after supper, the Constable had drawn aside a gentleman of Artois to tell him that King Henri wished for perpetual peace and would be bound by marriage alliances, from which one might hope for children; such alliances were the way to make friendship indissoluble. On 15 October (the first formal meeting) Lorraine had declared that marriages would solve everything (the problem of restitutions) and asked what dowry the Spanish wanted? A sum of 400,000 écus was agreed. A scheme to make Calais the dowry was, as has been stated, ruled out. Endowments for the marriage and for the expected children made for hard bargaining. By 7 November the Spanish feared that the French would 'envelop' their ancient claims in marriage settlements (the claims to Milan and Asti in particular).[122] The problems were not finally resolved at Cercamp, but at the French court. King Philip's Lord in Waiting inquired the height of the Princess. The

---

[120] Granvelle v, 261, 332–8; *Traicté*, pp. 63–6, 172–91 (text of the speech); J. Dumont, *Corps universel diplomatique du droit des gens* v, 23–7; letters of the Queen of Navarre in A. de Ruble, *Antoine de Bourbon et Jeanne d'Albret* (Paris 1881–6) I, 419–20. The King of Navarre was most deeply offended at not being included in the peace (Throckmorton's report, June 1559, in *Cal. For.* II, 309). King Philip continued to use the title King of Navarre.

[121] Gammon, op. cit., pp. 219–20.

[122] *Traicté*, pp. 2–3, 68, 161–75; Granvelle v, 221, 235, 243, 360.

Queen had her measured with a golden chain, which she then presented to King Philip's jester, who was in the party.[123]

The recess

At Cercamp all still hung on news from England. Already on 8 November the royal Council wrote to the ambassadors that they feared the worst for the Queen. She died on 17 November; the Spanish court knew by 19 November, by letters from Antwerp (although the Queen was reported still alive on 22 November). At Cercamp there was only suspicion and rumour. According to Henri II, the French ambassadors knew of the event before the Spanish. They cross-questioned the Duchess and the Spanish in the cloisters on 25 November, being certain that King Philip had heard by then.[124] They also bearded the English as they came from mass, their first public mass for several weeks; the Spanish had seen an English courier arriving late the night before. Perhaps the English were the last to know. Arundel, in any case, had left for England by this time, and Wotton had returned from Arras, where a conciliar letter of 4 November had not been received until 18 November.[125]

This event gave good reason for a recess. The French had been anxious to leave since mid-November; they said they were wasting their time and getting no more light from the Spanish about matters 'on the table' ('les choses qui ont esté mises sur le bureau'). They thought the Spanish played a procrastinating game; Granvelle was indeed stalling, asserting the difficulties of communication with England across the high seas. On 26 November there was an informal meeting in the cloisters at which all the Spanish ('toute la troupe') were present. Old problems resurfaced; the French would not proceed even on Savoy until Calais was settled, but tried to push the Spanish to a separate treaty, omitting or only generally including the English. They contended that, since Queen Mary was dead, the English had no powers. The Spanish still prevaricated; even if the Queen were dead, which they did not admit, their

---

[123] *Cal. Ven.* VI, 1547.

[124] *Cal. For.* II, 2; Emm. Phil., pp. 46–7; *Cal. Ven.* VI, 1562; *Traicté*, p. 75; Granvelle V, 363. The French King is said to have heard through one of the Queen's physicians (*Cal. Span.* XIV, 13).

[125] *Traicté*, pp. 74–7; *Cal. For.* II, 4.

treaties with England (1543, 1546, 1553) were perpetual. The French retorted that the Spanish were slaves of the English, the Spanish that, equally, the English were theirs (the Spanish), in view of the treaties.[126] The French then suggested a two to four months' recess under truce; the Spanish offered six weeks, during which time each side would visit their King. On Sunday 27 November, the English heard that the French 'began to truss and would remove'. However, even a recess needed agreement from the kings, King Philip accepting six weeks, or at most two months, provided a place for reassembly had been fixed. There were storms even over the letters of prorogation. The Spanish insisted that the English position be mentioned as the cause. The French were infuriated, Lorraine protesting that he knew the form of treaties, even though young, and that such matters were never mentioned. Eventually the Spanish, who had drafted articles of prorogation, to gain the initiative, accepted a generally worded prorogation until 31 January. The English agreed. The French prisoners were allowed to visit France, Montmorency going first to see the Duke of Savoy about his ransom.[127]

The final departures were speedy. On 1 December Lorraine, already booted for the journey, compelled the Spanish to 'conclude' before King Philip's final letter arrived; they had his letter to Alva personally, however. The next day, before dawn, the King's letter arrived; the Constable was already booted and spurred, so the Spanish did not tell him of the King's stiff terms for his ransom, leaving it for direct negotiation. Montmorency rode off, and the Spanish reached Arras the same evening.[128] The English travelled to Arras the same day to meet Lord Cobham, special envoy to King Philip. He was instructed to inform the King of Queen Mary's death, to emphasise the new Queen's desire to continue the old alliances and to make known her instructions to her ambassadors (a firm stand on Calais and the arrears). They had a secret interview with the King at Groenendael, Granvelle being present. The secrecy

---

[126] *Traicté*, pp. 74–7; Granvelle v, 361–78; *Cal. For.* ii, 16–18; *Cal. Span.* xiii, 437. Elizabeth signed herself, in letters to Philip, 'Soror et perpetuo confederata' (*Cal. Span.* xiv, 15–16).

[127] Granvelle v, 369–78; *Cal. For.* ii, 17; *Rel. Pol.*i, 349. Privately, Henri II admitted that all was in suspense over Calais (letter to the Cardinal of Tournon, printed in Ruble, pp. 331–3).

[128] *Cal. For.* ii, 25–7; Granvelle v, 379–80, 384; Emm. Phil., p. 48.

was reputedly because the King's mourning clothes, for Queen Mary, were not ready.[129]

The diplomats were doubtless glad to leave Cercamp. Wotton, who had retired from the abbey to lodge in the village at the end of November, declared that he was never wearier of any place 'saving only of Rome after the sack'.[130] The place was insalubrious and lodgings were cramped. In October there had been incessant rain. Illnesses were frequent: Thirlby before even reaching Cercamp; Ruy Goméz (fever or malaria?); Arundel (rheum) and Orange, at the insalubrious abbey. Granvelle succumbed to 'catarrh' at Groenendael.[131] Such hazards added to the difficulties of the negotiators, whose 'briefs' made for conflict and procrastination. Both monarchs needed peace, but intended to buy it as cheaply as possible. Given this and the complicating dimension of English involvement, the diplomats may be judged agile and alert, but also suspicious and at times cantankerous.

Diplomatic tactics at Cercamp and Le Cateau[132]

What is known of the diplomats' manners and manoeuvres? The French and Spanish tried the usual starting gambit: to make the other side put as much as possible 'on the table', and to reveal as little as possible of one's own intentions. One must avoid, at all costs, any impression that one was desperate for settlement; even at Lille the French were reporting home that the Spanish thought them in such straits that they (the Spanish) could lay the law down. Lorraine complained that the Spanish expected the French to beg 'with joined hands', i.e. in prayer. He recalled the methods of the

---

[129] *Cal. For.* II, 10–11, 29–30. The English instructions (23 November) did not arrive until 1 December, and thus could not be used at Cercamp. Cobham was given a gold chain by the King (Granvelle advised one of 900–1,000 écus, or exceptionally, of 1,500–2,000 écus, in value). He was reputed a great supporter of the new Queen (Feria's view, *Cal. Span.* XIV, 4). The obsequies for Queen Mary were celebrated in Brussels on 22 December, attended by the Duke of Savoy, the Duke of Alva, other Knights of the Golden Fleece, the ambassadors of Mantua and Venice, Ely and Wotton (but not Cobham, whose clothes were not adequate, he considered) (*Cal. For.* II, 38–9). The service was presumably in S. Gudule, as that for the Emperor on 29 December (*Coll. des voyages*, p. 35).

[130] *Cal. For.* II, 27. Perhaps lodgings in the village were easier for secret communication with England? (cf. Granvelle V, 375).

[131] Granvelle V, 235–7, 262, 277, 382; *Traicté*, p. 73; *Cal. For.* I, 405.

[132] This section draws on examples from both the Cercamp and Le Cateau negotiations.

late Admiral d'Annebault: to get the other side to make offers first, and keep silent about one's own.[133] Granvelle's ideal was conditions where the proposals of the other side were known before negotiations began. King Philip recognised that the French might follow normal practice: not to offer at first what they might offer at the end.[134] His ambassadors strove to make the French speak out, and put things in writing; in the second they had very limited success, for the French did not wish to do this until all points were agreed. However, interim written agreements were drawn up, on Savoy, on general terms, and on the dowry question.[135]

Each side commented on the others' deceits, and their manner at the negotiating table. The Spanish constantly feared that they had been too weak, too slow, and too irresolute with the French; harsh words were the only solution, for kindness made the French more insolent and difficult. It might even make them retract offers already made, for they were 'selling dear'. Granvelle commented, towards the end of negotiations, that the French did nothing out of generosity, but only if one showed one's teeth. When they were gentle one could be sure that they were finessing ('qu'il nous veullent faire quelque finesse'). His final word, at Le Cateau, was that the French were not susceptible to reason; as everyone knew, it was better to hit them than to negotiate with them, they were 'plus baptables que traictables'. Nevertheless, the Spanish made efforts; once they spoke with finished, or smooth-flowing, eloquence 'ore rotundo'.[136]

The French held that they had met obstinacy, coldness and opinionated views. They spoke of the 'darkness' of the negotiations: 'de la lumière que nous verrons en ce negoce, qui est iusques icy aux tenebres.' The Spanish (including the Duchess of Lorraine) were so opinionated that they would 'scorch the tail' of the negotiations. One must speak more bluntly with them. Several times, the French refer to the 'farce' being enacted: the negotiations with the English played out before the Spanish spectators, in February; the Duchess of Lorraine's own efforts at peacemaking in March,

---

[133] *Traicté*, p. 3, Granvelle v, 188, 204, 222. Granvelle reported that the French refused to give the Spanish 'carte blanche' (ibid, v, 188).

[134] Emm. Phil., p. 35; Granvelle v, 173.

[135] Granvelle v, 219, 240, 272–3; Emm. Phil., p. 47.

[136] Granvelle v, 257, 276, 282, 344, 346, 350, 352–4, 357–8, 514, 530. The expression is from Horace's *Ars Poetica* 323 (for the difficulties over this expression, cf. C. O. Brink, *Horace On Poetry: the 'Ars Poetica'* (Cambridge 1971) p. 348).

which they were sure had been 'arranged' by the Spanish. They saw the latter dragging out negotiations for their own purposes. This sentiment was reciprocated, and was true in both cases.[137] The French could see through Spanish tricks, which they called 'herbs of St John'.[138] There was a certain mocking tone on both sides: the Spanish laughed at the Anglo–French disputes, they feared, however, that the French sometimes mocked them. Bitterness and coldness were, on occasion, forgotten in the more private exchanges; the Spanish noted that the 'hopeful' proposals came when they met the French individually. 20 October is a case in point. The Spanish despaired of agreement and already threatened to break off, but, meeting Lorraine at the Duchess' lodgings (she had just arrived), they found that the Cardinal spoke more softly and promised better things on the morrow. He gave supper to all the company that evening.[139]

As for the English, they strove to put their case well, but seem to have failed in the final analysis. In the New Year, Granvelle reported that they put a good case badly, while the French did the reverse. This recalls the English admission, long before, to Philippe de Commynes that they always lost in treaty-making with the French, but usually won in war.[140] In 1558, Ely and Wotton, able and experienced diplomats, with full university training, seem to have faltered. They were inhibited, no doubt, by the situation at home, and made fearful (as what diplomat might not have been?) on waking to service of a new and unknown queen, who might bring political and religious change. Wotton reported of the French that they had the old hatred printed in their hearts; they even called the English 'noz anciens ennemyz'. English feelings may have been similar. Added to this, the problem of reaching any agreement was itself intractable and complex. Granvelle reported on the 'labyrinth'

---

[137] *Traicté*, pp. 29, 33, 35, 39, 42, 72, 83, 112; Granvelle v, 501.

[138] *Traicté*, p. 106. The herb, dedicated to Diana, is *Artemisia vulgaris*, mugwort in English, erba di S. Giovanni in Italian, armoise commune in French. It was thought to have magical properties, for instance to induce clairvoyance, and was used on St John's Eve. (C. F. Leyel, *Herbal Delights* (London 1937) pp. 163–4). The sense seems to be that the Spanish were trying to deceive the French by using tricks. Cf. the English proverb, 'Herb John in the pot doth neither much good nor hurt', i.e. it is worthless (W. G. Smith, ed., *The Oxford Dictionary of English Proverbs* (Oxford 1960, 2nd. ed.) p. 292).

[139] Granvelle v, 191, 276, 279–81, 303 (the Spanish ask for a private meeting, hoping to get more out of the French that way).

[140] Philippe de Commynes, *Mémoires*, ed. J. Calmette (Paris 1924–5) I, 221.

of Anglo–French disputes, a term he also applied to King Philip's finances.[141]

---

[141] Granvelle v, 455–6, 459; *Cal. For.* II, 4.

The Peace of Cateau–Cambrésis: negotiations at Le Cateau, February–April 1559

Attempts to bypass the negotiations

Before the diplomats reassembled, there had been considerable bilateral activity, first between England and Spain. Feria, returning to London, thought residence in the royal palace of Whitehall would help him to influence Queen Elizabeth and her Council; his request was refused. His instructions were to dwell on the need for peace, the lurid prospects if it failed, and the problem of the Queen's marriage. When he could, he counselled her strongly against marriage to an Englishman, and tried to move the Council individually. There were proposals for Elizabeth's marriage to the Emperor's son, to a prince of Denmark, or even to the Duke of Savoy, but Elizabeth now mocked at the revival of this old proposal. Feria was certain that the Queen would 'fix her eyes' on King Philip himself. He asked the King whether, if the subject came up, he should carry it further or throw cold water on it? He found his mission unbearable: the English were 'confused and inept' in all their affairs; the Queen and her people felt free to accept any marriage proposals; the Queen was more feared than her sister and 'gives her orders and has her way as absolutely as her father did'.[1] In late November the French already suspected that Feria had been sent to make a match for King Philip; early in December their ambassador in Rome was instructed to advise the Pope to refuse the necessary

---

[1] *Cal. Span.* XIII, 438; XIV, 1–3, 7–8, 13, 25; *Rel. Pol.* I, 273, 305–6; Feria's despatch in *Camden Miscellany*, XXVIII, 335. Feria pointed out that Elizabeth could not now be disposed of as in 1554 (when the Savoy proposal was first made).

dispensation. In November the whole Spanish court was reported to know of Philip's intention; by January the Diet of Augsburg was gossiping about the matter, most thinking that Elizabeth would indeed marry the King.[2] The latter did not, however, officially instruct Feria until 10 January, his masterly letter mentioning Elizabeth's recent assurances of the 'brotherhood, friendship and perpetual alliance between us'.[3] The marriage would be difficult for him to accept in conscience; he did not intend to be in England much, Elizabeth had not been 'sound of religion', and the marriage would appear to be 'like entering on perpetual war with France'. Yet it would be of enormous importance to 'Christianity' and the preservation of 'religion' in England. Philip would, therefore, 'render this service to God, and offer to marry the Queen of England'. Of course, she would need papal absolution, for her aberrant ways, and papal dispensation, for the marriage.[4] The match was still being discussed in February when King Philip stressed that it could not take place unless the old religion were preserved; everything hung on this, Spanish fears and English 'waywardness' increasing. By March, the Queen, who had seen Feria several times, explained that she had no desire to marry; her friendship with the King would preserve their states just as well, and her people did not wish her to marry a foreigner.

A few days later she was on another tack: she could not marry King Philip because she was a heretic. By 23 March he had accepted the refusal. His ambassador warned that the Queen intended to hold her own in her kingdom, as her father had done; she was much influenced by 'these heretics and the devil that prompts them'.[5] The proposal dropped out of sight, perhaps because of the many reasons against it, and Philip's own lethargy. The Duke of Parma thought that the King never took any pains to marry Queen Elizabeth, but

---

[2] Ruble, p. 17; *Cal. Ven.* vi, 1549; *Cal. For.* ii, 65, 71; *Traicté*, pp. 75–6. In a letter of December, to the Cardinal of Tournon, Henri II mentioned the problem of Elizabeth's Protestantism (Ruble, p. 333).

[3] Lord Cobham's mission was to stress this alliance (above, p. 166). On 4 December King Philip reciprocated. Queen Elizabeth would be a faithful ally and even more, an affectionate sister; the King would be her most devoted brother (Granvelle v, 405–7.)

[4] *Cal. Span.* xiv, 21–3. Philip was adamant that the Netherlands should not descend to any children of the marriage.

[5] Ibid., pp. 22–4, 27–8, 33–4, 37, 40, 43; *Cal. Ven.* vii, 62. The Bishop of Aquila (Alvarez de Quadra) visited England and Le Cateau on this matter (*Cal. Ven.* vii, 51).

treated the affair very coldly, and neglected it in many ways.[6] Elizabeth saw herself as a 'free princess', unlike her sister, and not bound to Spain.[7]

Meanwhile the King of France had approached her. His daughter-in-law, Mary Queen of Scots, the Dauphine (great-grand-daughter of Henry VII), had assumed the title and arms of England on Queen Mary's death, since she held Elizabeth to be illegitimate. If France actively supported this claim, the whole realm of England could be thrown into turmoil. It seems that there was a plan to send a secretary of state to England, to urge these claims, but that the King eventually decided to send privately some message that, if Elizabeth desisted over Calais, and did not marry 'outside the realm', he would keep quiet about the Dauphine's claim. Lord Grey fulfilled this mission,[8] but by December the King had another scheme. The Florentine merchant, Guido Cavalcanti, brought up in England, in Cecil's confidence, but at this time in the employ of the King's cousin, François de Vendôme, Governor of Calais and Vidame of Chartres,[9] was sent to the Queen, with messages of his desire for peace.[10] Despite the war her sister had levied, in which France had suffered, the King did not seek vengeance; he remembered his friendship for the King, her father, and for her brother King Edward. Henri favoured separate peace negotiations (at Blaenay (Blangy en Ternoise?), Ambleteuse, S. Valéry-sur-Somme, Étaples, or any place the Queen might choose). Cavalcanti returned with Elizabeth's refusal of secret negotiations; secrecy would, in any case, be impossible, negotiations should be either bit by bit through

---

[6] *Cal. Ven.* VII, 63.

[7] *Cal. For.* II, 107 (her letter to Henri II).

[8] *Cal. Ven.* VII, 1561, 1564; *Cal. For.* II, 44–6; Forbes I, 4–7. Lord Grey was Captain of Guines and captured when it was taken, hence the Queen's reluctance to see him. The Duke of Guise, who seems to have engineered his mission, released him for the purpose (cf. Sutherland, op. cit., pp. 91–2).

[9] The Vidame (lay official of the Bishop) became a leader of the French Prot-estants; he had been to England in 1550 as hostage under the treaty of Boulogne, and had been much involved in Protestant intrigues in Queen Mary's reign. Guido Cavalcanti was the son of Giovanni, a merchant and also gentleman usher to Henry VIII, for whom he undertook financial transactions (cf. F. J. Levy, 'A semi-professional diplomat: Guido Cavalcanti and the marriage negotiations of 1571', *Bulletin of the Institute of Historical Research* XXXV, 1962, pp. 212–14. This article, on the Anjou marriage negotiations, perhaps exaggerates Cavalcanti's role in 1558–9).

[10] Cavalcanti had been sent (in early December 1558) by the Vidame, with letters for the Earl of Pembroke about the peace negotiations. The letters were to be shown to the Earl of Bedford and to Cecil, with whom the matter was said to originate (*Cal. For.* II, 20). Cavalcanti was then sent again by Henri II.

Cavalcanti or through the English ambassadors at the peace conference. Elizabeth stressed that it was England which had lost in the
war, a war undertaken by her sister against the wishes of her people,
and without consulting the Council.

The good news of Elizabeth's friendship was thought to have
made the King think there would be no difficulty over Calais.
Cavalcanti was back in England in late January, the King having
chosen to negotiate through him. Henri accepted that negotiations
through the ambassadors (due to reassemble at Le Cateau) could
never be secret; all actions there would be 'spied out by so many
sharp eyes' that communications could not escape detection.[11] Sharp
eyes were also watching in London. On 31 January Feria was
reporting to King Philip that the man who had been hiding in the
Treasurer's chambers in Whitehall was called Guido Cavalcanti.
Should some trick be played on him when he returned from
France?[12] The French at Le Cateau had news of the mission of an
Italian to England, brought by the Vidame of Chartres; the English
also knew of some secret negotiations. Cavalcanti was at the French
court again from 13 to 19 February, seeing the King and the Duke
of Guise. The King remarked that if rough words had been used
by the French at 'Cambrai' (Le Cateau), they were intended for the
'imperialists' and not the Queen. Elizabeth had sent her portrait,
insufficient, she feared, to equal the King's present to her. Cavalcanti reported that her physical resemblance to her father was
matched by her deeds.[13] The French King still hankered for negotiations away from Le Cateau, where he feared that Lord Howard,
Elizabeth's new ambassador, was harming progress. The King, who
was in communication with Montmorency, wished for an
Anglo–French meeting, perhaps at Boulogne. The Duke of Guise
was to be one of the deputies, a clear indication that he had a hand
in the scheme. Cavalcanti, delayed by some 'sudden accident', was
back in England in late February, bearing the same offers as were
made at Le Cateau on 12 February. He came back to see the
King at Villers-Cotterêts, in early March, but another envoy then

[11] *Cal. For.* ii, 51–2, 80–1, 94–5; *Cal. Ven.* vii, 11.
[12] *Cal. Span.* xiv, 36. Feria thought that Lord Howard's departure for Le Cateau
had been delayed on this account (cf. below, p. 176).
[13] *Traicté*, pp. 89–90; Granvelle v, 444; *Cal. For.* ii, 140–3. Feria said that the
Queen had received a portrait of King Henri; there is a Venetian report that the
King's present was a diamond worth 12,000 écus (*Cal. Span.* xiv, 33; *Cal. Ven.* vii,
32).

proceeded to Le Cateau, although Cavalcanti declared that Queen Elizabeth wished him to go. His mission then appears to have terminated.[14] Direct negotiations were still, however, being canvassed in late March, when the Vidame despatched the Cornish adventurer and diplomatic agent, Henry Killigrew of Pendennis, to the Queen with the message, from the King, that better terms might be obtained in this way.[15]

A change of scene: the diplomats reassemble

These attempts at direct negotiation by both France and Spain reveal how many wires were crossed, and how complex the whole process had become. The diplomats from the conference had been due to reassemble on 25 January, but not at Cercamp, whose uncomfortable, cramped and insalubrious conditions called for a change. Cambrai (an imperial city, and therefore 'neutral') had often been favoured, but was ruled out, allegedly because of the troops in the vicinity.[16] In the end Le Cateau, a small township in the Cambrésis, south-east of Cambrai, was chosen at the suggestion of the Duchess of Lorraine. It had been attacked and devastated by Marshal S. André in 1555, and had been burnt during the S. Quentin campaign. In 1559 the bishop's château, dating from the eleventh century and adjoining the town, was reported to be partly

[14] *Cal. For.* II, 80, 140–1, 151, 166, 171; *Cal. Span.* XIV, 46, 48 (for the offers, see below, p. 186). Cavalcanti declared himself much in Mr Cecil's debt. He returned to Calais when the negotiations collapsed. His services to Queen Elizabeth were recognised by an annuity of £100 (February 1560) (*Calendar of Patent Rolls, Elizabeth vol. I 1558–1560* (London 1939) p. 254.

[15] Killigrew, a passionate Protestant, was much involved in Protestant schemes in the reign of Queen Mary, had served in war under the Vidame of Chartres and may have fought (on the French side) at the battle of S. Quentin. His memoir, written in 1573, to obtain a Cornish manor from the Queen, makes much (probably too much) of his visit to France during the Le Cateau negotiations, and his journey there, with the Vidame, to urge his compatriots not to surrender Calais. He had, apparently, been gulled into the belief that, in direct negotiations, the town might be regained. He was detained at Le Cateau by the Constable, and again at Calais on the King's orders (perhaps because of the complicated proceedings at Le Cateau?). He proceeded to England in late March, to advocate direct negotiations. (A. C. Miller, *Sir Henry Killigrew* (Leicester 1963) pp. 38–44; memoir in C. Howard ed., *Collection of Letters from the Original Manuscripts of many Princes . . .* (London 1753) I, 184–8; instructions from the Vidame, wrongly cited as from the Duke of Vendôme (King of Navarre), his relative (*Cal. For.* II, 185–6; Forbes, I, 67). These instructions are the only evidence for the mission, other than Killigrew's own memoir).

[16] Cambrai, as a neutral city, was to be the place chosen for meetings of arbiters under the treaty of Cateau-Cambrésis (Appendix B, articles 14, 17).

without windows. Paper windows with wooden frames were to be installed. A newer, sumptuous, episcopal residence, 'Mon plaisir', outside the town, had been built by the late Bishop, Robert de Croy. It had been richly embellished by Henri van Vermay.[17] 'Mon plaisir' had been abandoned after the Bishop's death in 1556. In general, King Philip's officials found much 'disrepair' in the buildings at Le Cateau, but it was nevertheless thought an improvement on Cercamp. Workmen were brought in from Valenciennes; King Philip warned that the lodgings for the ambassadors must be arranged carefully, in order not to upset the 'equality' which must be observed in these matters. The Duke of Savoy's marshal reported that the accommodation was piteous.[18] In fact the Spanish were probably the best housed (so said a Venetian report); they were at 'Beauregard' and 'Mon plaisir' outside the town. The Duchess was near them, at a house called 'Mon soulas'. Granvelle had the best kitchen. The French, also, were outside the town, at 'Mon secours' and 'Belle Image', near the 'Porte de Guise'. The Constable had the most prestigious of these lodgings, with 'plus de caquet' than the others. The English were in isolation, in the town, having the bishop's old residence (the château) near the 'Burgundy' gate. It was so bare that Lord Howard delayed in Cambrai to buy furnishings. The 'isolation' had partly been asked for; Ely told Secretary Courtewille that he did not mind where he was put, so long as it was not anywhere near the French. The English reported on the lodgings of all the others as outside the town gate, and that they themselves were housed 'very straitly'. The French felt that Cercamp had been more commodious, but that the air at Le Cateau was better.[19]

The diplomats assembled in early February, the suspension of arms having been prolonged till 10 February. The French had been delayed by festivities. The marriage of Charles Duke of Lorraine and Princess Claude de France was solemnised in Notre Dame of

[17] Cf. N. Bridgman, 'L'entrée de Charles Quint à Cambrai' in Jacquot, op. cit., II, 238.

[18] Granvelle V, 410–11, 419–21.

[19] Granvelle V, 420–1, 425, 426; *Cal. For.* II, 123–4; *Rel. Pol.* I, 420; *Cal. Ven.* VII, 33. It had originally been intended that the English should be lodged at Montègue, some distance from Le Cateau. There were disputes between the Spanish and French 'harbingers' (officials who arranged lodgings). The Bishop of Limoges, who arrived ahead of the other ambassadors, no doubt concerned himself with the lodgings problem.

Paris on 22 January with the 'state' normally reserved for a dauphin.[20] A second marriage was that of Montmorency's second son, the Baron Damville, with the daughter of the Duke of Bouillon (a grand-daughter of Diane de Poitiers). Montmorency travelled to the conference via his château at Chantilly; he was accompanied there by the King, who wished to enjoy his society in his own house more familiarly.[21] The Constable, whose release had been negotiated during the recess,[22] was now a free man, and had once more assumed direction of affairs, military and foreign.[23] He may have visited Calais, he sent letters, via Cavalcanti, to the Earl of Pembroke urging peace.[24] He did not neglect support for French interests in the Empire. To Granvelle he wrote on his high hopes of resumed peace negotiations.[25] The French arrived at Le Cateau on 6 February, having had 'baggage troubles' at Guise en route. They immediately thought of the approaching Lent, and asked that their fish carts ('chasse-marées') might come to Le Cateau two or three times a week, cross country. De Laubespine reported that the ambassadors had come with fuller powers.[26]

The English were now headed by the Queen's cousin, the Lord Chamberlain, Lord William Howard, Baron Howard of Effingham (in Surrey), Knight of the Garter. The two other ambassadors had pleaded that someone of 'great estate' be sent to replace Arundel, since the cardinals, constables and marshals (at the conference)

---

[20] Ronsard wrote an 'Envoy' for the knights competing in the marriage tournament (in front of the Guise palace.) He also wrote a pastoral eclogue celebrating the marriage and festivities at the Cardinal of Lorraine's château of Meudon. Both the Cardinal and the young Duke appear, in pastoral guise, as 'Charlot' (Ronsard IX, 75–100, 124–7). The marriage was not consummated, since the bride was only eleven years old.

[21] *Cal. Ven.* VII, 10, 20.

[22] The Duke of Savoy had at first demanded 300,000 écus ransom, then settled for 200,000. King Henri promised to pay half (Decrue, op. cit., pp. 220–2; Emm. Phil., pp. 47–8; Granvelle V, 326–7, 398, 408; *Cal. Ven.* VII, 6–7.) King Philip thought that Montmorency's release would help counteract the Guises, and promote divisions in France; there were also humanitarian reasons, his age and ill health (*Cal. Span.* XIII, 453; XIV, 16).

[23] Decrue, loc. cit. The Constable was reported as arranging for payment of troops, and for help for government creditors. (*Cal. Ven.* VII, 8).

[24] *Cal. For.* II, 89. Pembroke had been Captain of Calais, and in command of the English at S. Quentin. He showed Montmorency's letter to the Earl of Bedford. Peace hopes were reciprocated, and greetings sent from Cecil and from the Marquis of Northampton. Had Montmorency a following in England? (cf. the contacts of the Vidame of Chartres, above, p. 173n10).

[25] Decrue, op. cit., pp. 221–2.

[26] Granvelle V, 427–9.

thought it some derogation of their honour to be 'mated' with Ely and Wotton only. It is unlikely, in any event, that Queen Elizabeth would have acted otherwise. The ambassadors had powers to negotiate the renewal, by King Philip, of the treaties of 1543, 1546 and 1553; they were to enlarge upon the need for mutual traffic and defence against the common enemy of them both. They should also mention peace with Scotland.[27] For the Le Cateau meeting, they had powers to negotiate peace with Scotland and also powers to treat of peace with France (both were dated 20 January). Their instructions were to preserve at all costs the ancient amity with Burgundy (Queen Elizabeth's and Cecil's regular anachronism for the Netherlands). They were to temporise on Calais if they could not get it outright.[28] There had been some earlier powers, probably rushed off just before the Queen's accession, in Chancery hand (an English script not well understood by the French),[29] erased in parts, and with the seal of Philip and Mary appended. The ambassadors had complained that a covenant for 40*d.* between poor men would not be thought 'sufficient', outside England, if so erased. 'Roman' (Italic or humanistic) script, as used in their first commission, was requested, and presumably obtained, for the commission of 20 January. This script, usual on the continent, was only gradually coming into English official use.

Ely and Wotton arrived at Le Cateau on 6 February, Howard on the 9th, with his furnishings.[30] The English were in gloom. Ely had told Courtewille, amid sighs, that things might turn out badly for England; the Queen had young men in her counsels; the English loved novelty; there might be changes in religion, which the French would turn to their profit, engulfing England through Scotland. The English could rely only on King Philip; they would lose all if they turned from him. He added in Latin (they were presumably talking in French) that fear of death was worse than death itself.[31] Wotton had written to Cecil in January: his simple wit was now so decayed

---

[27] *Cal. For.* II, 59 (powers to treat for the renewal of the treaties of 1543 [1542 old style], 1546 and 1553), 76.

[28] T. Rymer, *Foedera, conventiones, litterae* xv, 510–11, 515–16; *Cal. For.* II, 109–10, 124; Forbes I, 36–40.

[29] Chancery hand was a debased Gothic, close-packed and difficult to read for those not used to it, for instance the French and Spanish ambassadors.

[30] *Cal. For.* II, 76, 123–4; Granvelle v, 429, 431.

[31] Granvelle v, 416–7. Ely was a conservative in religion; he was deprived of his bishopric in July 1559.

by age and travel that it was now 'most simple': in four months he
would reach the grand climacteric (sixty-three). He did not know
how to obtain a real peace with France, not just a 'piece of paper'
containing only words.[32] French hatred of England, ambition, desire
for revenge, their pretended claim to the Crown, their ability to
invade Scotland, were matched by England's lack of money and
good soldiers. He suspected the offers of the French; had not Cecil
written that one should fear even gifts from the Greeks? He feared
that France would sever England from Spain and then work her
purpose on the former. At school, his first lesson had taught him
'the pipe sounds sweetly while the fowler deceives the bird' (he was
quoting the Latin of the *Disticha Catonis*).[33] In King Henry VI's
time, the French had 'piped so sweetly' in the ear of Philip Duke
of Burgundy that he had forsaken the English alliance.[34] When
King Henry VIII was before Boulogne (1544) they had piped again,
sending the Cardinal du Bellay, 'as crafty a child as any in all the
college of cardinals', to deceive the King, while France made a
separate peace with the Emperor. The French were 'the cunningest
in casting bones betwixt friends' that he ever read of. The Guise
only wanted peace for the sake of their relative, the Queen of Scots;
if they acted otherwise it was only 'as men go a great way back
that they may leap the further'. With such a mixture of metaphor
went very deep despondency.[35] We need only add that Howard was,
at this time, very pro-Spanish. Before leaving England, Howard had
made great offers of service to King Philip; after arrival at Le
Cateau, he wrote to Cecil that he had never seen more dissimulation
nor craft used than they had on the French side, nor more plain
and true dealing than they had found on the King of Spain's
commissioners' part.[36] The Duke of Savoy, however, found Howard

---

[32] *Cal. For.* II, 82–7; *Rel. Pol.* I, 390–8. Cf. Wotton's fears, in November, that by
leaving Calais to the French, England would receive only a piece of parchment
sealed with a little wax (*Cal. For.* II, 3).

[33] *Disticha Catonis* I. 27. An edition by Erasmus (1514) was much used in schools.
The whole passage reads: 'Don't think well of people who are too flattering, the pipe
sounds sweetly as the fowler deceives the bird.'

[34] At the Congress of Arras, in 1435; (cf. my study: J. G. Dickinson, *The Congress
of Arras, 1435, a Study in Medieval Diplomacy*, Oxford 1955).

[35] *Cal. For.* II, 82–7. ; *Rel. Pol.* I, 390–8; Forbes I, 15–24. Wotton made his peace
with the new régime. He probably took the oath of supremacy in June (*Cal. Span.*
II, 79).

[36] *Cal. Span.* XIV, 2; *Cal. For.* II, 122.

more haughty with the Spanish than with the French.[37] He also thought him no diplomat: 'suited to all affairs, except those with which the Queen has now entrusted him ... no rhetorician', opinions in which Granvelle concurred, especially the last.[38] Henri II, for his part, indicated that Howard was obstructing progress. Perhaps, therefore, the Lord Chamberlain was a difficult customer to both sides.[39]

The mood of the Spanish is not well attested. Granvelle had urged the need for military preparedness, the best way to obtain peace. Money was, however, the eternal problem, the labyrinth. Troops may have been raised in Germany, as Granvelle had suggested,[40] but King Philip was reported as daily more and more disposed to peace; Ruy Gómez hoped that this next meeting would be more joyful than the last.[41] At court the news was that the King and the French were agreed on all points. The Duchess of Lorraine wrote the Cardinal a very 'loving letter', telling of Spain's urgent wish for peace, and hoping that all would be settled by the end of February. Prudently, however, the suspension of arms was approved until the end of negotiations plus six days.[42]

The negotiations recommence

Though there were these hopes of settlement, the meetings at Le Cateau were as difficult and as long-winded as at Cercamp. The English were again in the wings, the Spanish putting the English proposals to the French and the French proposals to the English.

[37] Emm. Phil., p. 49.

[38] Granvelle v, 457–8, 495 (letter of the Duke, 12 February 1559, and Granvelle's reply, 22 February).

[39] After the treaty-making in April 1559, ambassador Feria reported that Howard came back more French than a Parisian. In order to escape criticism for his bad management of the negotiations, he had tried to influence the Queen against marriage to King Philip, and had his head full of schemes of Montmorency's. This report must be treated with some caution (*Cal. Span.* xiv, 59).

[40] Granvelle v, 389–91, 447, 458–9. (the Duke of Savoy said that there was not a réal to hand); *Cal. Span.* i, 410. Thomas Gresham reported from Antwerp that the King was raising troops in the Netherlands; high prices were asked, no doubt in consequence, for arms and munitions (*Cal. For.* ii, 71, 110).

[41] *Cal. Ven.* vii, 6. By early February, there were said to be heavy wagers, at Antwerp, on peace (ibid., vii, 26).

[42] *Cal. For.* ii, 83; *Rel. Pol.* i, 391 (Wotton's report: he stated that the Spanish noblemen wished for peace, so that they could return home); *Cal. Ven.* vii, 20; Granvelle v, 428.

There were only two formal meetings of all three parties, face to face: a lengthy discussion on 11 February, before the Duchess, and a short encounter (for the English) on 12 March, when they were only present to be told that they would be 'informed' (outside the conference room) of the latest French proposals. This was done by the Spanish, and the English were called in again to hear the offers read out in the full assembly. In the same periods, there were twenty or twenty-one formal meetings of the Spanish and the French, eleven, certainly, before the Duchess. Between the Spanish and the English there were some ten meetings. There were informal meetings also. Between 15 February and 2 March there was a long 'recess', during which the first French proposals were sent to England; the Duchess and some of the diplomats dispersed.

As at Cercamp, formal meetings were in the Duchess' lodgings. She sat at one end of the table, 'at the board's end', flanked by the ambassadors on either side. For example, the French and English confronted one another across the table, and no doubt the French and Spanish did also. For more private discussions, the ambassadors left the table and then returned. The English, lodged in the town, had the furthest to go; on occasion they rode to the meetings. They had no room near the conference chamber, but waited in the Spanish lodgings until called. For private encounters, they were the least accessible; Montmorency walked down to the town, to the church there, to see Howard. Hunting was, however, a diversion which could occasionally be used for parleys.[43]

The isolation of the English and the intractability of the Calais problem did not augur well for a real settlement, though the Spanish strove to be even-handed, emphasising their role as mediators. Spanish and French were, by comparison, merely shadow-boxing. Montmorency was determined on peace, and took a strong part in the negotiations, often by private 'asides' or private meetings. He had entertained 'all' the diplomats on Shrove Tuesday (7 February), but perhaps this did not include the English, since Howard had not yet arrived? On Howard's arrival, a message came from the Constable that he would like some private meeting; Howard reciprocated, but on condition that it should be in some neutral place, because of their rank (i.e. neither could defer to the other), perhaps in the church, since the weather was inclement? A meeting in the

[43] *Cal. For.* II, 123, 158; *Traicté*, p. 83; Granvelle V, 343, 438–9, 442, 444, 520, 529, 531, 533, 535.

church in Le Cateau followed. The French were attempting a separate settlement with England, as Cavalcanti's mission indicated; if this failed, they wished for a separate and immediate settlement with Spain. These tactics threw the Spanish into dismay, given their obligations to the English and their urgent need for peace. They tried, even in the minutiae of negotiation, to remain mediators. For instance, when the French asked that they might meet the Spanish before the English were summoned, the Spanish ordered the Duchess' messenger to return with their request at a time when they would have the English with them. They repeatedly assured the English of their desire to preserve the friendship and mutual obligation between them.[44]

The Anglo–French agreement

Thus the complex web of negotiation and intrigue was woven. The French began by stating that they had nothing new to say to the English; they were determined to keep Calais, and hoped that the Spanish had persuaded the English to come back with some offer of settlement. They (the French) would never have returned to the conference if they had thought that the English would persist in their demands.[45] This, however, was just what the English instructions ordered. Elizabeth confirmed her instructions of 23 November: to demand Calais and the arrears (though the arrears might be waived if Calais were secured). If Calais were refused, then the ambassadors should 'entertain them [the French] with some other devises, without conclusion in that behalf', until they could receive answer from her again. They were to ascertain, as speedily as possible, 'the purpose of the French', informing the Spanish of their proceedings with the French, as far as convenient, without hindering the treaty with the French, 'and in such sort as the like goodwill may appear in the said King Philip toward themselves'.[46] Clearly, such negotiations were fraught with difficulty.

The formal three-party meeting before the Duchess on 11 February, went straight to the heart of the problem. French and

[44] *Cal. Ven.* vii, 29; Granvelle v, 438–9, 448.

[45] Granvelle v, 438–42; *Cal. For.* ii, 125; *Traicté*, pp. 80–2. There were rumours of a 'new Calais' being offered to the English (Granvelle v, 431).

[46] *Cal. For.* ii, 109–10; Forbes i, 40. In January the ambassadors had sent home their own draft treaty with France, which included the return of Calais in six weeks, the payment of the debts, and two pensions in perpetuity (*Cal. For.* ii, 74, 76–7).

English faced each other across the table, the Spanish sitting lower down, next to the English, as spectators of the farce to be enacted ('comme n'estans que spectateurs de la farce qui se devoit jouer').[47] Howard, apologising for his bad French, protested his Queen's wish for peace, on any reasonable conditions. Calais must, however, be restored, as should all places taken in the wars. The Queen could not, for her honour, and her subjects' contentment, make peace without it. Privately, he had stressed to the Spanish the seriousness of the loss. Calais should have been held, with its spacious, eminent and dominant ('seigneuriant') castle. Publicly, he affirmed that he would speak plainly: the French seemed about to cast a bone between the English and Spanish; the Queen would do nothing against the ancient treaties with the house of Burgundy, or the league with King Philip.[48] The Cardinal of Lorraine then spoke of his King's honour, which could not permit the loss of Calais, part of his ancient patrimony, won by conquest, and which the Estates of his realm had declared should never be restored. He stressed the expense and sufferings of the war.[49] English and Spanish then withdrew and the English spoke among themselves. Returning to the table, Wotton declared that they had not understood that the French would be so uncompromising on Calais. Did they wish to proceed by reason or by [the King's own] will?[50] If by 'reason' then the English had good titles to Calais, as they had shown at Cercamp. If by 'will', not to be used among princes, then the English could only submit and report to their Queen.[51] After French consultations, Lorraine replied: their King and the English Queen were both princes of honour, and would use the way of 'reason'. The French thought their claims as good as the English did theirs. The English had held Calais by force, interrupted by wars, which they had begun. Between princes there was no prescriptive right based on force, or bad faith (the French had denied rights of prescription,

[47] *Traicté*, p. 83.

[48] *Cal. For.* II, 126; *Rel. Pol.* I, 425; *Traicté*, pp. 83–4; Granvelle v, 448–9. Earlier, Howard asked for separate negotiations with the French, like the Spanish had. He had been angered by reports of the French hard-line attitudes (Granvelle v, 444).

[49] *Traicté*, p. 85; *Cal. For.* II, 126–7; *Rel. Pol.* I, 425–6; Granvelle v, 449–50. Lorraine referred to French 'protestations' on Calais, at Cercamp. When Wotton questioned this, he was told that 'protester' and 'affirmer' were the same in French. In diplomatic usage a protestation was a formal declaration.

[50] This seems the best way to render, in this context, the classic distinction between *ratio* and *voluntas* ('raison' and 'volonté').

[51] *Cal. For.* II, 127; *Rel. Pol.* I, 426; *Traicté*, p. 86; Granvelle v, 450.

entirely, at Cercamp).[52] Ely then spoke of the English claims, based
on good treaties of parchment, sealed with the seals of the kings of
France. French claims were but words. The French then re-asserted
their claims, and confused the argument. Wotton had based one of
the English claims on the right of arms; the French countered that,
if the English based their claims on conquest, they must accept the
French reconquest. The Spanish intervened to stop this line of
argument. There was silence, all waiting to see who would speak.[53]

It was then that Montmorency spoke out, stressing the French
King's honour and the wishes of his people. They must seek some
solution; perhaps, as earlier in the case of Boulogne, Calais could
be retained for some period while arbitration settled the dispute?
The English still demanded the return of the 'conquest'; they had
been talking together 'en leur Anglois'. They then asked about the
'means' of settlement. The Constable replied that there could be a
true accord which would allow both sides to live in friendship, or
they could leave the Calais problem and agree on the rest.[54] Howard
then reaffirmed England's links with Spain. The Cardinal, always
taking the lead, said that the French could not surrender, to which
the English replied that they had no other charge (i.e. mandate).
They kept pressing the Constable to elaborate on some 'means' of
peace. There were no other means, he replied, for he knew his
master's intentions very well. The English, on leaving, spoke among
themselves. Howard then spoke to each of the French in turn,
stressing his mistress' affection for the King; Henry VIII and François I had not ceased to love each other, even when at war. Elizabeth, although young and a woman, was very jealous of her
honour. He drew the Cardinal aside, telling him that he had seen
King Henri's letters to Elizabeth, and knew of Cavalcanti's mission.
He encouraged his mistress in her desire for peace, and the
Constable should do likewise with the King. Howard and the
Constable then arranged to meet on the morrow, Sunday, at
mass.[55]

The Spanish comments on the proceedings state that the English
were much roused by the idea of a truce, but that they had
dissuaded them, to make the French go further (in offers). The

[52] *Traicté*, p. 87; *Cal. For.* II, 127; Granvelle V, 451.
[53] *Traicté*, pp. 87–8; *Cal. For.* II, 127; *Rel. Pol.* I, 426–7; Granvelle V, 451.
[54] *Traicté*, p. 88; *Cal. For.* II, 127; *Rel. Pol.* I, 426–7.
[55] *Traicté*, pp. 88–90; Granvelle V, 451–2; *Cal. For.* II, 127–8; *Rel. Pol.* I, 426–7.

French had offered more when the English were firmer and more resolute. Granvelle wrote gloomily to the Duke of Savoy that the French were better advocates of a bad cause than the English of a good one. Their first hard, short, response had softened the French. But they had not pressed on, had spoken aside, in English, and then got into arguments among themselves. They used their 'weapons' very badly, and the Spanish could not speak out for them in case the French thought that they were preventing an accord.[56] King Philip wrote that the English were not responding to Feria's mission on the urgency of peace. He (the King) could not continue the war, having spent 1,200,000 ducats in the last two or three months, and needing another million for the period until the end of March. He *must* have an agreement; negotiations *must* not be broken off.[57]

Howard's private meeting with the Constable, in church, only served to reiterate the intransigence of both sides over Calais. Howard referred to the other restitutions being made to Spain; the Constable replied that these were part of the two marriage alliances. The French King could not tell whom Elizabeth might marry; she might marry an enemy of France, from Spain or Germany, so that to give up Calais would be like giving up the King's sword to an enemy, to be killed by it.[58] The two other English ambassadors and the two French bishops were then called in; the French then said that they should not even have discussed Calais, the English that they must refer home. The Constable rejoined that the French would not wait for a reply from England; their King must prepare for war, if he were not assured of peace. Montmorency warned the English against Spain; if King Philip had Calais 'on deposit', they might never have it again. The King would desert the English alliance. What was needed was a truce, or a meeting of English and French, in some other place. After this encounter, the Constable called two of Savoy's men to him; he urged a separate agreement between France and Spain, from which Savoy would profit. The English were the cause of all the hurt and evils. Reports on these encounters were made by both sides to the Spanish, who thought

---

[56] Granvelle v, 452, 455. (cf. Commynes' remarks, above, p. 169).
[57] Ibid., v, 453–4.
[58] The Spanish thought that the Constable said this in order to cast a shadow over King Philip's marriage to Elizabeth (Granvelle v, 461).

them suitably edited. The English were then warned, by the Spanish, of French 'ruses'.[59]

By further deliberations with the French, the Spanish drove them to make new offers on Calais on 12 February; they even offered to put the French proposals to the English and persuade them to accept, if the proposals were practical and reasonable. At first the only offer was a truce, Montmorency elaborating on how hard it was to obtain peace because of the English, and on how French and Spanish had treated before without them. The Spanish reiterated their commitment to England and the Queen's expectation of some 'offer', following King Henri's letter to her on her accession. Lorraine then suggested that they should let time settle their disputes ('querelles'), the French keeping Calais meanwhile. He mentioned, for the first time, the claims of Mary Queen of Scots to the English throne. To whom should they hand over Calais and pay arrears? The Spanish rejected the proposed truce; the English wished for a settlement of disputes, since Calais would always be the cause of further war. There were lengthy arguments and the French consulted apart; finally Lorraine made two proposals, so that the English would not refer home in vain, and to give room for manoeuvre.[60] The first was that there should be marriage alliances: between a son of Elizabeth and a daughter of the Dauphin and Dauphine, with Calais as dowry, and between a daughter of Elizabeth and a son of the Dauphin and Dauphine, with the 'arrears' owed by France as dowry. If this did not please, then the French should retain Calais for eight years, while the rival claims were considered by arbiters to be chosen by King Philip, provided that they were acceptable to France. The meeting continued until dark, Alva sending a message to the English that he would report to them in the morning.[61] The French offers, written down by the Spanish and checked with the French, were duly delivered to the English by the whole Spanish embassy. The English did not like the proposals, but agreed to transmit them; they refused a French offer

[59] *Cal. For.* ii, 128–9; *Rel. Pol.* i, 427–9; Granvelle v, 460–4; *Traicté*, pp. 90–1. The Spanish told the Savoyards that Granvelle himself had travelled to see Henry VIII, before the conclusion of the treaty of Crépy, to get his consent to a separate Franco–Spanish agreement.

[60] Granvelle v, 464–8; *Traicté*, pp. 92–6.

[61] Ibid. Howard had told the Spanish that Elizabeth was young and beautiful, and only needed a husband. He would search for one (at Le Cateau) (Granvelle v, 441–2).

of the route via Calais, deeming Dunkirk to be safer. The Spanish were to send a courier, with the English messenger, taking letters for Feria. Alva, in speaking to the English, and in the hope that the points would be reported, stressed the implications of the proposals: the first would have no result for fourteen years, the second for eight, while a third way was that of war. The great army and navy of Spain, and the English navy, had achieved very little in the last year. How could a war be sustained, at such excessive cost, when a six- or seven-year campaign would be needed? Should the new Queen not rather seek peace until she had established her realm in good order? The same arguments were put directly to Feria, also for use in England;[62] Alva probably paid for the posts.[63]

The Cardinal of Lorraine, for his part, could not resist a final piece of bravura ('une braverye'); he urged a speedy settlement without waiting for the English reply, which he thought was predictable. The French sent reports, and also the Bishop of Limoges, to their King. They had found the English hard and firm on Calais; the King should await the Bishop's arrival before writing to England and not leave Paris meanwhile. In fact the French proceeded to refuse to draw up written articles on their accord with the Spanish until England replied; negotiations were suspended and hung up ('accrochée').[64]

In the recess, the Duchess of Lorraine travelled with her son to meet King Philip. The young Duke had come to Le Cateau escorted by two brothers of the Cardinal of Lorraine, the Grand Prior of France and the Marquis of Elbeuf, with the Duke of Longueville, Léonor d'Orléans. The King had refused a formal meeting, which might delay negotiations; he would take exercise by hunting, near Binche (Mary of Hungary's Italianate palace), and the Lorraines could meet him there. They travelled to Mons, escorted by the

[62] Granvelle v, 469–80; *Traicté*, pp. 96–7; *Cal. For.* ii, 131–2. The ambassadors letter to Feria mirrored Alva's arguments, with added details on the need for peace, the growth of heresy, the Spanish dislike of fighting just for England, for a city so clumsily lost. The ambassadors feared that the English reports would not be explicit enough. Feria should give more weight to the arguments for peace than those for war. For his own ears, he was told that war would be Spain's ruin; there was penury surpassing all imagination (Granvelle v, 472–80; *Cal. Span.* xiv, 28–32).

[63] The master of posts in Brussels had only money for posts to Le Cateau; Alva twice paid for messengers to England (Granvelle v, 484–5).

[64] Granvelle v, 470, 484, 486; *Traicté*, pp. 96–7.

Prince of Orange.[65] Montmorency travelled to the French court, by now at François I's chateau of Villers-Cotterêts, north-east of Paris, for discussions with the King on 22 February. He had hoped for a meeting of the two kings in person, but the offer had been declined, perhaps by the Spanish only? Granvelle and Ruy Gómez thought such meetings often produced more evil than good.[66] According to the Venetian ambassador, Montmorency counselled the King to make public that he was raising large levies of troops, in case war came. He should despatch his commanders and make out that the levies were greater than they were. In fact, the Constable gave great hopes of peace, advising the King to stay at Villers-Cotterêts, near the assembly. S. André visited Paris.[67] Howard, meanwhile, threw the Spanish into consternation by asking to visit S. Quentin. The fortress was in a bad way; houses and fortifications were in ruins. The local commander asked whether Howard was to be given an artillery salute? Granvelle advised that although in the time of the late Emperor salvoes were not fired, to save powder, he thought that Howard merited them; this would also indicate that the Spanish had powder, if short on other things. The Lord Chamberlain, perhaps fortunately for the Spanish, dropped the scheme.[68] On the negotiations Granvelle was sunk in gloom. He wrote to the Duke of Parma of the 'softness' at court. He himself would have been short and dry with the French, and could have concluded by now. He had all along wished to take the lead. Musical analogies came to hand; the Spanish wrote to King Philip that they were hard put to bring the two viols (France and England) to accord. The Duke of Savoy, fearing the encounters between Howard and Montmorency, wrote that if Granvelle held the tambourine ('tambour de basque') in his hands, the matters would go differently.[69]

The Spaniards held the fort during the recess, Alva succumbing to fever from catarrh. The English had their answer, which they

---

[65] Granvelle v, 471, 487, 490–2; *Traicté*, pp. 96–7; *Cal. For.* ii, 155. For Binche, scene of the great festivities for Charles V and Prince Philip in 1549, cf. D. Heartz, 'Un divertissement de Palais pour Charles Quint à Binche', in Jacquot, op. cit., ii, 328–42.

[66] Granvelle v, 492–3 (cf. Commynes' similar views (*Mémoires* i, 135)).

[67] *Cal. Ven.* vii, 38–9. In December, the French had been reported as raising money for next year's campaign (Granvelle v, 389–91). The French ambassadors had always counselled preparedness, as in November, when they feared a rupture of negotiations (*Traicté*, p. 71).

[68] Granvelle v, 499–501.

[69] Granvelle v, 444, 458, 501.

had to decipher, by 25 February. They spent five long hours ('cinq grosses heures') discussing it with the Spanish, who alerted the Duchess and the French to return.[70] Queen Elizabeth had given her ambassadors a series of proposals, leaving timing and order of presentation to their discretion. They must first demand Calais, yet again; if possible, Alva should speak to the French on Spain's willingness to continue the war, rather than lose Calais. If he would not agree to speak, the English should point out how dangerous to the safety of the Low Countries and Flanders was French retention of Calais. If this failed, the Duke himself should be asked to devise some means of settlement. If he did not, then they should suggest that England should have the town and port of Calais, with the lands within the main river, from Newnham Bridge eastwards towards Flanders.[71] The French should have the County of Guines beyond the river, and all the high country westwards from the bridge towards France. This 'device' should be circumspectly opened, and seem to come from the Spanish, with the comment that it would, at first, be equally misliked by France and England.[72] If this failed, then the French might be allowed to retain Calais for five, six, seven or eight years; it should then be restored with 'recompense', pensions and arrears, as decided by arbiters to be chosen by King Philip. In all agreements there must be peace with Scotland; this was in fact a constant theme, for England feared a French invasion via Scotland, especially if France and Spain made a separate peace.[73] There should be an Anglo–Scottish agreement, or Scotland should be included in the treaty with France. If all else failed, the ambassadors should secure peace, as best and most honourably they could, including peace with Scotland (or hostages

[70] *Traicté*, pp. 102–4; Granvelle v, 495, 504–5; *Cal. For.* II, 158–9. The long meeting was in Alva's room, since he was in bed with the fever.

[71] For Newnham bridge and the waterways surrounding Calais, cf. the near contemporary map reproduced in *The Chronicle of Calais*. Newnham bridge was south-west of the town.

[72] Alva had, in fact, proposed such a division in November (above, p. 155n89).

[73] Feria's successor wrote 'it is incredible the fear these people are in of the French on the Scottish border' (*Cal. Span.* XIV, 76). On 10 February, Lord William Dacre, Warden of the West March, was writing from Carlisle to his son in London: he had received 'from his secret espialls' news that fifty cannon were being loaded on to ships at Le Havre, and that the Duke of Guise, with 10,000 Frenchmen, would cross to Scotland about Easter. He had also news of the two marriages proposed at Le Cateau (of Don Carlos and of the Duke of Savoy). His son must inform the Privy Council. He sent the letter 'poste haste with all possible diligence, haste haste' (*Cal. For.* II, 118–19.)

for its future conclusion), but reserving all England's claims to Calais, pensions and arrears. If possible, reference should be made to the Queen before this final proposal was made.[74]

Thus the ambassadors had a frighteningly wide set of options, agreed by the advice of the whole Privy Council. There was a sting in the tail of the letter: 'touching the device of the imagined marriages between Scotland and us;. . . we think the same scant worth the uttering of the French or the hearing of us.' In God's good time, the fruit of such marriages might serve for the 'corroboration of amities'.[75] Here the core of the French proposals, the double marriage alliances, was consigned to oblivion. When the English and the Spanish met, Queen Elizabeth's honour and her subjects' contentment were stressed; the Queen had consulted all her subjects, from highest to lowest, and they would expend life and goods to recover Calais.[76] There was much mutual recrimination on the contributions to a likely war; the Spanish said three or four years would be needed to regain Calais; the English thought it very hard that they should have to undertake an expedition by sea and the Spanish only a diversion on land. They always had Scotland to consider, having a feudal war ('guerre guerroyable') with her.[77] The Spanish agreed to put the English proposals, counselling that the French should be told that Elizabeth would have no peace without Calais. The English demurred: this would mean that the French would leave straight away. Not so, said the Spanish; we must try the uttermost with them, 'even till they be ready to put foot in the

---

[74] *Cal. For.* II, 137–9; Forbes I, 59–64. In December, Cecil advised the Queen that they should get Parliament to petition for the restitution of Calais, and to grant a subsidy for this. The Recorder of London should be persuaded to mention the City's feelings on this, in his speech when the Mayor was presented to the Queen on Twelfth Day (after Christmas) (*Cal. For.* II, 45). The Queen expressed a wish for reference to Parliament, in the instructions in question, but later told ambassador Mason that, in extremity, this might be omitted, for the French King would not depart from the offers he had made directly to her (via Cavalcanti) (*Cal. For.* II, 166; cf. below, p. 198).

[75] *Cal. For.* II, 137–9; Forbes I, 59.

[76] *Traicté*, p. 103.

[77] 'Guerre guerroyable' does not fit precisely into the typology of war as defined by medieval lawyers. Literally 'potential war', the term was used of 'feudal war', e.g. between lord and vassal, as opposed to 'Roman' war (to the death, and primarily against the Infidel) or 'public' or open war, between sovereign princes. In 1559 the English deemed their normal border warfare against Scotland to be 'guerre guerroyable'; they also recalled ancient claims to sovereignty over the Scottish kingdom (cf. M. H. Keen, *The Laws of War in the Late Middle Ages* (London 1965) p. 104; P. Contamine, *Guerre, état et société à la fin du moyen âge* (Paris 1972) p. 196).

saddle'. The Spanish drove the English, bit by bit, to reveal the full
detail of their instructions ('le secret de leurs instructions'), since
they wished to know all that the English could offer, as also all that
the French had in their throats ('dans le gésier'). Granvelle
despaired of the outcome; Spain must have a settlement, even a
bad one. The French were, however, not amenable to reason; better
to hit them than to negotiate with them.[78]

The Spanish had mentioned to the English the claim of Mary
Queen of Scots to the Crown of England; the French had raised
the subject, asking to whom they should deliver Calais. The English,
very unwisely, included this in their report home. Howard had
answered the French: make restitution to 'the Crown of England',
and if the Queen of Scots obtains it, she shall have Calais and all
the rest. Granvelle had told the ambassadors that the French
laboured at Rome for the 'disabling' of Queen Elizabeth to the
crown. The English ambassadors surmised that the French, in
suggesting arbiters on Calais and the arrears, would also bring
before them the title to the Crown. They had never, they wrote,
heard of arbitration on the titles of kings, but wished to know the
Queen's advice.[79] In fact, Elizabeth had heard of this claim from
the King of France himself, in the Cavalcanti negotiations. Lord
Cobham had warned her that the French mentioned it at Cercamp,
and had sent to Rome. By February her ambassador at the Curia,
Sir Edward Carne, knew of French machinations there. On 16
February he wrote that the French could not prevail on the Pope
to support the claim. His letter may not, however, have reached
the Queen by early March when the report came from Le Cateau.
This report, so meek in tone, roused her to fury. She also 'raved'
when Feria mentioned that the French had put forward the claims
of Mary Queen of Scots; she and her subjects were not so poor
that money and arms could not be got.[80] Howard's private letter,
mentioning private proposals for the Queen's marriage, may have
pleased her little better. Montmorency had said that he wished
King Henri's wife were dead, so that the King could marry Queen

---

[78] *Traicté*, pp. 102-3; Granvelle v, 505-14; *Cal. For.* II, 155-8; *Rel. Pol.* I, 447-56.
Ruy Gómez liked the eight-year proposal on Calais, for it would give peace for that
period. The proposal to divide Calais seemed good to the Spanish; the sea washed
over the land to the west, and would thus protect the French territory from English
incursions.

[79] *Cal. For.* II, 155-8; *Rel. Pol.* I, 447-56.

[80] *Cal. For.* II, 30-1, 135; *Rel. Pol.* I, 332-3; *Cal. Span.* XIV, 29.

Elizabeth. The Duchess of Lorraine and the Countess of Arenberg, out hunting, canvassed King Philip's candidature. Howard had replied that the King would be too much away, so that children of the match would not be likely.[81]

How did the Spanish handle, and the French receive, these proposals? There was a great deal of negotiation and bargaining, some formal, some informal, in the period 2 to 12 March. Montmorency walked down to the town to hear mass on 2 March and thus met the English; Howard spoke of his great wish to serve King Henri, saving only his duty to the Queen, but also of Calais. He spoke also of his small faith in the Spaniards and his hopes for separate negotiations.[82] Meanwhile Lorraine encountered the Spanish informally at the Duchess' lodgings, when Alva made a surprising new offer: that the Spanish would forego the restitutions to Savoy if Calais and other war conquests were handed over. The French noted this decline in Savoy's importance to Spain but refused the offer; it came too late and would show lack of resolution in their proceedings. Besides, they privately feared that the Spanish would include in this the demand for restitution of Metz, Toul and Verdun.[83] At the formal session, the same day, Granvelle reported on the English position and attempted to force another offer from the French. Lorraine contended that the ambassadors had gone as far as they could (the last offer was really their own suggestion). Calais could never be given up; no servant of the King would consent, no subject either, but would rather give up all that he had. Montmorency declared that to get Calais the English would have to take the crown off the King's head; he himself would rather lay his head on the table than consent. The Spanish said that they must be given other weapons to combat the English, and such other tricks ('herbs of St John'). After this formal session, the Duchess and her son walked in the garden with the Cardinal of Lorraine and talked of peace. The Duchess, moved by her own concern and by the Spanish (particularly Ruy Gómez, who had upset his colleagues by pleading for peace), made two proposals of her own.

[81] *Cal. For.* II, 158–9. Marguerite de la Marck, Countess of Arenberg (near Bonn) was the 'lady-in-waiting' to the Duchess (cf. her letter about the lodgings at Le Cateau, and possible dancing, in Granvelle v, 503).

[82] *Traicté*, pp. 97–100. (Ruble places the events of 2 March, mistakenly, under 3 March). Alva thought war inevitable; he was off to S. Quentin, no doubt to take stock of its defences (*Traicté*, p. 100).

[83] *Traicté*, pp. 101–8.

The marriage proposals were too long-term; could the French reduce the period for their retention of Calais, or could they not dismantle it, retaining it while arbiters reached a decision? She had seen the fortress, and it was not such a great one. The second offer being refused, the Duchess asked Lorraine to speak of it to no one; it was her own idea, and she would speak to the Spanish of the first. Even on this, the French had doubts; they reported that it could not be the Duchess' alone: 'n'estant pas cela sortiz de la boutique de ladite Dame seule.'[84]

Ely and Wotton took no comfort when told of these discussions, nor could they give way.[85] At a further session of French and Spanish before the Duchess on 4 March, each side pressed the other to find some way out. Montmorency was following royal instructions to delay matters, in the hope of pressing the English to reveal themselves, literally by 'skinning them'. A walk in the countryside resulted only in the refusal, by Lorraine, of the English proposal on the division of Calais, which the Spanish put informally ('par propoz familiers') as if it came from them, as Queen Elizabeth had asked.[86] The sight of an English courier on his way to Le Cateau[87] made the French hope that new proposals were arriving. The Spanish found Montmorency harder than usual; they supposed he feared to be blamed for the loss of Calais. Lorraine, on the other hand, was 'softer', perhaps because he expected the arrival of his sister-in-law, the Duchess of Guise, and the new Duchess of Lorraine.

French and Spanish continued negotiations before the Duchess on 8 March. She then put her own proposal, 'for the good of Christendom and in the service of the two kings'. Calais should be returned, in six or four years, without arbitration, unconditionally. The French found this very far from their instructions; their King was confident in his just cause. They asked the Spanish about the proposal, knowing full well that the latter were behind it, and were playing their part in the farce which they had devised ('ils devoient bien scavoir leur roolle, puis qu'ils avoient composé la farce'). The French finally agreed to refer the proposal to their King: the unconditional restitution, the period of years, and subsidiary points on

---

[84] *Traicté*, p. 108.
[85] Howard was ill with catarrh in the teeth (Granvelle v, 517).
[86] *Traicté*, pp. 109–11; Granvelle v, 517–21, 527.
[87] The courier in fact brought new instructions, mainly on peace with Scotland, and not new 'offers' (*Cal. For.* II, 150–1; Granvelle v, 520, 524).

the defortification of Eyemouth[88] and the sureties for a treaty. They told the King that they needed a reply to these 'master strokes' by Friday 10 March; the only point in favour of the offer was that it might bring peace for eight years. The Spanish had, in fact, been thrown into consternation. The Duchess, who was present, in their view, on behalf of King Philip, should not have acted on her own initiative. Any offers to the English must come from the French, or they might be called in question later. Granvelle and the others thought that the Cardinal of Lorraine was behind the Duchess' proposals, a clear indication that each side suspected her if she attempted an active role.[89] Granvelle was in despair; even the company of the ladies (the Duchess, her daughter-in-law, the Duchess of Guise, the Countess of Arenberg, and others) was a hindrance. For her part, the Duchess hoped for some amusement; she had asked for some dancing, and there was hunting: Howard with the Duchess, and also with Montmorency.[90]

The final French offer was hammered out in two sessions before the Duchess on 11 and 12 March. The French King had responded swiftly, as requested; he sent a secretary of state to assist, to show his 'concern for the peace of Christendom' and for King Philip's friendship. Judging by the proposals then made, the royal instructions must have been intricate, or his ambassadors had a fairly free hand. Never having thought to give up Calais except after arbitration, the King now offered it in eight years, unconditionally, provided that it was first defortified and made a merchant city. This should meet the frequent English argument that Calais was needed as a staple. Henri would, however, keep Guines; boundaries should be well defined, since war had almost resulted from such disputes in the past. He demurred over Eyemouth, adducing domestic need for its fortification. The Spanish referred this proposal to the English. They themselves were suspicious, since Courtewille had seen a courier go from the Constable to Howard,

[88] Eyemouth, six miles north of Berwick, across the border, had been fortified in time of truce, and had French troops under a Captain Gaillart. The English secured agreement for its defortification in the 1559 treaty, but this was not carried out. The same provision figured in the treaty of Edinburgh of 1560, which also provided for the withdrawal of French (and English) troops from Scotland. (*Cal. For.* II, 62, 101, 213, 218; Conyers Read, op. cit., p. 159; Wernham, op. cit., pp. 250–1. 256–7).

[89] *Traicté*, pp. 111–14; Granvelle V, 521–4. The French referred to the original, 8 year, proposal for Calais.

[90] Granvelle V, 502, 525, 528–9; *Cal. For.* II, 158–9; *Cal. Ven.* VII, 45.

and the two nobles had been out hunting alone. Howard thought it necessary to tell the Spanish that the two had only discussed hunting and old anecdotes of the French court,[91] but this only increased Spanish fears. As for the French proposal, the Spanish found it very far from the Duchess' (or rather Lorraine's, in Granvelle's view); it would necessitate reference to the Queen, a time-consuming process with which the French were trying to wear them (the Spanish) out. Lorraine even hinted that it would take a further six weeks to draw up an agreement. If, thought the Spanish, the French got away with this offer, which was too favourable to them, might they not go back on other agreed terms? One must show one's teeth, for there was no surety for French promises.[92] Evidently the Spanish had given hard looks and blunt responses, for Lorraine hinted privately to the Duchess that the French had not exhausted their offers. He asked to speak to Orange alone. The latter got Ruy Gómez to the meeting, fearing French variableness and unreliability. The two Spanish did not understand Lorraine very well, but were told that better offers would be made the next day.[93]

The final agreement came then, on 12 March. The English were summoned to the Spanish quarters to await their call to the assembly. At the meeting of French and Spanish before the Duchess, the Spanish declared that the English found the period for retention of Calais, eight years, too long. The French, deliberating first among themselves, refused to give way; they did, however, agree to hand over the town with fortifications intact, but less its artillery. They would also hand over Guines (i.e. the proposal to divide Calais and Guines had been dropped). Eyemouth should be defortified. Surety for the agreement should be the word of princes. The English were then summoned, having been warned beforehand by the Spanish not to reply to the offer, so that they could consult apart with the Spanish. They had also been told, by the secretary summoning them, of the discussions so far. When they came in to the assembly, they were simply told that the Spanish would inform them of the proposals. At separate discussions between the Spanish and the English, the latter holding their instructions in their hands, the Spanish agreed to press for less than eight years (on Calais) and for the artillery, or some pieces of it, to be handed over. They

[91] Granvelle v, 527–9.
[92] Ibid., 529–30.
[93] Ibid., 530–1.

prevailed on returning to the meeting; sixteen pieces of artillery
would be left: three cannon, three serpentines, three bastards and
lesser pieces, all of bronze. The Dauphin and Dauphine would ratify
the treaty, and hostages would be an additional surety. A penalty
of 500,000 écus, not the 1,000,000 the English hoped for, was agreed,
if the French did not fulfil the treaty. It would lapse if the English
went to war.[94]

The Spanish had almost won; they knew that these terms were
acceptable to the English, being more than they had asked for, and
that they had authority to agree. But when they retired to consult
with the English, they made deliberations spin out, so that the
French would think that lengthy persuasion had been necessary.
The articles of the treaty were then read out in full assembly so
that the English would not demur; however much they might be
grieved over the eight-year period, or would have liked to consult
the Queen, they had to accept, knowing that Feria and the Spanish
would support them in reports to the Queen. However, they put
in a protest that this treaty would depend on a Franco–Spanish
agreement, for they would do nothing without Spain. This provision
was incorporated in the text. The terms, in writing, were handed
to the English the next day, 13 March; they forwarded a French
version, keeping the original, subscribed by the French, from which
to draw up the Latin text. The wording omitted a preamble,
suggested by the Spanish, hoping that the disputes between England
and France would be healed by time, since Christendom must not
remain at war because of them.[95] The English remarked that there
had been 'some travail' for the penning and subscribing of the texts.
They considered that the Spanish had, in all the proceedings, used
themselves earnestly and honestly.[96]

The articles of agreement eventually formed a separate treaty
between France and England (see Appendix B). A peace with
Scotland was also vital to Elizabeth, for, as her instructions

---

[94] Ibid., v, 531–6. Sureties for the money were to be given at first by hostages,
and then by pledges from seven or eight foreign merchants. At first it was suggested
that the hostages be held by King Philip (fear of religious change in England
prompted this); eventually it was agreed that they should go to England, provided
they could all remain together.

[95] The final treaty 'reserved' all suits and claims between England and France
(Appendix B, article 16, pp. 250–1).

[96] Granvelle v, 535–7, 538–62 (full text); *Cal. For.* II, 170–2. Howard sent his son
to England with the news (ibid., II, 176).

affirmed, 'the greatest burden of these our wars resteth upon Scotland'. Indeed, she made clear that there must certainly be peace
with Scotland, even if only a temporary agreement were reached
with France. Peace with Scotland, she wrote, was even more
important than peace with France. By 2 April a separate treaty
with Scotland had been obtained, in addition to Scotland's inclusion
in the Anglo–French treaty (see Appendix B). Unfortunately we
have no details of the negotiations on the Anglo–Scottish agreement,[97] save for the frequent mention of the fortress of Eyemouth.

In the meantime a storm had broken over the heads of the English
ambassadors. Their letter, and Howard's, of 2 March produced a
furious reaction. They had referred to Mary Queen of Scots' claims,
and to their fear that these might be subsumed in the arbitration
process over Calais. The text of the royal reply of 7 March, a long
first version, and a shorter second version, survives in Cecil's hand.
The first mentions the Queen's anger that all is done through the
Spanish, as the French had complained. As for her title, how could
the ambassadors 'forbear' to hear of such matters, and to ask her
advice? They ought neither to hear of, nor reason of, nor once allow
such a matter to be 'opened' to them by anyone. The final version
ran 'we cannot well take it that our servants and subjects shall
either suffer others thus to speak, without due reprehension or
misliking', or make doubts over it, or require our pleasure about it;
'for true it is we like not the matter as it is handled'. Sir John
Mason, a Privy Councillor, experienced in diplomacy, was being
sent over to join them, and would have the same authority as they.[98]
The Privy Council added fuel to the flames: the ambassadors should
simply have declared their indignation to hear the subject
mentioned. There had been no mention of this scruple (on Elizabeth's title) in the French proposals; no doubt the Spanish had
introduced the matter to make the English more subservient. The
latter should have acted with the French, directly, more often;
action through Spain had only been convenient and profitable in

[97] *Cal. For.* ii, 138, 150.; Forbes i, 62. Feria wrote, in March, that the English
would even give up Calais, if peace with Scotland were obtained (*Cal. Span.* xiv,
38). A border truce was agreed that month (*Cal. For.* ii, 192).
[98] *Cal. For.* ii, 163–4; *Rel. Pol.* i, 460–1. Mason was a strong advocate of peace,
even without Calais (*Cal. For.* ii, 6–7). He had been, with Paget, one of the negotiators
of the settlement over Boulogne in 1550, and thereafter ambassador to France, and
to Brussels. He had started as a clerk in the Privy Council, being a protegé of Paget
(Gammon, op. cit., p. 172ff.).

Queen Mary's time. There could be no peace wherein the Queen's title was brought in question; it would be so far 'out of square' that any with English blood would better stand to their own defence and venture bodies, goods, and lands.[99] Ambassador Mason was to deliver a homily on these lines to the ambassadors. The ambassadors could treat 'apart' with the French. Reference to Parliament over Calais had been an extreme measure, threatened to secure delay, but not needed in practice.[100] Mason should see Montmorency and excuse the English if they were thought 'too much addicted' to the Spaniards. Separate negotiations were intended by the Queen.[101]

In fact, Mason and the intimidating letters did not arrive until 11 March, by which date the agreement was concluded. On reading the letters, the ambassadors were disconsolate; they felt 'great and importable grief, desiring rather to be out of this world' than that the Queen should be discontented with them. They had never intended to put her title in question, but merely to know whether she would accept discussion of Calais and the arrears by arbiters. Mason wrote that they had been 'appalled' at the Council's letters, which he had sent on ahead. As to the Queen's, he felt compelled to ask her on his knees to make them men again, for they could not be comforted, lamenting that by ten lines inaptly penned they should have run in danger of her indignation. An error of the pen should not, he argued, 'frustrate' the thanks their good work deserved. He wrote to Cecil that Ely and Wotton would carry this matter with them to their graves; one could see what great grief, entering suddenly into a man, could do. Wotton had fallen into an ague, more of the spirit than of the body, and was already 'sore broken'. Ely, although in health, was totally stunned ('factus totus stupidus'). He had worried at the rumours from England, and now the 'knot' was knit up. Whatever he had done in the past, he should not be overthrown now, for lack of a comfortable word, having served well and with judgment. Cecil must prevail on the Queen to relent. Mason, writing from this 'vale of misery', could do little. He spoke to the Spanish of his Queen's thanks to King Philip and

[99] *Cal. For.* II, 164–5; *Rel. Pol.* I, 461–2.

[100] *Cal. For.* II, 139, 166. Parliament met in January and was adjourned until 22 March. Its discussions centred on the royal supremacy over the church (Conyers Read, op. cit., pp. 130–2).

[101] *Cal. For.* II, 166–7; *Rel. Pol.* I, 458–9.

her constant amity. He visited the Constable, being welcomed with wine and presents. He stayed at Le Cateau until the end of the conference, as his colleagues asked, and to help with the 'drafting'. Queen Elizabeth forgave her ambassadors, although from the text of their letters she judged them at fault. She hoped to see cause, on their return, to accept their long travail and pain in good part.[102]

The Franco–Spanish negotiations

As soon as the Anglo–French problem was disposed of, the whole process of finalising a Franco–Spanish treaty started again. The Spanish hoped to gain the initiative, particularly in drafting: they wished, they reported, to wield the pen ('gaigner la plume'). There were at least eleven meetings of French and Spanish, including at least three before the Duchess (on 23 March, 24 March and 2 April) in the period 13 March to 2 April, when final agreement was reached, the treaty being promulgated on 3 April. A good six-hour meeting on 13 March began hard-working sessions on 14, 15 and 16 March, on which date articles of agreement were sent off to the two kings, Ruy Gómez travelling, 'in post', to Brussels, and Lorraine's two brothers (the Grand Prior and the Marquis of Elbeuf)[103] to King Henri at La Ferté Milon, a few miles south of Villers-Cotterêts. Mason reported that the agreement was concluded in general (the 'grosse') but that there were difficulties over penning and framing.[104] There were two crucial meetings, on 23 March (a good six hours), and on Good Friday (24 March), after which reference was again made to the kings. Ruy Gómez went to Groenendael, where Philip spent Easter, Lorraine travelled 'postwise' to La Ferté Milon.[105] He was with King Henri on 26 and 27 March. The final meetings at Le Cateau were on 29 March, 31 March, 1 April and 2 April. By 31 March Philip's comments, and those of his Council, had been received. The ambassadors had despatched the articles of 16 March in two versions: the Spanish

---

[102] *Cal. For.* II, 175–9, 184, 199; *Rel. Pol.* I, 471–4, 480. Elizabeth asked the ambassadors to try to obtain a higher indemnity, for non-compliance, from the French.

[103] François de Guise was Grand Prior of the Hospitallers in France; René de Guise was Marquis of Elbeuf, on the lower Seine.

[104] *Cal. For.* II, 177.

[105] *Cal. Ven.* VII, 49, 54; *Cal. For.* II, 183. A Venetian report suggests that Montmorency had not wanted Lorraine to undertake this mission, since he was averse to peace (*Cal. Ven.* VII, 58).

(the articles marked by alphabetic references), with French comments, and the French (marked by numbered references) with Spanish comments.[106] Presumably the King of France received a similar set of documents, but the French ambassadors' reports end on 8 March. The Spanish reports continued, but were less frequent. Venetian ambassadors continued to glean all they could, including unofficial information from Le Cateau; the English reported on what they saw and heard in the wings.[107]

Even when the articles were almost finalised, there were areas of contention and many minor differences. It seems best to consider these in relation to the final treaty (summarised in Appendix B). The French first refused the mention of any breaking of the truce, or of the previous meetings at Lille and Marcoing. There was then outright refusal, by them, of a clause committing the two kings to an expedition against the Turk. When the kings were firm friends and in accord, then the King of France would join in such a crusade.[108] On a future Council of the Church (article 2), the French would have no mention of the Emperor's obligation to procure it, for this might imply his right to convene it. The Spanish demurred, but could not prevail. On Montferrat, French agreement to hand it back to Mantua was conditional on an undertaking that neither France nor Spain would use the Marquisate for their troops, or put garrisons there. This was, as the Spanish reported, a considerable limitation on King Philip, and would pin down his garrisons to Milan; but they could not prevail. The French would not agree to any mention, in the treaty, of Saluzzo, whose sovereignty they still claimed.[109]

On two major problems, there was implicit, but not explicit, reservation of rights. The ancient French claims to the Duchy of Milan, and those of the Dukes of Burgundy (inherited by Philip) to the Duchy of Burgundy, had been mentioned, without French objections, in the discussions at Cercamp, according to the Spanish. Milan, renounced by the French in 1526 under the treaty of Madrid,

[106] Granvelle v, 547–66. Granvelle's comments were sent with the draft, but do not appear to have survived. The texts can, therefore, only be interpreted by reference to the treaty itself. The comments of the King, the Council, and Viglius, President of the Council, are dated 30 March (Granvelle v, 566–9).
[107] Granvelle's brother Thomas, Seigneur de Chantonnay, was at Le Cateau; the Venetian ambassador in Brussels had a report from him (*Cal. Ven.* vii, 61).
[108] Granvelle v, 549.
[109] Ibid., v, 549–50, 558–9.

had been a possible dowry for a Franco–imperial marriage in the treaty of Crépy in 1544. French claims had been 'reserved', if the marriage did not take place, which was the case. The Duchy of Burgundy was promised to the Emperor in 1526, but never delivered, when François I reneged on the treaty. In 1529, by the treaty of Cambrai, the Emperor's claims were left to 'justice'. In 1559, both these claims were left 'in limbo'.[110] Milan, the more likely revival, was not linked to any marriage proposal, as Calais had been.

There was agreement by 'postponement' on several items. The castle of Bouillon, to be restored to the Bishop of Liège, was also claimed by the de la Marck family, Seigneurs of Sedan.[111] There was to be arbitration on this claim. Arbitration would also deal with the abbey of S. Jean-au-Mont, near Thérouanne, which had possessions both in France and in the Netherlands. Likewise there would be arbitration over rival claims to the County of S. Pol.[112] Commissions of arbiters, who might choose a super arbiter, were to act within certain specified periods. The Spanish had consulted the President of the Council of Artois over the abbey and over S. Pol. The French were invited to send financial officials from Doullens, Amiens and elsewhere. Disputed boundaries in the northern lands, and between Franche Comté and France, would be left to arbitration by ministers of both powers, who were to meet in Cambrai next September.[113] On the vexed problem of the diocese of Thérouanne (which stretched across the frontier), there was to be a commission, in June, of royal representatives and a representa-

---

[110] Ibid., v, 556–7.

[111] Article 14 of the treaty. In the eleventh century, Bouillon was the principal stronghold of the Counts of Ardennes, some of whom were Dukes of Lower Lorraine. They styled themselves 'Dukes' of Bouillon. Godefroi de Bouillon sold the fortress to the Bishop of Liège, to raise money for the crusade. In 1482, Robert de la Marck, Seigneur de Sedan, obtained the fortress; it was restored to the Bishop in 1521, and then repossessed in 1552. The treaty re-awarded it to the Bishop, but the de la Marck continued to style themselves Dukes.

[112] Under article 18 of the treaty, S. Pol was to be repossessed by Marie de Bourbon, Duchess of Étoutteville (Pays de Caux, in Normandy). The County had passed from the house of Luxembourg by the marriage of the heiress Marie to François de Bourbon Count of Vendôme. Their second son, François I, Count of S. Pol, married the Étoutteville heiress, Adrienne, in 1534 and the fief was made a duchy. Their daughter, Marie, became the heiress of S. Pol and Étoutteville on the death of her brother, François II, in 1546. The County of S. Pol, devastated by the imperialists in 1535, came to the crown of France in 1659.

[113] Articles 14, 16 and 17 of the treaty; Granvelle v, 555–6.

tive of the metropolitan, the Archbishop of Reims (Lorraine himself), to decide on the allocation of lands and revenues. Benefices on one side had lands on the other, and thus the problem was complex, Lorraine summoning the Chantor of Thérouanne to advise. Eventually an even split of the total revenues was accepted. The French would have a new diocese, probably at Boulogne, and the Spanish another, probably at S. Omer. The French might rebuild a chapel in Thérouanne, where the mother church was in ruins.[114]

As might be expected, the real stumbling blocks were items on which instant action had to be taken: the restitutions and the marriage alliances. On the former, there were long discussions over the demolition of fortresses and withdrawal of artillery, generally on the basis of 'tit for tat'. The ruined condition of Thérouanne was to be matched by demolitions in Yvoir (article 12 of the treaty). Artillery, powder and arms could be withdrawn, before restitution of the great fortresses of Vermandois (S. Quentin, Ham and Le Catelet) on one side, and Thionville, Mariembourg and Yvoir on the other.[115] The French finally surrendered on Corsica; its restitution to Genoa was hidden in an article enjoining the King of France to receive Genoa into his good grace and friendship, restoring all he held on the island. The Genoese were to reciprocate, and not to punish those who had supported France.[116] King Philip consulted the Florentine ambassador on the restitutions to be made by the French in Tuscany and in Sienese territory. The ambassador declared, after the peace, that his master Duke Cosimo would be the greatest prince in Italy since Roman times.[117] The general plan was that all restitutions should first be made by the French, beginning in one month's time and being completed in two. Then the Spanish should make their restitutions, within one month from the date of completion by the French. In the intervening period (i.e. during the French period of restitution) the Spanish King would

[114] Granvelle v, 544–5; article 13 of the treaty. Boulogne had been the seat of a bishopric from the end of the fourth century; it was later united with Thérouanne. The part of the latter diocese in Philip's domains became two dioceses, under the 'new bishoprics' scheme: S. Omer, French and Flemish speaking, and Ypres, Flemish speaking. Papal authority was given in May 1559 and confirmed in January 1560.
[115] Articles 11 and 12 of the treaty.
[116] Article 24 of the treaty; Granvelle v, 560–1. The Spanish advised Philip to consult the Genoese ambassador on this subject.
[117] Article 25 of the treaty; Granvelle v, 565–5; *Cal. Ven.* vii, 61.

provide hostages for his compliance with the programme. The whole process was, therefore, to be completed in three months at maximum, a pious hope (see Appendix C).[118]

The general problem of individual property, ecclesiastic and lay, was covered by a clause allowing French and Spanish subjects to return to enjoy their immovable possessions and rents in the lands of either king, without claiming revenues for the period of 'seizure', and in spite of any grants made during this period. There was no provision, however, to allow the 'exiles' from Milan, Naples and Sicily so to reclaim possessions. Clerics provided to benefices, on either side, by the King or other laymen, should remain in possession. Lorraine, it was said, had taken alarm over a Spanish suggestion on this topic; as a pluralist abbot, he had made many provisions to benefices in Hapsburg territory.[119]

The minutes of drafting provoked contention and angry rejoinder. The French, for instance, in agreeing that Hesdin, ancient fortress of the Counts of Artois, and then of the Dukes of Burgundy, should remain in Spanish hands, would not swallow the Spanish reference to it as 'ancient patrimony' of their King. They offered 'pretended patrimony'; the matter was dropped.[120] As might be expected, there were peak periods of disagreement. On 23 March, Maundy Thursday, it was reported that all was broken up over Savoy. The Duke had been asked to send a representative on the question of the dowry for the marriage alliance and had done so. The Spanish were still bargaining over the number of Piedmontese fortresses to be retained by the French, and insisting that the King of Spain would keep his garrisons there while the French held their strongholds, eventually fixed at five. The Spanish told the English that towns like Chieri had as many as thirty or forty walled towns and castles under their rule; some, like Pignerolo, had as many as sixty. If the French kept these towns, they would gain by their pen in one hour more than their sword had won in twenty years. Final agreement was that King Philip's garrisons should remain in Vercelli and Asti. The meeting of the 23rd, however, ended with the French prepared to leave or threatening[121] to do so, sending their harbingers

[118] Article 44 of the treaty.
[119] Articles 6, 7, 8 of the treaty; Granvelle v, 551–2.
[120] Article 15 of the treaty; Granvelle v, 557.
[121] This is the modern translation of 'bravarono'. The editors of the *Calendar* give 'vapoured', which used to mean 'boast' or 'brag', and is now obsolete (*Cal. Ven.* vii, 55).

ahead to prepare new quarters, and even putting on their boots for the journey. Only the Duchess' intercession prevented a rupture; there was a meeting before her on Good Friday, reputedly for six to seven hours, followed by the reference to the two kings already mentioned. From this date, the Spanish reported that they gained ground. The French were, be it noted, to retain their strongholds (Turin, Chieri, Pignerolo, Chivasso, and Villanova d'Asti) only until France had settled her disputes with Savoy, which must be within three years.[122] Settlement on all this was reached on 28 March; on 29 March a courier went to Brussels, and a Spanish nobleman to the King at Groenendael. At Le Cateau, Lorraine embraced his nieces, the daughters of the Duchess. A Te Deum was sung, and bonfires were lit. Fires were also lit at Brussels and Groenendael.[123]

However, there was still wrangling (on 28 and 29 March) over the fortifications of Thérouanne and Yvoir. A session at the Cardinal of Lorraine's, he having purged himself and keeping to his room, seems to have settled the matter (31 March). By this time many of the articles were engrossed on parchment. But even on 1 April, two days before promulgation, the Bishop of Limoges was quibbling over S. Pol, Savoy's representatives argued about Pignerolo and Chieri, and there were disputes over the sureties (the hostages) for the restitutions. On 2 April King Philip wrote, yet again, about the release of prisoners.[124]

Central to the whole agreement were the two marriage alliances. That for Savoy with the Princess Marguerite was finalised in discussions over the dowry and dower. There was also need for papal dispensation; it was presumably already in hand, since by mid-April the English ambassador in Rome reported that the authority was on its way.[125] The great 'development' came over the marriage of Don Carlos. In the incomplete records of the March deliberations, we read that the French suggested the marriage of their Princess with King Philip himself, and not his son. On 1 April the Spanish visited the Constable who, they reported, had raised this proposal; they asked whether Milan would be the dowry, to

---

[122] Article 35 of the treaty; Granvelle v, 543, 561, 585; *Cal. Ven.* vii, 55, 58; *Cal. For.* ii, 186–8; *Rel. Pol.* i, 485–6. The English feared that the French would leave on Good Friday, and were prepared to leave themselves.

[123] *Cal. Ven.* vii, 59–61.

[124] Granvelle v, 570, 579; *Cal. For.* ii, 186, 219; *Cal. Ven.* vii, 59–61.

[125] Granvelle v, 579; *Cal. For.* ii, 219.

which Montmorency replied that his master would be content to leave the matter open (the Milan proposal had been his alone). It was agreed that the Constable would bring forward this matter, last thing, before the Duchess, when all other things had been concluded. This happened on 2 April at a meeting which began at 9 a.m. As the ambassadors rose from the table, the Constable and Marshal S. André took the Spanish towards the Duchess, and jointly proposed King Philip's marriage.[126] There followed a private discussion between the Duchess and the Spanish, at which they told her of 'the beginning, the progress, and the terms' of this marriage negotiation. The Spanish then announced that King Philip, despite his reluctance to remarry, having heard of King Henri's wish for the marriage and of the good that would come of it, and in order to consolidate the peace, had decided to accept the marriage freely, on the conditions agreed for Don Carlos (no stipulations about lands for the children). The Spanish hinted that the dowry might perhaps be increased; the French that Don Carlos might perhaps marry a younger sister. Straightway, we are told, and with joy and satisfaction, the articles of agreement were drawn up. King Philip was to give 50,000 écus worth of jewels to the Princess, in lieu of the 40,000 écus worth offered by Don Carlos. It was the equivalent of what Eleanor of Hapsburg had received when she married François I. Proxies for the marriage ceremony would be the hostages sent by King Philip (over the restitutions).[127]

This settlement, so briefly recorded, must have been the subject of detailed discussions and instructions. Perhaps it had not been a matter 'de longue haleine', for on 14 March King Philip was still writing of his son's marriage. On 16 March, Queen Catherine de' Medici told the Venetian ambassador that Philip was deliberating about a marriage, either for himself or for his son, and that he would see the Princess at the proposed meeting of the two kings. King Henri was reported as accepting the King's candidature if the latter thought his son too young (he was thirteen-and-a-half).[128] The matter was complex, for Philip did not finally acknowledge the failure of his marriage proposal to Queen Elizabeth until after mid-March. At some later stage, therefore, he must have accepted the

[126] Granvelle v, 576–80.
[127] Ibid. v, 580–1.
[128] Ibid. v, 544; *Cal. Ven.* vii, 49, 54, 61–2 (some interesting Venetian speculations on King Philip's motives); articles 27–33 of the treaty.

French proposal, which was no doubt put forward to counter another Anglo–Spanish alliance. The health, physical and mental, of Don Carlos may have suggested his father's change of plan.[129]

The manner of these negotiations was continual struggle over 'real' issues, often masked in jostling for advantage, however slight. The need for agreement was even more urgent as the spring season for campaigning approached. The Spanish maintained their policy of 'showing their teeth' to the French, and of trying to win control over the drafting process. The French thought that some of the Spanish 'devices', particularly the pretended independence of the Duchess of Lorraine, were a 'farce'. They themselves indulged in threats to break off, or posturing to that effect. The English, in their isolation, were no doubt in perpetual torment, given the new régime at home. It was hard to be abroad on mission when Elizabeth became Queen, and the future was so unpredictable. At Le Cateau, each side saw the others as frequently impossible, often deceitful. In such long and wide-ranging negotiations it was inevitable that agreement on one point be hung on another, and that rupture over a dominant issue, Calais or Savoy, for instance, might break up the whole. According to Alva, this had been expected at least four times, on account of Spain's allies (presumably England and Savoy).[130]

Ceremonies and ratifications

The final ceremonies on 3 April were soon over; the weary diplomats were doubtless impatient to be gone. In the morning, the treaty between France and Spain was read out and signed (the agreements between France and England, and between England and Scotland, were partly signed, and certainly dated, on 2 April). The Duchess and the diplomats then proceeded to the parish church, where a Te Deum and Mass were celebrated and the peace proclaimed. Unusually, for so great an event, we have scant detail of these final ceremonies.[131] There followed a 'dinner' with the Duchess, and the

---

[129] For Don Carlos, cf. Pierson, op. cit., pp. 54–6.

[130] *Cal. Ven.* vii, 63.

[131] *Cal. For.* ii, 202; *Cal. Ven.* vii, 61 (letter from Granvelle's brother, Thomas Perrenot, Seigneur de Chantonnay, referred to as M. de 'Sciampoli'); Granvelle v, 586–7.

departures. S. André, still a prisoner, went back to Brussels.[132] In Antwerp there were nine days of festivities.[133]

The subsequent ratifications by the monarchs themselves were followed in May by solemn ceremonies of oath-taking. The Cardinal of Lorraine travelled to Brussels, accompanied by his brothers the Cardinal of Guise[134] and the Marquis of Elbeuf, the Bishop of Orléans, and Montmorency's second son, Henri Baron Damville. They were lodged near the royal palace (the Coudenberg or Cold Hill), to which they could proceed by a specially built gallery. On Whit Monday, 15 May, King Philip and the ambassadors assisted at a solemn Mass, in the palace chapel, celebrated by Granvelle. The King and the ambassadors moved to the high altar for the oath-taking; the King took his oath to the treaty, his hand on a relic of the true cross. A banquet followed, at which the Dowager Duchess of Lorraine and her son sat on the King's right, the two French cardinals on his left. The Duke of Savoy, the Prince of Parma, the Duke of Alva, and many others were present at the ceremonies.[135]

In return, King Philip despatched the Duke of Alva and Ruy Gómez to the court of France, the latter en route for Spain. With them went the Prince of Orange and Lamoral, Count of Egmont, hostages under the treaty. Their suite was very large: Orange alone had 500 horse. The taking of oaths to the treaty by the King and the Dauphin took place in Notre Dame on Saturday 18 June, followed by a banquet at the palace of the Bishop of Paris nearby. Alva had the place of honour. On 21 and 22 June he stood proxy for his royal master at the ceremony of betrothal, and then of marriage, at the doors of Notre Dame, of the Princess Élisabeth.

---

[132] Granvelle v, 585–7, 589; *Cal. Ven.* vii, 64 (Philip remitted S. André's ransom, having acquired it from Henry Duke of Brunswick).

[133] Bells rang, artillery sounded. Notre Dame's spire was illuminated by cressets, there were celebrations in verse by the Guilds of Rhetoric, feasting, drinking and civic games (E. Van Meteren, *Historia Belgica nostri potissimum temporis* (Cologne 1597) p. 25.

[134] Louis de Guise, Bishop of Troyes and Albi.

[135] Ruble, p. 27; Emm. Phil., p. 50; *Coll. des voyages*, pp. 66–8 (the Duke of Lorraine was angry at his placing at the mass). Presents were given; for Lorraine a gilt service worth 10,000 écus; for Orléans one worth 3,000; for S. André remittance of his ransom, and silver gilt to the value of 2,000 écus. To the Constable the King sent gold and gilt vessels worth 15,000 écus.

His head-dress still proclaimed court mourning for Mary Tudor.[136] The Duke of Savoy had by then arrived, and there followed the fatal tournament celebrating the royal and ducal marriages. Henri II was wounded, and died on 10 July.[137]

The Anglo–French and Anglo–Scottish treaties were also ratified: the first by letters of the two sovereigns and the Dauphin, the second by letters of the Queen, the Dauphin and the Dauphine.[138] In May solemn embassies 'received' the personal oaths of the sovereigns. To England came Montmorency's eldest son, François, the Marshal de Vieilleville, and M. de Noailles, who was to remain as ambassador resident. On Corpus Christi (25 May), at a ceremony in the palace, prayers and psalms in English were followed by the Queen's oath to the treaty, and to that with Scotland.[139] To France went Lord Howard, Wotton, and Sir Nicolas Throckmorton, who was to remain as ambassador resident. Their train was reported to include a company of 'young sparks'. They were dined by the Constable at Chantilly, and again at Ecouen, 'a princely house . . . and worth the seeing', on which had been hung escutcheons of the English royal arms, the red rose and the white, and 'E's' for Elizabeth. On Sunday 28 May, Howard rode beside the King in the procession to Notre Dame, where the King took his oath after the Mass. The King took his oath on the word of a King, on his faith and honour, and on the Holy Gospels 'corporally touched'. In the evening, in the palace chapel, the Dauphin and Dauphine took their oaths. There was dancing at court that night. Howard found the

[136] Ruble, pp. 29, 33, 228–236. The Spanish were received, en route, by the Constable at Chantilly, and at Écouen (*Cal. For.* II, 307). At the banquet on 18 June, Alva, Orange and Egmont sat on the King's right, the Dauphin, the Duke of Lorraine and the Cardinal of Lorraine on his left. The Constable and his son entertained the other cardinals, young noblemen and foreign ambassadors. (*Cal. For.* II, 326). The secretaries of state had arranged not only the marriage contracts, but the festivities (Sutherland, op. cit., pp. 92–3). The marriage contract of Philip II and Élisabeth de France is printed in J. Dumont, *Corps universel diplomatique du droit des gens* V, 47–9.

[137] Savoy arrived in Paris accompanied by 150 gentlemen in red velvet, red satin, and gold (*Coll. des voyages*, p. 68). His marriage to Marguerite de France was celebrated without ceremony, at midnight, on 9 July, at the church of S. Paul, near the Tournelles (where the King died). Philip had sent his physician and surgeon, Andreas Vesalius, to minister to the King (*Cal. For.* II, 364).

[138] Rymer XV, 516; Forbes I, 82–3; *Cal. For.* II, 220. Elizabeth ordered 300 copies of the Anglo–French treaty to be printed (cost 20 shillings); the Anglo–Scottish treaty was speedily proclaimed on the border (*Cal. For.* II, 207, 214).

[139] *Cal. For.* II, 240, 249, 279–80, 433; *Cal. Span.* XIV, 59. Three of the four French hostages demanded under the treaty travelled to England at the same time (*Cal. For.* II, 283, 307).

mission expensive, for there was daily largesse to minstrels and the like.[140]

The treaty between the two kings, as many before and since, was to be reinforced by the adherence of many powers, should they wish to be included.[141] Both sides named the Pope, and the Apostolic See, the Emperor, the Prince Electors, the towns and Estates of the Empire, the King Dauphin and the Queen Dauphine, the Kings of Portugal, Poland and Denmark, the Dukes of Savoy and Lorraine, the Dowager Duchess of Lorraine, the Duke of Ferrara, the Republic of Venice, the Swiss Cantons, the Dukes of Mantua and Urbino. On the side of Philip II were named the Queen of England (as provided in the treaty between England and France), the Republic of Genoa, and the Duke of Florence.[142]

The Anglo–French treaty was to include the King of Spain, and the King, Queen and realm of Scotland, on the part of the King of France; for the Queen of England, the King of Spain was to be included. That between England and Scotland was to include the Kings of France and Spain for Scotland, and the King of Spain for England.[143] Queen Elizabeth and her Council had not wished the Pope to be one of the parties named on their side. The ambassadors at Le Cateau, in their fatal letter of 2 March, had asked whether the Pope should be included, since they had heard that supremacy of the Church was again to be the Crown's. The Council replied that the inclusion of the Apostolic See 'may be passed over in silence'.[144] There was to be no papal dimension for the English government's diplomatic agreements at this time. The English ambassador, Sir Edward Carne, lingered in Rome, but not as an effective voice for the England of Elizabeth.[145]

[140] *Cal. For.* II, 236, 240–2, 271, 275–7, 285, 289–91; Forbes I, 102–11; *Cal. Span.* XIV, 59; Rymer XV, 519–20 (the oath taken by the Dauphin and Dauphine). The English had travelled by way of Amiens, where the Mayor presented Howard with a great salmon, carp, pike, bream and perches, and with 30 great pots of wine (6 being hypocras) (*Cal. For.* II, 275).

[141] Articles 45 and 46 of the treaty.

[142] Ibid. Enumerated in these articles were certain nobles and ecclesiastics who had lands in the obedience of the other King; competent judges would adjudicate on any disputes.

[143] *Cal. For.* II, 195, 198.

[144] Ibid. II, 157, 165.

[145] He protested that he was detained by the Pope, since England had 'rebelled' against the Apostolic See. In fact, he had asked the Pope to detain him, since, as a staunch Catholic, he feared to return to England and thereby lose his lands (*Cal. For.* II, 193–5, 199; *Dictionary of National Biography*).

The achievements of the treaty of Cateau-Cambrésis

England and Scotland

It is time to draw back from these negotiations. Had a real peace been achieved, and at what price? For England, the peace with Scotland, a first priority, was but a temporary respite; all 'claims' on either side were 'reserved'. Hence the Dauphin and Dauphine continued to style themselves King and Queen of England and Ireland, and to flaunt the royal arms.[146] Elizabeth feared a French invasion via Scotland, where Mary of Guise, the Regent, had French garrisons.[147] The problem became horrendous when the Protestant 'Lords of the Congregation' rebelled in May 1559 and deposed the Regent in October. English help was expected, and when, reluctantly, Elizabeth authorised armed intervention, a general conflagration was feared, most of all by the Spanish.[148] Elizabeth could argue that as suzerain over Scotland[149] her treaty with the Scots was merely one of mutual defence (against a French conquest of Scotland, the union of Scotland with France, and a possible invasion of England), and for the defence of Scottish freedoms and liberties.[150] The French held England's intervention to be open war. Their ambassador in London reported that the Queen wished to unite the two crowns under the style of 'Great Britain'; indeed Cecil had written to the Lords of the Congregation that the 'best felicity' for

[146] There were continual English complaints on this score. The arms had been seen at the jousts, in June 1559, on the plate on which the English ambassador was served, on hangings, and seals, and again at the 'triumphs' at Tours and Chénonceaux, after Easter 1560. (*Cal. For.* II, 347–8, 521, 524; III, 209–12, 322, 406–10: Forbes I, 334, 339, 420). The College of Arms pronounced that the arms were not only wrongfully used, but 'falsely marshalled' (*Cal. For.* II, 313–14). Montmorency, to whom Throckmorton complained (showing him a coloured drawing), replied that Queen Elizabeth used the arms of France (which indeed she did) (*Cal. For.* II, 324). Cecil heard from Throckmorton of Latin verses on the gate at Blois, constituting a breach of the 'peace'; unfortunately he did not leave us the details (*Cal. For.* II, 210–11).

[147] Queen Elizabeth bought arms and munitions at Antwerp, hoping that the 'peace' would have brought the price down (*Cal. For.* II, 28, 60, 105, 152). A short-term border truce with Scotland had been agreed in March (ibid., II, 192).

[148] Already, in April 1559, Philip and his Privy Council had decided against any Spanish involvement in Scotland. Open war must be avoided at all costs; Spanish shipping, Netherlands' trade and the herring fishing would be threatened; most of all, opposition to France, the main enemy, would be dissipated (*Cal. For.* II, 213–14).

[149] Cecil and the Council deliberated on English sovereignty over Scotland (*Cal. For.* III, 519).

[150] Treaty of Berwick (February 1560). Cf. W. C. Dickinson, *Scotland from the Earliest Times to 1603* (London 1965) pp. 326–9.

Scotland was either perpetual peace with England, or to be made one monarchy with England, as they were one island.[151] French armed intervention, according to Henri II, would be in support of the Regent in her struggle with 'heretics and schismatics'.[152] The eventual victory for the rebels secured withdrawal of French troops and the promise that Queen Mary's English claims would be abandoned.[153] However, the treaty had been negotiated by the French, and not by the Queen herself; she never ratified it. Her claims, therefore, remained a threat, which she later used in efforts to win public recognition, by Queen Elizabeth, of her right to the English succession. The 'postern' gate of Scotland, now a Protestant power, had, however, been closed to the French.

England and France

For England, the treaty with France heralded the probable loss of Calais; Feria reported that the common people mocked at the idea that the French would surrender it.[154] Ambassador Throckmorton indulged in wishful thinking (February 1560); he tried to tell the Cardinal of Lorraine that the Queen could have had Calais in 1559, had she not been moved towards the universal peace of Christendom. At this, the Cardinal 'put his finger to his nose and scratched it a little, where, I think, it did not itche'.[155] The legal and political reality on the subject was unpromising. It was all too likely that, during the eight-year period, the French would discover some English act which violated the treaty and thus released them

[151] *Cal. For.* III, 209 (report to Catherine de'Medici, December 1559); Cecil's memorandum of August 1559 printed in A. Clifford, ed., *The Papers of Sir Ralph Sadler* (Edinburgh 1809) I, 375 (cf. Conyers Read, op. cit., p. 145).

[152] *Calendar of State Papers Relating to English Affairs Preserved Principally at Rome in the Vatican Archives, vol. I, Elizabeth 1558–1571*, ed. J. M. Rigg (London 1916). pp. 11–13. Henri II informed the Pope that the nobility and third estate in Scotland manifested a seditious, insolent and irreligious spirit (ibid.). Cf. François II's protest, through his ambassador to England, in April 1560 (Forbes I, 410).

[153] The treaty of Edinburgh (July 1560), made possible by the failure of French reinforcement plans, the Huguenot conspiracy of Amboise, the surrender of Leith, and the death of the Regent (in June), was negotiated by Cecil and Wotton, and by the Bishop of Valence (Jean de Monluc) for France. The latter was escorted and 'watched' by Henry Killigrew, who played a considerable part behind the scenes (cf. A. C. Miller, op. cit., pp. 55–67; Wernham, op. cit., pp. 248–58; Conyers-Read, op. cit., pp. 173–93). The English fleet had anchored in the Forth in January (before the treaty of Berwick), but the army did not cross the border until April.

[154] *Cal. Span.* XIV, 43.

[155] Forbes I, 340; *Cal. For.* III, 409.

from its terms. In 1560 the English were demanding Calais and the 500,000 crowns indemnity, in retaliation for French intervention in Scotland (taken as a breach of the treaty of 1559), and the price of their defeat.[156] In 1563, during the first religious war in France, the tables were turned: English troops were landed at Le Havre and at Dieppe, towns offered by the Huguenots in return for promised military support and a large loan, and as guarantees of the eventual return of Calais.[157] This could be construed as an act of war, even though Cecil wished it to be regarded otherwise: the English would enter 'quietly' into these places, intended no war with France, but only to stay the power of the Guises and to regain Calais.[158] However, Elizabeth's envoy to the Huguenots had revealed: 'if the Queen succoured them, how much they were bound to God considering that thereby she lost her interest in Calais and entered into war with France, Scotland and Spain'.[159] Indeed, this intervention, and the loss of Le Havre after nine months, meant diplomatic and political failure at the peace negotiations in April 1564.[160] The loss of Calais had to be accepted; a renewed diplomatic effort in 1567 was rebuffed.[161]

This loss was a national humiliation, but had compensations. To retain Calais on a war footing cost £15,000 a year, a disproportionate drain on English financial resources. To retain it without adequate defences, perhaps again as a Staple, invited early recapture. To retain it, on any terms, invited further military involvement on the continental mainland, in France or in the nearby Nether-

---

[156] Conyers Read, op. cit., pp. 174, 176, 181, 190.

[157] This agreement (the treaty of Hampton Court, September 1562) was preceded by considerable secret activity, Henry Killigrew travelling to France to sound out opinions and possibilities (Mason, op. cit., pp. 74–83). Cession of towns had been proposed by the Huguenots in 1560; in April 1562 ambassador Throckmorton was arguing that the Huguenots should hand over Newhaven (Le Havre), Dieppe, or Calais, or all three, just as the Spaniards were to be offered strongholds by the Catholics (Conyers Read, op. cit., pp. 246–60; Wernham, op. cit., pp. 264–7). To avoid 'open war' the Queen refused to allow her troops to go to the relief of Rouen, although the commander at Le Havre, Sir Adrian Poynings, permitted a token force to set out. The Huguenot contingent went under Killigrew's command.

[158] Conyers Read, op. cit., pp. 251–2 (letter, probably to Sir Thomas Chaloner, ambassador to Spain. Full text in T. Wright, ed., *Queen Elizabeth and Her Times* (London 1838) I, 96.

[159] Letter to Killigrew (Mason, op. cit., p. 79).

[160] A small indemnity of 120,000 écus was to be paid for the return of the hostages held in England under the 1559 treaty. The 500,000 écus indemnity was not now on offer (treaty of Troyes, April 1564; cf. Conyers Read, op. cit., pp. 285–8).

[161] Ibid., p. 390.

lands. By its loss, England became Shakespeare's island fortress,
built by Nature against 'infection and the hand of war', the precious
stone set in the defensive moat of the sea.[162] England could, if she
wished, distance herself, except on her own terms, from continental
broils and conflicts. A bastion or bastions on the continent had
their dangers: in 1560, Cecil wrote (of Huguenot offers) 'no strength
is tenable that is farre distant',[163] and warned of the 'bottomless
pit' of expense of force and treasure, with no help but some popular
religious support.[164] The same was even truer of Calais. Elizabeth
and Cecil were islanders; the Queen never travelled abroad, Cecil
made only two brief journeys in 1554 and 1555, early in his career.[165]
Both had 'island', rather than 'European' mentalities, even if some
of their subjects did not. The treaty of 1559 presaged this condition.
It did not remove the obverse, the possibility of invasion, which
could and did threaten this increasingly Protestant power. Sea
power and guile would overcome this, with a close watch over
Scotland and Ireland. There was little prospect of Throckmorton's
fears being realised: that the alliance of France and Spain would
make England another Piedmont.[166]

France and Spain

England and Scotland were two lesser, though important, participants in the 'balance of power' first delineated by Guicciardini in
fifteenth-century Italy, but now a European equipoise, projected
even into the New World. Of the two 'super-powers', France and
Spain, the former seemed to have met defeat in the 1559 treaty. At
home it was bitterly resented; the Spanish envoy in London heard
it said that the peace had been made by prisoners (Montmorency

---

[162] *Richard II* II, i, 40ff. Cf. Ronsard's England, the son of Neptune, surrounded
completely by waves, and separated from the malice of the world (Ronsard VI, 423).
Leo X's views are mentioned above.

[163] Wright, op. cit., I, 31 (letter of 21 June).

[164] Cecil's words were: 'God forbid that your majesty should enter into that
bottomless pit of expense of your force and treasure, within the French King's own
mainland . . . there your majesty should have no more to further you but a devotion
popular upon opinions of religion.' (Quoted by A. Froude, *The Reign of Elizabeth*
(London 1911) I, 181, the only printed source to give the full text.)

[165] To Brussels to fetch Cardinal Pole to England (1554), and in 1555 to the
conference at Marcq, in the Calais pale, and on a three-week journey in Flanders
and Brabant (Conyers-Read, op. cit., pp. 103–6).

[166] *Cal. For.* II, 357 (report of July 1559); Forbes I, 153. Feria reported the general
gloom at the English Court (*Cal. Span.* XIV, 48–9).

and S. André) and that 'had it been made by others, King Philip would not have won such good terms.[167] Blaise de Monluc who, like many, had won fame and fortune in the wars, was indignant: France had given up all King François and King Henri had won, equivalent to one third of the French kingdom; he had read in a book in Spanish that it was 198 fortresses.[168] There was considerable validity in these complaints. The treaty marked the end of Italian dreams and commitments; the loss of Piedmont highlighted this, for here was the bridgehead for Italy. Only Saluzzo remained under French domination, and even here Savoy's claims were 'reserved'. The loss of Corsica disabled French schemes in the Mediterranean, particularly any break through Spanish encirclement. In the north, however, gains were solid and lasting: the great fortress of Calais, 'that jewel', as the English called it; the three fortresses of Vermandois, S. Quentin, Ham and Le Catelet; the three 'imperial' bishoprics, Metz, Toul and Verdun, quietly omitted from the discussions and from the treaty, but not surrendered.[169] Queen Elizabeth's envoy to the Diet of Augsburg saw the danger to Germany: France was 'enlarging the kingdom' under pretence of friendship for the Emperor.[170] The King wished to possess all the lands lying towards France on the Rhine, so that the river might be the frontier, or *limes Galliae*.[171] France had, indeed, to break through the encircling block of Spanish territories and Spanish client states to the north and east. There was rich scope for French designs and intervention in the much divided Empire; there was also opportunity in the north and west, above all in England. France might, therefore, advance yet again on a wider front. Yet her limited gains in 1559 concealed a desperate situation. There was financial bankruptcy, exhaustion after the wars and the menace of a yet more powerful internal threat: the growth and vigour of Protestantism. There were over

[167] *Cal. Span.* XIV, 135.

[168] Monluc II, 318.

[169] French possession of these towns was not formally acknowledged until 1648. Discussions, in 1559, had been refused by the French as not pertaining to the Franco–Spanish talks, and a projected embassy from Emperor Ferdinand had been refused. The French said that they would discuss the matter at the Diet of Augsburg, then in session, to which they sent representatives. (*Cal. For.* II, 134; *Cal. Ven.* VII, 32).

[170] *Cal. For.* II, 134. The Emperor was promised French help with the Pope, who had not yet confirmed his title (since the Electoral college had included Protestants). In fact, he never went to Rome for coronation.

[171] *Cal. For.* II, 212. Cf. Ronsard's eulogy of the King, who had campaigned, since his accession, to extend the 'empire of the French' (Ronsard IX, 103).

sixty Huguenot churches at this date, conversions (or temporary adherence) among the highest in the land, and much fear of political and social upheaval. One observer thought that the King had been forced to peace by the religious troubles.[172]

For Spain, the victory seemed substantial, 'so excellent a peace and profitable', in the words of William of Orange. Spain's hold over Naples, Sicily, Sardinia, and the fortresses of Tuscany, and over Genoa and Corsica (through Milan) seemed assured. Spanish hegemony in the Western Mediterranean was a base for the struggle against the Turk, which King Philip had intended to proclaim in the treaty itself. For twenty years, the King's principal preoccupation was to be the defence of the Mediterranean against the Turk; negotiations (with the Turk) for peace were called off on 8 April 1559 precisely, and the expedition to Tripoli, which met with such disaster, was planned.[173]

When King Philip left for Spain in August 1559, the northern dominions seemed secure. Yet armed force would soon be needed to stem growing disaffection, religious disunity, and disenchantment with rule from and by Spain. In 1556 there had been protests from the nobles over wars with France, not thought to be in the interests of the Netherlands.[174] Other protests, political, religious, and economic, would follow. Spanish control of the Provinces came to depend on her armies and they on the overland route, since English and French shipping menaced the sea. The 'Spanish road', suggested by Granvelle in 1563, ran from Genoa (or its other ports, Savona and La Spezia), to Milan, through Savoy, via the Mont Cenis, through Franche Comté and Lorraine, to Luxembourg, Liège and Brabant.[175] This was the artery of Spain's military might, a way through the King's own lands, or those of his allies, Genoa, Savoy, Lorraine, and Liège. The 1559 treaty gave security in these areas; broadly, it was an attempt to sustain Spain's northern and her Italian power, and to link the two.

---

[172] *Cal. Ven.* vii, 63. Large Huguenot gatherings in Paris were reported in May 1558, for instance, and March 1539 (ibid., vi, 1500–5; vii 51, 63). Monluc saw heretics everywhere (ii, 338–9).

[173] Cf. Pierson, op. cit., pp. 151–2. The imperial ambassador in Constantinople (Ghiselin de Busbecq) reported that the Turks were much annoyed at the peace (of Le Cateau), in which they had hoped to be included (*The Turkish Letters of Ogier Ghiselin de Busbecq*, trans. E. S. Forster (Oxford 1927) p. 214).

[174] H. Pirenne, *Histoire de Belgique* (Brussels 1912) iii, 381–2; G. Parker, *The Dutch Revolt* (London 1977) pp. 38–9; P. Geyl, *The Revolt of the Netherlands* (London 1958) p. 70.

[175] Pierson, op. cit., pp. 134–6; Parker, op. cit., p. 292, n. 26, and his detailed study, *The Army of Flanders and the Spanish Road* (Cambridge and New York 1972).

The peace also promised co-existence, if not understanding, with France, in an alliance cemented by marriage. But Catherine de' Medici found King Philip's political and religious policies antipathetic. Her interview with Alva at Bayonne in 1565[176] only served to accentuate the differences, and her daughter, the instrument of any rapprochement, died in 1568. King Philip's aggressive support for French Catholics, and for his own daughter's claim to the throne,[177] culminated in open war in 1595. This was, however, a short interlude. Peace with Henri IV was negotiated at Vervins (in the Thierache district, north of Laon) in 1598. This peace substantially reaffirmed that of 1559, some testimony to its merits.

The religious implications

There is, finally, the religious dimension of the peace, and the historical myths surrounding it. Protestants were convinced that the treaty included some secret agreement between France and Spain to undertake a systematic extermination of heretics. William of Orange, one of the Spanish hostages under the treaty, wrote in his *Apology* (1580) that while in Paris he went riding with the King in the Bois de Vincennes. Henri spoke of the increasing number of heretics in his realm; there were plans to exterminate all suspected Protestants in France, in the Netherlands, and throughout Christendom. The Duke of Alva was negotiating on the means to do this.[178] At this encounter, Orange's evasive silence (he had not yet resumed the Protestantism of his childhood) earned him his title 'the Silent'. In France Huguenot reports were categoric; in 1558 a letter to Calvin affirmed that if the King made peace, he would turn all his power against the Protestants, to extirpate the 'race' and the 'name'. By June 1559 the King was said to have a long list of heretics whom he intended to pick off one by one.[179] In May 1559 ambassador Throckmorton, always attuned to Huguenot fore-

---

[176] See below, p. 219.

[177] Despite her mother's renunciation of any claim in the 1559 agreement (art. 29).

[178] *Apologie ou Défense de Tres Illustre Prince Guillaume par la grace de Dieu Prince d'Orange* . . . (Leyden 1581) pp. 49–51; *The Apologie* . . . *ed. after the English edition of 1581* by H. Wansink (Leiden 1969), p. 61, cf. Pontus Payen, op. cit., I, 7–9. Orange had instructions, on King Philip's departure from the Netherlands, to extirpate heretics in Holland, Zealand and Utrecht, where he was Stadtholder. Orange's position is discussed by N. M. Sutherland, 'William of Orange and the Revolt of the Netherlands', *Archiv für Reformationsgeschichte* LXXIV, 1983.

[179] E. Lavisse, *Histoire de France* . . . *V (ii)*, par H. Lemonnier (Paris 1903?) 246.

bodings, reported on the King's intention to use extreme measures of persecution against Protestants in France and in Scotland. He was informed by the Vidame of Chartres, a few weeks later, that there was to be a new league between France and Spain, who were troubled by Queen Elizabeth's league with the Scots; the French King hoped that the King of Spain would endeavour to repress rebels and heretics, rather than suffer them to wax so strong and to increase.[180] In England Henry Killigrew, the Protestant adventurer, who had visited Le Cateau during the conference, referred (in a personal memoir of 1573) to a clause in the treaty of 1559 under which both kings undertook to root out heresy from their dominions and from other lands in which the Pope's authority was not absolutely obeyed.[181] Killigrew and a colleague, on the embassy staff in Paris in 1560, asserted the same belief.[182] The story became part of Protestant propaganda, and even a 'conspiracy' theory. At the same time, there is more sober testimony. De Thou, the French historian, usually reliable and impartial, wrote in his history (published in 1605), of the 1559 negotiations: 'This [concord] was soon turned to the ruin of France and Belgium through the perverse judgment of both kings and the counsel of their ministers, internal disorders arising far worse than foreign war. For from this time were renewed the secret plans of the Cardinal of Lorraine and Granvelle, Bishop of Arras, concerning the hunting down of sectaries and punishing them by the sword; in connection with which secret agreements were entered into on both sides, which finally broke out into open wars against the King's majesty [the wars of religion].'[183] In England William Camden, historian and antiquary, writing for James I, stated that Queen Elizabeth knew that 'the treaty of Cambrai was undertaken on purpose for the rooting out of the Protestant religion'.[184] Camden, a convinced Protestant, showed considerable impartiality on religious matters

---

[180] *Cal. For.* ii, 272; Forbes, i, 181; *Cal. For.* ii, 419.

[181] Miller, op. cit., pp. 27, 45–7, quoting Killigrew's memoir of 1573, which is printed in L. Howard, ed., *A Collection of Letters from the Original Manuscripts of Many Princes* . . . (London 1753) i, 184.

[182] Forbes i, 297.

[183] J.-A. de Thou, *Historiarum sui temporis volumen primum*, xxii, 9. In January 1559, the Council of Castile had indeed proposed mutual extradition of heretics by France and Spain as part of a peace settlement (Parker, op. cit., p. 285n38).

[184] W. Camden, *The History of the Most Renowned and Victorious Princess Elizabeth*, ed. W. T. MacCaffery (Chicago 1970) p. 24. The original Latin edition was published in 1615. The King asked Camden to obtain emendations to De Thou's account of Mary Queen of Scots, but there is no evidence that he did (ibid., xxxv–xxxvi).

(save for his treatment of Puritans); he would have read de Thou, with whom he corresponded, and to whom he sent his history in manuscript.

Could this belief have rested on fact? Already in 1544 the ill-fated treaty of Crépy (Laonnais) between Charles V and François I had been supplemented by a secret treaty under which François I undertook to help the Emperor in the work of church reform, to further the meeting of a General Council, and to bring back German heretics into the Church.[185] Granvelle knew personally of these negotiations, being one of the Emperor's plenipotentiaries. In 1545 Charles V established special inquisitors in the Netherlands, and his edict of 1550 ordered the execution of heretics. The edict was re-enacted by King Philip on Granvelle's advice. In August 1559 King Philip's parting message to the States General, delivered by Granvelle, commanded immediate action 'for the extirpation of all sects and heresies'.[186] In France the reign of Henri II was a period of repression; the 1547 edict established a new tribunal of the Paris Parlement, the *chambre ardente*, and an edict of 1551 forbade the holding of municipal or judicial office by heretics, condemning also heretical books and teachers. The growing number and strength of Huguenots caused royal alarm. By June 1559, in a stormy session of the Parlement of Paris, an influential minority of the judiciary were demanding a reforming Council and the suspension of the pursuit of heretics. The King came to the court, and his spokesman, the Cardinal of Lorraine, demanded the execution of heretics and confiscation of their goods.[187] The arrest of the four leaders of the minority showed how far the King would go; one, Anne de Bourg who remained intractable, was subsequently executed. In a letter

---

[185] K. Brandi, *The Emperor Charles V*, Eng. trans. (London 1967) p. 521; R. J. Knecht, *Francis I* (Cambridge 1982) pp. 370–1.

[186] Granvelle IX, 478–9; Pieter Bor, *Nederlandsche Oorlogen* (Utrecht 1595) I, f. 9; L. P. Gachard, *Collection de documents inédits concernant l'histoire de Belgique* (Brussels 1833) I, 313–22; Pirenne, op. cit., III, 390.

[187] J. H. Shennan, *The Parlement of Paris* (London 1968), p. 207; Lavisse, op. cit., v (ii) 244–6. Ambassador Throckmorton reported Lorraine's speech, as also the rumours that one reason for the King's action was the money which confiscation would bring (*Cal. For.* II, 309). Étienne Pasquier, advocate in Parlement, reported that the Cardinal addressed the full Parlement, as soon as peace was proclaimed, informing them that the King would have made peace, on any conditions, so that he could proceed to the extermination and banishment of the heresy of Calvin. It is possible that this speech was made on an earlier occasion, not that at which the King was present (Étienne Pasquier, *Les Lettres* (Paris 1619) I, 174; letter to M. de Fonsomme).

written shortly afterwards to the French ambassador to the curia, the King asserted that, now there was peace, he hoped to employ his time in the punishment and extirpation of all heretics, of whatever rank or degree.[188] At the same time, the Duke of Alva was writing from Paris to King Philip that the French King welcomed his help in the reform of the church and the suppression of heresy in France. Geneva must be the target, King Henri thought, since it was the refuge and home of those of 'the religion'.[189]

There is no doubt, therefore, that Philip II and Henri II shared the opinion of the Emperor Charles V that the suppression of heresy 'is more important for the service of our Lord and the good and preservation of these realms than any other [affair]'.[190] Both also held heresy to be potential rebellion. It may be that their ambassadors discussed the problem at the conference in 1558–9. There is the tradition that they did so at Marcoing; a secret agreement at Cercamp and Le Cateau cannot be ruled out. It would have conformed with the religious and political stance of both monarchs. Secrecy may have been partly a by-product of the English presence. Joint action by France and Spain, encouraged and applauded by Catholic propagandists such as Peter Canisius (1 July 1559), might well have followed had King Henri lived.[191] His widow, however, was no zealot; her emblem, the Rainbow, symbol of Peace,[192] indicated her desire for concord and peaceful reconciliation, as she made abundantly clear to Alva in 1565 at Bayonne.[193] She had, fortunately for her, not inherited a public undertaking of an anti-heresy campaign. The 1559 treaty had provided only that the two

---

[188] Quoted by Lavisse, op. cit., v (ii) 247.

[189] Ruble, pp. 199–200.

[190] Letter from the former Emperor to Juana, Regent of Spain, May 1558. H. Kamen, *The Spanish Inquisition* (London 1965) pp. 78–9.

[191] The Jesuit leader was then Provincial of Upper Germany, and attended the Diet of Augsburg (cf. *Beatri Petri Canisii . . . epistulae et acta*, ed. O. Braunsberger (Freiburg im Bresgau 1898) ii, 469).

[192] For Queen Catherine's emblem, cf. F. A. Yates, *Astraea* (London 1975) p. 218. The Queen used the emblem with the motto, in Greek, 'It brings light and serenity'.

[193] Alva told the Queen that King Philip wished the heretics to be expelled from France. He found her 'indifferent' on these matters, preferring a league against the Turk to the league against heresy, which the Pope had urged. She and her Chancellor, de l'Hopital, favoured moderation. Alva feared that the disease of heresy would spread to Spain; the Huguenots would stir up the Moriscos, and they the Turk. He, at other times, recommended extermination as the remedy (Granvelle ix, 280–99; N. Sutherland, *The Massacre of St Bartholomew and the European Conflict, 1559–1572* (London 1973) pp. 34–46; Pierson, op. cit., p. 137).

kings should work for a General Council, to bring about the 'reformation and reduction of the entire Christian Church into one true
union and concord' (article 2).[194] In fact it was the new Pope, Pius
IV (Gian Angelo de' Medici), ardent reformer and conciliator of
princes, who secured this. Having promised at the election conclave
to resummon the Council of Trent, he proceeded to do so. It met,
in final session, from January 1562 to December 1563.

The Peace in art and literature

What of the visual and literary records of the peace-making? In the
Ashmolean Museum in Oxford there is a contemporary drawing by
Jan van der Straet (Stradanus) (see Plate 7). In it King Philip,
flanked by two female figures (Peace and Christian Piety on his left,
Magnanimity or Generosity on his right) is setting fire to the figure
of Fury, chained at his feet on a pile of martial trophies. In the
foreground, on the right, France and Spain, in martial costume,
clasp hands; on the left Germany and Italy, seated on trophies and
arms, do the same. In the background a man is closing the door of
the Temple of Janus, the god of the doorway ('janua'), a door closed
in peace and open in war.[195] The drawing is in pen and ink, with
grey wash, and is dated 1565. From its Italian inscription, it seems
intended for an Italian patron;[196] since the artist was often in Flor-

[194] To the German Protestants, whom he wished to support his claims to Metz,
Toul and Verdun, the French King affirmed that he was not, in reality, working
with the King of Spain to procure a Council at which the Pope should be president
and judge. The Council he wanted should decide all disputes according to the word
of God, and the precedents of the primitive church (report of Queen Elizabeth's
envoy to the Diet of Augsburg, Christopher Mundt, *Cal. For.* II, 323).

[195] K. T. Parker, *Catalogue of the Collection of Drawings in the Ashmolean Museum*
(Oxford 1938) I, 30. The figure of 'il furore', or Madness, is one of the symbolic
personages often accompanying War. This figure, and the closed door, suggest a
reference to a famous passage of the *Aeneid* (1. 294ff.) in which the Gates of War
are closed, and Furor sits on a heap of arms, his hands bound behind his back.
Dryden's version runs:

> Janus himself before his fane shall wait,
> And keep the dreadful issues of his gate
> With bolts and iron bars: within remains
> Imprisoned Fury, bound in brazen chains:
> High on a trophy raised, of useless arms,
> He sits, and threats the world with vain alarms.

[196] The author of the Ashmolean catalogue quotes the suggestion that the figure
of Italy refers to the Pope. This is unlikely; it was the temporal powers of Italy,
above all Florence and Genoa, which benefited from the treaty.

ence, it may perhaps have been intended for Duke Cosimo, who benefited so much from the peace. King Philip's triumph is clearly that of peace and the Christian religion, linked in one allegorical figure.

A 'triumph' picture for King Henri may have been precluded by the King's sudden death and the subsequent troubled period. There were some 'ephemeral' triumphs celebrating the royal marriage in June; Ronsard mentions masques, mommeries, and dancing. There was to have been a comedy played at the Guise Palace, on the command of the Cardinal of Lorraine. Ronsard wrote 'inscriptions', lauding the royal family and King Philip, short four-line verses, in which King Henri is hailed as great Jupiter, the King of Spain as heir to Janus, Élisabeth de France (now Queen of Spain) as a beautiful lily, whose body a goddess might enter, the Dauphin as Achilles, the Dauphine as Venus, Marguerite de France (now Duchess of Savoy) as Minerva, and the two Lorraines, Duke and Cardinal as Mars and Mercury.[197] We do not know if the entertainment took place. The King's accident and death called for other themes.

Queen Elizabeth, hearing of a slight accident only, wrote on 10 July to Montmorency in sententious vein, that great monarchs are subject to great misfortunes; we must thank Almighty God, who daily preserves us from greater.[198] The Huguenots had their own picture of King Henri. They saw his sudden death as divine punishment for his religious persecution: 'the judgments of God are like a deep abyss, which is sometimes lit up by a light brighter than the sun; the tempest of persecution is over.'[199] Nostradamus had a different, secular, vision: of an old lion (the King, it was thought), overcome by a young lion in a duel (the fatal tournament) and of the death of the older, in a golden cage.[200] Ronsard had counselled the King, in the New Year of 1559, that France itself was a sufficient New Year present; he had no need of the skies, or the empire of

---

[197] Ronsard IX, 131–41.
[198] *Cal. For.* II, 368.
[199] Letter to Calvin, 1 July 1559, quoted in Lavisse, op. cit., v (ii) 248.
[200] Michel de Nostre Dame, astrologer and physician. His book of prophecies, in quatrains grouped in hundreds, was called *Centuries*. The first edition of 1555 was followed by a second in 1558, dedicated to the King. (The prophecy is *Centurie* I, no. 35). Blaise de Monluc records (June 1558) that the King had the prophecies read to him (II, 287).

the seas.[201] After the peace, the poet wrote of the King's many conquests. Now fortune's wheel had turned. He should cultivate the peace which Lorraine and Montmorency[202] had bought. Kings should be content with their own; France was so great. What profit could there be in a victory over the Flemings, with King Philip led in chains through Paris? King Henri was getting old; he should govern his household, live in peace, that is live well, building his Louvre, reading his books, and hunting. He should guard the peace, and seek knowledge, as his father did.

> Pensez-vous estre Dieu? L'honneur du monde passe,
> Il faut un jour mourir, quelque chose qu'on fasse.

The poem could serve as a valediction.[203] In the comedy for the marriage festivities, one 'inscription' for the King had again counselled content; the King should have had the sun for an emblem, for his honour could not be increased.[204] This was a reference to the King's emblem, the crescent moon (perhaps a compliment to his mistress Diane de Poitiers?), and his motto, 'Donec totum impleat orbem' ('until it [the moon] waxes full').[205] The emblem itself had, perhaps, a transitory quality; it lacked the vigorous confidence of the winged stags of Charles VII, the salamander of François I, or the sun emblem of later kings.

The immediate hopes of this peace-making had, however, been great. The two marriage alliances were pledges of concord; by a happy coincidence there is a charming portrait of Marguerite de France as Minerva. The enamel, in the Wallace Collection in London, was made by Jean de Court in 1555. Minerva, daughter

---

[201] Ronsard x, 66.

[202] For Ronsard, Lorraine was the 'pilot' of the ship of France; he had healed the divisions at Le Cateau, unravelling, by his long speeches, the disputes between the kings, the rights and wrongs of the wars, and of the claims to territory (Ronsard ix, 149). Montmorency, bringing peace and the marriage alliances, returned to France which had been ill, in his absence, as a child whose wet-nurse was away. His return was like the coming of spring, and all the population rejoiced (ibid., ix, 117–23). Thus the poet hedged his bets.

[203] Ronsard ix, 113–14. ['Do you think you are a God? Worldly honour passes. Death must come one day, whatever one does'].

[204] Ibid., ix, 193.

[205] For the device and the motto, cf. the King's entry into Paris in 1549 (decoration at the gate of S. Denis) (quoted in A. Denieul Cormier, *The Renaissance in France 1488–1559* (London 1969) p. 248). In December 1558, captains being discharged from the army were given gold medals, with this device and motto (*Cal. For.* ii, 22).

of Jove, was the Goddess of Peace and Wisdom. The portrait shows the Princess seated upon the orb of the world, a helmet at her side, holding a lance, her left hand on the *aegis* (shield) with the Gorgon's head. At her feet, upon two heavy volumes, sits the owl, the bird of learning (see Plate 8). Marguerite herself took as her emblem an olive branch wound about with a serpent (another symbol of knowledge)[206] and the motto 'Rerum custos sapientia' ('Wisdom, guardian of all things'). This was the way Ronsard saw the Princess, who was his patron; for him she was the learned princess, 'la colonne et l'espérance des Muses', the new Pallas, whose virtue equalled her wisdom, and whose eyes, like the Gorgon's, would turn sinners to stone. At the peace, she, who was Minerva, was inflamed by love, for the first time, for her future husband the Duke of Savoy.[207] Ronsard's paeans for the peace show the bright hopes it had engendered. Peace had taken up her abode in the Duchess of Lorraine's eyes; the golden age had returned; Mars had been chained in Hell. Let him who broke the peace die, dogs eating his brains in the fields.[208] It had seemed that Minerva's peace and wisdom were in the ascendant.

However, political realities soon darkened the scene. Pontus Payen, writing of the Netherlands, could also have been describing France: with the ending of the war, and the royal marriage alliances, the nations of Europe enjoyed repose in another golden age; all was then changed to an age of iron by a very bloody civil war.[209]

[206] Marguerite was a learned Princess; she knew Latin, Greek and Italian, reading Plutarch in the original with Jacques Amyot, whom she brought to the University of Bourges (when she was Duchess of Berri, from 1550). Michel de l'Hopital was her Chancellor in Berri and subsequently Chancellor of Savoy, before becoming Chancellor of France (Stephens, op. cit., pp. 114–15, 121, 135–44).

[207] Ronsard III, 98, 101; IX, 170–1, 197–8.

[208] Ibid., IX, 131–41, 113–14.

[209] Pontus Payen I, 1–2.

Epilogue

Paix et guerre sont toujours en balance;
Ils s'enclinent tout ainsi qu'on les boute[1]

Do some general conclusions emerge from this study? Certainly it is clear that the search for peace, however potent as an ideal, however firm as an obligation, was overshadowed by other aims, other political realities. Peace by its very nature is an ever-changing phenomenon, fragile and always under threat. It depends upon compromise, concessions, restraint and continual vigilance. To be effective it has to be enforced, and may therefore be deeply resented. The threats to its continuance are the greater, the wider the peace network and the more numerous the participating powers. This is true whether the peace is based upon the dominance of a super-power (as the *Pax Augusta*, or the *Pax Britannica*), or on an *ad hoc* balance between powers (accidental or by consent), or on an attempted co-existence through neutrality, *détente*, or other disengagement. The peace will always be threatened, as the power structure varies, so that the conqueror or dominant power of today becomes the weakened or client state of tomorrow. Any peace depends upon immobility, and this is not the normal state of living societies. It depends also upon the harnessing of human greed, ambition, and search for excitement, and its apostles, like those of a great religion, must win men's minds and hearts and offer some 'participation'. War, in the pre-atomic age, offered honourable, and even pleasurable activity, and rewards, for nations and individuals. Even if it went badly, there was the gamble of future victory, which excited and sustained. Hence the disposition to continue fighting, the view of war and peace as open choices, complementary actions. Only the horrendous discoveries of modern times have weighted the balance towards peace.

---

[1] 'War and peace are always in the balance; they tip the way one pushes them'. Pierre Gringoire, *Oeuvres complètes* i, 27 (from *Les folles enterprises*).

The peace efforts of the Renaissance reflect, and respond to, changing conditions: the breakdown of any universal authority, whether papal or imperial; the emergence of new political forces. Papal arbitration had become a thing of the past, as Bodin observed in 1576.[2] There was a brief flicker at the Congress of Munster in 1648. Papal censures had been invoked in the peace treaties of 1521 and 1522, in the later stages of the Franco–imperial conflict, but not in the 1559 settlement, to which the Pope was simply an 'adherent'. Such censures were, however, invoked by papal allies, as another weapon to be used against their enemies. The Pope himself, by his commitment to a territorial policy, had forfeited his claim to 'neutrality' and thus (for many) his right to arbitrate. Even in his native Italy he had brought ruin; Guicciardini wrote of Julius II as the 'fatal instrument' of Italy's ruin.[3] By the time that the Papacy had reformed and rearmed for war on heresy, its neutrality was under fire for still deeper causes. The Protestants would not attend the Council of Trent. For Robert Ascham, tutor to Elizabeth I, the Pope was 'the disturber of Christendom';[4] for others he was Evil Incarnate, the Anti-Christ.

The crumbling of papal power and influence was paralleled by the divisions of Charles V's empire so that, more and more, the secular powers had many and ever-changing options in their international relations. Peace was still an ideal, more earnestly invoked when war become more cruel, but war was an ever-present alternative which could always be 'justified'. The growing power of the Turk had complicated and enlarged the area of conflict. Henry VIII's bastions in France, Henri II's on the Rhine and Moselle, Philip II's in the Mediterranean, might be chauvinistic attempts at empire-building. All Europe, however, had cause for alarm at Turkish advances. Yet even here, peace or war were viable options which could be 'justified' in terms of political and economic realities, if not on ideological and religious grounds.

Venetian reactions are instructive. In 1621 James Howell praised Venice (applauded in seventeenth-century England for many virtues): 'a city that all Europe is bound unto, for she is her greatest rampart against that huge Eastern tyrant the Turk by sea, else I

[2] Bodin, p. 177.

[3] Guicciardini, *Storia d'Italia* i, 65 (Lib.i, cap.ix).

[4] Roger Ascham, *English works*, ed. W. A. Wright (Cambridge 1970) (*A discours . . . of the state of Germainie, 1553*), p. 137.

believe he had over-run all Christendom.'[5] Venice, however, did
not relish this role, nor consistently play it. She needed peace, and
peace with the Turk above all, to sustain her trade, already under
threat. Other observers saw this. In the early seventeenth century
William Bedell wrote: 'Their Arsenall is indeed a shop of warr; but
it serveth them more for the guard of their peace with the opinion
of it, than the use.'[6] In the same period Paolo Sarpi himself castigated his fellow citizens for their supineness: 'This republic desires
peace and avoids war as a sick man avoids medicine' (one must
accept contemporary views of physicians).[7] The Turk, therefore,
was an ever-present threat for some, for others a potential or
necessary ally, as the French 'special relationship' proved. Others
might imitate the French; Walsingham advised Queen Elizabeth to
invoke Turkish attacks on Spain in 1585.[8] Many of the powers were
'French' or 'Venetian', psychologically, in their treatment of the
Turks or their reactions to the division within Christendom itself.

If the Turkish presence confused and interpenetrated the old
unity of Christendom, still worse and more bitter were the divisions
among Christians. Blaise de Monluc wrote, with good reason, 'other
quarrels are easily composed, but that for religion has no end'.[9]
The lamentable divide between Catholic and Protestant was demar-
cated for all to see by the emerging pattern of diplomatic representation. In the Swiss cantons, ambassadors from Catholic powers
turned Solothurn (near Basel) into the 'town of the ambassadors';
papal nuncios took up residence at Lucerne. The ambassadors of
Protestant powers congregated in Zurich. This diplomatic 'divide'
had been commanded for Catholic powers by Pius V (1556–1572)
whose updated version of the bull *In Coena Domini* (against heresy)
forbade Catholic rulers to receive or to correspond with non-Cath-
olics.[10] It was not entirely because of this that the Venetians allowed
their embassy in England to lapse from 1558 to 1602 (they had
'residencies' only, in Protestant countries), but the act was sympto-
matic of changed conditions. As Mattingly pointed out, 'by 1589
European diplomatic contacts were interrupted everywhere except

[5] James Howell, *Epistolae Ho-Elianae, Familiar Letters* (London 1754) p. 59.
[6] Quoted in Bouwsma, op. cit., p. 109.
[7] Ibid., p. 528.
[8] Conyers Read, *Mr Secretary Walsingham and the Policy of Queen Elizabeth* (Oxford 1925) III, 224.
[9] *Commentaires et lettres* III, 513.
[10] Pastor, op. cit., XVIII, 35–6, 441; Bouwsma, op. cit., pp. 327–9.

between ideological allies'. England, for instance, kept a resident in France, but her older network contracted to residents with non-Catholic powers (after 1589) and a newly established ambassador with the Turk; unofficial agents worked elsewhere. The networks were partly rebuilt in the period after the peace between France and Spain in 1598 and that between Spain and England in 1604.[11]

The 'divide' permeated diplomatic practice also. For Protestant powers there was no more solemn promulgation of treaties at high mass, with oaths on the sacrament, or on some relic. In 1559, Elizabeth I's ratification of the treaties was by oath after prayers and psalms in English.[12] In 1572 the Anglo–French treaty was ratified by the King of France after evensong 'to avoid all offence that might chance on either party rather than at mass'. The English ambassadors retired to a side chapel, leaving the King to 'such ceremonies as were used in their Romish evensong' (but in hearing of the good music). The King then advanced with them to the high altar, and laid his hand on 'the book open', which he then kissed.[13]

Yet alliances, as this example proves, spanned the religious 'divide', as they did the divisions between Christian and Infidel. France was a pastmaster at both, and Elizabeth I, like her 'successor' Cromwell, trod warily in the international religious antagonisms. At Elizabeth's accession Queen Sophia of Denmark and Norway had offered close alliance; kingdoms were to be preserved not so much by arms as by the friendship of neighbouring Princes, especially those who had the same religion. Queen Sophia hoped that Elizabeth's known zest for 'the religion' would prompt her to expel the 'entire doctrine of Anti-Christ'.[14] But harder realities prevailed in the struggle with the ambitions of France, or Spain, both for Queen Elizabeth and later for Oliver Cromwell. It was these realities that were behind the emergence of *politiques*; Giovanni Botero, in the late sixteenth century, wrote of them: 'They profess to prefer temporal to ecclesiastical peace and the political state to the Kingdom of God, to exclude Christ, our Lord and his Holy Gospel from the councils of state, and finally to adapt their deliber-

---

[11] Mattingly, op. cit., pp. 204ff.
[12] See above, p. 208.
[13] Ambassador Thomas Smith to Burghley (H. Ellis, *Original Letters* (London 1827), Series II, III, 12–22 (quoted in M. Dewar, *Sir Thomas Smith: a Tudor intellectual in office* (London 1964) p. 247).
[14] *Cal. For.* II, 90–1.

ations not to the law of God but to present occasions.'[15] Zealots on
both sides would condemn, on this score, Machiavelli and Bodin,
and secular rulers whose actions fitted into a secular scheme of
politics. Yet the Christian ideals and inspirations remained, even
in the turbulent struggles of the later sixteenth and seventeenth
century, even if more narrowly defined, as befitted the sectarian
religious attitudes of the time. Religion could be a mask, as it always
can, and it is as hard to assess this factor as to assess personal piety,
from the outside. The Venetian statesman and historian, Nicolò
Contarini, wrote of Philip II: 'The inner recess of a man one cannot
penetrate; the effects of this piety, however, were of marvellous
profit to the King . . . It was most notable of all in Philip, King of
Spain that, being most religious, religion never impeded him from
any advancement of the State . . . and whatever he did was always
put forward as being in the service of God and for the aggrandisement of the Catholic faith.'[16]

Religious divisions, and alliances between co-religionists across
national frontiers, did not exclude intensely felt national differences
and traditions, perhaps more strongly held to in the many
dangerous conflicts of the time. These loyalties might appear unim-
portant to idealists like the Benedictine poet Alexander Barclay: at
Heaven's gate one would not be asked whether one was French,
English, Scot, Lombard, Picard or Fleming, but only about one's
merit and one's life.[17] More realistic and also unusual was the
tolerant understanding of Robert Gaguin, poet and diplomat. In
1489 he pleaded for an end to Anglo-French enmity: let English
and French to follow their own traditions and be at peace; French
couldn't swear 'By God' or 'By our Lord', nor English pronounce
Picquigny.[18] For the most part, however, there was pride but with
it chauvinism and intolerance. Roger Ascham thanked God that he
had been only once in Italy, and then only for nine days; in that

[15] Quoted from *Relationi universali* (Venice 1640) p. 442, by Bouwsma, op. cit.,
p. 300.

[16] Quoted from the *Historie Viniziane* (written in the 1620s and never published),
by O. Logan, *Culture and Society in Venice 1470–1790* (London 1972) p. 121.

[17] Alexander Barclay, *Mirror of Good Maners*, quoted in *Eclogues*, ed. B. White
(*Early English Text Society*) (London 1928) p. v.

[18] Robert Gaguin, *Epistulae et orationes*, ed. L. Thuasne (Paris 1903–1904) II, 4,
415–16. Gaguin, General of the Trinitarian Order, humanist and diplomat, wrote
Le passetemps d'oysiueté (from which this passage is taken) while in England on a
protracted embassy.

time in one city (Venice), he had found more liberty to sin than he had heard tell of in 'our noble citie of London' in nine years. The Venetians were unlike the English in religion, and hence in 'honestie of living'.[19] On his last great embassy to France, in 1527, Wolsey instructed his retinue that the French would approach them very familiarly, and speak French to them, as if they could understand every word. Let the English speak English in return, 'for if you understand not them, they shall no more understand you'. Rice, the Welshman, should speak Welsh, which would be as obscure ('diffuse') to the French as their language to him.[20] In these anti-pathies of French and English, of Germans and Italians, of French and Spaniards, there were those who revived ancient traditions of climatic causes. For Bodin, the people of the extreme south (he thought of the Spanish) were more 'ingenious' than those of the middle regions; they could gain, by subtlety, without striking a blow. Southerners, like foxes, relied on diplomacy and finesse or appeals to religion to get what they wanted.[21]

The diplomats and their masters still struggled with this basic problem of communication, given national antipathies and linguistic barriers. There was pride and obstinacy in this latter context. For some, the division of language had become, not the biblical story of sin, but a positive benefit. Ronsard, in the preface to his *Franciade*, termed it *lese majesté* to abandon the language of one's own country, which was alive and flourishing, to disinter the ashes of the Ancients.[22] In 1552 Sebastian Munster wrote in his *Cosmography*: 'Formerly regions were bounded by mountains and rivers . . . but today languages and lordships mark the limits of one region from the next, and the limits of a region are the limits of its language.'[23] In 1549 Joachim du Bellay wrote his *Déffense et illustration de la langue Françoyse*; northern vernaculars were now being praised and expounded as Italian had been and still was.[24] The 'Germanitas' of Luther, and his use of the language, is a theme in itself, as is the long development of English 'identity' in prose and verse.

---

[19] Ascham, *English Works*, p. 234.
[20] Cavendish's Life, in *Two Tudor Lives*, pp. 50ff.
[21] Bodin, pp. 149–52.
[22] Ronsard xvi, 351 (preface to the 1589 edition).
[23] Quoted G. Parker, *The Dutch Revolt* (London 1977) p. 35.
[24] Cf. V. Ilardi, '"Italianita" among some Italian intellectuals', in *Traditio* xii, 1956.

In all these struggles, there was a time for peace, as for war. In the endeavours for peace, the use of 'summitry' was less and less in favour. Cloak-and-dagger diplomacy was often the method of communication as Europe became more divided, less aware of any common cause. Secrecy was at a premium, expense a burden, and travel cumbersome and unimproved. The extravagant retinues of princes or of grand embassies were at fault on all three counts. Not only the meetings themselves, but the endless receptions *en route* made such 'summits' more occasions of display, entertainment and rivalry than means for diplomatic parley. In 1522 for instance, when the Emperor journeyed to England to conclude the offensive alliance against France, his journey and his reception were enormously expensive to both sides. Met with solemnity at Gravelines, he was received at the Milk Gate of Calais by all the notables, on the right 'all the parsons, curates, priests, copes, crosses and reliques as may be gotten within the Pale'. Wolsey went to Dover with heralds and the King's trumpets; at Canterbury, the King and his great suite waited, as also the Cardinal's following. The Queen, with others, was to be on the wharf at Greenwich.[25] In 1527 Wolsey's great embassy to France (when he hoped to achieve 'perpetual peace') highlighted the temptations and dangers of summitry. The Cardinal explained to his retinue that he was the King's lieutenant-general, and as such must receive the honour and service due to the King.[26] In 1532 the meeting of Henry VIII and François I, which was intended to avoid the prodigality of 1520, nevertheless brought more than 2,700 in the King of England's train.[27]

Hence the normal exchange of less publicised, less spectacular embassies, or the 'working' conferences of diplomats (as in 1558–9). The experience and powers of endurance of the 'professional' ambassadors and civil servants, and their personal talents, made them the normal peacemakers. The possession of such qualities meant burdensome and prolonged service. In 1585, for instance, Walsingham wrote to the English ambassador to the Turk that his experience made his service invaluable. Although he had exceeded the agreed period of service, the Queen could not yet release him 'thinking it necessary that you stay one year longer at least for

[25] *L.P.* iii (ii) no. 2288; Rymer XIII, 767–8.
[26] Cavendish, loc. cit., pp. 50ff.
[27] Hamy, op. cit., p. l.

compassing a matter of such importance (help against Spain)'.[28] It was, and still is, a familiar ploy.

The work of the diplomats was perilous yet full of opportunities, as the careers of Richard Pace, Gasparo Contarini, Antoine Duprat, Nicolas Wotton or Antoine Perrenot de Granvelle reveal. Essentially, their success depended upon the ability to communicate and to interpret the communications of others, far from home and in the hot-house atmosphere of a court, or a diplomatic conference. At least there was a degree of secrecy now unknown, so that compromise by concession or genuine concern for an agreement could be reached. If the sayings and doings of diplomats were the subject of rumour, very often quite well-informed, they were free from the interview by the media, at each stage of the day's proceedings, to which their modern successors are subjected. It was, however, felt then, as now, that there was weakness in suing for peace, and that in any case, treaties were all too often but words. Such a climate was well described by Scottish envoys meeting the English early in 1559: 'Princes always stand too much on their reputation to crave peace, but by meaner persons such things have their beginning.'[29] The result was all too often what Commynes had observed: people deceive themselves that they can reconcile great princes.[30]

The search for peace went on, intermittently and with frequent reluctance. Wars came through a whole *catena* of tensions. Some were short eruptions, frontier incidents, violence on the high seas, breaking of truces, which could as quickly be healed (if the will was there). These incidents were what Henry VIII termed 'an excorse'. Others sprang from longstanding grievances, over disputed territory, over unkept treaties, over broken promises (of alliance, of marriage, of transfer of territory). The states of Europe were burdened with inherited conflicts, with all their potential for covert or open conflict, intervention, or bargaining. It was true then, as now, that 'war begins in the minds of men', and peace also. The whole machinery of propaganda, of distrust or hatred of the foreigner, of military and political ambition, and of religious bigotry, could be brought into play. The essential combativeness and competitiveness of men, whether rulers or ruled, adapted to

[28] Conyers Read, op. cit., III, 228.
[29] *Cal. For.* II, 120. Louis XI, a pastmaster in diplomacy, held it self-evident that one should negotiate with an enemy by proxy (Louis XI, *Lettres* XI, 25–6).
[30] Commynes I, 92.

changing ideals of chivalry (July 1559 saw the last Chapter of the
Golden Fleece),[31] and of warfare. Diplomacy adapted itself also.
For many it was, as has often been said, 'war by other means'.
Charles V once said 'Peace is beautiful to talk of, but difficult to
have, for as everyone knows it cannot be had without the enemy's
consent'.[32] The Venetians remarked in 1522 that they should not
be governed by timidity and immoderate desire for peace: 'peace is
desirable and holy when it is above suspicion, when it does not
augment the danger, . . . there should not be war, under the
insidious name of peace.'[33] In truth, war and peace could hardly
be separated; they were alternatives and, all too often, alternating
conditions. War to gain peace, preparedness as a weapon to preserve
peace, were often quoted arguments. There were those who hoped
to exile war or at least to keep it far from home, as Bodin advised;[34]
others concentrated on defence.

Perhaps a propagandist of 1559 should be given the last word.
Guillaume Aubert, advocate in the Paris Parlement and an associate
of the *Pléiade* poets, published an *Oraison de la Paix* (Prayer for
Peace) in May 1559, addressed to Philip II and Henri II.[35] It is
strongly Erasmian, but has its own momentum. The two princes,
whose fathers were at war for thirty years, are reminded that the
tranquillity of Christendom depends on them. The horrors of war
are graphically depicted, and the rarity of any peace being kept.
Wars spring up again, as a tree which is not properly uprooted.
Secret war is prepared under cover of peace; sometimes the very
trumpet which announced the peace proclaims the war. There are
then Erasmian arguments that man is made for peace, as his
physical helplessness shows. Aubert makes Mother Nature lament,
seeing her children at war. Then there comes a savage from La
France Antarctique, instructed in the Christian faith by Ville-

[31] It was no accident that Philip II's parting words to the knights were on the
fight against heresy, and that the knights agreed that no heretics should be elected
(F. A. de Reiffenberg, *Histoire de l'ordre de la Toison d'or* (Brussels 1830) pp. 473–4).

[32] Brandi, op. cit., pp. 219, 501.

[33] Guicciardini IV, 180–1, (Lib. xv, cap.ii).

[34] Bodin, p. 169. Henry VII had hoped that the French would be occupied in
Italy (*Cal. Milan* I, 601); in 1514 Italians in Rome hoped that the French and English
would kill each other, while they (the Italians) made merry. (D. S. Chambers, op.
cit., p. 59); Navagero, ambassador in Rome in 1558, counselled avoidance of war
or its deflection far from home (Alberi, 2nd series, III, 407–8).

[35] G. Aubert, *Oraison de la paix* (Paris, Benoist Prevost, 1559).

gaignon.[36] On visiting the camp at Amiens, he exclaims in dismay on the war between Christians. Aubert then gives the reasons for war: ambition,[37] vengeance, desire for grandeur, desire for honour and glory, recovery of territory (neat summaries are given of the disputes over Burgundy, Milan and Naples). Princes should accept arbitration; they do not permit their subjects to resort to force in their disputes. Judgment must come, in the end, after war. There should be two governing principles. First, there should be no war to settle disputes. Second, action should be taken[38] by all other princes against any who break the first rule. Such a prince is an enemy of Christendom. If these rules had been upheld, there would have been no Turkish conquests recently, and no Mohammedan conquests in times past. War, if it be necessary to avoid the 'slumbers' of peace, should be against vice.[39] A third principle is recommended: let the princes choose wise and experienced counsellors. They will, no doubt, counsel peace and turn the princes away from war. One of them will perhaps advise some secret league for war against the Turk. Aubert will speak of this another time, and remind them of Godefroi de Bouillon.

The treatise is a fitting testament not only to the writings of Erasmus, Vives and their followers, but to the efforts of the peacemakers themselves: Wolsey, Margaret of Austria, Christina of Denmark, and many lesser figures, the toiling, dispirited ambassadors of the great powers. The peace so much talked of, so little sustained, proved (as it still proves) elusive. Yet men could always hope that the war they were fighting would be the last:

> The time of universal peace is near.
> Prove this a prosperous day, the three-nooked world
> shall bear the olive freely.[40]

---

[36] Huguenots under Nicolas Durand de Villegaignon founded a settlement in the bay of Rio de Janeiro, which they called *La France Antarctique*. Its fort was Fort Coligny.

[37] The two princes have been left war, by their fathers, as an inheritance (*Oraison*, f.12r.)

[38] Nowadays princes waging war are calculating profit and the chance of getting richer as if they were merchants, crossing and recrossing the Equator, and the two tropics, cornering Africa to get to the spices of Calicut (ibid., ff.14r and v.)

[39] Reference is then made to the two marriage alliances which bound together the peace of 1559 (ibid., f.21r).

[40] Shakespeare, *Antony and Cleopatra*, IV, 6, 5–8 (Octavius Caesar's speech before the battle of Actium).

Appendix A

Richard Pace's oration
(translated from the Latin original by D. A. Russell)

Oration of Richard Pace, given in the Church of St Paul at London
on the occasion of the peace lately concluded and treaty struck between
the Most Invincible King of England and the Most Christian King of
the French.

Most sacred and most invincible King, since it is recorded in history
that not only the common orators of ancient times but also the
most learned and eloquent were sometimes struck dumb in public
assemblies, when there was only the people to see and hear them,
no one—in my judgment—should feel surprise if, in this assembly,
so venerable and so full of majesty, he perceives and sees that I am
smitten not only with fear but with sheer terror; especially as my
learning is much less than small, when compared with the consummate knowledge of those ancients, my natural abilities none, and
my tongue so rude, uncultivated and unpolished that, even if an
extreme effort were made, it could not arrive at the smallest part
of their eloquence; especially also as I must deliver my speech not,
as they did, to the people, but to you, Most Excellent King, who
are both pre-eminent in excellence among the greatest and most
potent monarchs and also are wont to contend often, to your great
honour and glory, with all men of learning in contests of letters,
and that with such success that no one has taken the palm from
you. And further: who is so expert in speech, who has such boldness
born in him, that such a throng of men of wisdom and letters should
not terrify him? Nevertheless, most sacred King, putting my trust
in your clemency and the humanity of all my hearers, I will attempt,
as far as my powers allow, to put forth something which, as I hope,
will not appear altogether alien to the matters which have been
concluded here to-day.

Our ancestors displayed their admirable prudence in many ways, but most especially in the devising of holy treaties. Were we to examine and weigh all human affairs, no one could find a thing more laudable, more splendid, more necessary and useful than the giving and receiving of faith; for if faith be kept inviolably—and this is what a treaty entered into and struck in holiness most ensures—it removes all dissension and discord, and all tearful and ruinous war; in their place it substitutes welcome ease, and pleasant tranquillity, and (what is greatest of all) perpetual peace. And the fruit of peace is so ample and abundant that no orator has ever been found learned or eloquent enough to match the blessings of peace with worthy praise. Hence comes the common saying: 'By discord do great affairs dissolve, by concord and peace do small affairs grow.'[1] If the cause be asked, nothing can be plainer. For peace it is that most of all makes human minds tranquil and quiet; and a tranquil and quiet mind is far removed from doing any wrong, committing any crime, or perpetrating any wickedness, and from all murder, slaughter and rapine, which are the services of abominable war; instead, it turns all its intention towards what is right, just, pious and honourable. Hence what St Paul writes most religiously (as he does all), being himself made tranquil and a teacher of peace out of a turbulent Saul.[2] What therefore is more welcome or acceptable to immortal God than that a man should practice the good things of which peace is the sole guide and author? With good reason therefore did Isocrates,[3] a good philosopher no less than an eloquent orator, when he was about to address the people of Athens on peace, state at the beginning that he was to speak of a matter most great and most useful to all mankind. In agreement with him is Silius, also a pagan, who writes in this wise: 'Peace, best of all things that nature has given to man.'[4] But why do I cite the pagans, when Christ himself set peace so far above all other things, that he said to his disciples 'Peace be unto you', as though in this one greeting of peace he included all blessings? The prophet David too says: 'Scatter the nations which desire war.'[5] What else is signified

---

[1] Sallust, *Bellum Jugurthinum* 10.6.

[2] The text of St Paul which Pace presumably quoted here is not given; perhaps *Romans* 14:19: 'Let us therefore follow after the things which make for peace.'

[3] Isocrates, *de pace* 2.

[4] 'Pax, optima rerum quas homini novisse datum est': Silius Italicus, *Punica* 11.591. Pace has 'quas homini natura dedit', a variant perhaps due to a slip of memory by himself or an intermediate source.

[5] Psalms 67:31 (Vulgate): 'dissipa gentes quae bella volunt.'

by this than that all who are enemies of peace should be scattered and destroyed? Again, if a man considers more deeply and with keener eye, and weighs with all care, the whole life of our Redeemer Christ, he will find it nothing but the teaching of concord, charity and peace. The holy prophet Isaiah has given you a most abundant testimony of this: for when, inspired by the divine spirit, he proclaimed the coming of Christ the creator of all things, he promised us neither a leader skilled in war nor a strenuous warrior nor yet a triumphant commander riding gloriously on a white horse after gaining the victory, but a Prince of Peace[6] sent to reconcile the world to the Father and to instil into human hearts mutual love and indissoluble charity. But the strength of the peace, of which I speak, will shine forth more clearly if we set against it the abominable calamity of war. The acts of war are these: unbounded greed for possession, by means both right and wrong; monstrous and barbarous cruelty; insatiable thirst for human blood and mutual slaughter; spoliation of poverty; overthrow of towns and cities; in a word, instant ruin of piety and religion beyond anything that can be described. To achieve all these ends the more easily, the warlike have devised the most ingenious stratagems, and constructed wonderful machines out of a mind that is acute and yet too prone to evil. To these, not many years ago, were added what we call Bombards, truly a diabolical invention; not only does the blow from these lay low and slay a man, but the noise is so horrendous and terrifying that it brings with it bewilderment, hallucination, the total alienation of the senses; it takes a man entirely out of his own control and makes him not to know himself.

But if not even tigers plot this manner of destruction against themselves, ought not men, who are endowed with reason, to do better than the beasts in any virtue? Who ever saw a lion fighting a lion? Who has heard of a serpent that was the enemy of another serpent? Does dragon rage against dragon? Has not the concord of wolves given room for an adage?[7] Since these things are so, I cannot—such is my judgment—speak better than to say that some fury gave birth to war at an ill-omened and unhappy birth; for this madness of fighting could not have been implanted in human hearts

---

[6] Isaiah 9:6. Is the reference to a white horse a sly dig at Pope Leo X's white stallion, which he rode at the battle of Ravenna, and in the procession to the Lateran, after his election?

[7] 'Friendship of wolves', a Greek proverbial expression, signifies a false friendship.

without the help of some internal fury. Hence I cannot but strongly approve the etymology of 'bellum' proposed by those who say that it is named by *antiphrasis* from no lovely (*bella*) or good thing.[8] There is a celebrated Greek proverb too, most apt to express the plague of war: 'War is sweet only to those who have not experienced it.'[9] So I shall say in few words that war is, as it were, a vast sea, a measureless ocean of all evils, discovered from the utter ruin of mankind; peace on the contrary is the heap and accumulation of all good things, which the great and good God has generously bestowed for the preservation of that same mankind. Since therefore it is abundantly clear from the comparison of the countless advantages of fruitful peace and the infinite evils of pestilential war which of the two is to be preferred to the other, I cannot think any man can be so blind as not to see and judge that peace is to be loved, desired, embraced and cherished by all mortal men. If it was needful at any other time, surely nothing can be so needful in these times of ours, when the whole Christian world is tossing and heaving like a ship at sea blown about by the wind, and a vast inexplicable danger to the Christian republic threatens from the external enemy of Christ's name. For who does not know with what zeal and vigilance the monstrous tyrant of the Turks tries to advance and extend his frontiers, and with what speed he has thrown down and worn out two powerful armies of the Sultan, and—fearful to tell—destroyed in barely three months that great empire of the Sultan which has flourished, it is said, five hundred years?

Awake then ye Christian princes, holding—as the apostle says—the same wisdom, the same charity, the same unanimity![10] Awake, I say, and rouse yourselves at last from deep slumber, and judge it a great disgrace to you if you let your walls burn when you could keep the fire far off and drive it away—especially as you have been urged to the Turkish expedition by so many weighty letters and pious warnings and prayers from his Holiness the vicar of Christ on earth, and have been challenged by him to undertake, if not the protection of your own honour and renown, at least that of the faith of Christ; to shake the hard yoke of slavery from your

[8] Pace takes this from Erasmus' *Dulce bellum inexpertis* (*Adagia* IV.v.1). For Greek sources, see Diogenianus 3.94 (= *Paroemiographi Graeci* i.231, Leutsch-Schneidewin).
[9] I.e. *glukus apeirois polemos*, the Greek proverb which Erasmus (loc. cit.) took as his text.
[10] Romans 12, esp. v. 16.

necks, to fight bravely for your children, your hearths, and for the altars of God and all the saints. Yet by what means or manner or counsel the universal peace among all Christian princes, so long and so earnestly desired, could be brought about, I know not, unless the two Kings who are the chief of all were energetically and faithfully to address themselves to the work, as indeed they do. I speak of you, most invincible King Henry, whom Almighty God has endowed with so rare a genius, so deep a wisdom, so notable a piety and care for religion; and whom He made such a vigilant guardian to preserve the treasure of His faith, that, despising and scorning all glory and increase of fortune, which all could see you would have won had you chosen to continue in the war, you applied all your heart and all your mind, moved as you were by the frequent exhortation of the Holy Father, to the initiation of universal peace among all Christian princes. The sanctity of your pure heart is all the more cause of wonder because Nature herself, when she was bent on creating you, seems to have thought of nothing other than to fashion a great general to undertake wars with prudence and bring them to an issue with success. He who looks closely upon you cannot but see that the beauty of your splendid body, the incomparable aptness and compactness of your limbs, all breathes war: you are tall, brave, active, powerful, and so strong that you leave far behind you all who seek to display their bodily strength in earnest or in play. There is no need for me to speak of wealth, which is held to be the sinews of war, or of the warlike nation that is your subject; these are too well known to the whole world for me to need to say one word about them. Yet I will add how gloriously and marvellously you conducted yourself in the war which you lately undertook; in which you so humbled your royal greatness as to match any common soldier in the endurance of hardship, surpassed the greatest and most experienced commanders in wisdom, and displayed such skill in siting your camp to best advantage and drawing up your army bravely that the enemy spies and all others (and their number was great) who had resorted thither to observe your strength, confessed with one voice that the camp was impregnable and the army invincible, and preached and spread this account in all places. None the less, as I said, you despised and rejected all these incitements to the waging and continuing of the war, you set aside every enmity you had formed, you put behind you all grounds of quarrel, your buried in deep oblivion whatever

causes of hatred there were, and, zealous only for the common
tranquillity and health of all Christians, you turned all your
thoughts to health-bearing peace. In this endeavour, it was the
Most Reverend Lord Cardinal of York who, as they say, stuck the
spur into you when you were running hard already.[11] This loyal
and sound counsel never failed you in any noble or laudable action.
This pious intention of your heart was further augmented by the
most Christian King of France, Francis, when you knew for sure
and felt certain that he too was most eager for this same peace, in
order that he might show himself to be the most Christian King in
deed as well as in name, and that he was going upon the matter
with such pure and unsullied faith that he sent here to you the most
magnificent and prudent ambassadors and did not disdain to ask
that your only daughter, the most illustrious Lady Mary, should
be given in marriage to his only son, the most excellent Prince of
the Gauls; by which means the knot of this most honourable peace
and treaty of mutual defence is made altogether indissoluble and
unbreakable, secured by the bond of this new and greatest affinity.
Moreover, that nothing should ever enter our minds that might
tend to the breaking off of this most noble marriage, it has been
enacted by our common consent that it should be strengthened by
the sanctions of the church, and that against him who should violate
this promise should be spoken the dreadful sentence of excommunication, while his kingdom and all his dominions should be cut off
by interdict from water and fire and all Christian rites, and under
this dreadful curse should be rendered altogether profane. O good
and mighty God, how much do we all, the followers of Thy holy
religion, owe to Thee, who hast put into the hearts of these two
mighty Kings such piety that, treading in Thy divine footsteps, they
think of nothing but of that healthful peace which Thou, in leaving
this world, didst leave as a common and universal good to all who
faithfully worship Thee! Your strength, most sacred Kings, is so
great and formidable, your wealth so ample, your counsels so sound
and weighty, that you will easily draw all other Christian princes
over to your opinion, and without question hold the reins of the
whole Christian Empire as you please. But why do I say 'draw
over', when already, at this present time, this same treaty has been
struck, in so far as it lies in you, as a result of your pious affection

[11] From Erasmus, *Currentem incitare* (*Adagia* II.i.78), where this form of words is
cited from Pliny *Epist.* 1.8.1.

towards the religion of Christ, between the most sacred Imperial
Majesty and the most serene Catholic King, who is the beloved
kinsman of you both; and when also there has been left a most
convenient place for all princes and rulers to accept this peace and
treaty on a day already determined? How great and memorable is
this deed of yours, O most noble Kings! You are most powerful,
most wealthy and most warlike; you are flourishing in the prime of
your youth; and yet you have repressed by reason and counsel all
that youthful spirit that is wont to be intent on gloriously extending
frontiers; you have laid down your arms and sheathed the drawn
and blooded sword in the scabbard, so that peace, which is both
necessary and healthful, peace which has long fared miserably in
exile, should be happily restored to her dominion over the Christian
world by your doing.

Most worthy father, Cardinal of York, Legate of the Apostolic
See: were I to pass you over in this place in silence, I should no
doubt be committing a very great error. You, in this business which
has been completed, have displayed such shrewdness of mind, such
prudence and dexterity, that both Kings have granted you the
fullest authority to effect the whole matter. All posterity, most
reverend father, will laud your success to the skies. Posterity will
marvel too that England has produced a man such that not only
her own King but foreign kings as well judged it right to commit
their business to him. O happy day, to be marked, in Cretan
fashion,[12] with a white stone; on which (as David foretold with
prophetic mouth[13]) 'abundance of peace shall arise'—a peace, as is
apparent, which is firm and will endure, because it is universal! O
happy pair of Kings! You are today about to give a most auspicious
beginning to three things: to the treaty; to faith; and to peace: to
the treaty, that it shall be entered into in holiness; to faith, that it
shall be sincere and inviolable; to peace, that it shall be perpetual
—that is, not only shall all war be removed, but suspicion of any
war shall be totally taken away.

So may immortal God bring it to pass that the joy we feel at this
most healthful peace, formed and entered into in this church to-

---

[12] The Cretans are supposed to have originated the practice of marking lucky
days by white pebbles, unlucky by black: Erasmus, *Creta notare. Carbone notare* (*Adagia*
I.v.54); see A. Otto, *Die Sprichwörte und sprichwörtlichen Redensarten der Römer*, 1890, p.
64.
[13] Psalm 71:7 (Vulgate): 'orietur in diebus eius iustitia et abundantia pacis.'

day, shall be solid and perpetual for all Christians. Of this inesti-
mable blessing the sacred oaths with which this holy treaty has
been confirmed give me a secure hope. He who shall not fear to
violate these oaths shall sink his body and soul together into the
depths of hell and the Gehenna of fire.

Look therefore, princes, you who are the authors of this most
religious treaty, friendship and peace, look to the giving and taking
of your faith: persuade yourselves that nothing can be more alien
from great princes than to violate their faith. Finally, consider in
your minds what venerable witnesses you have present of all the
matters you have here treated and concluded. To say nothing of
the countless multitude of people, here are present two most worthy
and reverend Legates of the Apostolic See;[14] here is the most holy
church of St. Paul; here is God himself, the guardian of this famous
temple; to whose divine majesty and to all the powers of heaven I
humbly pray, beg and beseech in all prayers, that whatever you
have piously done here this day they may aid, prosper and render
happy and fortunate.

END

Printed at London, in the Year of the Word Incarnate, MDXVIII,
on the Nones of December, by Richard Pynson, King's Printer,
with privilege granted by the King, that none shall print this speech
in the kingdom of England within two years, or if printed elsewhere
import and sell it in the same kingdom of England.

[14] The second legate is Cardinal Lorenzo Campeggio.

Appendix B

The treaties of Cateau-Cambrésis, 2 and 3 April 1559: summaries

I. The treaty between King Philip II and King Henri II (3 April 1559)[1]

God has moved the two great Princes [the Catholic King Philip and the Most Christian King Henri II][2] to seek an end to the disputes and differences of the war between them, and to transform it into a good, final, complete, sincere and durable Peace. [The ambassadors, who had full powers, are then named.]

1. Without derogating from treaties made, before 1551, between their predecessors, there shall be a sure and stable peace, confederation and perpetual alliance between the Kings and their children, heirs and successors, and their realms.
2. For the good of Christendom, and the maintenance of religion ... the two Princes will work for a General Council, so necessary to reform and reduce to unity the Christian Church.
3. The subjects of either side may come and go, and trade, in the lands of both, by land or sea, while observing local laws and customs ...
4. All letters of marque[3] and reprisals are to cease, except for manifest denial of justice ... according to the requirements of law.
5. The towns and inhabitants of Flanders and Artois are to enjoy the rights and privileges granted them by the Kings of France,

---

[1] Full text in *Traicté*, pp. 119–60; J. Dumont, *Corps universel diplomatique du droit des gens* v, 34–41.

[2] Philip II bore the title 'the Catholic King', Henri II that of 'the Most Christian King' in contemporary usage.

[3] A licence, granted by a sovereign to a subject, to take reprisals (for injuries done by the enemy's subjects), usually by capturing enemy merchant shipping.

and the towns and inhabitants of France are to enjoy the rights and privileges granted them in the lands of the Catholic King.

6. All subjects, ecclesiastical and lay, of one side and the other, may return to possession of their immoveable goods, rents . . . seized and occupied during the wars . . . without claiming any of the intervening revenues.

7. This restitution is to be despite any gifts or grants made in the interval, except for the exiles from Naples, Sicily and Milan, who are not covered by this treaty.

8. Those provided to benefices at the disposition of the Kings, or other lay persons, will remain in possession.

9. The Dauphin shall enter into possession of the Seigneurie of Crèvecoeur . . .[4]

10. Mary, daughter of the late Queen of France, Eleanor of Portugal, shall enjoy the dowry which the Queen had in France.

11. The King of Spain shall restore to the King of France S. Quentin, Le Catelet and Ham, with their dependencies . . . The King of France shall restore to the King of Spain Thionville, Mariembourg, Yvoir, Damvillers and Montmédy, with their dependencies. . . . The Princes may remove all artillery, powder, arms, provisions, from these places . . . which shall be restored in the state they are at present, without any demolition of fortifications.

12. The town and city of Thérouanne, ruined and demolished when seized from the King of France, shall be restored by the King of Spain in its present state. Yvoir may be defortified by the King of France before restitution. Neither place shall be refortified.

13. Since there has been no divine service in the ruined and demolished city and church of Thérouanne, and there has been long concern for the division of the diocese . . ., there shall be appointed two commissioners to discuss the matter with a representative of the Archbishop of Reims [the metropolitan], at Aire, on 1 June next. They shall decide on the equal division of the revenues between the new diocese in France (at Boulogne or

---

[4] Crèvecoeur, an ancient chatellenie which was obtained by the Crown in 1337, was given to Jean, Duke of Normandy as heir to the throne. It remained under the suzerainty of the Bishop of Cambrai, to whom Jean did homage. In 1435, under the treaty of Arras, it had been ceded to the Duke of Burgundy. The French crown was now reclaiming its former possession (A. Longnon, *La formation de l'unité française* (Paris 1922) pp. 200–2, 235).

elsewhere) and that in the dominions of the Catholic King (at
S. Omer or elsewhere). The Pope shall be asked to approve
this division.

14. The town of Couvin shall be returned to the Bishop of Liège,
and Frahan, and generally all that the Most Christian King
now occupies, which was the property of the Bishop, Chapter,
Church and land of Liège, and especially the castle of Bouillon
(in its present state, without demolition or withdrawal of artillery) . . . the claims of the Seigneur de Sedan, and the members
of the de la Marck family, shall be decided by commissioners
who shall meet at Cambrai on 1 September next.

15. Hesdin and its baillage and appurtenances shall remain the
Catholic King's.

16. Arbitration shall take place on the claims of the Princes over
the abbey of S. Jean-au-Mont . . . and its lands in French and
Spanish dominions [arbiters on each side, plus a super-arbiter,
if necessary].

17. Disputes between the two Princes on actions since the treaty of
Crépy [1544], and border disputes and others, shall be decided
by ministers deputed by both sides who shall meet at Cambrai
on 1 September next.

18. The Dame d'Étoutteville shall repossess the County of S. Pol
from the Catholic King. His claims, and those of the Most
Christian King, shall be decided within six months by two
commissioners from each side, and if necessary a super-arbiter.

19. The King of Spain shall regain possession of the County of
Charolais, under the sovereignty of the King of France.

20. Disputed lands, between the County of Burgundy [Franche
Comté] and the possessions and lands of the Most Christian
King, shall be allocated by commissioners, having visited the
territory and heard the parties. The half of these lands nearest
to the County of Burgundy shall be put under the obedience of
the Catholic King, the other half under the obedience of the
Most Christian King.

21. The Marquisate of Montferrat shall be restored to the Duke of
Mantua. The French and Spanish are to withdraw.

22. The subjects of Montferrat, and especially those living in
Casale, shall not be penalised for serving either of the two Kings
. . .

23. The Most Christian King shall depart from the town of Valenza

in the Duchy of Milan, and restore it to the Catholic King. No demolition is to take place and the Most Christian King is to withdraw his artillery, munitions, and provisions, as also is to be done in other places occupied by either side.

24. The Most Christian King is to receive the Genoese into his good grace and friendship . . . and will restore all the places he holds in Corsica. The subjects of the King and the Genoese will live in friendship, and will trade with each other. The Genoese shall not take proceedings against any of their subjects who followed the Most Christian King.

25. The Most Christian King is to withdraw all troops, of whatever nation, from Montalcino and other places in Sienese territory and in Tuscany. He is to withdraw artillery, munitions and provisions. Any Sienese who fled to these places are to be pardoned by the Sienese government.

26. All such Sienese are to be restored to their possessions. The Duke of Florence is to ratify this treaty. Likewise any in Tuscany who followed the late Emperor, the present King, or the Duke, are to be pardoned.

27. For the greater confirmation of this peace, and to render the friendship . . . firmer and more indissoluble, there has been agreed the marriage of Madame Élisabeth, eldest daughter of the Most Christian King, and the Catholic King . . .

28. Madame Élisabeth shall be escorted to the frontiers and received into the lands of the King of Spain. She shall have a dowry of 400,000 écus du soleil. A third shall be payable upon consummation of the marriage, a third one year later, and a third six months after that. The whole amount shall be payable, within the eighteen months specified, at Antwerp.

29. Madame Élisabeth shall not claim anything else of the goods and possessions of her father or her mother, which she must expressly renounce . . .

30. The King her future husband shall give Madame Élisabeth jewels to the value of 50,000 écus, as an inheritance.

31. The King shall maintain her as befits the daughter and wife of such great kings.

32. In lieu of dower, which is not usual in the Spanish kingdoms, she shall have 133,333 écus (one third of her dowry) which shall be her inheritance, if she survives her husband.

33. If she survives her husband, she may leave Spanish dominions,

whenever she wishes, and return to France, taking her servants, her possessions, jewels, furnishings . . .

34. Since the greater part of the recent wars have been over the claims of the Most Christian King to the lands of Savoy, Bresse, Piedmont and other territories held by the Duke of Savoy, and since the Duke has shown goodwill [to come to a settlement] and recognises the King with all possible honour, service and friendship . . . the marriage between the Duke and Madame Marguerite de France, only sister of the King, Duchess of Berri, is agreed. She shall have, for life, the Duchy of Berri and other lands she holds at present, with (in addition) a dowry of 300,000 écus, renouncing all other claims . . . and a dower of 30,000 livres a year . . .

35. The marriage shall be solemnised within two months, with the necessary papal dispensation. Then the Duke shall be given full possession of the Duchy of Savoy, the Pais de Bresse, Bugey . . . the Principality of Piedmont, the County of Asti . . . which the King holds . . . except the towns and places of Turin, Chieri, Pignerolo, Chivasso and Villanova d'Asti, which the Most Christian King shall hold until the disputes between him and the Duke are settled, which is to be done within three years at the latest.[5] The places will then be returned to the Duke. The disputes are to be settled as customarily, or else arbiters are to be chosen within six months of the marriage.

36. The Most Christian King may, when restoring these lands to the Duke, demolish fortifications built by him or his father, and withdraw artillery, provisions, and other munitions.

37. All benefice holders in these lands, appointed while the Most Christian Kings, father and son, held them, shall remain in possession, as shall office-holders.

38. All legal judgments made while the Most Christian King, or his father, held these lands are to remain in force . . .

39. The Duke of Savoy shall pardon all inhabitants of these lands who have followed the Most Christian Kings . . . during their possession of these lands.

40. At the time of the Duke's marriage the King of the Spains shall leave him in free possession of all towns, places and fortresses

[5] The towns were to be retained, with their dependent territories (in the case of Turin, Chivasso and Villanova d'Asti); in the case of Pignerolo and Chieri, with as much dependent territory as was necessary for the nourishment of the towns.

in his lands and shall evacuate all garrisons and troops . . . But the Catholic King may keep garrisons in Vercelli and Asti while the Most Christian King holds the five places [article 35]. Afterwards, he shall restore them. The Duke of Savoy, with his lands and subjects, shall remain neutral and the common friend of both Kings.

41. All grants, alienations . . . made by the Most Christian Kings, during their occupation, of domains or patrimonies in these lands, or of lands of vassals or subjects of the Duke of Savoy, deprived for having served him, shall be cancelled.

42. All other grants made by the Most Christian King and his father shall be maintained.

43. Those who were admitted, by fee or homage, into possession of fiefs or lordships in these lands, by the King or his officials, shall not be molested or disturbed.

44. Restitutions on both sides, under this treaty, shall be made as follows: the Most Christian King shall make restitutions, of the lands of the Duke of Savoy, and also in Italy, Corsica and elsewhere, within two months of the date of this treaty, beginning within one month. Before this restitution commences, the Catholic King shall provide four hostages, such as the Most Christian King shall choose, to guarantee his own restitutions. Within one month of the Most Christian King's restitutions, the Catholic King shall make his, both beyond the mountains [the Alps] and on this side of them. This month's period shall begin as soon as the Catholic King is notified of the Most Christian King's restitutions. The hostages shall then be returned.

45. There shall be comprised in this treaty, if they wish, on the part of the Catholic King: the Pope and the Apostolic See, the Roman Emperor [the Holy Roman Emperor], his children, and their lands, the Prince Electors, the towns and states of the Empire, especially the Bishop of Liège, the Duke of Cleves, the Bishop and city of Cambrai and the land of Cambrésis, the maritime towns of East Frisia . . . these Princes shall renounce all practices against the Emperor, or against the states of the Empire, provided that the Emperor and his states comport themselves in friendship with the two Kings. Also included shall be the Cantons of the Confederation of High Germany, and the Grisons . . . the Queen of England (according to what has been

agreed between the Most Christian King, the King and Queen Dauphin, King and Queen of Scotland, and her, and reserving the agreement which the Catholic King has with the Kings and realm of England) . . . the King of Portugal, the King of Denmark, the Duke of Savoy, the Duke of Lorraine and the Duchess his mother, the Doge and Signory of Venice, the republics of Genoa and Lucca, the Dukes of Florence and Ferrara . . . the Dukes of Mantua and Urbino, the Duke of Parma . . .

46. On the part of the Most Christian King shall be included, the Pope and the Apostolic See, the Emperor, the Prince Electors, towns, communities and states of the Empire, especially the Dukes of Savoy, the Duke of Württemberg, the Landgrave of Hesse . . . the Countess of West Frisia and her son, the maritime towns (according to ancient alliances), the King and Queen Dauphin, King and Queen of Scotland, the Dowager Queen of Scotland and the realm of Scotland (according to ancient alliances), the King of Bohemia . . . the Kings of Portugal, Poland, Denmark and Sweden, the Queen Elizabeth, widow of John Vayvoda, and her son the King [of Hungary], the Doge and Signory of Venice, the thirteen Cantons of the Swiss Confederation, the Lords of the Grison Confederation, . . . the Duke of Lorraine and the Dowager his mother, the Duke of Savoy, the Duke of Ferrara . . . the Marquis of Montferrat, the Duchess Dowager and the Duke of Mantua, . . . the Republic of Lucca, the Bishops and Chapters of Metz, Toul and Verdun, the Abbot of Gorze,[6] the Seigneurs de la Marck . . .

47. Others, agreed by both Kings, may be included in the treaty . . . if they provide letters to this effect within six months of the treaty.

48. The King Dauphin shall ratify the treaty, and it shall be enregistered by the Parlement of Paris and other Parlements of France . . . and also by the Chambre des Comptes of Paris. Officials of the King shall be released from any oaths they may have taken not to consent to the alienation of crown lands. These ratifications shall be made and delivered to the King Catholic within three months. The Catholic King shall have

---

[6] The great Benedictine abbey in Lorraine. As an 'advance post' of Metz, it had been fortified by the imperialists, and taken by the French in 1552. By 1559 two claimants to the abbacy, adhering respectively to the French and Spanish sides, were in dispute (cf. Granvelle v, 563).

similar ratifications of the treaty made by his Great Council, other councils, and Chambres des Comptes, with release of his officials from any oaths, within the same period.[7] Within six months, the treaty shall be ratified by his son, the Prince of the Spains.

All the above articles have been accorded and agreed by the ambassadors [the ambassadors at the conference], in virtue of their powers; they undertake to obtain the ratifications of their masters within eight days. They also undertake that the Catholic King shall, as soon as can be, take an oath to the treaty, in the presence of the representatives of the Most Christian King, on the Holy Gospels, and the Canon of the Mass, and on his honour. The Most Christian King shall do likewise, in the presence of representatives of the Catholic King . . .
In witness to which the ambassadors have subscribed the present treaty, and signed their names, at Cateau-Cambrésis, 3 April 1559, after Easter.

II. The treaty between King Henri II and Queen Elizabeth I (2 April 1559)[8]

1. There shall be peace between King Henri and Queen Elizabeth and their subjects.
2. Neither shall invade the realm of the other.
3. Neither shall assist any prince or people who invade the realms of the other.
4. The treaty shall remain in force even if violated by the subjects of either realm . . . (the offenders to be punished).
5. The inhabitants of each kingdom shall have liberty to trade with the other.
6. No armed vessel shall leave any of the ports of France or England without giving previous security to the Admiral of France or England that the peace will not be violated.
7. The King of France shall have peaceable possession for eight

[7] Enregistering by the Great Council of Malines (Mechelen), and the Chambre des Comptes at Lille, is on record (Dumont v, 43).
[8] Full text in Dumont v, 31–4; Rymer xv, 505–10; summary in *Cal. For.* ii, 196–8. In the summary, the reference to English violation of the treaty (article 14) mistakenly omits 'the Queen of England' from the relevant passage.

years of Calais, Ruysbank, Nyhuse, Merk, Oye, Hammes, Sandgate and Guines, with their appurtenances, acquired by the King of France during the late war with Queen Mary. At the end of eight years, the premises shall be restored to England.

8. Along with the town of Calais shall be restored 16 brass pieces of artillery (3 cannon, 3 demi-cannon, 3 bastards, and 7 smaller pieces called mayennes).

9. The King of France shall cause 7 or 8 substantial merchants (not subjects of France) to become bound to the Queen of England in the sum of 500,000 crowns of gold of the sun for the restitution of the premises at the end of the specified period.

10. The securities mentioned in the last article may be changed, from time to time.

11. The King of France shall surrender to the Queen, as hostages for the ratification of the treaty, 4 hostages [they are named] who shall become bond for the sum of 500,000 crowns until the merchants (article 9) shall be produced.

12. The hostages shall not be detained in custody in England, but shall take oath that they will not depart from England without the Queen's licence.

13. The King may change these hostages every two months.

14. During the period of eight years, it shall not be lawful either for the King of France, or the King and Queen of Scotland, or the Queen of England, to make any hostile attempt upon the realm or subjects of the other. If this be done by the Queen of England, or her subjects on her command, the King of France and the King and Queen Dauphin and the merchants and hostages shall be free from their promises and bond. If it be done by the King of France, or the King and Queen Dauphin, or their subjects on their command, then the King and the King and Queen Dauphin shall be bound to surrender Calais and the places aforesaid, and if this be not done the merchants or hostages shall be bound to forfeit the 500,000 crowns aforesaid. Private individuals violating the treaty shall be punished by their own sovereigns.

15. The port of Eyemouth in Scotland, and all buildings erected by the French, the Scottish or the English, in violation of the treaty of Boulogne [1550], shall be demolished within three months from the date of this treaty.

16. All suits and claims between the King of France and the King

and Queen of Scotland, on one hand, and the Queen of
England, on the other, shall remain whole and entire. It is
hoped that they will be speedily terminated.

17. Neither of the contracting parties shall harbour rebels or traitors
of the other . . .

18. Letters of marque[9] shall be given only against the chief delin-
quents, their goods and factors, and only after denial of justice.

19. In this treaty shall be included, on the part of the King of
France, the King of Spain, and the King and Queen and realm
of Scotland; on the part of the Queen of England, Philip King
of Spain.

20. [proclamation of the treaty].

21. The King of France and the Queen of England shall swear to
observe the articles of the treaty.

*III. The treaty between François and Mary, King and Queen of Scotland,
and Elizabeth, Queen of England (2 April 1559)[10]*

1. There shall be peace between Scotland and England.

2. Neither shall invade the territories of the other.

3. Neither shall assist the enemies of the other.

4. Neither shall shelter the rebels, traitors, murderers, thieves,
robbers or fugitives of the other.

5. The fortress of Eyemouth shall be rased, and all other violations
of the treaty of Boulogne [1550] shall be remedied.

6. All other claims, on either side, shall be reserved, for the
present.

7. Certain articles, respecting which the ambassadors are not
sufficiently informed, shall be arranged within two months by
commissioners appointed for this purpose.

8. Until this is done, the treaty between Edward VI and Queen
Mary shall be observed.

9. In this treaty shall be comprehended, on the part of Scotland,
the Kings of France and Spain, and on the part of England,
Philip King of Spain.

10. [proclamation of the treaty].

11. Each of the contracting parties shall confirm the treaty within
ten days of being required to do so by the other.

[9] See above, p. 242n3.
[10] Full text in Dumont v, 29–30; Rymer xv, 513–15; summary in *Cal. For.* ii, 195.

Appendix C

Restitutions made under the treaty of Cateau-Cambrésis

Piedmont

When the treaty was published in Piedmont on 11 April, the French governor, Marshal Charles de Cossé Brissac, had about 10,000–12,000 troops under his command, many unpaid and strongly opposed to peace. Demolition of the 'French' fortresses was often savagely done, so that Savoy had cause for grievance. The Duke, returning to Savoy in December 1559, imposed heavy customs tolls and dues on the five towns retained by France, and forbade trade with them. His subjects were forbidden to reside there, so that the towns suffered from depopulation and extreme difficulty over food supplies. It had been understood that the French could only retain the towns, plus the immediately surrounding territory (article 35 of the treaty; see above, p. 246n5); corn had to be brought in from Provence and Lyonnais. There was a revolt in Turin in February 1560, and savage reprisals. Brissac returned to France heavily in debt through payment of his troops; his successor, the Seigneur de Bordillon, found the situation intolerable. By 1562, Catherine de'Medici had resolved to cede the five towns,[1] in exchange for Savigliano and Perosa; the treaty of Fossano was concluded by the Cardinal of Lorraine, on his way to the Council of Trent.[2] At the same time, the Marquisate of Saluzzo was 'detached' from Dauphiné and returned to Savoy's sovereignty. By 1574 the 'exchange' towns had been ceded to the Duke; after further

---

[1] The detailed provisions for restitution to the Duke of all his lands, and the marriage agreement, were incorporated in letters of 2 July 1559 from Henri II (Dumont v, 52).

[2] The 1559 treaty had, in any case, envisaged only a three years' retention by France.

conflict, Saluzzo was finally abandoned in 1601, in exchange for the Duke's lands across the Rhone: Bresse and Bugey.[3]

Tuscany

Under the treaty, the French troops were to retire from Tuscany and Sienese lands, with a general amnesty for all Sienese subjects. The treaty implicitly confirmed Philip II's possession of the Tuscan *praesidi*, the group of coastal fortresses so vital for defence, some also providing havens for his galleys sailing north from Naples. The fortresses were Talamone, Orbetello, Ansedonia, Porto Ercole, Monte Argentaro, Porto San Stefano, and (on Elba) Porto Longone.[4]

Corsica

The return of the island to Genoa was long delayed. The French had taken the island in 1553, when the Corsican patriot Petro de Bastelica (Sampiero Corso) had, with the aid of French troops from Italy, French galleys, and the Turkish fleet under Dragut Reis, driven the Genoese from Bastia, Ajaccio, and other towns. The Genoese, aided by Andrea Doria's expedition, held out in some towns. Corsican envoys demanding French help against the terms of the 1559 treaty were in Paris in July 1559. No help was forthcoming, and the French troops, who had been aiding Sampiero, had to leave the island in November. Sampiero continued the struggle for three years, the Spanish suspecting French complicity. He was forced to leave the island and to live in Marseilles on a French pension. He offered to reconquer the island for France in 1561, and was authorised to seek help from the Turk. The Genoese countered this mission, and attempted to take his wife and children hostage. An accusation of her infidelity roused him to revenge; he strangled her. In Corsica, Genoese rule was oppressive, there were heavy tolls and other exactions, and interference with ancient rights; the fighting was brutal on both sides. Catherine de'Medici financed Sampiero's son and gave him a banner 'Pugna pro patria', for an

---

[3] Ruble, pp. 31–7. Valenza, in the Duchy of Milan, was handed over (July 1559) after complaints by the Duke of Alva over delays (Ruble, pp. 39–40).

[4] Ruble, pp. 60–1; cf. Pierson, op. cit., pp. 33, 77, 132, 150.

expedition in 1564; officially, she denied all complicity. Granvelle feared war, and Spanish troops were despatched to aid the Genoese. In 1567 Sampiero was attacked treacherously, in an ambush, by his wife's relations, and killed by one of his squires and Genoese soldiers. His head was sent to Ajaccio. His son fought on, with French subsidies, but had to capitulate in 1569; he died a Marshal of France. Sampiero is remembered as the first 'French Corsican'.[5]

The northern lands

Thionville had been handed over by 21 June; its artillery, arms and munitions were taken to Metz. The Count of Mansfeld,[6] Governor of Luxembourg, received the city, the Seigneur d'Andelot (François de Coligny-Châtillon) having arrived with express royal orders. Montmédy, Damvillers and Mariembourg were handed over at about the same time; the latter was uninhabited, wells foul, mills burnt, houses roofless, the church desecrated.[7] Charolais was handed over in July. Granvelle's brother, Thomas Perrenot, Seigneur de Chantonnay, ambassador to France, had to excuse Spanish delays over restitutions. The journey of the King to Spain was one excuse; in reality, it seems that Spain feared another war between France and England. Le Catelet was to be held, on the King's orders, as a counter to French disputes over some villages in Luxembourg. The Cardinal of Lorraine, who had protested to the ambassador in October, witnessed a bitter royal interview with de Chantonnay in November. King and Cardinal inveighed against Spanish delays; in addition, Spanish troops were causing untold hardship. In fact Philip could not pay the troops; already, in June, Granvelle had reported on the payment overdue to Walloon troops in S. Quentin. Margaret of Parma, Regent after the King's departure, borrowed money and made payments. The fortresses of S. Quentin, Ham and Le Catelet, were handed over in January 1560. There were still disputes over frontier villages, and over the abbey of S. Jean-au-Mont.[8] Spanish troops remained in the Netherlands after the peace; there were probably some 3,000 of them, despite the protest at the Estates General that the King should guard the

[5] Ruble, pp. 63–84.
[6] Peter Ernst I, Count of Mansfeld in Saxony.
[7] Granvelle v, 602; Ruble, pp. 217–19.
[8] Ruble, pp. 215–24; Granvelle v, 593, 596, 609–10; Decrue, op. cit., pp. 732–3.

frontiers and man his fortresses with Netherlandish forces.[9] The Spanish troops did not leave until January 1561.

Prisoners

The treaty itself did not cover the subject, but at the conference there was considerable discussion on terms of release. This centred not on the prisoners of rank (whose ransoms were negotiated with their captors), but the ordinary soldiers, mounted or foot, who had been imprisoned, or sent to the galleys, during the wars. Montmorency and Alva agreed that those unfortunates should be released without ransom; if they were in debt recovery of the amount would be pursued afterwards. Commissioners on both sides would visit the towns, fortresses, ports and ships, to identify their own.[10] Many French prisoners were released in Flanders and the north; hommes d'armes were classified as gentlemen, and ransomed for one year's pay. Prisoners had been released from each town where the Duchess of Lorraine passed after the Congress. The position in Spain and Italy was not so favourable; harsh treatment and delays were common. Some French prisoners were detained on Philip's ships, about to sail on the Barbary expedition. For the Spaniards detained on the galleys at Marseilles, release was negotiated when the Admiral of Spain, the Duke of Sessa,[11] visited the town. Nine hundred and seventy-five prisoners were released from thirty-five ships in October 1559. The whole operation was the subject of endless inquiries and protests on both sides,[12] the French being apparently more generous in their responses.

[9] Henri Pirenne, *Histoire de Belgique* (Brussels 1912) III, 388.
[10] Ruble, pp. 205–6.
[11] Don Gonzalo Fernandez de Cordoba, Governor-General of Milan, Duke of Sessa (Campania).
[12] Granvelle V, 569, 571, 581; *Cal. Ven.* VII, 64; Ruble, pp. 205–14.

Appendix D

The position of the Duchy of Lorraine
(Summary of a document presented at the conference)

Lorraine wished to preserve its 'neutrality'. In October, the Duchess submitted articles on the points in dispute with the King of France, who had announced himself protector of Lorraine when he seized the three bishoprics in 1552/3. There were French garrisons in Malatour and Busy; the King retained Stenay; royal officials from the baillages of Sens, Chaumont and Langres, and those of the Parlement of Paris, intervened in the baillage of Bar, Condrecourt, Conflans, Châtillon and La Marche, where the Duke had not only 'regalian' but 'sovereign' rights. The officials summoned cases to the Parlement or to the Privy Council. These territories should be left in peace or neutral judges appointed. Officials from the Duchy of Luxembourg (in King Philip's domains) also attacked her son's lands. The Duke and his lands should be included in the peace treaty 'comme voisons de leurs majestez'. In fact, the Duke and his mother were included in the treaty, as allies of both kings.[1]

---

[1] Granvelle v, 290–1; articles 45 and 46 of the treaty (see above, Appendix B).

Select bibliography

1. Primary sources

Alberi, Ed., ed., *Le relazione degli ambasciatori Veneti al Senato*, 14 vols (Florence 1839–63).

Asham, Roger, *English Works*, ed. W. A. Wright (Cambridge 1970).

Aubert, G., *Oraison de la paix* (Paris, Prevost, 1559).

Bacon, Roger, *Opus majus*, trans. R. B. Burke (Pennsylvania 1928).

Barrillon, Jean, *Journal*, ed. P. de Vaisière, *Societé de l'Histoire de France*, 2 vols (Paris 1897–9).

Basin, Thomas, *Histoire de Charles VII*, ed. C. Samaran, 2 vols (Paris 1933–44).

Bisticci, Vespasiano da, *Vite di uomini illustri del Secolo XV*, ed. L. Ferati (Bologna 1892–3).

Bodin, Jean, *Six Books of the Commonwealth*, English trans., ed. M. J. Tooley (Oxford 1967).

Bor, Pieter, *Nederlandsche Oorlogen* (Utrecht 1595).

Bouchet, Jean, *Le panégyric du Seigneur Loys de la Trimoille*, in J. A. C. Buchon, *Choix de chroniques* (Paris 1838).

Brantôme, Pierre de Bourdeille, Seigneur de, *Oeuvres complètes*, ed. L. Lalanne, *Societé de l'Histoire de France*, 10 vols (Paris 1864–81).

Busbecq, Ogier Ghiselin de, *The Turkish Letters of Ogier Ghiselin de Busbecq, Imperial Ambassador at Constantinople 1554–1562*, trans. E. S. Forster (Oxford 1968).

Calendar of Letters, Despatches and State Papers Relating to the Negotiations between England and Spain, Preserved in the Archives at Simancas and Elsewhere, ed. G. A. Bergenroth, P. de Gayangos, M. A. S. Hume & Royall Tyler (London 1862–1954). *Further Supplement*, ed. G. Mattingly (London 1940).

Calendar of State Papers, Foreign Series, of the Reign of Mary, 1553–1558, ed. W. Turnbull (London 1861).

Calendar of State Papers, Foreign Series, of the Reign of Elizabeth, ed. J. Stevenson (London 1863–   ).

Calendar of State Papers . . . in the Archives and Collections of Venice, ed. Rawdon Brown & G. C. Bentinck (London 1864–   ).

Calendar of State Papers Relating to English Affairs Preserved Principally at Rome in the Vatican Archives, vol. I, Elizabeth 1558–1571, ed. J. M. Rigg (London 1916).

Camden, W., *The History of the Most Renouned and Victorious Princess Elizabeth*, ed. W. T. MacCaffery (Chicago 1974).

Carloix, M., 'Mémoires sur Vieilleville', in *Nouvelle collection de mémoires . . .* ed. J.-F. Michaud & J. J. F. Poujolat, 1st series, vol. IX (Paris 1854) (there is doubt over whether Carloix, secretary of Vieilleville, wrote these memoirs).

Caxton, William, *The Prologues and Epilogues*, ed. W. J. B. Crutch, *Early English Text Society* (London 1928).

Collection des voyages des souverains des Pays Bas, pub. par L. P. Gachard & C. Piot, 4 vols (Brussels 1876–82).

Commynes, Philippe de, *Mémoires*, ed. N. Lenglet du Fresnoy, 4 vols (Paris 1747).

———, *Mémoires*, ed. J. Calmette, 3 vols (Paris 1924–5).

Corpus Christi College Cambridge, Manuscript 111, pp. 383–95 (anonymous English narrative of the 1521 negotiations at Calais and Bruges).

Corpus Iuris Canonici, ed. A. Friedburg, 2 vols (Leipzig 1879–1881).

Cusa, Nicolas of, *Opera Omnia* (Leipzig-Hamburg 1939–1959) vol. XIV, *De Concordantia Catholica*, ed. G. Kallen.

Dante Alighieri, *The Monarchy and Three Political Letters*, ed. D. Nicholl & C. Hardie (London 1954).

Desjardins, A., ed., *Négotiations diplomatiques de la France avec la Toscane*, 6 vols (Paris 1859–86).

'Diarii d'Emmanuel-Philibert duc de Savoie', extracts ed. L. Romier, in 'Les guerres d'Henri II et le traité de Cateau-Cambrésis (1554–1559)', *Mélanges d'archeologie et d'histoire*, 1910.

Du Bellay, Joachim, *Poematum Libri quatuor* (Paris 1558).

———, *Oeuvres françaises*, ed. C. Marty-Leveaux, 2 vols (Paris 1866–7).

Dumont, J., *Corps universel diplomatique du droit des gens*, 8 vols (Amsterdam 1726–31) vols IV & V.

Erasmus, Desiderius, *Adagiorum opus* (Basel, Froben, 1528).

———, *Adages I.i.1 to I.v.100*, ed. M. M. Phillips & R. A. B. Mynors (Toronto 1982) (part of the collected works of Erasmus).

————, *The Adages*; cf. M. M. Phillips, *Erasmus and his Times: a shortened version of the Adages* (Cambridge 1967).

————, *The Colloquies*, trans. N. Bailey (London 1878).

————, *The Complaint of Peace*, ed. and trans. W. J. Hirten (New Govt. 1946).

————, *Dulce bellum inexpertis*, ed. Y. Rémy & R. Dunil-Marquebreucq (Brussels 1953).

————, *The Education of a Christian Prince*, trans. L. K. Born (New York 1936).

————, *Opus epistolarum*, ed. P. S. Allen, 12 vols (Oxford 1906–58).

————, *Opuscula*, ed. W. K. Ferguson (The Hague 1933).

Feria (Don Gómez-Suárez de Figuerosa), Count of, 'The Count of Feria's dispatch to Philip II of 14 November 1558', ed. and trans. by M. J. Rodriguez-Salgado and Simon Adams, *Camden Miscellany*, XXVIII (London 1984).

Forbes, P., ed., *A Full View of the Public Transactions in the Reign of Queen Elizabeth*, 2 vols (London 1740).

Four Years at the Court of Henry VIII, ed. Rawdon Brown, 2 vols (London 1854) (despatches of Sebastiano Giustiniani).

Gachard, L. P., ed. *Collection de documents inédits concernant l'histoire de Belgique*, 3 vols (Brussels 1833).

Gaguin, Robert, *Epistulae et orationes*, ed. L. Thuasne, 2 vols (Paris 1903–4).

Gesta Henrici Quinti, trans. F. Tayler & J. S. Roskell (Oxford 1975).

Gringoire, Pierre, *Oeuvres complètes*, ed. d'Héricault & Montaiglon, vol. 1 (Paris 1858).

Guicciardini, Francesco, *Storia d'Italia*, ed. C. Panigada & R. Palmarocchi, 9 vols (Bari 1929–36).

————, *Maxims and Reflections of a Renaissance Statesman*, trans. M. Domandi (New York 1965), (translation of the *Ricordi*).

Guise, François, Duc de, 'Mémoires' in *Nouvelle collection de mémoires . . .* ed. J.-F. Michaud & J. J. F. Poujolat, 1st series, vol. VI (Paris 1854).

Hall, Edward, *The Triumphant Reigne of Kyng Henry VIII*, ed. C. Whibley, 2 vols (London 1904).

Hooft, P. C., *Nederlandsche Histoorien*, 2 vols (Amsterdam 1650).

Howard, C. Ed., *Collection of Letters from the Original Manuscripts of Many Princes*, 2 vols (London 1753).

Howell, James, *Epistolae Ho-Elianae, Familiar Letters* (London 1754).

Kendall, F. M., & Ilardi, V. ed., *Dispatches with Related Documents of Milanese Ambassadors in France and Burgundy 1450–1483*, 3 vols, (Athens, Ohio 1970).

Kervyn de Lettenhove, Le Baron, ed., *Relations politiques des Pays-Bas et de l'Angleterre sous le règne de Philippe II*, 11 vols, (Brussels 1882–1900).

Legazione di A. Sessistori, ambasciatore di Cosimo I, ed. G. Canestrini (Florence 1853).

Le Glay, A. ed., *Négotiations diplomatiques entre la France et l'Autriche*, 2 vols (Paris 1845).

Lemaire de Belges, Jean, *Oeuvres*, ed. J. Stecher, 4 vols (Brussels 1882–91).

Letters and Papers, Foreign and Domestic, of the Reign of Henry VIII, 1509–47, ed. J. S. Brewer, J. Gairdner & R. H. Brodie (London 1862–1938).

Louis XI, *Lettrés de Louis XI*, ed. E. J. V. Charavay & B. de Mandrot *Société de l'Histoire de France*, 11 vols (Paris 1883–1909).

Letters and Papers of the Reigns of Richard III and Henry VII, ed. J. Gairdner, Rolls Series, 2 vols (London 1861).

Machiavelli, Niccolò, *Le Opere*, ed. P. Fanfani, L. Passerini & G. Milanesi, 6 vols (Florence 1873–7).

Mandrot, B. de & Samaran, C., ed., *Dépêches des ambassadeurs milanais en France sous Louis XI et François Sforza*, 4 vols (Paris 1916–23).

Marot, Clément, *Oeuvres diverses*, ed. C. A. Mayer (London 1968).

————, *Les Épitres*, ed. C. A. Mayer (London 1958).

Memorials of King Henry VII, ed. J. Gairdner, Rolls Series (London 1958).

Meteren, E. Van, *Historia Belgica nostri potissimum temporis* (Cologne 1597).

Monluc, Blaise de, *Commentaires et lettres*, ed. A. de Ruble, *Société de l'Histoire de France*, 5 vols (Paris 1866–72).

————, *Military Memoirs*, ed. Ian Roy (London 1971).

Nichols, J. G., ed., *The Chronicle of Calais in the Reigns of Henry VII and Henry VIII, Camden Society* (London 1846).

Orange, William of, *Apologie ou Défense de Tres Illustre Prince Guillaume par la grace de Dieu Prince d'Orange . . .* (Leyden 1581).

————, *The Apologie of William of Orange . . .*, ed. after the English edition of 1581 by W. Wansink (Leiden 1969).

Pace, Richard, *De Fructu* (Basel 1517).

————, *Oratio Richardi Pacei in pace* (London, Pynson, 1518).

Paget, William, *The Letters of William, Lord Paget of Beaudesert 1547–1563*, ed. B. L. Beer & S. M. Jack, *Camden Miscellany* xxv (London 1974).

Parker, Mathew, *De antiquitate Britanniae ecclesiae* ('Hanoviae' 1605).

Pasquier, Étienne, *Les lettres*, 2 vols (Paris 1619).

Payen, Pontus, *Mémoires*, ed. A. Henne, 2 vols (Brussels 1861).

Pollard, A. F., *The Reign of Henry VII from Contemporary Sources*, 3 vols (London 1914).

Popham, E., ed., *Illustrium virorum elogia sepulchria* (London 1778).

Pyne, H., trans., *England and France in the Fifteenth Century: the debate between the heralds of France and England* (London 1870). [French text, *Débat des hérauts*, ed. L. Pannier and P. Meyer (Paris 1877)].

Recueil des traittez de paix, treves et neutralité entre les couronnes d'Espagne et de France, ed. J. J. Chiflet (Antwerp 1645, 2nd. ed.)

Ribier, G., *Lettres et mémoires d'Estat . . .*, 2 vols (Paris 1666).

Ronsard, Pierre de, *Oeuvres complètes*, ed. P. Laumonier, 20 vols (Paris 1914–75).

Rymer, Thomas, *Foedera, conventiones, litterae*, 20 vols (London 1704–35), vols x, xiii, xv.

Sanderus, Antonius, *Flandria illustrata*, 2 vols (Cologne 1641).

Seyssel, Claude de, *La monarchie de France*, ed. J. Poujol (Paris 1961).

Skelton, John, *The Poetical Works: with some account of the author and his writings*, by A. Dyce, 2 vols (London 1843).

Sylvester, R. S. & Harding, D. P., ed., *Two Early Tudor Lives: The Life and Death of Cardinal Wolsey by George Cavendish, The Life of Sir Thomas More by William Roper* (New Haven 1962).

Traicté de paix fait à Chateau-Cambrésis l'an MDLIX le iii d'avril (Paris, Camusat, 1637).

Thou, Jacques-Auguste de, *Historiarum sui temporis volumen primum* (London 1733).

Valdes, Alfonso de, *Dialogue of Lactantius and an Archdeacon*, trans. J. E. Longhurst (Albuquerque 1952).

Vives, Juan Luis, *Ioannis Ludovici Vivis, Valentini, opera omnia*, ed. G. Majansio, 8 vols (Valencia 1782–90).

Vynckt, Van der, *Nederlandscher Beroerten* (Amsterdam 1823).

Weiss, G., ed., *Papiers d'État du Cardinal de Granvelle, Collection de documents inédits sur l'histoire de France*, 9 vols (Paris 1841–52).

2. Secondary sources

Ady, C. M., *The Bentivoglio of Bologna* (Oxford 1937).

Ady, C. M., *A History of Milan under the Sforza* (London 1907).

————, *Lorenzo dei Medici* (London 1955).

Alvarez, M. F., *Charles V* (London 1975).

Anglo, S., *Spectacle, Pageantry and Early Tudor Policy* (Oxford 1969).

Appelbaum, S., ed., *The Triumph of Maximilian* (New York 1964).

Armstrong, E., *The Emperor Charles V* (London 1910).

Bataillon, M., *Erasme et l'Espagne* (Bordeaux/Paris 1937).

Benecke, G., *Maximilian I* (London 1982).

Bonardi, A., 'Venezia e la lega di Cambrai', in *Nuovo Archivio Veneto*, new series, VII, 1904.

Blair, Claude, 'A royal swordsmith and damascener: Diego de Çaias', in *Metropolitan Museum Journal* III, 1970.

Bonenfant, P., *Du meurtre de Montereau au traité de Troyes* (Brussels 1958).

Bouwsma, W. J., *Venice and the Defense of Republican Liberty* (Berkeley 1968).

Brandi, K., *The Emperor Charles V*, English trans. (London 1967).

Bridge, John S., *A History of France from the Death of Louis XI*, 5 vols (Oxford 1929).

Bruchet, M., *Marguerite d'Autriche* (Lille 1927).

Buisson, A., *Le chancelier Antoine Duprat* (Paris 1935).

Calmette, J., *La question des Pyrénées et la Marche d'Espagne au moyen âge* (Paris 1947).

Calmette, J. & Périnelle, G., *Louis XI et l'Angleterre* (Paris 1930).

Catalogue of the Medici Archives which will be sold by auction by Messrs. Christie, Manson and Woods Monday February 4 1918 (London 1918).

Chamard, H., *Joachim du Bellay 1522–1560* (Lille 1900).

Chambers, D. S., *Cardinal Bainbridge in the Court of Rome 1509–1514* (Oxford 1965).

————, 'Cardinal Wolsey and the papal tiara', in *Bulletin of the Institute of Historical Research* XXXVII, 1965.

Chrimes, S. B., *Henry VII* (London 1972).

Clarette, G., 'Notice pour servir à la vie de M. de Gattinara', in *Mémoires et documents publiés par la societé savoisine d'histoire et d'archéologie* XXXVII (Chambéry 1898).

Combet, J., *Louis XI et le S. Siège* (Paris 1903).

Contamine, P., *Guerre, état et société à la fin du moyen age* (Paris 1972).

Cooper, C. H., *Memoir of Margaret Countess of Richmond and Derby* (Cambridge 1874).

Cruickshank, C. G., *The English Occupation of Tournai 1513–1521* (Oxford 1971).

Cruickshank, J., ed., *French Literature and its Background . . . I. The Sixteenth Century* (London 1968).

David, M., 'Le serment du sacre du IXᵉ au XVᵉ siècle', in *Revue du Moyen Age Latin* VI, 1950.

————, *La souveraineté et les limites du pouvoir monarchique du IXᵉ au XVᵉ siècle* (Paris 1954).

Decrue, F., *Anne de Montmorency, connétable et pair de France sous les rois Henri II, François II et Charles IX* (Paris 1889).

Danieul-Cormier, A., *The Renaissance in France 1488–1559*, English trans. (London 1969).

Devonshire-Jones, R., *Francesco Vettori, Florentine Citizen, and the Medici Government* (London 1972).

Dewar, M., *Sir Thomas Smith: a Tudor intellectual in office* (London 1964).

Dickinson, Joycelyne G., *The Congress of Arras (1435): a study in medieval diplomacy* (Oxford 1955).

Dickinson, W. C., *A New History of Scotland from the Earliest Times to 1643* (London 1961).

Evenett, H. O., *The Cardinal of Lorraine and the Council of Trent* (London 1930).

Fernández-Santamaria, J. A., 'Erasmus on the just war', in *Journal of the History of Ideas* XXXIV, 1973.

————, *The State, War and Peace: Spanish political thought in the Renaissance, 1516–1559* (Cambridge 1977).

Febvre, L., *Philippe II et la Franche Comté* (Paris 1970).

Fischer-Galati, S. A., *Ottoman Imperialism and German Protestantism 1521–1555* (New York 1972).

Folz, R., *The Concept of Empire in Western Europe from the Fifth to the Fourteenth Century* (London 1969).

Fowler, K., ed., *The Hundred Years' War* (London 1971).

Froude, J. A., *The Reign of Queen Elizabeth*, 3 vols (London 1911).

Gammon, S. R., *Statesman and Schemer: William First Lord Paget, Tudor Minister* (London 1973).

Geyl, P., *The Revolt of the Netherlands* (London 1958).

Gilbert, F., *Machiavelli and Guicciardini* (Princeton 1965).

Griffiths, R. A., *The Reign of Henry VI* (London 1981).

Guillemin, J. J., *Le Cardinal de Lorraine* (Paris 1847).

Gundersheimer, L., ed., *French Humanism 1470–1600* (London 1969).

Hale, J. R., 'Gunpowder and the Renaissance' in *From the Renaissance to the Counter-Reformation*, ed. C. H. Carter (London 1966).

————, ed., *Renaissance Venice* (London 1973).

Hamy, P. A., *Entrevue de François premier avec Henry VIII à Boulogne-sur-Mer en 1532* (Paris 1898).

Hauser, H., 'Le traité de Madrid et la cession de la Bourgogne à Charles Quint', in *Revue Bourguignonne* XXII, 1912.

Head, C., 'Pope Pius II and the Wars of the Roses', in *Archivium Historiae Pontificae* VIII, 1970.

Heer, F., *The Holy Roman Empire*, English trans. (London 1968).

Hutton, J., 'Erasmus and France, the propaganda for peace', in *Studies in the Renaissance* VIII, 1961.

Iongh, J. de, *Margaret of Austria* (London 1954).

Izbicki, T. M., 'The canonists and the treaty of Troyes' in *Proceedings of the Fifth International Congress of Medieval Canon Law, Salamanca 1976* (Citta del Vaticano 1980).

Jacquot, J., ed., *Fêtes et cérémonies du temps de Charles quint*, 3 vols (Paris 1960–1975).

Jedin, H., *A History of the Council of Trent*, trans. E. Graf, 2 vols (London 1957–1961).

Kamen, H., *The Spanish Inquisition* (London 1965).

Keen, M. H., *The Laws of War in the Late Middle Ages* (London 1965).

————, *Chivalry* (New Haven and London 1984).

Knecht, R. J., *Francis I* (Cambridge 1982).

Levy, F. J., 'A semi-professional diplomat: Guido Cavalcanti and the marriage negotiations of 1571', in *Bulletin of the Institute of Historical Research* XXXV, 1962.

Livet, G., *L'équilibre européen de la fin du XVe à la fin du XVIIIe siècle* (Paris 1976).

Lynch, J., *Spain under the Hapsburgs* (Oxford 1964).

Loades, D. M., *The Reign of Mary Tudor* (London 1979).

Logan, O., *Culture and Society in Venice 1470–1790* (London 1972).

Lot, F., *Recherches sur les effectifs des armées françaises des guerres d'Italie aux guerres de réligion, 1496–1562* (Paris 1962).

Lupton, J. H., *A Life of John Colet* (London 1887).

Luzio, A., 'Isabella d'Este di fronte a Giulio II', in *Archivio Storico Lombardo*, series IV, XVIII, 1912.

————, 'I preliminari della lega di Cambray', in *Archivio Storico Lombardo*, series IV, XVI, 1911.

Lynch, J., *Spain under the Hapsburgs* (Oxford 1964).

McConica, J. M., *English Humanists and Reformation Politics under Henry VIII and Edward VI* (Oxford 1965).

Mallet, M., *The Borgias* (London 1971).

————, *The Mercenaries and their Masters: warfare in Renaissance Italy* (London 1974).

Maltby, W. S., *Alba: a biography of F. Alvarez de Toledo, 3rd Duke of Alba, 1507–1582* (California 1983).

Mattingly, G., 'An early non-aggression pact', in *Journal of Modern History* X, 1938.

————, *Renaissance Diplomacy* (London 1955).

————, 'The reputation of Dr De Puebla', in *English Historical Review* L, 1980.

Maulde-la-Clavière, M. A. H. de, *La diplomatie au temps de Machiavel*, 3 vols (Paris 1892–3).

Mayer, D. Moulton, *The Great Regent, Louise of Savoy, 1476–1531* (London 1966).

Miller, A. C., *Sir Henry Killigrew* (Leicester 1963).

Motley, J. L., *The Rise of the Dutch Republic* (London 1897).

Negri, P., 'Studi sulla crisi Italiana alla fine del secolo XV', in *Archivio Storico Lombardo* LI, 1974.

Nitti, F., *Leone X e la sua politica secondo documenti e carteggi inediti* (Florence 1892).

Nores, P., 'Storia della guerra di Paolo IV', in *Archivio Storico Italiano*, series I, XII, 1847.

Palmer, J. J. N., *England, France and Christendom 1377–1399* (London 1972).

Parker, G., *The Army of Flanders and the Spanish Road* (Cambridge and New York 1972).

————, *The Dutch Revolt* (London 1977).

Parker, K. T., *Catalogue of the Collection of Drawings in the Ashmolean Museum, vol. I, the Netherlandish, German, French and Spanish schools* (Oxford 1938).

Partner, P., *The Lands of St Peter: the Papal State in the Middle Ages and the early Renaissance* (London 1972).

Pastor, L., *The History of the Popes*, English trans. by F. I. Antrobus & R. Kerr, vol. VI–XV (London 1928–50).

Perret, P. M., *Histoire des rélations de la France avec Venise* (Paris 1896).

Pierson, P., *Philip II of Spain* (London 1975).

Phillips, M. M., *Erasmus and his Times: a shortened version of the Adages* (Cambridge 1967).

————, *Erasmus and the Northern Renaissance* (London 1949).

Pins, J. de, 'Autour des guerres d'Italie. Un ambassadeur français à Venise et à Rome (1515–1525). Jean de Pins, Eveque de Rieux', in *Revue d'Histoire Diplomatique* LXI, 1947.

Pirenne, H., *Histoire de Belgique* vol. III (Brussels 1912).

Pope-Hennessy, J., *The Portrait in the Renaissance* (London 1966).

Porter, H. C., *Erasmus and Cambridge: the Cambridge letters of Erasmus*, trans. D. F. S. Thomson (Toronto 1963).

Quellen, D. E., *The Office of Ambassador in the Middle Ages* (Princeton 1967).

Read, Conyers, *Mr Secretary Cecil and Queen Elizabeth* (London 1955).

————, *Mr Secretary Walsingham and the Policy of Queen Elizabeth*, 3 vols (Oxford 1925).

Recueils de la société Jean Bodin XIV, XV, *La Paix* (Paris 1961).

Reiffenberg, F. A. de, *Histoire de l'Ordre de la Toison d'Or* (Brussels 1830).

Ridolfi, R., *The Life of Francesco Guicciardini*, English trans. C. Grayson (London 1967).

————, *The Life of Niccolo Machiavelli*, English trans. C. Grayson (London 1963).

Romero Murube, J., *L'Alcazar de Séville* (Madrid 1971).

Romier, L., *La carrière d'un favori. Jacques d'Albon de S. André, Maréchal de France* (Paris 1909).

————, *Les origines politiques des guerres de réligion*, 2 vols (Paris 1913–1914).

Ross, J., *The Lives of the Early Medici as Told in their Correspondence* (London 1910).

Ruble, A. de, *Antoine de Bourbon et Jeanne d'Albret*, 2 vols (Paris 1881–6).

————, *Le traité de Cateau-Cambrésis* (Paris 1889).

Russell, F. H., *The Just War in the Middle Ages* (Cambridge 1975).

Russell, Joycelyne G., *The Field of Cloth of Gold: men and manners in 1520* (London 1969).

————, 'The search for Universal Peace: the conferences at Calais and Bruges in 1521', in *Bulletin of the Institute of Historical Research* XLIV, 1971. cf. also Dickinson, Joycelyne G.

Scarisbrick, J. J., *Henry VIII* (London 1968).

Schenk, W., *Reginald Pole Cardinal of England* (London 1950).

Schwoebel, R., *The Shadow of the Crescent: the Renaissance image of the Turk* (1453–1517) (Nieuwkoop 1967).

Shennan, J. H., *The Parlement of Paris* (London 1968).

Shirley, T. F., *Thomas Thirlby, Tudor Bishop* (London 1964).

Sigmund, P. E., *Nicolas of Cusa and Medieval Political Thought* (Harvard 1963).

Stephens, W., *Margaret of France, Duchess of Savoy* (London 1912).

Strieder, J., *Jacob Fugger the Rich*, English trans. (New York 1966).

Sutherland, N., *The French Secretaries of State in the Age of Catherine de Medici* (London 1962).

————, *The Massacre of St Bartholomew and the European Conflict, 1559–1572* (London 1973).

Vale, Malcolm, *War and Chivalry* (London 1981).

Van Durme, M., *El cardenal Granvela (1517–1586)* Barcelona 1957).

Vaughan, H. M., *The Medici Popes* (London 1908).

Waas, G. E., *The Legendary Character of Maximilian* (New York 1941).

Wauters, A., *Histoire des environs de Bruxelles*, 3 vols (Brussels 1855).

Wedgwood, C. V., *William the Silent* (New Haven 1944).

Wegg, J., *Richard Pace: a Tudor diplomatist* (London 1971).

Wernham, R. B., *Before the Armada: the growth of English foreign policy 1485–1588* (London 1966).

Wilkie, W. E., *The Cardinal Protectors of England* (Cambridge 1974).

Williams, H. Noel, *The Brood of False Lorraine: the history of the Ducs de Guise (1496–1588)*, 2 vols (London, n.d.).

Wright, T., ed., *Queen Elizabeth and her times*, 2 vols (London 1838).

Yates, F. A., *Astraea: the imperial theme in the sixteenth century* (London 1975).

Index

Index